The International Guide to
Building a Classical Music Library

Bill Parker

The Cimino Publishing Group
Carle Place, New York

ISBN 1-878427-59-8

First printing: October 1997

Printed in Canada

01 00 99 98 97   6 5 4 3 2 1

Cover and interior design by *Mori Studio*

Table of Contents

Acknowledgments   *v*

Introduction   *vii*

A Classical Music Primer   *viii*
The Purpose of This Book   *xvii*
The International Edition   *xviii*
How the Recordings Were Selected   *xix*
How to Interpret the CD Listings   *xx*
About "Super Budget" Recordings   *xxii*
About Technology   *xxiii*
Keeping This Book Updated   *xxv*

The Middle Ages and Renaissance   1

Gregorian Chant   1
Medieval Collections   3
Renaissance Collections   4

Byrd, William   5
Dowland, John   6
Gabrieli, Giovanni   7
Josquin Desprez   8
Lassus, Orlandus   8
Monteverdi, Claudio   9
Palestrina, Giovanni Pierluigi da   10
Praetorius, Michael   11
Tallis, Thomas   12
Victoria, Tomás Luis de   13

The Baroque Era   15

Albinoni, Tomaso   16
Bach, Johann Sebastian   17
Corelli, Arcangelo   25
Couperin, François   26
Handel, George Frideric   26
Pachelbel, Johann   30
Purcell, Henry   31
Rameau, Jean-Philippe   32
Scarlatti, Domenico   33
Telemann, Georg Philipp   34
Vivaldi, Antonio   35

The Classical Period   39

Bach, Carl Philipp Emanuel   39
Beethoven, Ludwig van   40
Boccherini, Luigi   52
Gluck, Christoph Willibald von   53
Haydn, Franz Joseph   54
Mozart, Wolfgang Amadeus   58

The Early Romantics   71

Bellini, Vincenzo   72
Berlioz, Hector   73
Chopin, Frédéric   76
Donizetti, Gaetano   78
Glinka, Mikhail   80
Mendelssohn, Felix   81
Paganini, Niccoló   84
Rossini, Gioacchino   85
Schubert, Franz   87
Schumann, Robert   95
Weber, Carl Maria von   100

The Mainstream Romantics   103

Bizet, Georges   104
Borodin, Alexander   106
Brahms, Johannes   108
Bruch, Max   119
Bruckner, Anton   120
Chabrier, Emmanuel   123
Chausson, Ernest   124
Delibes, Leo   125
Dvořák, Antonin   126
Franck, César   131
Grieg, Edvard   133
Edouard Lalo   135
Liszt, Franz   136
Mussorgsky, Modest   139
Offenbach, Jacques   142
Rimsky-Korsakov, Nikolai   143

The Mainstream Romantics (cont.)

Saint-Saëns, Camille   146
Smetana, Bedřich   151
Strauss II, Johann   153
Tchaikovsky, Piotr Ilyich   154
Verdi, Giuseppe   162
Wagner, Richard   166

The Late Romantics   171

Debussy, Claude   171
Delius, Frederick   176
Dukas, Paul   178
Elgar, Edward   179
Fauré, Gabriel   182
Humperdinck, Engelbert   184
d'Indy, Vincent   185
Leoncavallo, Ruggero   186
Mahler, Gustav   187
Mascagni, Pietro   191
Puccini, Giacomo   192
Strauss, Richard   195

The Moderns   203

Barber, Samuel   206
Bartók, Béla   207
Berg, Alban   210
Bernstein, Leonard   212
Bloch, Ernest   214
Britten, Benjamin   215
Copland, Aaron   217
Enesco, Georges   220
Falla, Manuel de   221
Gershwin, George   224
Grofé, Ferde   227
Hanson, Howard   228
Hindemith, Paul   229
Holst, Gustav   231
Honegger, Arthur   233
Ives, Charles   235
Janáček, Leoš   236
Khachaturian, Aram   238
Kodály, Zoltán   239
Milhaud, Darius   240

The Moderns (cont.)

Nielsen, Carl   241
Orff, Carl   242
Poulenc, Francis   244
Prokofiev, Serge   245
Rachmaninov, Sergei   251
Ravel, Maurice   255
Respighi, Ottorino   265
Rodrigo, Joaquin   266
Satie, Erik   267
Schoenberg, Arnold   268
Shostakovich, Dmitri   271
Sibelius, Jan   275
Stravinsky, Igor   279
Thomson, Virgil   283
Vaughan Williams, Ralph   285
Villa-Lobos, Heitor   287
Walton, William   289
Webern, Anton   291

A Minimal Epilogue   293

Adams, John   293
Glass, Philip   294
Górecki, Henryk   294

Anthologies   295

Classical Music in the Movies   305

About the Author   313

Index   315

Acknowledgments

Immeasurable thanks are due for benefactions received from Rex Levang, Minnesota Public Radio; John Michel, American Composers Forum; Forrest Faubion, Allegro Corporation; David Belote, PolyGram Classics and Jazz; John E. Ryan, BMG Classics; Henry Peters, EMI Classics; John Kulstad, Koch International; Phil Melitta, Nimbus Records; Laurence Vittes, Naxos of America; Sean O'Sullivan, Sony Classics; Richard Schweer, Qualiton Imports; Gerry Fisher, Warner-Elektra-Atlantic; Jim Glay, Harmonia Mundi USA; Bob Morris, my literary agent; Jack Caravela, my editor; Ed Cimino, my publisher, and (as always) above all, my attorney, Edward F. Rooney!

Thanks equally to those steadfast friends who egged me on, consoled me in crisis, called me at 3 a.m. to make sure I was typing, sat patiently with me over lunch and dinner while I bewailed my burdens, forced down my pills, made me take my daily walk, propped up my eyelids, wiped away my scowls, and dragged me kicking and screaming to the final deadline: Steve Birkeland, Scott Alan Herbert, Laura Waterman Wittstock, Garrett Johnson, Thomas P. Kunesh, Brian and Natasha Tice, Brooke Creswell, Gloria Sewell, Dr. Philip Blackburn, Ku-Tsang Lin, Dr. Alvin C. Holm, Melissa Metzler, and the Prince of Patience, Roberto Ramon Aviña, Jr.

To all of these, this book
is gratefully dedicated

Introduction

For many people the word "classical" suggests music that is relaxing. You have probably heard it said: "I can't listen to that classical stuff, it puts me to sleep." For others, it means music that is stiff and formal, music that you can't dance to. For yet others it signifies music written in and for other cultures and times, not theirs, and therefore not understandable and of no interest.

It may be hoped that in the course of your explorations you will come to believe that none of the above are true. There is quiet classical music, to be sure, but one would be hard pressed to sleep through Tchaikovsky's *1812 Overture*. If you think classical music has no beat, try Ravel's *Boléro*. And although classical music was often originally written for wealthy aristocrats, today it is the universal property of everyone, thanks to its ever-increasing use in films and commercials, and its ready availability on recordings.

The term "classical" is somewhat misleading to begin with. More precisely it should refer to the period of about 1750-1820, the age of Haydn and Mozart and early Beethoven. The way you keep its two uses apart is to notice that when the specific era is denoted, it is spelled with a capital "C." Generically, with a small "c," classical is a loose term for music that has the cachet of history and respectability. Nowadays it could apply to Beatles songs as well as to the Bruckner symphonies.

But for our purposes, and in the common usage, we are referring to what might better be called "art music," works of music that are deliberately written down, i.e., composed, by professional musicians, in an acknowledged tradition that can be traced just like a genealogy from the late Middle Ages and Renaissance to the present, from the masses of Guillaume Machaut to the cantatas of Bach, from the piano concertos of Mozart to the tone poems of Franz Liszt, from the ballets of Stravinsky to the symphonies of Gorecki.

It is music that ultimately rests on a set of academic rules—no matter how often the rules are transgressed—regarding melody, harmony, rhythm, tempo, and other technical devices. Above all, and what sets it emotionally apart from other types of music, is its relative sense of philosophical distance. It is designed to last beyond the present moment. It is meant to be not only listened to, but concentrated on.

Another term for it is "concert music," that is, music one deliberately goes into a room or hall to sit down and pay attention to. It is not intended for dancing or marching (although there are very often dances and marches in it), or even for putting yourself to sleep or waking yourself up, though no one can stop you from putting it to whatever use you may like. Its real purpose is to either make you feel deeply, or think deeply, or both. If you can accept these as conditions for liking classical music, you are ready to make a stab at it.

A Classical Music Primer

You are probably reading this book because you're already at least a little interested in classical music, but also a little uncertain about it. You may have heard some classical music you liked, but got discouraged going any deeper when you ran into tech-talk or foreign phraseology. Some classical people do tend to talk to each other in jargon. Some even use their knowledge of classical music to assert their "superiority."

This is very bad. It comes from a snobbish attitude, something that's been handed down from the days of the royal courts and believe me, most people who act snooty about classical music have no connection whatsoever with the ancient nobility.

So forget about that. The Millennium is upon us. The world is wired. We're all connected by fax or phone or Internet. There are thousands of recordings of every kind of music, and we now have a world-wide web of radio broadcasts.

Any music you want is yours for the dialing, and you're quite smart enough to decide what music you like all by yourself. You don't need to belong to any certain social class or economic group.

Maybe a little guidance is welcome in unfamiliar territory, but learning about classical music shouldn't be like taking nasty medicine. Often you get the feeling it must be impossible to listen to or enjoy classical music unless you take a course or read a book or study very hard. It doesn't sound like *fun* to get into classical music. So no wonder you don't do it!

Therefore I'm not going to give a course here in the technical aspects of classical music. I'm not going to tell you what *allegretto grazioso* means, or define a Picardy third, or discuss the various editions of Bruckner's symphonies. All that sort of stuff can be interesting, but you don't *have* to know it to enjoy classical music. All you need at first is to get your bearings, to find some point of reference so you can navigate a little on your own.

That's where I may be able to assist. I can't turn Beethoven into Jimi Hendrix or Kenny G or Smashing Pumpkins, but even so, I think I can make Beethoven seem less like somebody from an entirely different planet.

Beethoven is dead. I'm sorry about that. (So is Jimi Hendrix, by the way.) Some people think classical music is music by dead people. Not too swift: Jim Morisson was definitely not classical, Philip Glass (living) is.

What? You knew that? You knew that Jim Morisson was pop and Philip Glass was classical? Think of it: you could be a person who claims to "know nothing" about classical music, but you might have known that. So maybe you know more than you think you know! When it comes to music, a *lot* of people know more than they think they do. You're likely to be one of them. There's a simple reason for that. Words, like the ones you are reading now, are only one form of language communication. Music is another. The language of music isn't the same as words. Because we often haven't read about music in a book, we think we're not informed about it. But music can be its own teacher. It can get through to the brain without any intermediary.

Music expresses feelings and emotions in ways that words often can't. That's why we humans *need* music. Sometimes words are put to music, as in songs (both pop and classical), but only when it seems the music *adds* something, when it *enhances* what the words say.

Sometimes music can tell a whole story that words don't, as in a movie score. The shower scene in Hitchcock's *Psycho* would not be half as scary without that famous Bernard Herrmann music. The same goes for opera. (Bernard Herrmann wrote an opera, by the way.) A lot of people think they don't like opera because they can't understand the words. The fact is, you can usually tell what's going on just fine without the words, because the music makes everything clear all on its own.

Some people don't believe this when you tell it to them, but then they experience it themselves and believe. That's the bottom line with any music, including classical: experience it. Don't (necessarily) take a course in it, read about it, study it hard. Just experience it. Reading and studying will enhance enjoyment down the road, just as music enhances words in a song, but you don't have to read or study a lot to get started, to make a friendly acquaintance with classical music.

We'll take care of that here.

Hello. Allow me introduce you to classical music. That's with a small "c." Maybe we ought to think up a better term, but that's all we've got at the moment. The word "classical" tends to evoke something very old, as when we refer to the Classical Period in history (ancient Rome and all that). True, a lot of classical music *is* old—but some of it isn't. What is called classical music spans far more than a thousand years, from the beginnings of Gregorian Chant (around A.D. 600) to the present.

To make classification easier, scholars have divided this long history up into periods. You will constantly hear these mentioned when people talk about classical music, so you might as well be familiar with them right away:

Medieval (600-1450)
Renaissance (1450-1600)
Baroque (1600-1750)
Classical (1750-1820)
Romantic (1820-1915)
Modern (1915-now)

The dates are approximate, and some reference books will give them slightly differently, but they are significant because there is a degree of similarity within each period as to how the music sounds. After only a short study of classical music it's amazingly easy to hear a piece and guess correctly which period it comes from, even though you can't name the exact composer.

One odd thing you have to note: in the middle of the list is a period called the Classical (1750-1820). It's confusing, but there's nothing to be done about it. You just have to remember that in the field of classical music, covering some 1,400 years, there is one period—the shortest of all—that is known as the Classical period, with a capital C, and unlike as in other disciplines, such as history, it does *not* indicate the *oldest* period!

In a history or art class the periods run like this: Classical, Medieval, Renaissance, Baroque, Romantic, and Modern. But not in classical music. Weird, but that's how it is.

A lot of people have misconceptions about classical music that I'd like to clear up once and for all. Let's put classical music on trial. I'll be the defense attorney and you be the judge.

Charge: Classical music poses as "holier than thou."

Defense: No music poses as anything. Some *people* make claims for types of music, and they're entitled to their opinions. There are, for certain, people who will try to make you feel stupid and inadequate if you don't like classical music. This makes them feel better about themselves. The truth is, there are different types and styles of music for different temperaments, times, and tastes. No one of them is higher or lower than another; they're just different from each other.

Pop music is "about" what's happening in people's lives and emotions *right now*. It's deliberately crafted to be short, powerful, and to the point. The words resonate with modern everyday life and its current issues. If it's dance music, it has a strong and regular beat to keep you in the groove. Pop music is deliberately targeted towards the needs and feelings of the young and those nostalgic for youth.

"Easy listening" is music that *used* to be pop music but has grown old along with its listeners. It may seem out-of-date to a teen, but to mom and dad it's still "where it's at."

Jazz is a distinctively American art form that grew out of the melodies and rhythms of traditional African music, mixed with other elements as it developed. In some ways it's very similar to classical music except for its surface sound, because of the different rhythms, instruments, and tonal colors. The main technical difference is that jazz depends on improvisation while classical is carved in stone (with a few rare exceptions).

Classical is not, as often assumed, the popular music of a bygone age, which because it is now old is considered "a classic." An old car is "a classic," but the term "classic" (without the -al on the end) should be avoided in talking about music. A lot of people use "classic" and "classical" interchangeably, but don't do it; you will expose yourself as an amateur. "Classical" is a distinct category of music, not *higher* or *better* than others, but *different* based on certain accepted standards and definitions, and not because it is (often but not always) "old." You have to be old to be "a classic," but not to be "classical."

Recently I saw a puff piece in a record company ad for a Mozart CD claiming that "In Mozart's day, the split between classical and popular music hadn't happened...Mozart WAS pop music!" This is not only an outrageous attempt to patronize non-classical people and trick them into listening to Mozart, it's also an outright untruth.

Pop music didn't suddenly "split off" from classical music in recent times. Actually, a better case can be made that it was the other way around. As I indicated above, classical music "as we know it" is traced back only to about the year A.D. 600, the beginning of

Gregorian Chant. Of course, there was music long before that—probably for many thousands of years before—and I think that "popular" would be a more accurate term for most of that ancient music.

What "popular" music would have meant for eons was what we today would call "folk" or "ethnic" music. It was the Music of the Masses, made up and sung by common folk and played on household instruments. By the early Middle Ages, both the Catholic Church and the royal courts were beginning to have a sense that music could, or even should, receive more serious and academic attention than before, when it wasn't taken too seriously as part of humanity's makeup. (In ancient Greece, Plato had condemned music as effeminate and enervating.)

A new theory began to take hold: that music could be ennobling, that it could be more than merely something to dance to or row a boat to, that it could be raised to the level of dignity already held by literature and sculpture and painting, that it could be something worthwhile admiring on its own terms and not just as accompaniment to some other activity. It could have a refined structure and be listened to with respect and devotion for its own sake. It should be uplifting and elegant in tone.

These ideas took hold in the Church under the initial guidance of Pope Gregory the Great, who specified that if music was to be part of holy ritual, then it must be worthy of its keep. The courts, eager to be on good terms with the Church, took pains to refine and improve the quality of their own secular music.

The result of this symbiotic relationship was a burgeoning tradition based on a new sense of music as a high and noble art, suitable for stimulating reflection and profound emotion rather than mere kinetic energy. The earliest medieval composers, such as Perotin and Machaut, took this assignment seriously and produced music that could be written down and performed over and over again the same way. This innovation, the permanent writing-down of music, was revolutionary and became the signpost of what today we call "classical music."

By the Baroque era (1600-1750) these sacred and secular streams had pretty much merged into one definable category of "serious" or "concert" music that people actually paid a ticket for and went to a concert hall to sit down and just listen to, as they used to watch a play, or before that, the Mass in church.

All of this music, and all of its descendants in a clear line to the present, evolved out of the earlier "popular" (folk and ethnic) music. This is clearly seen in many of the medieval Masses, with titles such as *Missa L'homme armé* ("The armored man"), indicating a sacred piece based on a popular tune of the time.

So although it had its roots in popular music, it became a separate art form which came to be called "classical" because of several distinguishing earmarks: it was "composed" by professional musicians, rather than just evolving through the ranks of amateurs; it was meant to be listened to as one would look at a great painting, not just danced to or played as the accompaniment to a ceremony; it used elements of melody, rhythm, and (later) harmony calculated to evoke a serious, philosophical, or timeless reaction in the listener; and it was so fixed in form that it was usually played in exactly the same way every time, not improvised or altered from one performer to another.

In the earliest days, "classical music" was pretty much reserved to the Church; a little later it worked its way into the royal courts and the homes of the aristocracy; by the Industrial Revolution it became available to the bourgeoisie—that part of the public with money for expensive tickets, a merchant class who aspired to the dignity formerly reserved for nobles. Only in our own time has it become available to *everyone* through the media of radio, television, film, and recordings. But through all these centuries it has been distinct in its characteristics, as defined in the paragraph above.

It was *not* "popular music," and Mozart was not a "pop composer." To say that is patently ridiculous. People in Mozart's day below the bourgeois class had their own types of dance, folk, ethnic music, although a handful of Mozart opera tunes might filter down by way of simple arrangements for crude instruments. Mozart's great contemporary, Franz Joseph Haydn, made a particular point of "elevating" many folk tunes and ethnic songs by incorporating them into his serious concert compositions, and other classical composers have made a specialty of this in later times as well.

We can see that though classical music was devised and developed by an educated and wealthy class, there is nothing to limit it to any one social class today. It is a distinct type and form of the musical art which can be enjoyed by anyone, regardless of social or economic class, race, religion, or origin, if he or she finds it attractive. There is no need to think that classical music can only be listened to by pinheads, dorks, or snobs. That is imputing to music a power it simply does not have. If we do not like a certain kind of music—any kind, I again emphasize—the fault is not in the music, but in ourselves.

That concludes my defense of classical music. I hope I have been a good enough attorney to win the jury's heart. If so, I will proceed now to an even more daunting task: to try to elucidate some of that intimidating classical-music terminology.

Over many years as a classical music radio announcer I had a lot of amusing experiences with listeners. One oft-repeated scenario involved playing a little-known (but very good!) piece of music and having the phones light up. As I answered each line the caller would enthusiastically ask what "that wonderful piece of music" was and I would say (to give a real example): "That was the Polka and Fugue from *Schwanda der Dudelsackpfeiffer* by Jaromir Weinberger." Usually, complete silence would ensue, followed by some nervous throat-clearing, after which the caller would mumble something like "Er...yes...thank you," and hang up.

There were a couple of things this indicated to me: (1) people have preconceived notions; they expect that if a composition sounds great to them it ought to be by somebody they've heard of, such as Beethoven or Mozart, and if it isn't, perhaps their enthusiasm was misplaced; and (2) people become discouraged in pursuing classical music when they are confronted by foreign languages and unfamiliar technical terminology. It's just all too intimidating and confusing.

The hardest things I've had to do in interesting people in classical music have been to get them to trust their own taste and instincts, and to stop worrying about the techno-talk. If you recognize yourself in this situation, give me a chance to disabuse you of your self-doubts.

As with anything in life, the best approach to success is one step at a time. You really don't have to stop everything you're doing, sign up for a university course, and immerse yourself in Music Appreciation for months or years in order to start enjoying classical music. More than likely you would just end up hating it all, because it had become *work* instead of pleasure.

The easiest, most painless way to get started is to learn a few of the most basic terms and then just pick up more jargon as you go along. As the pieces of the puzzle start fitting together, you'll most likely experience a comfortable, gradual sense of accomplishment and satisfaction.

Classical music has its own vocabulary, it's true. Some of it is shared with other types of music, but a lot of it isn't. There are reasons both historical and practical for this. It isn't because classical artists are trying to be different or superior. It's just how it developed, and since some aspects of classical music are uniquely different, different terms are necessary.

One of the terms you hear most often is "opus." Since becoming the name of a penguin in a popular cartoon strip, even this word has become less intimidating. It's a Latin word that means "a work," in the sense of a completed, lasting creation. Most composers have had their compositions (their "works") catalogued for posterity, and these are usually listed in chronological order as opus no. 1, 2, 3, and so on. This is especially useful in identifying classical pieces because often they have only generic designations, unlike pop music in which everything has a sort of "song title," like "Lucy in the Sky with Diamonds." In classical, there are a lot of pieces simply called Sonata in D-flat, sometimes many of them by the same composer. If it weren't for good old "opus" it would be hard to explain which one you're referring to without whistling it.

Since classical music is written down with a view to lasting for centuries in a fixed form, it's only natural that certain forms have developed which comply with its needs. Some of these are the symphony, the concerto, the sonata, the opera, the oratorio, and the string quartet. There are dozens more, but if you learn these half dozen you will have a handle on at least 50% of the forms of classical music.

In its simplest definition, the symphony is a work for full orchestra, usually in four sections (called "movements"), which takes some simple melodies or themes and develops them according to a set of guidelines and rules into a coherent structure. It is a sort of novel in tones. It almost seems to tell a story, but there are no human characters, just abstract relations of musical tones. Nevertheless, it can seem as theatrical and overpowering as any spoken drama.

The concerto is closely related to the symphony. It too is for full orchestra, but features a solo instrument—most commonly the piano or violin—which stands out from the orchestra and "solos" much as a singer does against the background of a band. Concertos tend to have three movements instead of four; it's another way to spot them.

Sonatas are works for much smaller ensembles, usually one or two instruments. They are really very much like concertos but without the full orchestra background. The violin may play a three-movement musical drama, accompanied by the piano only.

An opera is a dramatic musical work much more like a literary play. It has characters who sing lyrics, accompanied by a full orchestra. There is a plot, and there are costumes and scenery.

An oratorio is a "sacred" work very similar to an opera in form and effect, but without costumes and scenery, and without a "plot" as such. Handel's *Messiah* is the best-known oratorio.

In addition to these forms, one may speak of "chamber music," referring to classical pieces that are written for small groups of instruments, i.e., smaller than an orchestra. The most common forms here are easy to remember because they are usually basically sonatas, but with specialized names indicating how many instruments are in the group. Thus we refer to trios, quartets, quintets, sextets, septets, and so on up. If you add these self-evident "chamber" forms to the basic half dozen above, you now account for the majority of the classical music you are most likely to hear.

As you go along you will add in the tone poem, the fugue, the lied, the overture, and a number of others, but just take one at a time and it won't seem very burdensome.

You'll also come across a host of terms in Italian which merely indicate the tempo of a piece of classical music, or a part of it. Some of these, such as *largo*, *adagio*, and *lento*, indicate various degrees of slowness; others, such as *allegro*, *allegretto*, and *presto* indicate fast tempos. You will see these often in references to classical music, but you really don't need to pay any attention to them. It will be obvious to you whether a piece is slow or fast; nobody will have to tell you that it's *adagio* or *allegro*! But I mention these terms to demystify them, as they often creep into titles. You need only tip your hat to them, smile, and pass on.

The same could be said of "key signatures," i.e. C Major, B Minor, and the like. Those designations are important to know if you're a performing musician, and remembering whether a generic title, such as a sonata, is in C or B might help you identify it in a catalog, but it has absolutely nothing to do with enjoying the music. Millions of people listen with pleasure to classical music without any idea of what key the piece is in. You just don't need to know that.

In fact, you don't need to know any of the technical terminology of classical music to enjoy it, any more than you have to know how to write a popular song to enjoy one. Leave the technical part to professional musicians. To be a good listener, you need only receive the abstract, emotional message coming from the composer's brain via the medium of the written notes. How the composer makes his or her effects is no more necessary to your enjoyment than knowing how the special effects are produced in a movie—although figuring those out some day can certainly enhance and deepen your enjoyment.

I've said that the best thing you can do to get familiar with classical music is "just listen to it." I've also said that classical music is a vast subject, encompassing about 1,400 years of music. So the question naturally arises, "where do I start?" If the terminology, the foreign languages, and the rep aren't intimidating enough, how about those 1,400 years worth of compositions to plow through?

The good news is: you don't have to listen to all of them. There really isn't any bad news, except that you won't *like* all of them either—but of course you don't have to feel guilty about that. I can't tell you how many people have told me "OK, I tried classical, I listened to the Overture to *The Barber of Seville* but I didn't like it, so I guess classical isn't for me."

Now just a minute! Out of the thousands of classical pieces available to listen to, you heard *one* and blew the whole thing off? All right, it is *possible* that you could listen to 100 classical pieces and not like *any* of them, but the more you listen, the less likely that becomes. In fact, if you listen a couple of times over, you might even start liking *The Barber of Seville*. It's kind of like developing a new taste in ethnic food. Your success depends on two factors: how adventurous you are, and how persevering.

Here are some ideas for approaching your experiments in listening:

PLAN A—*Listening by Period*

Many people find that they prefer the music of one period in music history over many of the others. Usually the compositions of one period all have quite a few features in common, a "sound" that you can instantly recognize. This often creates a cozy sense of familiarity so that if a person really likes the music of Handel, they will find they gravitate next to music by Bach, Vivaldi, Pachelbel, and Scarlatti. Sometimes they are surprised to discover that all these composers lived about the same time (the Baroque Period).

This is an acceptable way to start finding your way around classical music, as it provides a feeling of comfort and safety. Many listeners find "their" period and stick with it loyally forever, and I can't say they're wrong to do it. My only regret would be that they may cheat themselves out of the great music of other periods, just as they used to cheat themselves out of classical music...period.

PLAN B—*Listening by Brand-Name Composer*

In our commercial culture we tend to go by brand names, so it's only natural that we want to listen to Albinoni and Bizet and Chopin rather than Arriaga and Boismortier and Castelnuovo-Tedesco. The first three make a nice ABC of music indeed, whereas the second trio are known to only a few connoisseurs.

I am the first to acknowledge that where there is smoke there is fire, i.e., there is a *reason* that the "Great Composers" are so called. Some old hands in the classical field get so jaded with time that they wouldn't be caught dead listening to somebody so "common" as Mozart or Beethoven.

I find that attitude pretty silly. Just because millions of listeners have liked something doesn't mean it's bad or low-brow. What's really strange is how full the world is of people who are so awed and intimidated by classical music they think it's too far "above" them, while some classical aficionados are looking down their noses at classical pieces they consider "beneath" them!

I think we should all stop worrying about Above and Below and concentrate on keeping our minds open. Personally I get a little turned off by people who are obsessed with rating everything and everybody they meet. Long ago I tired of the questions "Who is your favorite composer?" and "What is your favorite composition?" which I am inevitably asked the very moment my love of classical music becomes known.

The only honest answer I can give is that there are so many wonderful composers and pieces of music over a span of 1,400 years that I don't find it very useful to rank them in numerical order. My favorite may change with the time of day and the mood I'm in. This isn't a sales contest, a race for the presidency, or a football game—it's music! It's a private matter between you and your inner Muse. It's like love. You are not required to explain it or give it a grade. Just make it your own.

I approve completely of starting out by listening to the "Great Composers." Just remember that although they probably *are* great for very good reasons, that doesn't mean the less-famous composers are "bad" or not worth listening too. And it doesn't mean that if you find yourself liking Castelnuovo-Tedesco better than Chopin there is anything wrong with you. In my opinion, they're *both* great! Chopin had a better agent, but I don't begrudge him his fame; he deserves it. Just give the other guy a chance too!

PLAN C—Listening by Artist

Many listeners are more attuned to the performer than to what music is being played. There is really nothing intrinsically "wrong" with this approach. There are people who are crazy about the pianism of Vladimir Horowitz or Van Cliburn, and have only a secondary interest in what they may be playing. It could be anything from Chopsticks to Chopin—so long as Vlad or Van is at the keyboard, their respective fans will be all ears.

I do consider this approach less satisfactory than those above because it puts a premium on personalities to the possible neglect and detriment of the music itself; but if it entices the listener to pay more attention to great music, it has some value.

It does bother me, I admit, when I see crowds screaming for Pavarotti, buying his every album (yes Virginia, compact discs are "albums," too!), watching his every TV appearance excitedly, and then being unable to recall a single melody he sang, or otherwise identify it. In such a case, the music almost seems to become irrelevant, a mere appurtenance. One suspects Pavarotti might be as big a star if he were a bullfighter or a politician. Nevertheless, a portion of his audiences surely must come to care about the music apart from its presenter, and for that one may be grateful.

PLAN D—The Movie Connection

Many people come to classical music from hearing a composition in a movie or TV show they loved. Classical music has been a staple of films since early days. The French composer Saint-Saëns wrote a score for a silent movie (*The Assassination of the Duc de Guise*) in 1908! Tchaikovsky's *Swan Lake* ballet music made a spooky accompaniment to Bela Lugosi in the classic 1931 version of *Dracula*. Richard Strauss's once-obscure *Also sprach Zarathustra* became widely known only after it opened *2001: A Space Odyssey* in 1968, and a scene from Puccini's opera *La Bohème* became a virtual pop hit after being used in the film *Moonstruck* almost 20 years later.

I could list hundreds of other examples (and do, in an appendix at the end of this book). Although this is only a shotgun method of meeting great music, it works for a lot of people. My only caution is that you have to realize that the association you have with this music from a movie may have little or nothing to do with the composer's original intentions. Whether that is important or not may be argued, and it certainly can vary in significance. If you visualize tumbling spacecraft when you hear *The Blue Danube*, I guess it's all right. If that makes the famous waltz stick in your craw better than thinking of bewhiskered *bourgeoises* squiring demure maidens in ball gowns across a Viennese dance floor, I'm all for it.

The important thing, after all, is to find whatever method works for you to come to grips with classical music. Have faith that your efforts will be rewarded richly in the long run.

[The foregoing Classical Music Primer uses material by the author which originally appeared on the Internet site of the NetRadio Network at http://www.netradio.net. It is reprinted here with permission.]

The Purpose of This Book

This book is not written, as I feel some guides to classical music are, from one aficionado to another. I have tried to avoid speaking a "secret language," striving for relatively plain English instead. So many music books sound to me like music professors writing for colleagues down the hall. Others are patronizing and embarrassing for grownups to read. What I have tried to do is write a book on classical music and its recordings that a person of average intelligence, but without a degree in music, can read with profit and comfort, yet without shame.

I have not included a glossary because I have tried to explain any specialized terms as they occur in the narrative. If I have neglected any it is because I hope their meaning will be fairly clear from the context. In any case, I do not think people like to read glossaries, or to have to interrupt their reading constantly to look up unfamiliar terms.

In selecting the composers and their works I have tried not to be shallow while emphasizing breadth over depth. I have sought to touch on as wide a spectrum, from the Middle Ages to recent times, as I could without abandoning the principle that I should stick to the proven classics.

Already a friend has berated me for omitting Olivier Messiaen while including Arthur Honegger. I can only say I have a reason for everything I do. In this case I agree with Charles Osborne, who has written that "Messiaen is clearly not in the main-stream of contemporary composition, wherever that stream may be wandering, but has made a safe place for himself in one of its backwaters." (*The Dictionary of Composers*, 1981, ed. Osborne.) No two people would ever compile a book like this exactly the same way and I do not claim my selection is right and others are wrong.

I am merely satisfied that I have come close to what I intended to do: to cover as wide a spectrum as the paper allotted to me could hold, to avoid musicological jargon, to make the composers come to life as real humans as best I could, to suggest the emotions most people have when they hear the various works of music, and to recommend recordings that have wide consensus as to their merits.

When Sir Neville Marriner endorsed my first edition 17 years ago, he wrote that "Parker is positive; this is a slim volume of suggestions, not derogatory comparisons." The book is not quite so slim today, but I have kept the maestro's compliment firmly in mind. Just as then, I have tried not to "waste ink on invective." My purpose is not to show how I can trash my nemeses and *bête noires* (although I have let my opinions and prejudices show through when it seemed appropriate), but to point out good things that listeners may like.

Since there are countless new recordings coming out every year, record recommendations date fairly quickly. Fortunately, classical recordings are somewhat insulated from obsolescence since (1) the repertory changes only very slowly over long time spans, and (2) the acknowledged greatest recordings tend to stay in print, and to retain their status as classics, over a period of many years.

Still, recordings come and go, and even as we go to press wonderful new things are coming on line, and great old ones disappearing, or being reissued with new catalog numbers or on new labels. Keep these things in mind if you use these listings in your shopping; your record store clerk may help sort out what is still in print and what is not. All I can guarantee is that every record listed here was in print when I typed it into my computer.

The International Edition

Previous editions of this book limited the record listings to those available in the United States of America, using the Schwann *Opus* catalog as the standard reference. It has now become desirable to expand the selections to include those available on both sides of the Atlantic, and in some cases, the Pacific.

This has become easier in the last few years by a great increase in international availability of classical recordings, made possible through the activities of import-export firms, and by the ease of purchasing CDs via phone and mail order, and through the Internet.

In the past, recordings by the same artists on the same labels were often marketed under different logos and with different catalog numbers in different countries. With the shrinking of our globe, these practices have become increasingly unnecessary and cumbersome. With a few exceptions, record companies now use the same label names and catalog numbers worldwide. Therefore in this edition, although you will usually find only one listing per recording, you will notice names and/or numbers in brackets when there is an alternate identification. In such cases the U.S. name or number is given first, and the most common U.K. or European name or number in brackets, e.g.: London [Decca], or IMP 6700872 [Carlton Classics 30367 00872].

One important point to keep in mind is that some albums are not released simultaneously in all markets. Quite a number of European releases are either not released in the U.S., or are made available only on a very limited basis, sometimes exclusively through specialist importers. Even those, however, have become relatively easy to obtain through mail order or the Internet. In any case, I have tended in this book to favor those recordings readily available in all markets at the same time. This is, however, a fluid situation which changes often, and I cannot guarantee that each listing will be accurate at the time you see it, or in the country where you reside.

This fourth edition includes some new composers and works of music not previously included (e.g. Lalo, Mozart's "Great" Mass, the Ravel Piano Trio), and hundreds of new or additional recordings to choose from when you are buying. The listings have been completely revised and updated as of press time. There are also new sections on "Classical Music in the Movies," and "Anthologies" of classical music.

How the Recordings Were Selected

Only standard compact discs are listed in this book. No attempt is made to distinguish other formats, as they are either extinct or nearly so, or have not yet become widely accepted. Music cassettes still exist, but they are such a small proportion of the classical music catalog that listing them adds little, if anything.

My goal was to list neither too few nor too many discs. Some books give as few as one recommendation per work; this implies to many readers that only one worthwhile recording exists of each piece, and if the record store is out of that one the shopper should skulk home disappointed. Others recommend so many, with so many qualifications, that sorting through them can make it seem that the purpose of such a book—to narrow choices down—is being defeated.

My view is that there are three principal things a buyer is likely to be looking for: the best-sounding recording, the greatest performance, or the best price—or, of course, any combination of these. For each work of music I have looked for an outstanding recording in each of these three categories.

Sometimes there have been more than one in each of approximately equal value. Sometimes one recording encompasses two or, rarely, three of the criteria, as when a budget recording is the best performance as well. Sometimes I could not in good conscience list any recording for one of the criteria, as when there simply is not a good budget recording. I have chosen not to list a mediocre performance just because it is cheap, or a brilliant digital recording of an inferior artist.

If a recording is not listed, it may be out of print, or it may just not have fit the arbitrary (but consistent) criteria I set for myself. Many fine recordings are not listed in this book because they have "non-basic" couplings, or are excessively expensive, when another version essentially as good exists with better couplings or better price. It is very important to understand that I do not present these listings as a tabulation of the "greatest recordings ever made," but as a practical guide to widely-praised versions that are likely to be currently obtainable (i.e., during the useful lifetime of this edition).

I cannot list every good recording ever made in the confines of this book, nor can I guarantee that one not listed is good or bad. All I can do is say with confidence that all those which are listed have a great deal going for them, and you will not, I hope, have to regret purchasing any one of them.

As for my judging of the recordings themselves, it is based primarily on the common consensus among critics. I do read, and have read for many years, the reviews in all the leading music magazines, and other publications judging recordings, and get a sense of what recordings are widely admired and which are not. In addition, I have been in the record business and/or classical radio broadcasting for more than 30 years, and am keenly aware, often by osmosis, of what is happening in classical recordings. I keep copious and detailed notes on all the pieces that I cover in my book, and all the recordings of them, in and out of print, their changing labels and numbers, and whatever else is relevant.

And of course, there is my personal judgment; but I never allow this to overrule the general consensus. If there is a recording that only I like, it is not listed in this book. And there are a few recordings here that I don't like, but list anyway because everybody else likes them. There are no marginal choices here; all are "central" selections. To be listed, a disc must give good value all around, fulfill the criteria for an excellent first purchase, be fairly easy to find, not be unduly expensive, have received very high marks from at least one or two eminent music critics (and no low ones from anybody), and not give a highly controversial view of the music. Much safer than that, a recommendation cannot be.

How to Interpret the CD Listings

In past editions I listed the recordings "in approximate descending order of desirability," going on to hedge my choices by noting that since I do not intend to list any inferior or questionable recordings at all, a CD that is last on the list might be only slightly less optimal than the items above it. I advised not giving the sequence much weight when using the list as a buying guide. In this edition I have thought better of the old method. I was reminded of that person we all know who says "Needless to say..." and then says it. Why indicate a hierarchy of preference and then insist that it is next to useless? And so it is, in truth, because the fine judgments that cause me to put one great version a hair above another might justifiably be reversed by another listener/collector with slightly different priorities.

Therefore in this edition I have preferred not to quibble over fine points, or encourage the natural tendency to assume there is a vast gulf between two items listed as first and second choices. I have eliminated the paragraphs preceding each set of listings which formerly tried to distinguish among them—paragraphs which sometimes only fomented confusion instead of clarifying, and which necessarily often fell into a routine employment of empty adjectives. The order I have chosen now is strictly alphabetic.

I have also eliminated the old designations indicating relative pricing, such as (mid-price) and (budget), since in considering a disc on an international basis such information may vary. Many a CD considered a "budget" recording in Great Britain, for example, becomes a premium-priced item once it is imported into the U.S., and vice versa. Pricing varies so much from one market to another, and changes so often within each market, that I have felt these price designations to be no longer useful. Some labels, such as Naxos and Sony Essential Classics, are definitely lower-priced in all markets, but whether they should be considered "mid-price" or "budget" can be a relative matter depending on where you purchase them.

I do not want to cause situations where I proclaim a record to be a "budget" item only to find that a month later it has been moved by the manufacturer to a different label or series at a higher price, making an innocent retailer look like a thief and liar. I will leave considerations of price up to you, the buyer, as you will obviously be able, once you examine the tags on various items, to judge for yourself whether they are high or low in price. I can only advise you in a general way that the quality of all the records in each listing in this book are deemed to be of approximately similar quality *relative to their pricing*. You may presume that the cheapest record in a list is not appreciably inferior to the most expensive one, and that in the latter case you are usually paying for more famous artists, or for more sophisticated sonic quality. The intrinsic artistic value of the cheaper record, and its enjoyability, are in most cases quite comparable.

For each recording, the soloist's last name is given first, (if there is a soloist), followed by the conductor's last name, then the name of the orchestra or other ensemble. Next is the name of the record label (occasionally preceded by a generic album title, if any, in quotation marks), followed by the selection number, and number of discs in a set, if any, in parentheses.

A word about catalog numbers: you will often see on the disc itself a number that is considerably more complex than the one given in this book. In the interests of simplicity I have opted to list the absolute minimum information needed to identify the item. In most cases the excess on the disc is simply a printout of the barcode for retail pricing purposes; the actual catalog number is merely a part of the barcode, and that is the only part I list, or you need. For example, on the album *Canticles of Ecstasy* from Deutsche Harmonia Mundi you will see on the back the number 05472 77320 2. The only part of that number I list is 77320, as that is all that is necessary to find and purchase the disc. You will also often see alpha prefixes before numbers. In most cases these merely distinguish one series within a label from another, and are mainly intended for the internal use of the record company. On the rare occasions that I include the alpha prefix, it is to clarify between two catalog items that have identical numbers and otherwise would be confused in the computer database.]

Next, the "pedigree" of the recording is given in brackets—if definitively known by me. The "pedigree," also known as the Spars Code, is the three-letter code showing on virtually all compact discs to indicate (1) whether the original master was analog or digital, (2) whether or not that master has been digitally remastered for this release, and (3) the current format. Thus, [DDD] means the recording is digital from the first step to the last;

[ADD] means the original analog master has been digitally remastered for issue on compact disc; [AAD] means the original analog master has not been digitally remastered for issue on compact disc. (The final letter will always be a "D," since a compact disc is by definition a digital format.)

When there is no pedigree listed, it usually means that the manufacturer does not list the pedigree in the standard Schwann *Opus* catalog, it is not listed on the recording, or I have serious doubts about the accuracy of the information given. Lack of a pedigree often means the recording is analog, but not always; records from Harmonia Mundi France, for example, are most often digital, but are not so identified on the sleeve or in their catalog, and since it is apparently not a matter of importance to them I prefer to remain noncommittal.

All recordings are stereo unless specifically marked (mono) after the pedigree; I have allowed only a tiny number of monophonic recordings into this book, as not fulfilling the criteria for a first purchase. Later on, as an in-depth collector, you may wish to acquire many great performances which are in older sound—but not, usually, the first time around.

If there are additional pieces on the disc besides the featured item, a plus sign (+) will be followed by their titles. If no composer is given, the pieces are by the composer under discussion. I have tried to indicate changes in artists for coupled works if doing so clarifies the description.

Following is an imaginary sample listing which shows all the features explained above:

Parker, Bourbon Symphony Orchestra. *Tales from the Crypt,* Rusty Dagger Records 911 (2) [AAD] (mono) + *Ale and Farewell,* Variations on "Louie, Louie" (conducted by Armstrong); Gorgonzola: Mad Scene from *Clair de Loony*

About "Super Budget" Recordings

This book discusses in detail only recordings that have list prices of about $6 or more; the great majority are at least $8. But there is another kind of compact disc being carried in many stores these days, known in the trade as the "super budget." These discs retail at $5 or less, and often are treated as "in and out," or promotional, merchandise; that is, they appear in mass quantities, sell for a limited period, and then disappear.

Generally these are recordings by artists with no name recognition, or from countries with no copyright laws or where the economy is distressed (often Eastern European) and masters are available very cheaply. Whatever the reason, the record company has little or no expense involved with recording costs, royalties, or advertising, and it is possible for them to sell the discs at a very low price.

Most of these recordings are actually 100 percent digital [DDD] and are manufactured with the same quality standards as high-priced discs. Very few of them are returned to stores as defective; fewer than normal, in fact, since when they are defective, people are more likely to simply use them for coasters considering the price.

It is true that most of these performances fall short of the genius or inspired level. Still, some of them are excellent, and even when they are not they may make a reasonably acceptable introduction to a piece of music which you may wish to replace later with a greater artist. In any case I did not think it a good use of space to discuss the merits of individual super-budget discs. I assume that it is when you are considering spending larger amounts of money that you most look for detailed information and guidance.

About Technology

An article in *Insight* magazine dated March 28, 1988, noted that "The demise of the long-playing record is at hand, some say, but such forecasts may be rash. True, some stores have cut orders of vinyl and grant more space to compact discs, but records won't vanish, except perhaps from classical bins." A record executive was quoted as predicting that customers would not be able to buy LPs in five years, but the article treated this as exaggeration.

Unless you have been in a galaxy far, far away for the past decade, you know that the record executive was much too optimistic. Long before his deadline, LPs were virtually extinct, and not just in the classical bins. An article in the St. Paul Pioneer Press dated June 21, 1991 (three years and a month after the foregoing prognosis) asked "Buy any good records lately? Probably not. Major "record" companies have virtually stopped selling them in the United States, and few retailers carry them."

The little silvery wafer that finally drove the vinyl LP into the Jurassic period was the compact disc, or CD. (May I plead plaintively for you to spell it "disc"? The spelling "disk" is reserved for computer disks—or more properly, diskettes.)

The CD was designed to be a format, or carrier, for digital recordings. The term "digital" refers to a computerized technology for recording which was introduced to the public in 1982. Unlike the previous standard system, in which sound waves were mechanically inscribed on wax or plastic, the digital system converts the sound waves to numerical values. These are expressed as electrical pulses which are magnetically recorded onto tape.

When the CD is manufactured, the numerical values are decoded back into the sounds (music) which they represent. This process involves no friction and so eliminates the background of noise, or "tape hiss," inevitable with the old analog system; it also eliminates the need for artificial compression of the music, thus capturing the full dynamic range of a performance. Besides all this, digital recording can guarantee accuracy of pitch (eliminating "flutter" and "wow"), and greatly reduce distortion.

The compact disc, unlike the vinyl LP, does not wear out from repeated plays, as there is no physical contact between the laser beam which reads and reflects the encoded information on the disc, and the disc itself. The old stylus tracked the LP from the outer edge inward, at a constant speed of 33 1/3 revolutions per minute; the laser reads the CD from the center out, at speeds varying from 500 rpm near the center to 200 rpm near the outer edge.

Compact discs completely eliminate pops and ticks and the other assorted noises endemic to LPs, and hold about 50 percent more music in a much smaller space.

Despite these advantages, there are listeners who insist that they prefer the sound of analog recordings, even with their little noises and distractions. They say the sound is "warmer," and there is no reason to doubt or dismiss the claim; all hearing is subjective to begin with, and in listening to recordings we can grow fond of what we are most used to, whether it is the newest-fangled invention or not.

It is even more clearly true that there was a black, liquid beauty to the old LP, and one could experience a certain comfort in watching it spin on the turntable. Nowadays the CD is rather disconcertingly swallowed up by the player and not seen again till the concert is over. And although the music is no longer compressed, the artwork is; I don't think I will ever enjoy looking at a CD cover as much as an LP sleeve.

Ironically, the worst charge leveled against digital recordings is that they are too clear and undistorted—extraneous sounds such as the player's throat-clearings, or even the fingers striking the keys, can suddenly become intrusive on a CD. Many early CDs were marred by such oddities, but as time passes the sound engineers have learned to compensate.

It is important to remember that while digital technology has eliminated noise and distortion, and expanded dynamic range and frequency, the real point of a recording is not technology. It is music. An expensive camera does not guarantee a great photograph. It is the photographer who has to manipulate the camera artistically. In the recording studio there are many factors besides digital technology that affect the final product, such as microphone placement and tonal balance, and above all the quality of the musicians who are playing.

There is no point in buying a new digital recording of a lousy performance, when you can get a beautifully produced analog recording of a great artist that has been well reprocessed digitally. Many buyers make the mistake of refusing to consider anything but an all-digital [DDD] recording, regardless of the many complex considerations that go into a great disc. That is why I have tried in this book to include all-digital recordings only when they are testaments to really good music-making; and why I have included many analog recordings that are so good you would be foolish to pass them up just because they are not all-digital.

The compact disc has become the standard home audio format, fending off feeble challenges from Sony's mini disc (MD) and the digital compact cassette (DCC) from Philips. Another threat, digital audio tape (DAT), became a staple tool of radio stations and professional recording studios, but never caught on with the general public. The most interesting new technology coming along at the moment is Virtual Surround Sound from Dolby Laboratories, in alliance with Microsoft, which will make possible high quality stereo reception through your home computer. This promises to make audio CDs playable on your CD-ROM drive with a quality comparable to the best hi-fi system.

Almost from the beginning of the CD era there has been a rumor abroad that in a matter of a few years the music on a disc would fade out to silence. Nobody could prove this or disprove it because presumably no CD was old enough to start decaying. In the spring of 1994, however, there were confirmed reports of some discs eroding. The latest information would seem to indicate, however, that the phenomenon is limited to a small percentage of discs made prior to about 1991 involving a particular chemical reaction among ingredients used in one non-standard manufacturing process. As of this writing, there does not appear to be any mass degradation looming on the horizon.

This is a book about classical music and its recordings, not audio equipment, and so I am afraid I can't go into more detail here about CD players and related technologies. For that (as well as to learn about those passacaglias and Picardy thirds) you will just have to get another book.

Keeping This Book Updated

Since recordings are constantly going in and out of print and new ones are introduced each month, this book is necessarily starting to become outdated before the ink is dry. The records listed herein were current when the text was written, but some will have disappeared, or been superseded, before the book gets to the store shelves.

In order to get an idea of monthly developments you can visit my Internet web site, *The Classical Music Preview,* at **http://cmp.orbis.net** . Here I look monthly at those new releases that I might have put in my book had they been available before going to press, and note those that have disappeared, or merely changed labels or numbers. I also offer information on how and where to buy classical recordings.

The Middle Ages and Renaissance
(ca. 600-1600)

Since very little contemporary concert music has won a wide audience in the past 30 or 40 years (except possibly for some of the current "minimalist" music), the gap has been filled by a renewed interest in very old music—the songs and dances and chants whose authors, as often as not, are unknown, but which form the basis for all Western classical music.

Gradually we have learned that these works are not only historically important, but also direct in expression and delightful to listen to. In response to this, record companies have issued hundreds of recordings of the pre-Bach repertoire.

A collective rubric for the tonal works created in Europe from about A.D. 800 to 1600 is "early music," though some writers extend this term, quite unreasonably as I think, to include composers as late as Mozart, who died in 1791. Much early music is anonymous in origin, and has come down to us through oral tradition, or in a written form whose authenticity is very much in doubt; and what early music actually sounded like is a topic of often acrimonious dispute.

None of this music is part of what is considered the standard modern concert repertoire. If you attend an evening of the Boston Symphony, or the Los Angeles Philharmonic, you may hear Bach, Mozart, Beethoven, Brahms, Berlioz, or Stravinsky on the program, but you will not hear any troubadour songs, Gregorian chants, or Renaissance dances (unless re-orchestrated by Respighi). For these you must seek out occasional special recitals, often in museum galleries.

Nevertheless, a few names stand out with whom any person interested in these founding times should become familiar. A generous selection of them and some of their most representative compositions are offered in this chapter, along with a few collections that attempt to honor in some small fashion that most prolific of all composers, "Anonymous."

Gregorian Chant (fl. ca. 600-1150)

This music, intended for use in the liturgy of the Roman Catholic Church, evolved from the psalm-singing and intoned rituals of the Jewish temple, with additional influences from Greek and Roman choral traditions. The four original church *modes* (roughly analogous to our *scales*) seem to have been taken over from the secular music of the Greeks in about the fourth century A.D.

It took another seven centuries before our modern system of musical notation was developed, so the early chants were either handed down orally or transmitted by a rather inexact system of signs called *neumes*, whose quaint and pretty diamond shapes we admire in medieval manuscripts.

There were several different styles of chanting in the earliest days, but the system attributed to Pope St. Gregory I (540-604), with the addition of four new modes, became dominant throughout Christendom. The original style of singing this music (also known as *plainsong*) degenerated over the centuries, but since the 1830s the Benedictine monks of the Abbey of Solesmes, France, have succeeded with admirable scholarship in restoring this ancient art to its first glory.

With its monodic melody, unhampered by either barlines or harmonization, Gregorian chant is ideally suited to its intended function of suggesting an austere and mystical beauty not of this earth. Ironically, it has all but disappeared from the liturgy of the Church today, while it has found new favor with many as an accompaniment to such activities as painting and Zen meditation.

In the spring of 1994 one might say a miracle happened: a recording of chants sung by the Choir of the Benedictine Monastery of Santo Domingo de Silos in Spain became a commercial phenomenon. Starting out as a favorite early-morning album of a radio disc jockey, it garnered media attention unprecedented for such an item, getting reviews and interviews on *Good Morning America*, the *Tonight Show*, the *Today Show*, and *Newsweek*. It hit the pop charts and was being merchandised in many record stores right alongside the latest rock albums. Would old Pope Gregory be pleased or appalled?

Less media-savvy, but more musically sophisticated, are the choir of monks from the Abbey of Saint-Pierre de Solesmes, directed by Dom Gajard, who have made about 20 fine recordings demonstrating their rigorous adherence to the highest standards of Gregorian chant performance. Excellent singing is also preserved in recordings by the others listed below.

Monastic Choir of St. Peter's Abbey, Solesmes. *Gregorian Sampler*, Paraclete 829

Nova Schola Gregoriana, Turco. *Mass Propers for the Church year*, Naxos 8.550711 [DDD]

Pro Cantione Antiqua, O'Donnell. *The Essential Gregorian Chant*, United 88035 [DDD]

Ruhland, Munich Capella Antiqua. Sony 53899 [DDD]

Santo Domingo de Silos Monks. *Chant*, EMI 62735 [DDD]

Schola Hungarica. *Gregorian Chant According to the Aquitaine Tradition*, Harmonia Mundi 1903037

————— *Since CDs can change label and number, use artists as main reference.* —————

Medieval Collections

What historians call the High Middle Ages and musicians the Gothic Era (ca. 1150-1450) is a period rich in the development of secular song and dance music. There are the chivalrous lyrics of the Troubadours, Trouvères, and Minnesingers—wandering minstrels with evocative names such as Bernard de Ventadorn and Walther von der Vogelweide. And there are countless irresistible little dances for instruments such as the nakers, rommelpot, cow horn and clappers.

Sacred music also evolved further in this period, with the appearance of *polyphonic* choral compositions; in these, two or more melodies were sung simultaneously to create a richer and more varied effect than the old plainsong. Polyphony was in effect an intermediate stage between the monody of chant and the development of modern harmony.

Altramar Medieval Music Ensemble. *Saint Francis and the Minstrels of God*, Dorian Discovery 80143 [DDD]

Anonymous 4. *An English Ladymass*, Harmonia Mundi 907080

Anonymous 4. *The Lily and the Lamb: Chant and polyphony from medieval England*, Harmonia Mundi 907125

Azéma (soprano), et al. *The Unicorn: Myth and Miracle in Medieval France, 1200-1300*, Erato 94830 [DDD]

Clemencic Consort. *Carmina Burana* (sel.), Harmonia Mundi 90335

Cohen, Boston Camerata. *A Medieval Christmas*, Nonesuch 71315 [ADD]

Ensemble Organum, Peres. *Laudario di Cortona: A Medieval Mystery*, Harmonia Mundi 901582

Ensemble P.A.N. *Ars Magis Subtiliter*, New Albion 021 [DDD]

Hillier, Hilliard Ensemble. *Proensa* (Troubadour songs), ECM 21368 [DDD]

Hillier, Hilliard Ensemble. *Sumer is Icumen In*, Harmonia Mundi 901154

Jaffee, Waverly Consort. *Douce Dame: Music of Courtly Love from Medieval France and Italy*, Vanguard Classics 8201 [ADD]

Kirkby, Page, Gothic Voices. *Hildegard von Bingen: A Feather on the Breath of God*, Hyperion 66039 [DDD]

Martin Best Medieval Ensemble. *Songs of Chivalry*, Nimbus 5006

Munrow, London Early Music Consort. *Music of the Crusades*, London [Decca] Jubilee 430264 [ADD]

Munrow, London Early Music Consort. *The Art of Courtly Love: French Secular Music (1300-1475)*, Virgin Veritas 61284 (2)

Munrow, London Early Music Consort. *Music of the Gothic Era*, Archiv 415292 [ADD]

Oberlin (countertenor), Barab (viol). *Troubadour and Trouvère Songs: Music of the Middle Ages Vol. 1, The 12th and 13th Centuries*, Lyrichord 8001

——— *Artists are listed alphabetically, not in order by critical ranking.* ———

Orlando Consort. *Popes and Antipopes: Music for the Courts of Avignon and Rome,* Metronome 1008 [DDD]

Oxford Camerata, Summerly. *Machaut: Messe le Nostre Dame; Songs,* Naxos 8.553833 [DDD]

Page, Gothic Voices. *The Study of Love: French songs and motets of the 14th Century,* Hyperion 66619 [DDD]

Page, Gothic Voices. *Music of the Lion-Hearted King,* Hyperion 66336 [DDD]

Pickett, New London Collective. *The Pilgrimage to Santiago,* L'Oiseau-Lyre 433148 (2) [DDD]

Pickett, New London Consort. *The Feast of Fools,* L'Oiseau-Lyre 433194 [DDD]

Sequentia. *Hildegard von Bingen: Canticles of Ecstasy,* Deutsche Harmonia Mundi 77320 [DDD]

Wishart, Sinfonye. *The Sweet Look and the Loving Manner: Trobairitz Love Lyrics and Chansons de Femme from Medieval France,* Hyperion 66625 [DDD]

Renaissance Collections

The Renaissance period (ca. 1450-1600) in music corresponds to the great flowering of secular and humanist ideals in Europe after the fall of Constantinople to the Turks and the subsequent flight of Eastern scholars to the West, which resulted in the rediscovery of much long-lost literature and philosophy. Secular works gained even more attention from composers. Huge repertoires were built up for solo instruments such as the lute and virginals. Splendid brass music was written for processions at the royal courts. Little proto-orchestras, such as "consorts of viols," came into being. Secular part-songs, particularly the Italian madrigals, became larger, more complex, and infinitely richer, as heard in the cosmic-sounding masses of Palestrina, Byrd, and Victoria. Four nations were dominant at this time in producing music in the European Classical tradition: England, Spain, France, and Italy.

Barlow, Broadside Band. *English Country Dances,* Saydisc 393 [DDD]

Bassano, Gentlemen of the Chappell, His Majesties Sagbutts and Cornetts. *Venice Preserved,* ASV Gaudeamus 122 [DDD]

Calliope. *Calliope Dances: A Renaissance Revel,* Nonesuch 79039 [DDD]

Chance (countertenor), Wilson (lute). *The Sypres Curten of the Night: Elizabethean and Jacobean lute-songs,* Chandos Chaconne 0538 [DDD]

Christophers, The Sixteen. *The Eton Choirbook, Vol. 3: The Pillars of Eternity,* Collins Classics 1342 [DDD]

Deller Consort. *Shakespeare Songs and Consort Music,* Harmonia Mundi 190202 [ADD]

———— *[DDD] indicates newest recordings; [ADD] or [AAD] are reissues.* ————

Fretwork. *The English Viol,* Virgin Veritas 61173 [DDD]

Hill, Westminster Cathedral Choir. *Treasures of the Spanish Renaissance,* Hyperion 66168 [DDD]

Hillier, Hilliard Ensemble. *The Old Hall Manuscript (early English Renaissance music),* EMI 54111 [DDD]

Jaffee, Waverly Consort. *1492: Music from the Age of Discovery,* EMI 54506

La Nef. *Music for Joan the Mad: Spain 1479-1555,* Dorian 80128 [DDD]

McCreesh, Gabrieli Consort & Players. *Venetian Vespers,* Archiv 437552 (2) [DDD]

Minstrelsy. *Vieni o Cara,* Lyrichord 8023

Page, Gothic Voices. *The Service of Venus and Mars (French motets and Mass movements),* Hyperion 66238 [DDD]

Paniagua, Atrium Musicae de Madrid. *Musique Arabo-Andalouse,* Harmonia Mundi 90389

Pickett, New London Consort. *Elizabethan and Jacobean Consort Music,* Linn 011 [DDD]

Ragossnig, Ulsamer Collegium. *Dance Music of the Renaissance,* Archiv 415294 [ADD]

Rooley, Consort of Musicke. *The Monteverdi Circle,* Musica Oscura 070989 [DDD]

Summerly, Oxford Camerata. *Lamentations,* Naxos 8.550572 [DDD]

Summerly, Oxford Camerata. *Renaissance Masterpieces,* Naxos 8.550843 [DDD]

William Byrd (1543-1623)

Byrd was a devout Catholic whose musical genius protected him in an England where Catholics were ruthlessly persecuted. His royal patron, Queen Elizabeth, pointedly ignored his religious views. In gratitude, he created some of the greatest masterpieces of English Protestant church music, including *The Great Service.* For many years Byrd was a close associate of Thomas Tallis, the "father of English Cathedral music." The Queen granted the pair a joint license which allowed them to virtually monopolize music publishing.

Byrd also contributed significant instrumental music, including some 140 pieces for the virginals (an early keyboard instrument whose repertoire is now often performed on the harpsichord). These are widely anthologized in two famous collections, *Ladye Nevell's Virginal Booke* and the *Fitzwilliam Virginal Book.* William Byrd is often considered the most versatile composer of his time, and the first great genius of the keyboard.

——— *CDs go in and out of print; availability of all listed items is not assured.* ———

Choral Music

Byrd is best known for his Latin Masses for 3, 4, and 5 Voices (i.e. vocal ranges). Two or more are featured on each recording listed.

Phillips, Tallis Scholars. Gimell 454945
Summerly, Oxford Camerata. Naxos 8.550574 [DDD]

Consort Music

Music for a small group of viols (old string instruments).

Fretwork. Virgin Classics 59539 [45031] [DDD]

John Dowland (1563-1626)

A younger contemporary of William Byrd, Dowland was England's other most famous Elizabethan composer. After a visit to Paris at age 17, he converted to Catholicism, but fared less well in the Virgin Queen's favor than Byrd. As a result he spent considerable time abroad, moping, as was his wont, in the courts of Brunswick and Denmark.

His reputation for melancholy was so pervasive that he adopted as his motto "Semper Dowland Semper Dolens" ("Always Dowland, Always Sorrowing"). It is no surprise that among his best-known titles are "Flow my tears," "I saw my lady weep," "In darkness let me dwell," and "Forlorn hope." One of his texts reads: "My wailing Muse her woeful work begins, sounding nought but sorrow, grief and care." Not a party animal perhaps, but a touching poet.

He was a master of the lute, and more importantly, the song with lute accompaniment. His sensitivity in matching words and music has carried his reputation as one of the greatest song writers down to the present day.

Lachrimae, or Seven Teares

This unique instrumental work calls for five viols and a lute to play seven pavans (slow dances), each beginning with a sorrowful descending figure, and covering the gamut of weeping including "teares, and sighes, and grones." An additional 14 pieces in the collection abandon the "lachrimae" motif; a few of them are actually quite cheerful!

Fretwork. Virgin Classics 59539 [45005] [DDD]
Holman, Parley of Instruments. Hyperion 66637 [DDD]
Lindberg, Dowland Consort. BIS 315 [DDD]

——— *Some CDs may be available only through importers.* ———

Lute Music

McFarlane. Dorian 90148 [DDD]
O'Dette. Complete Lute Works, Vol. 4, Harmonia Mundi 907163

Lute Songs

Agnew (tenor), Wilson (lute). *Flow my Teares*, Metronome 1010 [DDD]
Agnew (tenor), Wilson (lute). *In Darkness let me Dwell*, Metronome 1011
   [ADD]
Müller (tenor), Wilson (lute). *First Book of Songs*, ASV Gaudeamus 135 [DDD]
Oberlin (countertenor), Iadone (lute). Lyrichord 8011

Giovanni Gabrieli (ca. 1554/57-1612)

Gabrieli, about whose life little is known, became the most important composer of grandiose ceremonial music in Renaissance Italy. As organist of St. Mark's, Venice, following the death of his uncle and teacher, Andrea, he had free rein to compose in an ornate and brilliant style. Contemporary visitors to the church described being overwhelmed by the antiphonal pealings of organ and brass echoing back and forth across the chancel. Late in life Gabrieli became the teacher of Heinrich Schütz, who was to become known as the "father of German music" and the greatest German composer before Bach. Gabrieli's music fell into oblivion for centuries, being revived only in recent years.

Canzoni for Brass

These short, gleaming pieces work well on either modern or historical brass instruments.

Empire Brass and Friends. Telarc 80204 [DDD]
Parrott, Taverner Consort Choir and Players. EMI 54265
Biggs, Edward Tarr Brass Ensemble, Gregg Smith Singers, Texas Boys' Choir.
   The Glory of Venice/Gabrieli in San Marco, CBS 42645 [ADD]
McCreesh, Gabrieli Consort and Players. *A Venetian Coronation 1595*, Virgin
   Classics 59006 [DDD]

Josquin Desprez (ca. 1440-1521)

Considered almost universally by his colleagues to be the greatest composer in the world around the year 1500, Josquin during his long life produced a large number of masterpieces, mostly sacred works such as masses and motets. He commanded large salaries and was sought after by princes and kings, one of whom chafed that Josquin would compose "only when it suits him, not when you wish." His mature works exhibited an admirable balance among the elements of euphonious sound, formal symmetry, vigor of expression, and fresh imagination. They were regarded respectfully everywhere as models of composition.

We think of him today as a Frenchman, but that is scarcely cosmopolitan enough for one who had a Flemish upbringing, spent the better part of 40 years in Milan and Rome, and maintained close contacts with the court of the Holy Roman Emperor. He won the praise of the author Rabelais, and of Martin Luther, who called him "the master of notes— they have to do what he wants.' His tomb was destroyed during the French Revolution along with other hated symbols of the past; his music survives undefiled.

Footnote: in searching catalogues for this composer's works, keep in mind that most sources alphabetize him under "J," with just a few opting for "D"—though never under "P". It is not quite certain whether or not Desprez (or Despres, or des Prez, or des Prés) should be considered a surname in the modern sense, or if he is just "Little Joe from Picardy." I incline towards the latter.

Masses and Motets

Herreweghe, La Chapelle Royale Chorus. *Motets,* Harmonia Mundi 901243
Hillier, Hilliard Ensemble. *Motets and chansons,* Virgin Veritas 61302 [DDD]
Phillips, Tallis Scholars. *Missa L'homme armé,* et al., Gimell 454919 [DDD]
Turner, Pro Cantione Antiqua. *Missa L'homme armé,* Deutsche Grammophon
415293 + Ockeghem: *Missa pro defunctis*

Orlandus Lassus (ca. 1532-1594)

Lassus was a close counterpart to Josquin Desprez one century later, and could be considered his direct musical descendant in the field of counterpoint. Though less of a melodist than the earlier master, Lassus compared favorably in form, fecundity, energy, and attention to detail. He even had similar name problems: born in Mons (now part of Belgium), he was christened Roland de Lassus; from a sojourn in Rome (as master of music at the Basilica of St. John Lateran) he gained the alternate spelling of Orlando di Lasso. His name shows up in various catalogues under either "D" or "L."

——— *All CDs listed are considered approximately equal in (high) merit.* ———

Along with Palestrina he dominated his era, and was the last great composer of the Flemish School. Emperor Maximilian II granted him a patent of nobility, Pope Gregory II created him a Cavalier of St. Peter. When he died, in Munich, of depression and fatigue, all Europe mourned him as the Belgian Orpheus, and the Prince of Music.

Vocal and Choral Music

Lassus is equally noted for masses, madrigals, motets, and chansons—all beloved types of vocal music in his era.

Higginbottom, Choir of New College, Oxford. *Choral Music,* Collins Classics 1494 [DDD]
Hillier, Hilliard Ensemble. *Chansons and Motets,* Virgin Veritas 61166 [DDD]

Claudio Monteverdi (1567-1643)

Born in Cremona, Italy, Monteverdi showed an early aptitude for music and by age 23 was employed as a string player in the court of Mantua, where he worked for over two decades, beginning composition of the madrigals which were to represent the core and paradigm of his creative life. Ever an experimenter, Monteverdi added instrumental accompaniments to the traditionally a capella choral works. Singlehandedly he created the first true orchestra. Eventually his efforts made it possible for the madrigal to evolve into the cantata. He became the first genius of opera, creating *Orfeo* only seven years after the form was invented, and producing one of the greatest of all operas, *The Coronation of Poppea,* at the age of 75.

Monteverdi was to Italian Renaissance music what Michelangelo was to its visual art. In 1613 he took over the most coveted post in his country: music director of St. Mark's in Venice. During the next thirty years he accomplished the miracle of metamorphosing from the last great composer of the Renaissance to the first great composer of the Baroque era. During his long and highly productive life he suffered often from depression, especially for several years after the death of his wife. In 1630 he took ordination as a priest.

The scope and inspiration of his music mark him as one of the greatest composers of the 17th century, and one of the greatest of all time. The intense beauty of his melodies, his forceful expression of emotion and humanity, make his music seem astonishingly modern even today.

L'Incoronazione di Poppea

For an example of Monteverdi's great operas most record guides start with his first, *La Favola d'Orfeo.* Although it is obviously historically important, *The Coronation of Poppea,*

———— *CDs listed are solid, central choices, not necessarily "the greatest."* ————

his last opera, written when in his 75th year, is infinitely richer and more interesting in every way, and is far more likely to make you sit up and understand why this very ancient composer is still so alive. It has pageantry, intrigue, tragedy, comedy, and it's completely amoral—the evil Nero and his conniving wife Poppea are triumphant at the end. But, they win us over by singing one of the most sublime love duets in any opera ever written (although some scholars believe this was actually written by another composer!).

Augér, Hickox, City of London Baroque Sinfonia. Virgin Classics 59524 (3) [DDD]
Borst, Jacobs, Concerto Vocale. Harmonia Mundi 901330/32 (3)
McNair, Gardiner, English Baroque Soloists. Archiv 447088 (3) [DDD]

Madrigals

The madrigal is a vocal work for small choral ensemble, popular in the Renaissance period. Its form and content varied considerably, but for Monteverdi it signified an elaborate polyphonic setting of the poems of Petrarch. His several published volumes of madrigals are considered the high point in the development of this musical form.

Alessandrini, Concerto Italiano Vocal Ensemble. Book 6 complete. Arcana 66 [DDD]
Christie, Les Arts Florissants. Sel. from Books 7 and 8. Harmonia Mundi 1901068
Rooley, Consort of Musicke. *Madrigals of Love,* Virgin Classics 59621 [DDD]
Stubbs, Tragicomedia. *Madrigali concertati,* Das Alte Werk 91971 [DDD]

Vespro della Beata Vergine (Vespers of 1610)

This long and magnificent choral paean of evening prayers to the Virgin Mary has had a surprising number of complete recordings. Those listed here have been especially praised.

Gardiner, English Baroque Soloists, London Monteverdi Choir. Archiv 429565 (2) [DDD]
Parrott, Taverner Consort, Choir and Players. EMI 47078 (2)

Giovanni Pierluigi da Palestrina (ca. 1525-1594)

He was in some ways the diametric opposite of his fellow Italian Renaissance composer Claudio Monteverdi—Palestrina had almost no interest in innovation or musical revolu-

———— Some famous CDs are not listed because currently out of print. ————

tion. Far from indulging in the vivid expression of human emotion, he reserved his creativity for flights of spiritual ecstasy. He had no interest in instruments or vertical harmony; his great compositions are all a capella and represent the culmination of the polyphonic style. They may sound over-refined to some listeners, but there is no denying the purity and power of Palestrina's seamless "cathedrals in sound." He wrote nearly a thousand such works, many of them commissioned by princes, potentates, and popes.

Missa Papae Marcelli

This melodically and harmonically beautiful mass written for Pope Marcellus, clear and noble in its lineaments, has long been the most famous and beloved of Palestrina's more than 100 masses.

Hill, Westminster Cathedral Choir. Hyperion 66266 [DDD] + other works by Palestrina

Preston, Westminster Abbey Choir. Deutsche Grammophon 415517 [DDD] + Allegri: *Miserere*, et al.

Michael Praetorius (1571-1621)

Like Monteverdi, Praetorius spanned the Renaissance and Baroque periods. He was the youngest son of a Protestant pastor who had studied directly under Martin Luther. During his relatively short life he dedicated himself mainly to the composing and publishing of Lutheran church music, producing more than 1,200 chorales (the Reformation-era counterparts to the medieval Catholic plainsong). Ironically, Praetorius is remembered today mostly for his delightful instrumental settings of secular French dances, giving some credence perhaps to the medieval adage that "the Devil has the best tunes."

Terpischore

Published in 1612, this collection of 78 merry, lilting, foot-stomping dances sounds as fresh today as four centuries ago. No particular instruments are specified in the score, but all reputable performers now employ a colorful array of authentic period fiddles, winds, and percussion.

Munrow, London Early Music Consort. EMI Studio 69024 [ADD] + Motets
Munrow, London Early Music Consort. Virgin Classics 61289 + Motets
Pickett, New London Consort. L'Oiseau-Lyre 414633 [DDD]

——— *Catalog numbers are subject to change without notice.* ———

Thomas Tallis (ca. 1505-1585)

When he was buried at Greenwich, Tallis was recommended to eternity by some verses on a tombstone no longer extant:

> *Enterred here doth ly a worthy Wyght*
> *Who for long Tyme in Musick bore the Bell:*
> *His Name to shew, was Thomas Tallys hyght,*
> *In honest vertuous Lyff he dyd excell.*

Prophetic, perhaps, in fixing his musical fame in the past, for he has the dubious distinction of being better known as part of another composer's title rather than on his own merits. For years, the *Fantasia on a Theme by Thomas Tallis* (by Ralph Vaughan Williams) was the only way most people were reminded of him, and one might wonder why a theme so haunting did not sooner spark curiosity about his own works.

He was an organist at Waltham Abbey when Henry VIII shut down the monasteries in 1540. Like his friend and colleague William Byrd, he made his peace with necessity and joined the King's own Chapel Royal, where he composed music and played the organ through the reigns of three more Tudors: Edward VI, Mary, and Elizabeth I. He and Byrd were granted a monopoly of music paper and printed music by the staunchly Protestant Elizabeth, for which they thanked her by dedicating a major printed collection of their hymns and motets. The fact that she graciously ignored the ill-disguised Catholicism of two of her best composers has justified her nickname of Good Queen Bess, at least among music lovers.

Tallis wrote much music for the Anglican service, but ironically, most of it is lost and his surviving works are principally in Latin, including two settings of *The Lamentations of Jeremiah,* and the 16 motets dedicated to the Queen. His works are distinguished by dark sonorities and thick textures. They are richly expressive, although limited in range by an emphasis on sombre and melancholy emotions.

His long career encompassed nearly all of the 16th century. We know of no tragic or dramatic incidents in his life, or whether any personal losses contributed to his morose muse, but his very personal idiom has guaranteed him a place in the pantheon of great composers which no one, and nothing, can take away. As his tombstone concluded:

> *As he dyd lyve, so also did he dy,*
> *In mild and quyet sort (O! happy Man).*
> *To God ful oft for Mercy did he cry,*
> *Wherefore he lyves, let Death do what he can.*

—— Since CDs can change label and number, use artists as main reference. ——

Church Music

An introduction to Tallis should include some of his anthems, plus the astounding 40-part motet Spem in Alium, a tour de force if there ever was one. This is the ultimate in polyphonic composition: the music is laid out for eight choirs singing simultaneously, each having five separate melodic lines. The piece begins with each of the 40 parts entering one by one, and then singing together at a dramatic point in the text with a breathtaking change of harmony.

Parrott, Taverner Choir and Consort. EMI 49563
Phillips, Tallis Scholars. *Spem in Alium,* Gimell 454906 [DDD]

Tomás Luis de Victoria (ca. 1549-1611)

The most famous Spanish composer of the High Renaissance, Victoria spent more than 20 years in Rome; some believe he studied with Palestrina, although that influence may have been only indirect. Whatever the case, there is no denying a flavor in Victoria's music that evokes the sombre Spanish court of Philip II and his forbidding palace, the Escorial. His religious music combines a dark mystical intensity with the unbending severity of the Inquisition. There is also often a sense of drama—some say melodrama—that is totally absent from the ethereal music of Palestrina.

Requiem Mass

In its striking blend of seriousness and serenity this work projects a galvanizing and granitic strength. Hearing it, one cannot argue with those who draw parallels between Victoria's music and the religious paintings of his contemporaries, El Greco and Velazquez.

Phillips, Tallis Scholars. Gimell 454912 [DDD] + A. Lobo: *Funeral Motet for Philip II of Spain*
Hill, Winchester Cathedral Choir. Hyperion 66304 [DDD]

——— *Artists are listed alphabetically, not in order by critical ranking.* ———

The Baroque Era
(ca. 1600-1750)

Several qualities distinguish the Baroque era, and the dictionary is the best place to begin. "Baroque: anything extravagantly ornamented, especially something so ornate as to be in bad taste." Lovers of Baroque music will be offended by the second half of the definition, but keeping the possibility in mind can serve as a useful corrective when examining this music.

A great expansion of instrumental resources around 1600, particularly through the creative efforts of Claudio Monteverdi (see preceding chapter), led to a decline of interest in the purely vocal style. Art music grew larger and louder. Changing political events led to a growing patronage of the arts by the nobility, who favored grandiosity in all things.

The Catholic Church, battered by the Lutheran Reformation, lost much of its influence in the arts; the emphasis on polyphony gave way to homophony, a texture in which a single melody predominates, accompanied by subordinate harmonies. The old church modes faded from the scene, generally replaced by a new system of tonality based on "keys," major and minor; at the end of the period, J. S. Bach threw all his weight on the "modern" side with the publication of his *Well-Tempered Clavier,* a demonstration both practical and artistic of the new system's superior technical potential.

While adventurers were exploring and colonizing the world beyond Europe, musicians were busily creating new and more complex forms in which to express their ideas. The concerto and "concerto grosso," the dance suite, the sonata, the cantata, and the oratorio all were new in the 1600s—as was opera, perhaps the most influential form of all. Monteverdi, again, was the main force behind the success of this form, whose vivid portrayal of dramatic conflict insinuated itself into most of the other forms, not excepting the Mass. But by the end of the Baroque era, most composers interested in vocal music had stopped writing Masses and were concentrating on the theater.

Whatever the form, sacred or secular, ornate grandeur is the hallmark of the Baroque style. It is virtually impossible to miss. You can "drop a needle" on just about any piece of Baroque music, by any composer from any country, and its "Baroqueness" is immediately identifiable. It is this fact which leads its detractors to dismiss much of it as "musical wallpaper." It is true that a huge amount of Baroque music was written rapidly, under commission, and according to formula. Telemann's *Tafelmusik,* Handel's *Water Music,* and thousands more were composed to order as background music for some sybaritic king's dinner party or Sunday outing. Genius, however, will out. Bach and Couperin, Scarlatti and Purcell conformed to the rigid rules of their time, but they were able to bend the system to their wills, and create from its raw materials music that still stuns the senses, engages the intellect, and often, in its rather extroverted way, touches the heart.

A rebirth of popular interest in Baroque music has occurred over the last 30 years thanks largely to a return to the use of period instruments, and a renewed scholarly attention to authentic performance traditions. Many current recordings adhere to these ideals, a fact frequently reflected in the recommendations.

Tomaso Albinoni (1671-1750)

Albinoni was not really a very important composer, but his one "hit," emasculated as it is, is so big we can't leave him out. He was born in Venice just seven years before his neighbor, the far more significant Antonio Vivaldi (*q.v.*). Eldest son of a prosperous paper manufacturer, he did not even claim to be more than a dilettante for the first half of his life. Nevertheless, Bach admired much of his work and even "borrowed" some of it as grist for his own mill.

Adagio for Strings and Organ

Ironically, Albinoni provided only the seed from which his "masterpiece" sprouted. A 20th-century Italian, Remo Giazotto, took a fragment of Albinoni's music and worked it into a full-length pseudo-Baroque Adagio. This magnificent forgery shows up on innumerable recordings, frequently coupled with other "greatest hits" of the Baroque.

I Musici. Philips Digital Classics 410606 [DDD] + Mozart: Serenade No. 13 *Eine kleine Nachtmusik;* Pachelbel: Canon in D; Boccherini: Minuet, *et al.*

Karajan, Berlin Philharmonic Orchestra. Deutsche Grammophon 413309 [DDD] + Pachelbel: Canon in D, short works by Bach, Gluck, Mozart, and Vivaldi

Karajan, Berlin Philharmonic. *Karajan Adagio,* Deutsche Grammophon 445282 [DDD] + slow pieces and movements by other composers

Marriner, Academy of St. Martin-in-the-Fields. EMI 47391 + Pachelbel: Canon in D, other short pieces

Münchinger, Stuttgart Chamber Orchestra. London [Decca] 411973 [DDD] + Pachelbel: Canon in D, other Baroque favorites

Paillard Chamber Orchestra. RCA Victor 65468 [DDD] + Pachelbel: Canon in D, selections by 9 other Baroque composers

Warren-Green, London Chamber Orchestra. Virgin Classics 59563 [DDD] + Pachelbel: Canon in D; Vivaldi: *The Four Seasons*

——— *CDs go in and out of print; availability of all listed items is not assured.* ———

Johann Sebastian Bach (1685-1750)

Along with Mozart and Beethoven, Bach is one of the leading candidates for Greatest Composer. He is the hands-down winner among performing musicians, who appreciate more than the general public the solid professionalism behind his art. All his life he was the grudging "most obedient servant" of one princely or clerical employer or another, being required to churn out occasional and functional pieces by the hundreds. Despite this he seemed constitutionally incapable of shoddy work, insisting on filling his compositions with deep ideas, sonic splendors, or heartwrenching emotions, as his muse dictated.

Like many composers of his time, Bach came from a family which had produced musicians as if they were tradesmen through several generations. His biography produces no very colorful events, no titillating scandals—unless you are obsessed, as many seem to be, by the fact that his two wives bore him a total of 20 children. Far more amazing than that is the fact that three of them became excellent composers in their own right. Bach did spend about a month in jail once, but only because he had irritated one of his royal employers over his desire to take a better-paying job elsewhere.

Many of his contemporaries spoke of his being stubborn and difficult. He once compared the playing of one of his bassoonists to a nanny-goat, and barely escaped being drawn into a duel. He was a perfectionist, yet was quick to praise those he admired. As a young man he walked more than 200 miles to hear the great Buxtehude play the organ. He liked the instrumental music of the Italians, especially Vivaldi, and paid them the ultimate compliment of rewriting some of their works in his own style. And he was a sincere family man: he nurtured his musical sons, compiled a remarkable genealogy of his musical ancestors and collected their manuscripts, and wrote a delightful collection of pieces for his second wife to play, the *Anna Magdalena Bach Notebook*.

Bach's death in 1750 has stood ever since as the marker ending the Baroque era. It was he who fulfilled its ideals and burst its limits. After him, most composers felt there was nothing more to be done in the old style, and new ideas began to evolve. The reaction was so severe that Bach's music itself seemed to disappear almost overnight. Not until 1829, when the 20-year-old Felix Mendelssohn conducted a highly successful performance of the *St. Matthew Passion,* did Bach's music start its slow march back into the affections of the public. Even at that, it was only in the 1960s that it had truly a vigorous revival among musicians and on records.

On purely musical grounds, and in terms of the Baroque parameters, Bach's music is considered virtually a model of perfection. Marvelous in its logic, it is highly favored by intellectuals; Bach was Albert Einstein's favorite composer. Most of it is noble and serious in tone, and there is a certain weightiness even in the movements based on popular songs and dances. Some listeners find Bach's approach overly severe and are uncomfortable with the often hymn-like sonorities and the music's measured Teutonic tread; but no one denies

——— *Some CDs may be available only through importers.* ———

the awesome intelligence which must have been necessary to create works of such complexity and power.

Brandenburg Concertos (6). S.1046/51

Commissioned by the Margrave of Brandenburg, these six concerti blend French, Italian and German stylistic elements into a colorful mix of courtly entertainment music that has remained, with Handel's *Water Music* and Vivaldi's *The Four Seasons,* the most popular orchestral music of the Baroque. Each concerto allows a different instrument(s) of the ensemble to have a starring role.

Britten, English Chamber Orchestra. London [Decca] Double 443847 (2) [ADD]

[For some time now the Schwann Opus catalog has unaccountably insisted on listing the Britten version as performed by the Scottish Chamber Orchestra. This error has subsequently multiplied like rabbits in Australia, showing up most recently in (perhaps appropriately?) *The Complete Idiot's Guide to Classical Music* (Alpha Books, 1997, p. 347). A year ago I listed this recording in an article I was commissioned to write for a national magazine. When the magazine hit the stands I found *English* changed to *Scottish.* I called the magazine immediately and was told that their "fact checker" had called a record store in New York where the (high-school age) clerk had looked it up in the Schwann catalog and triumphantly reported that I was "wrong." I was, in fact, banned from writing further for the magazine by a senior editor who said it was obvious that I "didn't know what I was doing." This has cost me potentially thousands of dollars in income. I call this to the attention of those who flippantly maintain that people who concern themselves with minutiae and accuracy are nothing more than "anal retentive" obscurantists. I also mention it to save anyone the trouble of writing me—ever again!—to "inform" me of my "error." It is the English Chamber Orchestra, as printed on the album cover, and the copyright holder, London Records (Decca in the U.K.), will tell you the same. You may now return to the listings.]

Harnoncourt, Vienna Concentus Musicus. Das Alte Werk 77611 (2) [ADD]
Koopman, Amsterdam Baroque Orchestra. Erato Bonsai 91935 (2) [DDD]
Lamon, Tafelmusik. Sony Vivarte 66289 (2) [DDD]
Leonhardt Consort. Sony Seon 62946 (2) [ADD]
Linde, Linde Consort. EMI Studio 63434 (2) + *Musical Offering*
Marriner, Academy of St. Martin's-in-the-Fields. Nos. 1-4, EMI Red Line 69877 [DDD]; Nos. 5-6 + Orchestral Suite No. 1, EMI Red Line 69878 [DDD]
Marriner, Academy of St. Martin's-in-the-Fields. Nos. 1-3, Philips 400076 [ADD]; Nos. 4-6, Philips 400077 [ADD]
Pearlman, Boston Baroque. Nos. 1-3, Telarc 80368 [DDD]; Nos. 4-6, Telarc 80354 [DDD]
Pickett, New London Consort. L'Oiseau-Lyre 440675 (2) [DDD]
Pinnock, The English Concert. Archiv 423492 (3) [DDD] + Suites for Orchestra 1-4

———— *U.S. labels and numbers are given first, U.K. in [brackets] when needed.* ————

Cantatas

Bach wrote about 300 of these half-hour choral works for soloists, chorus, and orchestra, of which some 200 survive. They were written for use in the Lutheran Church services of Bach's day, in lieu of the Latin Mass, no longer considered theologically acceptable. Some of the favorite short pieces by Bach, such as "Jesu, Joy of Man's Desiring," "Sheep May Safely Graze," and "Sleepers Wake" come from the cantatas.

Failoni Chamber Orchestra, Budapest and Hungarian Radio Choirs. Cantatas 80, 147, Naxos 8.550642 [DDD]

Gardiner, English Baroque Soloists, Kirkby. Cantata 51, Philips 411458 [DDD] + Magnificat

Gardiner, English Baroque Soloists, Monteverdi Choir. Cantatas 140, 147, Archiv 431809 [DDD]

Gardiner, English Baroque Soloists, Monteverdi Choir. *Jesu, Joy of Man's Desiring: Great Bach Choruses,* Archiv 439885 [DDD]

Herreweghe, La Chapelle Royale, Concerto Vocale. Harmonia Mundi 901326 + Magnificat

Koopman, Amsterdam Baroque Orchestra and Choir. *Complete Cantatas,* Vol. 1, Erato 98536 (3) [DDD]

Leonhardt Consort, Harnoncourt, Vienna Concentus Musicus. Cantatas 5-8, Das Alte Werk 42498 (2) [AAD]

Concertos (7) for Harpsichord. S.1052/8

These are among the earliest masterpieces of music for keyboard instrument with orchestral accompaniment. Bach wrote them during a break from his church music duties, while directing a group called the Collegium Musicum. These were students and Leipzig townspeople who got together to play in a local coffeehouse.

Actually, it appears that virtually all these concertos are Bach's transcriptions from earlier works, such as violin or wind pieces, which are now lost. They are noted for the technical virtuosity of the "outer" movements (1 and 3) and the soulful expressiveness of the slow middle movements.

Kipnis, Marriner, London Strings. Sony 53243 (2) [ADD]

Koopman, Amsterdam Baroque Orchestra. Erato Duo Bonsai 91929 (2), 92930 (2) [DDD]

Pinnock, English Concert. Archiv 415991 (Nos. 1, 2, 3) [ADD], Archiv 415992 (Nos. 4, 5, 6) [ADD]

——— *All CDs listed are considered approximately equal in (high) merit.* ———

Concertos (2) for Violin, S.1041/2; Concerto in D Minor for 2 Violins, S.1043

These are the first great violin concertos in European history. They are packed with beautiful themes, clever details of construction, and opportunities for bravura display. That is what great violin concertos have striven for ever since. The "double" concerto is especially beloved for its ravishing slow movement. All three can fit conveniently on one CD, so look for a good version that does not split them over two or more discs.

> **Grumiaux, Krebbers, DeWaart, Philharmonia Orchestra.** Philips Silver Line 420700 [ADD] + Double Concerto for Violin and Oboe in D Minor, S.1060
> **Kuijken, La Petite Bande.** DHM Editio Classica 77006 [DDD]
> **Mutter, Accardo, English Chamber Orchestra.** EMI 47005 [DDD]
> **Perlman, Stern, Mehta, New York Philharmonic Orchestra.** Sony 38487
> **Schroeder, Hirons, Hogwood, Academy of Ancient Music.** L'Oiseau-Lyre 400080 [DDD]
> **Wallfisch, Bury, Orchestra of the Age of Enlightenment.** Virgin Veritas 59319 [DDD]
> **Zukerman, Sillito, English Chamber Orchestra, Los Angeles Philharmonic Orchestra.** Sony Essential Classics 48273 [ADD] + Vivaldi: miscellaneous violin concertos

Harpsichord Music

Listed below are some of the more famous of Bach's numerous solo works for harpsichord (or often, originally, clavichord), and some of their best and most representative recordings.

Chromatic Fantasy and Fugue in D Minor, S.903

> **Banowetz, Duphil (pianos).** Naxos 8.550066 [DDD] + *Italian Concerto, Capriccio on the Departure of a Beloved Brother*, French Suite No. 6, et al.
> **Rousset (harpsichord).** L'Oiseau-Lyre 433054 [DDD] + Partita in B Minor, S.831, 4 Duets, S.802-5, *Italian Concerto*

Goldberg Variations, S.988

> **Aldwell (piano).** Biddulph FLW 001 [DDD]
> **Cole (harpsichord).** Virgin Veritas 59045 [DDD]

————— *CDs listed are solid, central choices, not necessarily "the greatest."* —————

Gould (piano). Sony 38479 or 52685 (single discs) or 52594 (coupled with *Well-Tempered Clavier* (3) [ADD]
Pinnock (harpsichord). Archiv 415130 [ADD]
Rousset (harpsichord). L'Oiseau-Lyre 444866 [DDD]
A. Schiff (piano). London [Decca] 417116 [DDD]

Italian Concerto in F, S.971

Banowetz, Duphil (pianos). Naxos 8.550066 [DDD] + Chromatic Fantasy and Fugue in D Minor, *Capriccio on the Departure of a Beloved Brother*, French Suite No. 6, et al.
Kipnis (harpsichord). Sony 53263 [ADD] + other short pieces
Pinnock (harpsichord). *The Harmonious Blacksmith*, Archiv 413591 [DDD] + short favorites by Handel, Couperin, Rameau, Scarlatti and others
Rousset (harpsichord). L'Oiseau-Lyre 433054 [DDD] + Partita in B Minor, S.831, 4 Duets, S.802-5, *Chromatic Fantasy and Fugue* in D Minor

Partitas for Harpsichord Nos. 1-6, S.825-30

Rousset (harpsichord). L'Oiseau-Lyre 440217 (2) [DDD]
Verlet (harpsichord). Philips Duo 442559 (2)

Well-Tempered Clavier, S.846-893

Gilbert (harpsichord). Archiv 413439 (4) [DDD]
Gould (piano). CBS 52594 (3) [AAD] + *Goldberg Variations*
Moroney (harpsichord). Harmonia Mundi 901285/88 (4) [DDD]
A. Schiff (piano). Book I, London [Decca] 414388 (2) [DDD]; Book II, London [Decca] 417236 (2) [DDD]

Instrumental Music—Miscellaneous

Bach wrote a considerable variety of pieces for solo instruments or for small ensembles. Aside from the *English* Suites and *French* Suites (whose names mean nothing anyway!), most of these look rather boringly generic in the catalogs, what with an endless litany of suites, partitas, sonatas, and trio sonatas. A prudent approach might be to focus on an already favored instrument and try one of Bach's more famous works written for it. If you already have a taste for a specific artist, indulge it as well. To get you started here are some of the best-known works along with well-known performers.

——— *Some famous CDs are not listed because currently out of print.* ———

Lute Music

Bream (tr. guitar). RCA Victor Gold Seal 61603 [ADD]
Isbin (tr. guitar). Virgin Classics 59503 [DDD]
Kirchhof (Baroque lute). Sony Vivarte 45858 (2) [DDD]
J. Williams (tr. guitar) Sony 42204

Sonatas (3) and Partitas (3) for Solo Violin, S.1001-1006

Grumiaux. Philips Duo 438736 (2) [ADD]
S. Kuijken. DHM Editio Classica 77043 (2) [ADD]
Milstein. Deutsche Grammophon 423294 (2) [ADD]
Mintz. Deutsche Grammophon 445526 (2) [ADD]
Perlman. EMI 49483 (2) [DDD]

Suites (6) for Solo Cello, S.1007-1012

Casals. EMI 66215 (2) (mono)
Fournier. Deutsche Grammophon 419359 (2) [ADD]
Kirshbaum. Virgin Classics 45086 (2)
Ma. CBS 37867 (2)
Rostropovich. EMI 55363 (2)
Starker. Mercury Living Presence 432756 (2) [ADD]

Magnificat in D. S.243

A joyful choral Christmas classic, the *Magnificat* takes its text (in Latin) from the story of the angel's revelation to Mary that she will bear the Savior, and her poetic response, "My soul shall magnify the Lord." The work has complex textures and demands careful choral singing to avoid becoming a jumble.

Christophers, The Sixteen, Orchestra of the Sixteen. Collins Classics 1320
    [DDD] + Vivaldi: *Gloria* in D. Rv.589; Caldara: *Stabat Mater*
Gardiner, English Baroque Soloists, Kirkby. Philips 411458 [DDD] + Cantata 51
Herreweghe, La Chapelle Royale, Collegium Vocale. Harmonia Mundi
    901326 + Cantata 80
Hickox, Collegium Musicum 90. Chandos 0518 [DDD] + Vivaldi: *Gloria* in D,
    R.589
Marriner, Academy of St. Martin-in-the-Fields. EMI 54283 + Vivaldi: *Gloria*,
    Rv. 589

————— *Catalog numbers are subject to change without notice.* —————

Preston, Academy of Ancient Music, Christ Church Cathedral Choir.
L'Oiseau-Lyre 414678 [ADD] + Vivaldi: *Gloria* in D, R.589

Mass in B Minor, S.232

This pinnacle of Bach's vocal and sacred music is in many ways a paradox. The composer spent more than fifteen years cobbling it together from bits and pieces of earlier works, polishing it into a veritable treatise of choral composition. There is no record of its performance as a complete work, since its curious construction fits neither the Catholic nor Protestant liturgy. It is difficult to deny the theory that Bach wrote it out of pure idealism, heedless of its impracticality, much as some believe Shakespeare wrote *Hamlet,* which is twice as long as Elizabethan plays were allowed to be. In any case, it is not only Bach's greatest choral work, but one of the greatest ever written by anyone. And some would agree with the Swiss critic Nageli, who as early as 1817 called it the "greatest work of music of all ages, and of all peoples."

> **Christophers, The Sixteen, Orchestra of the Sixteen.** Collins Classics 7032 (2) [DDD]
>
> **Gardiner, English Baroque Soloists, Monteverdi Choir**. Archiv 415514 (2) [DDD]
>
> **Hengelbrock, Freiburg Baroque Orchestra, Balthasar Neumann Choir.** DHM Editio Classica 77380 (2) [DDD]
>
> **Hickox, Collegium Musicum 90 Chorus and Orchestra.** Chandos 0533/4 (2) [DDD]
>
> **Karajan, Berlin Philharmonic Orchestra and Vienna Singverein.** Deutsche Grammophon 439696 (2) [ADD]
>
> **King, King's Consort and Choir, Tölz Boys' Choir.** Hyperion 67201 (2) [DDD]
>
> **Klemperer, New Philharmonia Orchestra, BBC Chorus.** EMI Studio 63364 (2) [ADD]
>
> **Leonhardt, La Petite Bande.** DHM Editio Classica 77040 (2) [ADD]
>
> **Parrott, Taverner Consort and Players.** EMI 47292 [47293] (2)

Organ Music

Each recording listed contains at least the popular Toccata and Fugue in D Minor, S.565.

Alain. Erato Bonsai 45922
Biggs. *Great Organ Favorites,* CBS 42644 [ADD]

———— *Since CDs can change label and number, use artists as main reference.* ————

Fox. RCA Victrola 7736 [ADD]
Hurford. London [Decca] 443485 (2) [ADD]
Kee. Chandos Chaconne 0527 [DDD]
Koopman. Deutsche Grammophon 447292 [DDD]
Murray. *Bach Organ Blaster,* Telarc 80316 [DDD]
Rübsam. Naxos 8.550184 [DDD]

St. Matthew Passion, S.244

For many listeners, four hours of solemn music telling the grim story of Christ's sufferings may seem daunting. Perhaps being a devout Christian helps to undertake the project, but anyone might be affected by the powerful drama that Bach creates from his mighty polyphonic arsenal. This is not mere pious reflection, but a wrenching enactment of the Gospel story, alternately heartrending and consoling. Musically it is astounding in that despite the vast canvas, the painting is not done in broad strokes, but is finely etched down to the minutest detail. It has been called a compendium of all the techniques of composition which preceded it.

Gardiner, English Baroque Soloists, Monteverdi Choir. Archiv 427648 (3) [DDD]

Herreweghe, Chapelle Royale Orchestra, Ghent Collegium Vocale. Harmonia Mundi 901155/57 (3) [DDD]

Harnoncourt, Vienna Concentus Musicus, Choir of King's College, Cambridge, Regensburg Cathedral Choir. Das Alte Werk 42509 (3) [AAD]

Klemperer, Philharmonia Orchestra. EMI 63058 (3) [ADD]

Koopman, Amsterdam Baroque Orchestra. Erato 45814 (3) [DDD]

Oberfrank, Hungarian Festival Chorus and State Symphony Orchestra. Naxos 8.550832/34 (2) [DDD]

Willcocks, Thames Chamber Orchestra and Chorus. ASV Quicksilva 324 (3) [DDD]

Suites (4) for Orchestra, S. 1066/9

Sometimes also listed as "Overtures," these Suites are uniformly fine, though No. 3 is best known since it contains the beloved "Air on the G String." Along with the *Brandenburg* Concertos, these constitute the "easiest" Bach listening.

Gardiner, English Baroque Soloists. Erato 99615 (2)
Goebel, Musica Antiqua Köln. Archiv 415671 (2) [DDD]

——— *Artists are listed alphabetically, not in order by critical ranking.* ———

Goodman, Brandenburg Consort. Hyperion 22002 (2)
Hogwood, Academy of Ancient Music. L'Oiseau-Lyre 417834 (2) [DDD]
Kuijken, La Petite Bande. DHM Editio Classica 77008 (2) [DDD]
Marriner, Academy of St. Martin-in-the-Fields. London [Decca] Jubilee
    430378 [ADD]
Pickett, New London Consort. L'Oiseau-Lyre 452000 (2) [DDD] + orchestral
    movements from cantatas, and Sinfonia from the *Easter Oratorio*
Pinnock, The English Concert. Deutsche Grammophon 423492 (3) [DDD] +
    Brandenburg Concertos

Arcangelo Corelli (1653-1713)

Corelli was an elegant Italian composer of wealthy family, whose works for violin or strings were among the most popular in the 18th century. He seems to have enjoyed a life of almost unlimited luck and success, even though there were others who could play or conduct better than he. For nearly 25 years he was paid handsomely by the wealthy Pietro, Cardinal Ottoboni, to serve as his private music director. When Corelli died, rich and in possession of a fabulous art collection, the Cardinal saw to it that he was buried in an elaborate tomb in the Pantheon of Rome. His exceedingly Baroque monument can still be seen here.

Concerti Grossi (12), op. 6

By far Corelli's most famous works, these tuneful and colorful short concertos rival Handel's wonderful set (also op. 6) in popularity.

Banchini, Ensemble 415. Harmonia Mundi 901406/07 (2)
Biondi, Europa Galante. Opus 111 30-147 (2) [DDD]
Goodman, Brandenburg Consort. Hyperion Dyad 22011 (2) [DDD]
Krecheck, Capella Istropolitana. Naxos 8.550402/3 (2) [DDD]
Lamon, Tafelmusik. Nos. 1, 3, 7-9, 11, DHM Baroque Esprit 77445
Marriner, Academy of St. Martin's-in-the-Fields. London [Decca] Double
    443862 (2)
McGegan, Philharmonia Baroque Orchestra. Nos. 1-6, Harmonia Mundi
    907014; Nos. 7-12, Harmonia Mundi 907015
Pinnock, The English Concert. Deutsche Grammophon 423626 (2) [DDD]

——— *[DDD] indicates newest recordings; [ADD] or [AAD] are reissues.* ———

François Couperin (1668-1733)

Known as "le grand," Couperin was only the most famous of a dozen musicians in his family who contributed to French music in the 17th and 18th centuries. The Great François is principally remembered for his works for harpsichord, including 27 suites ("ordres") of dance movements with picturesque titles. Another collection, *L'Art de toucher le clavecin*, offers detailed instructions on how to play the instrument, including not only proper posture but also the correct way of making affecting grimaces.

At the young age of 25 he was appointed by the Sun King, Louis XIV, to the post of organist in the Royal Chapel at Versailles. For years he was music teacher to the king's children. He was the first composer to insist that his music be played exactly as written, without further embellishment or improvisation. His frequent use of markings such as "gracious, naive, tender, breezy" seems to reflect his own charming character no less than the spirit of his times. When he died, his post as royal harpsichordist (by then under Louis XV) was inherited by his daughter, last of a distinguished line.

Harpsichord Music

The *ordres* of Couperin are full of wit and refinement, and they established a tradition of understatement which became one of the fundamentals of French music thereafter. There are 27 *ordres*, or suites, in all, but our listings feature only selections of the most famous pieces.

[*Les baricades mistérieuses* ("The Mysterious Barricades") is a piece less than two-and-a-half minutes in length from the sixth ordre of Book II, *Pièces de clavecin*. If I had to pick one work of music to take to my desert island—one piece of jewel-like formal, melodic, and harmonic perfection—one work I could slip into my pocket which yet contains all the mysteries of the universe within its tiny precincts, this would be it.]

Baumont. Selections, Erato 11471 [DDD]
Christie, Rousset. Selections, Harmonia Mundi 901269 [DDD]
Cuckston. Sel. from Book 2, Naxos 8.550460 [DDD]
Pinnock. *The Harmonious Blacksmith*, Archiv 413591 [DDD] + Bach: *Italian Concerto*, short pieces by Handel, Rameau, Scarlatti and others
Sempe. Selections, DHM 77219 [DDD]

George Frideric Handel (1685-1759)

Handel is universally considered to be, along with J.S. Bach, the greatest Baroque composer. Ironically, though they were both Germans, and born in the same year, the two masters never met. Handel nevertheless became close friends with several other famous composers, including Telemann and Domenico Scarlatti.

——— *CDs go in and out of print; availability of all listed items is not assured.* ———

A child prodigy, Handel spent his early twenties studying in Italy. He became adept at the "Italian Style," putting it to good use after his move in 1711 to London, where for several years he composed and produced highly successful Italian operas. Handel's official patron, the Elector of Hanover, succeeded to the English throne in 1714 as George I, providing the composer with one of the most fortuitous job opportunities in history.

Handel remained in England for the rest of his life, becoming a citizen and anglicizing his name—though, as you can see above, without perfect aptness. The British rage for Italian operas waned in the 1730s, and Handel moved on to other things such as his great religious oratorios. His later years were plagued by ill-health, including blindness and a severe stroke, afflictions which he bore with characteristic dignity. When he died, he was given a state funeral in Westminster Abbey.

Handel was often described as stubborn and autocratic: "He disdained," we are told, "to teach his art to any but princes," and reputedly he could swear in five languages. At the same time he possessed a lively, if somewhat caustic, wit, and as often as not was given to impromptu turns of kindliness. Altogether, an oddly endearing character, his comically corpulent frame invariably clad in the most costly garments, and topped off by an enormous white wig which, a contemporary critic claimed, when things were going well at a performance, had "a certain nod, or vibration" of its own.

Handel's music makes a fascinating contrast to Bach's. Less profoundly thought through, it nevertheless can make a more immediate impact, and the melodies are more singable—less "instrumental"—than Bach's. Before consigning him to second place in the Baroque, as many musicologists do today, we might pause to remember Mozart saying he "strikes like a thunderbolt," and Beethoven calling him "the greatest, ablest composer that ever lived."

Concerti Grossi (12), op. 6

In Europe, these tuneful, glowingly orchestrated pieces are almost as popular as Bach's *Brandenburg* Concertos. For some reason they are not so well known in America. You only impoverish yourself by not knowing them.

Hogwood, Handel & Haydn Society. L'Oiseau-Lyre 436845 (3) [DDD]
Pinnock, The English Concert. Archiv 410897/9 (3) [DDD]
Turovsky, I Musici di Montreal. Chandos 9004/6 (3) [DDD]

Concertos (16) for Organ

Although Bach remains the most famous (and copious) composer of solo organ music, Handel was the inventor of the organ concerto, pitting the instrument brilliantly against a

——— *Some CDs may be available only through importers.* ———

battery of strings and winds. There is no "churchiness" in this organ music, as you can verify by sampling, for instance, the scintillating Concerto No. 13, nicknamed "The Cuckoo and the Nightingale."

> **Haselböck, Németh, Capella Savaria.** (5 sel.) Hänssler Classic 98940 [DDD]
> **Koopman, Amsterdam Baroque Orchestra.** Erato Duo Bonsai 91932 (2) [DDD]
> **Preston, Pinnock, The English Concert.** (4 sel.) Archiv "3D Baroque" 431708 [DDD]

Messiah

If Bach's *Mass in B Minor* and *St. Matthew Passion* are often the musician's usual top choices for greatest choral works, we still need not apologize for adoring the people's choice in sacred music. The Bach may be both more intellectual and truly spiritual, but Handel's *Messiah* is more infectiously celebratory, more hummable. Though its text is in English, its musical manner is unapologetically Italian, abandoning Teutonic brooding in favor of joyful extroversion. If there is anything in all music that makes you want to leap to your feet and cheer more than the "Hallelujah Chorus," I cannot think of it. And yes, Handel really wrote it all in three weeks. (This was possible only before television.)

There is no composition of comparable length and scope that has had more recordings. There are several different editions of the score, so that whether you select "traditional" or "authentic" performances you may run into sections that sound rather different from the version you hear at your local church each Christmas; be prepared to keep an open mind.

> **Christie, Les Arts Florissants.** Harmonia Mundi 901498/99 (2)
> **Christophers, The Sixteen, Orchestra of The Sixteen.** Hyperion 66251/2 (2) [DDD]
> **C. Davis, London Symphony Orchestra and Chorus.** Philips Duo 438356 (2) [ADD]
> **Gardiner, English Baroque Soloists, Monteverdi Choir.** Philips 411041 (3) [DDD]
> **Mackerras, English Chamber Orchestra, Ambrosian Singers.** [EMI] Studio 69040 (2) [ADD]
> **Mackerras, Royal Philharmonic Orchestra, Huddersfield Choral Society.** (Mozart orchestration) ASV 230 (2) [DDD]
> **Malgoire, La Grande Ecurie et la Chambre du Roi.** Sony 63001 (2) [ADD]
> [Proceeds from the Malgoire recording go to support hospices in 40 nations.]

———— U.S. labels and numbers are given first, U.K. in [brackets] when needed. ————

Marriner, Academy of St. Martin-in-the-Fields. Philips 434695 (2) [DDD]
Parrott, Taverner Choir and Players. EMI 49801 (2) [DDD]
Pearlman, Boston Baroque. Telarc 80322 (2) [DDD]
Pinnock, The English Concert. Archiv 423630 (2) [DDD]
Shaw, Atlanta Symphony Orchestra and Chamber Choir. Telarc 80093 (2) [DDD]
Solti, Chicago Symphony Orchestra and Chorus. London [Decca] 414396 (2) [DDD]

Royal Fireworks Music/Water Music

The first is brilliant trumpet-and-drums music to celebrate the signing of a peace treaty, the second outdoorsy winds-and-strings music to accompany King George's royal barge cruises up and down the Thames. They appear so often together on recordings that they are difficult to separate; there are complete versions, and complete suites, and individual suites, and selections put together helter-skelter. How much you should get on a disc is a function of how much you enjoy either or both.

For the *Royal Fireworks Music* alone:

Fennell, Cleveland Symphonic Winds. Telarc 80038 [DDD] + Bach, Holst
King, King's Consort, Choir of New College, Oxford. Hyperion 66350 [DDD] + Four Coronation Anthems
Pinnock, The English Concert. Archiv 447279 [DDD] + *Alexander's Feast* Overture

For the *Water Music* alone:

Gardiner, English Baroque Soloists. Philips 434122 [DDD]
Lamon, Tafelmusik. Sony Vivarte 68257 [DDD] + *Il Pastor Fido*
McGegan, Philharmonia Baroque Orchestra. Harmonia Mundi f907010 [AAD]
Malcolm, English Chamber Orchestra. ASV Quicksilva 6152 [DDD]
Marriner, Academy of St. Martin-in-the-Fields. Philips 416447 [ADD]
Pinnock, The English Concert. Archiv 410525 [DDD]

For suites from each, together on one disc:

Hogwood, Academy of Ancient Music. L'Oiseau-Lyre 400059 [ADD]
Leppard, English Chamber Orchestra. Philips Solo 442388 [ADD]

———— *All CDs listed are considered approximately equal in (high) merit.* ————

Marriner, Academy of St. Martin-in-the-Fields. Argo 414596 [ADD]
Paillard, Paillard Chamber Orchestra. Erato 45931
Warchal, Capella Istropolitana. Naxos 8.550109 [DDD]

Johann Pachelbel (1653-1706)

Pachelbel was an eminent organist in the generation before Bach, some of whose relatives were his students. He was not, however, a significant composer. Most of his works are considered prolix, repetitive, and uninspired. His name is omitted from several standard dictionaries of composers. All the more amazing then that one tiny piece, the *Canon* in D, revised, augmented, and reorchestrated by other hands, has in just recent years become possibly the most popular, most often played and recorded classical composition in the world!

Canon in D

Originally scored for three violins and continuo, the "celebrated Canon" is now ordinarily heard in a version for string orchestra. Part of its mass appeal is surely that it is repetitive; its clear beat and hypnotically undulating melody have a powerfully relaxing effect. Some listeners claim it re-calibrates their biorhythms, or puts them in touch with higher harmonies.

The *Canon* in D has become such a cult item that people have developed fierce loyalties to one or another performance, and refuse to listen to any competitors. One label has even put out an album called *Pachelbel's Greatest Hit*, containing several different versions of this one piece, so it can be listened to over and over in slightly different versions without changing records. With dozens of recordings to choose from, much depends on what other music comes in your package (the *Canon* itself is only about seven minutes long).

I Musici. Philips 410606 [DDD] + Mozart: Serenade No. 13 "Eine kleine Nachtmusik"; Albinoni: Adagio; Boccherini: Minuet, *et al.*

Karajan, Berlin Philharmonic Orchestra. Deutsche Grammophon 413309 [DDD] + Albinoni: Adagio, short works by Bach, Gluck, Mozart, and Vivaldi

Marriner, Academy of St. Martin-in-the-Fields. EMI 47391 + Albinoni: Adagio, other short pieces

Münchinger, Stuttgart Chamber Orchestra. London [Decca] 411973 [DDD] + Albinoni: Adagio, other Baroque favorites

Paillard Chamber Orchestra. RCA Victor Red Seal 65468 [DDD] + Albinoni: Adagio, selections by 9 other Baroque composers

Paillard Chamber Orchestra, various other artists (including Cleo Laine!). "Pachelbel's Greatest Hit," RCA Victor Red Seal 60712 (9 versions)

——— *CDs listed are solid, central choices, not necessarily "the greatest."* ———

Pinnock, The English Concert. *Baroque Music,* Archiv 415518 [DDD] + short pieces by Handel, Vivaldi, Purcell, Albinoni, Avison, and Haydn (who wasn't Baroque!)

Warren-Green, London Chamber Orchestra. Virgin Classics 59563 [DDD] + Albinoni: Adagio; Vivaldi: *The Four Seaons*

Henry Purcell (1659-1695)

Purcell lived a life almost exactly as brief as Mozart's, and in some ways it was almost as brilliant. He wrote an extraordinary amount of quality music in that short span and took his place in music history as the greatest native English composer during more than two centuries.

Born into a musical family, Purcell early became a chorister, then a composer, to the Chapel Royal, and a little later on, organist for Westminster Abbey. Although adept at writing organ and harpsichord pieces, odes and anthems, songs and sonatas, it was in theater music that he excelled.

We could call him the first great English opera composer except that his stage works are not what we would call operas today. Handel, with his full-blown Italianate operas, was a generation away from arriving on the London scene, and until then the English seemed most reluctant to fully embrace such a foreign art form. They were more likely to use the term "masque" than "opera" to describe a pastiche of music, dancing, talking, and singing that is closer to what we would call "incidental music." Whatever it was, it was a stunning visual and auditory entertainment, and though few of Purcell's masques are staged today we can relive their splendor vividly through recordings.

Purcell remained more talked about than heard for many decades after his death. The first rush of revival began after Benjamin Britten in the 20th century used one of Purcell's haunting harpsichord themes as the basis for his *Young Person's Guide to the Orchestra* (alternate title: *Variations on a Theme by Henry Purcell*). A second spurt of interest followed the dramatic use of Purcell's *Funeral Music for Queen Mary* in the film *A Clockwork Orange.* The latter music was played not only at Queen Mary's funeral, and in the classic movie, but also at Purcell's own untimely obsequies in Westminster Abbey.

Dido and Aeneas

This is Purcell's masterpiece—his greatest theater work and the one closest to a true opera. Although it is now more than 300 years old it is still often performed and has had an amazing number of recordings. The final lament of Dido, the ill-fated Queen of Carthage, "When I am laid in earth," has never been surpassed for noble poignancy.

——— *Some famous CDs are not listed because currently out of print.* ———

Christie, Gens, Les Arts Florissants. Erato 98477 [DDD]
Hogwood, Bott, Academy of Ancient Music and Chorus. L'Oiseau-Lyre
   436992 [DDD]
Leppard, Norman, English Chamber Orchestra. Philips 416299 [DDD]

Music of Purcell

Christie, Les Arts florissants; A. Deller, Deller Consort; London Baroque.
   Prelude Baroque VII, Harmonia Mundi 290807
Christophers, The Sixteen, Orchestra of the Sixteen. *Complete Funeral Music
   for Queen Mary,* et al., Collins Classics 1425 [DDD]
King, King's Consort. *Essential Purcell,* Hyperion KING 2 [DDD]

Jean-Philippe Rameau (1683-1764)

Rameau acquired a reputation in France as a far less engaging person than François
Couperin, but an even greater composer. Surprisingly little is know of his life. Except in
music, he appears to have been a poor student. He was nearly 40—quite a late age in those
times—before making a name for himself in Paris. Like Couperin, he wrote volumes of
harpsichord music, but also chamber works and some 30 theater pieces, including ballets
and operas, and hybrid forms of each.

His music is more complex than Couperin's, and his contemporaries tended to find it
demanding and difficult. Nevertheless, he commanded respect for his mastery of orchestration and his bold experiments in harmony. Only recently have his masterpieces begun to be
heard with pleasure outside France, thanks to scholars and musicians who have restored his
scores, and who play his music with style and vigor.

Harpsichord Music

Pinnock. *The Harmonious Blacksmith,* Archiv 413591 [DDD] + Bach: *Italian
   Concerto,* short pieces by Handel, Couperin, Scarlatti and others
Rousset. L'Oiseau-Lyre 425886 (2) [DDD]
Rowland. Naxos 8.553047 [DDD]

Orchestral Music

Herreweghe, Chapelle Royale Orchestra; Christie, Les Arts Florissants.
   Harmonia Mundi 290808

McGegan, Philharmonia Baroque Orchestra. Orchestral suites from *Naïs* and
   Le temple de la gloire, Harmonia Mundi 907121
Rousset, Les Talens Lyriques. *Overtures*, London [Decca] 455293 [DDD]

Domenico Scarlatti (1685-1757)

Scarlatti was born, you will note, in the same miraculous year as Bach and Handel, and one
might be forgiven for considering this a lucky omen. His father Alessandro, though now
largely forgotten, was once the world's most famous composer of oratorio and opera, and a
major influence on Handel. Naturally he was his son's teacher, and went far beyond that in
vigorously promoting Domenico's career; in this he did his job too well, for the fame of the
younger Scarlatti all but wiped out the elder's memory.

   Scarlatti met Handel while the latter was working in Italy. They became good friends,
and it is said that years later, whenever Handel's name was mentioned, Scarlatti crossed
himself reverently (we do not know what the good Lutheran Handel thought of that).

   About 1720 Scarlatti became music-master to a Portuguese princess who later became
queen of Spain, taking her beloved teacher with her. Scarlatti spent the second half of his
life at the Spanish court, virtually disappearing from public view, though we know he married twice and had nine children. We are also told he became addicted to gambling and was
repeatedly saved from ruin by his devoted royal patroness.

   Obviously, however, he did not spend all his time in lovemaking and dicing. In addition to operas, oratorios, cantatas, serenades, and assorted other works, he composed the
555 sonatas (or as he called them, "essercizi") for the harpsichord for which he is particularly remembered.

Sonatas for Harpsichord

   These short pieces—full of Latin dance rhythms, harmonically unpredictable, dramatic and poetic by turn—were aptly called by that peripatetic music-maven of the 18th century, Dr. Charles Burney, "original and happy Freaks." Even in faraway England they had
become wildly popular well before the composer's death, to the point that critics spoke of a
"Scarlatti sect." Today they are played also on the piano with great success.

Beauséjour (harpsichord). 18 selections, Analekta Fleur de Lys 3041 [DDD]
Horowitz (piano). 18 selections, Sony 53460 [ADD]
Perahia (piano). 7 selections, Sony 62785 [DDD] + Handel: Keyboard Suites 2,
   3, 5 (including "The Harmonious Blacksmith"), Chaconne in G Major
Pinnock (harpsichord). 14 selections, Archiv 419632 [DDD]
Pletnev (piano). 31 selections, Virgin 45123 (2) [DDD]

——— *Since CDs can change label and number, use artists as main reference.* ———

A. Schiff (piano). 15 selections, London [Decca] 421422 [DDD]
Staier (harpsichord). 18 selections, Das Alte Werk 12601 [DDD]
Wilson (harpsichord). 14 selections, Teldec 46419 [DDD]

Georg Philipp Telemann (1681-1767)

In his day, Telemann was one of the most famous composers in Europe, and possibly the most prolific of all time. He wrote an estimated 2,000 works—more than Bach and Handel put together—including some 40 operas, 44 passions, 600 overtures, 700 songs, and stacks of chamber music.

He was a man of letters, founding the first German music magazine, and authoring three somewhat contradictory autobiographies. He had a university education in languages and science. At almost 60 years of age he discovered, like Handel, a love of botany, developing an "avarice for ranunculi, and particularly, anemones." Handel thereafter often sent plant specimens to Telemann from England.

Telemann incorporated both French and Italian principles in his compositions, and even wrote works based on Polish folk dances. He lived to the ripe age of 86 and achieved universal adoration in his own time, his music being performed even more widely than Bach's. He was forgotten in the 19th century, then revived under questionable auspices in the 20th as a "pioneer of the classical style."

It is sad that such a fine musician has been both egregiously under- and over-rated. Let us admit that he falls short of the sublimities of Bach and Handel, and is in fact perhaps the least of the composers in this chapter. But there is little in his recorded output that is less than pleasant to hear, and the lover of the Baroque is sure to find countless gems in Telemann's treasure chest of music.

One of my own favorites is a children's opera called *Der Schulmeister*, in which an incompetent pedagogue attempts to teach scales to an unruly boys' choir; at the end they all good-naturedly admit defeat and bray like jackasses. Natures less innocent than mine might prefer his suite *The Prostitute*, which contains the song "Come up and see me sometime."

I would like to say that Telemann's range was unique in music but it was not. Mozart, as everyone now knows, wrote scatological songs in between his sublime masterpieces, and Brahms played the piano in a whorehouse. May I add to these examples that of the Czech-American composer Paul Reif, author of distinguished music for wind ensemble and string quartet, a song cycle on poems of T. S. Eliot, and so on, who while on duty in Africa during World War II managed to eclipse his intellectual accomplishments with the popular soldiers' song "Dirty Gertie from Bizerte."

———— *Artists are listed alphabetically, not in order by critical ranking.* ————

Suite in A Minor for Recorder and Strings

This is the one piece among Telemann's thousands that has come closest to becoming a chestnut. It is very representative and has had quite a few fine recordings.

Brüggen, Friedrich, Southwest German Chamber Orchestra, et al. Das Alte
Werk 77620 [ADD] + other Telemann selections
Stivin, Edlinger, Capella Istropolitana. Naxos 8.550156 [DDD] + other
Telemann selections

Antonio Vivaldi (1678-1741)

Vivaldi had a life colorful enough to match his vividly red hair. Though trained early as a musician, his first career was as a Catholic priest. Before the first year of his pastorate was out he developed a mysterious chest ailment which frequently prevented him from finishing the saying of Mass. Just as mysteriously, the malady seemed to disappear when he was conducting an orchestra or playing the violin.

At this same time he became music director for a Venetian school for orphaned girls and unwed mothers. Many of Vivaldi's more than 400 instrumental concertos apparently were written for, and first performed by, this precocious and highly competent "all girls' orchestra." History records no scandal involving the "red priest" and his presumably vulnerable charges; that was to come years later when he took up with Anna Giraud, a soprano who was to star in many of his operas, and her sister, who became his traveling companions during the height of his international fame.

After about 1730 Vivaldi's popularity began to fade. Although he had once performed for the Pope himself, his operas were banned by the Church in 1737 because of his inattention to priestly duties and his association with the two women. The next year the Foundling School refused to renew his contract. Four years later, desperately seeking work in Vienna, he died, and was buried there in a pauper's grave.

His surviving works number about 750. This is picayune compared with Bach or Telemann, but impressive in the level of general high quality. He was acknowledged as the master of the concerto, a form to which he apparently first brought the concept of one instrumental virtuoso engaging in dramatic conflict with an orchestra. One of Vivaldi's most ardent admirers was J. S. Bach, who transcribed and arranged many of his concertos, or incorporated parts of them in his own works.

Aside from *The Four Seasons,* the rest of the 400 concertos are often difficult to differentiate one from the other. This is not because, as the tired taunt goes, "Vivaldi wrote the same concerto 400 times," but because they are all about equally good. He composed 37 concertos just for the bassoon, more than anyone else in history; and there are dozens more for cello, flute, guitar, horn, mandolin, oboe, piccolo, recorder, trumpet, viola d'amore, and violin, plus combinations of these, as well as "concertos for orchestra," and "concertos for diverse instruments." The astonishing thing is that there are none for harpsichord, nor any solo pieces for that ubiquitous instrument of the Baroque. Perhaps he shared the disdain of Sir Thomas Beecham, who said that to him the harpsichord sounded "like two skeletons copulating on a tin roof in a hailstorm."

Vivaldi's music remained largely forgotten by the public from his death until about 1960, when it experienced a veritable explosion of renewed popularity. That happened in part, no doubt, because much of it can be listened to with one ear as a kind of elegant dinner music. But this is the listener's fault, not Vivaldi's; there is plenty in his output to satisfy the most discriminating audience.

The Four Seasons

In one sense, these are nothing more than four of those 400 concertos (here featuring the violin as soloist), taken out of context and highlighted with a programmatic title. The context is a set of 12 violin concertos, Op. 8, bearing the collective label "The Contest between Harmony and Invention." These demonstrate Vivaldi's characteristic sense of the dramatic in contrasting traditional rules of composition with wilder flights of imagination.

In *The Four Seasons* the composer contrives, by purely musical means, to suggest singing birds, raging thunderstorms, barking dogs, squawking bagpipes, buzzing flies, hunters' gunshots, and the cracking of ice on frozen ponds. Who could resist? (Well, there are some; perhaps no classical music is so reviled by self-appointed sophisticates and esthetes. Or is it aesthetes?) A quick check of a recent Schwann Opus Catalog showed 81 recordings of *The Four Seasons* in print. Listed below are only those most praised by critics.

Blankestijn, Chamber Orchestra of Europe. Das Alte Werk 91683 [DDD] + other concertos

Carmignola, Sonatori de la Gioiosa Marca. Divox Antiqua 79404 [DDD] + 2 miscellaneous concertos

Hogwood, Academy of Ancient Music. L'Oiseau-Lyre 410126 [DDD]

Gunzenhauser, Capella Istropolitano. Naxos 8.550056 [DDD]

Lamon, Tafelmusik. Sony Vivarte 48251 [DDD] + other concertos

Loveday, Marriner, Academy of St. Martin-in-the-Fields. Argo 414486 [ADD]

Manze, Koopman, Amsterdam Baroque Orchestra. Erato 94811 [DDD] + 2 oboe concertos

Shaham, Orpheus Chamber Orchestra. Deutsche Grammophon 439933 [DDD] + Kreisler: *Concerto in the Style of Vivaldi*

———— *CDs go in and out of print; availability of all listed items is not assured.* ————

Sparf, Drottningholm Baroque Ensemble. BIS 275 [DDD]
Standage, Pinnock, The English Concert. Archiv 400045 [ADD]
Warren-Green, London Chamber Orchestra. Virgin Classics 59563 [DDD] +
  Albinoni: Adagio; Pachelbel: Canon in D

Gloria in D. Rv.589

The most famous of Vivaldi's choral works, and justly so. The celebrated opening bars
are among the most joyfully triumphant in Baroque music. If the *Gloria* doesn't make you
feel good, you are suffering too much.

Christophers, The Sixteen, Orchestra of the Sixteen. Collins Classics 1320
  [DDD] + Bach: *Magnificat*; Caldara: *Stabat Mater*
Hickox, Collegium Musicum 90. Chandos Chaconne 0518 [DDD] + Bach:
  Magnificat
Marriner, Academy of St. Martin-in-the-Fields. EMI 54283 + Bach: *Magnificat*
**Marriner, Academy of St. Martin-in-the-Fields, King's College Choir,
  Cambridge.** London [Decca] Jubilee 421146 [ADD] + Haydn: *Lord Nelson*
  Mass
Muti, New Philharmonia Orchestra and Chorus. EMI 47990 [ADD] +
  Magnificat in G Minor
Pinnock, The English Concert and Choir. Archiv 423386 [DDD] + A.
  Scarlatti: *Dixit Dominus*
Preston, Academy of Ancient Music, Christ Church Cathedral Choir.
  L'Oiseau-Lyre 414678 [ADD] + Bach: *Magnificat*
**Willcocks, London Symphony Orchestra, Choir of King's College,
  Cambridge.** London [Decca] 421146 [ADD] + Haydn: Mass No. 11 "Nelson"

——— *Some CDs may be available only through importers.* ———

The Classical Period
(1750-ca. 1820)

In the generation following the death of J. S. Bach, several influences came together to create what Goethe was to denominate the Classical period in music. The tremendous popularity of Italian opera was reflected, in every form of composition, in an emphasis on dramatic expression and a simpler, broader melodic style. Harmonies were simplified, counterpoint abandoned, and polyphony replaced by broken-chord accompaniment. A new structural principle, sonata form, established itself as the basis for most instrumental composition. A new orchestral form, the symphony, began to replace the Baroque orchestral suite and concerto grosso. Regional and national differences in style began to melt away as French, Italian, and German techniques became widely diffused and tended to merge with each other.

Not all of the new characteristics came solely from within the musical establishment. Rationalist philosophy as exhibited in the writings of Rousseau, Kant, and Voltaire was favored among the educated and cultured classes. The old system of court patronage for the arts was breaking down in the wake of the democratic movement, which was to result in the American and French Revolutions. Composers were swept up in the ideals of the age, which stressed the importance of the individual and his feelings.

Meanwhile, the beginnings of modern technology were forcing changes in musical style, simply by making available new possibilities through improvements to existing instruments, and the introduction of entirely new ones. Most notable was the advent of the piano, which during the classical period gradually supplanted the harpsichord. Not only did the piano have greater sonority, but gradations of expression were possible by varying the pressure on the keys. Mechanical changes of this type left their mark on how composers viewed their materials, and what they decided to give their audiences.

Carl Philipp Emanuel Bach (1714-1788)

Carl Philipp Emanuel was J. S. Bach's second oldest son, and in every opinion is the greatest of the four Bach progeny who themselves became composers. He is also the perfect transitional figure between the Baroque and Classical periods. As a Bach he obviously was heir to the greatest glories of the Baroque, but he was not content to merely copy his father. He had a lively intellect of his own and struck out in bold new directions.

For 27 years he worked in the Baroque manner as a court musician (for Frederick the Great of Prussia). In 1767 he took over the position in Hamburg of his just-deceased godfather, Georg Philipp Telemann, and in the speech accepting his appointment he uttered these prophetic words: "It seems to me that music must, above all, touch the heart." For the rest of his life he strove to find ways to base musical compositions upon poetic ideas. Although C. P. E. Bach was partial to the clavichord and harpsichord to the last, his skill and innovation in developing personal expression had a profound impact on both Haydn and Beethoven.

Perhaps this is the place to point out that C. P. E.'s youngest brother, Johann Christian, influenced in a similar way the music of Mozart. After studying opera in Italy, J. C. Bach moved to London, where the eight-year-old Mozart met him during his tour as a child prodigy. In later years Mozart was to acknowledge the lessons he learned from the "London Bach." Thus we see that, contrary to. the conventional opinion that Johann Sebastian Bach's art stagnated and died with him, his legacy lived on through his children, and later was transmuted into the masterpieces of Haydn, Mozart, and Beethoven.

"Hamburg" Symphonies (6), W.182

These are C. P. E. Bach's finest orchestral works, along with the equally good but lesser known set of four, W.183.

Haenchen, C.P.E. Bach Chamber Orchestra. Capriccio 10106
Hengelbrock, Freiburg Baroque Orchestra. Nos. 3-5, DHM Editio Classica 77187 [DDD] + Harpsichord Concerto in C Minor, Oboe Concerto in E-flat
Rémy, Les Amis de Philippe. cpo 999418 [DDD]

Ludwig van Beethoven (1770-1827)

Like C. P. E. Bach, Beethoven was a transitional figure, but between two different eras—the Classical and the Romantic. We place him here only because the tendency in recent years has been to stress his roots with Haydn (with whom he studied, however intractably) and his affinities with Mozart, not to mention (as we did in the previous chapter) his worship of Handel. This view is, I think, to the good; but it does not compel us to abandon the view that Beethoven was also the first great Romantic composer.

Born in Bonn, then only a small provincial town, Beethoven removed to Vienna when in his early 20s. There he became famous as a piano virtuoso and composer, and hobnobbed with those members of the aristocracy who were to support him financially for years to come, despite his unwillingness to show them the customary deference. No composer, indeed, was more devoted to the ideals of rationalism and revolution. Many of his greatest works have at their core the themes of democracy and brotherhood, e.g. *Egmont*, Symphony No. 9, and *Fidelio*.

——— *All CDs listed are considered approximately equal in (high) merit.* ———

Beethoven's career as a pianist fell victim to increasing deafness, a condition which was total by 1818. Always brusque and impatient by nature, be became positively antisocial after this time. His refusal, however, to give up music, his determination to continue composing ever greater works in the face of despair, his well-publicized policy of staring down the Fates and shaking his shaggy mane at the gods, all contributed to the romantic image we now all know as the "suffering artist." More than any composer before him he insisted on his prerogatives as a creative genius. When reminded of his obligations to royalty, he countered by describing himself as a "prince of Art."

Shy and introspective, Beethoven never married, though he loved several women. He often sat for hours, plunged in thought, so unaware of his surroundings that his rooms degenerated into rank squalor. "Never," said his admirer Goethe, "have I seen an artist with more concentration, more energy, more inwardness" (apparently the great poet had not seen his apartment).

Critics of Beethoven's day often found his works impossibly wayward and incomprehensible. He returned their scorn, often filling his next work with the very qualities they had condemned in his last. To this day there are people who believe the elliptical arguments of his late string quartets are not the musings of genius, but the ravings of madness. By the end of his life Beethoven had covered more ground, from his first simple pieces for mandolin to the cosmic cries of the Ninth or "Choral" Symphony, than any composer who had lived until then.

Within a few years of his death, he was widely considered the founding father and greatest genius of the Romantic movement in music. Though he is still probably the most popular of the great composers, there has been a reaction in recent years by those who resent his role, by extension, as greatest composer of all. Heretical detractors have pointed to his lack of ease in composing, his struggle to think up great melodies, his difficulty with vocal writing, his reliance on melodramatic contrasts and military rhythms to make an effect.

But to others—most others—he is, and no doubt always will be, in his sense of inevitability, poetic depth, dramatic cogency, and force of expression, the musical corollary of Shakespeare in literature, and of Michelangelo in art. Whatever the opinion, one thing seems certain: even if Bach or Mozart before him was greater, no one has surpassed him since. Two centuries later, there is no composer who has even a remote chance of achieving consensus as Beethoven's equal.

Concertos (5) for Piano and Orchestra

Written by Beethoven between ages 25 and 39, before deafness finally ended his love affair with the piano, these concertos have no earlier rivals than Mozart's, and few later ones except for Brahms's. The first two, indeed, have several affinities with Mozart, though even here we can frequently discern the young lion roaring. The third is more characteris-

———— CDs listed are solid, central choices, not necessarily "the greatest." ————

tic, but still conservative. By No. 4, Beethoven has become the more familiar iconoclast: traditional rules are broken, drama is heightened, poetic ideas are developed with grandeur and eloquence. And the fifth is so majestic, so symphonic in breadth, that it has earned the nickname "Emperor."

Complete sets:

Ashkenazy, Cleveland Orchestra. London [Decca] 421718 [DDD] + *Choral Fantasy*

Brendel, Levine, Chicago Symphony Orchestra. Philips 456045 (3) [DDD]

Fleisher, Szell, Cleveland Orchestra. Sony Essential Classics 48397 (3) [ADD] + Triple Concerto

Lubin (fortepiano), Hogwood, Academy of Ancient Music. L'Oiseau-Lyre 421408 (3) [DDD]

Perahia, Haitink, Concertgebouw Orchestra. CBS [Sony] 44575 (3) [DDD]

Pollini, Abbado, Berlin Philharmonic Orchestra. Deutsche Grammophon 439770 (3) [DDD]

No. 5 in E-flat, Op. 73 "Emperor"

Arrau, C. Davis, Dresden Philharmonic Orchestra. Philips 416215 [DDD]

Ashkenazy (pianist and conductor) Cleveland Orchestra. London [Decca] 421718 [ADD] + *Choral Fantasy*, Op. 80

Brendel, Haitink, London Philharmonic Orchestra. Philips 434148 [ADD] + Fantasia in C Minor

Cliburn, Reiner, Chicago Symphony Orchestra. RCA Living Stereo 61961 [AAD] + Rachmaninov: Piano Concerto No. 2

Fleisher, Szell, Cleveland Orchestra. Sony Essential Classics 46549 [ADD] + Triple Concerto

Gilels, Szell, Cleveland Orchestra. EMI Doublefforte 69509 (2) [ADD] + Variations; Dvořák: Symphony No. 8, 2 *Slavonic Dances*

Kempff, Leitner, Berlin Philharmonic Orchestra. Deutsche Grammophon Originals 447402 [ADD] + Piano Concerto No. 4

Kovacevich, Australian Chamber Orchestra. Classics for Pleasure Eminence 2184 [DDD] + Grosse Fuge, Op. 133

Levin (fortepiano), Gardiner, Orchestre Révolutionnaire et Romantique. Archiv 447771 [DDD] + *Choral Fantasy*

Perahia, Haitink, Concertgebouw Orchestra. CBS [Sony] 42330 [DDD]

Schnabel, Stock, Chicago Symphony Orchestra. RCA Victor Gold Seal 61393 + Piano Concerto No. 4

———— *Some famous CDs are not listed because currently out of print.* ————

R. Serkin, Bernstein, New York Philharmonic Orchestra. Sony 47520 [ADD]
+ Piano Concerto No. 3

Concerto in D for Violin, Op. 61

Now regarded by many as the crown of violin concertos, this work was proclaimed
"tedious and repetitious" by its first reviewer. Beethoven wrote it with uncharacteristic
speed and apparently the soloist at the 1806 premiere, Franz Clement, sight-read the score.
It was mid-century before the piece really caught on.

Chung, Tennstedt, Concertgebouw Orchestra. EMI 54072 + Bruch: Violin
Concerto No. 1
Heifetz, Munch, Boston Symphony Orchestra. RCA Victor Red Seal 5402
[ADD] + Brahms: Violin Concerto
Menuhin, Furtwängler, Philharmonia Orchestra. EMI 69799 (mono) [ADD]
Nishizaki, Jean, Slovak Philharmonic Orchestra (Bratislava). Naxos 8.550149
Perlman, Barenboim, Berlin Philharmonic Orchestra. EMI 49567 [DDD] + 2
Romances for Violin and Orchestra
Perlman, Giulini, Philharmonia Orchestra. EMI 56210 [DDD]
Schneiderhan, Jochum, Berlin Philharmonic Orchestra. Deutsche
Grammophon 447403 [ADD] + Mozart: Violin Concerto No. 5
Szeryng, Haitink, Royal Concertgebouw Orchestra. Philips Solo 442398
[ADD] + 2 Romances for Violin and Orchestra

Concerto in C Minor for Violin, Cello, Piano and Orchestra, Op. 56

This "triple concerto" reminds us how little removed Beethoven was in time from the
Baroque. It is less dramatic, more chamber-like, than most of his concertos, and it takes a
while to really get going. But it has an appeal all its own, and should win you over by the
end.

Beaux Arts Trio, Masur, Leipzig Gewandhaus Orchestra. Philips 438005
[DDD] + *Choral Fantasy*
Oistrakh, Oborin, Knushevitzky, Sargent, Philharmonia Orchestra. EMI
Doublefforte 69331 [ADD] + Brahms: Double Concerto, Mozart: Violin
Concerto No. 3, Prokofiev: Violin Concerto No. 2
Oistrakh, Rostropovich, Richter, Karajan, Berlin Philharmonic Orchestra.
EMI 66219 [ADD] + Brahms: Double Concerto
**Perlman, Ma, Barenboim (piano and conductor), Berlin Philharmonic
Orchestra.** EMI 55516 [DDD] + *Choral Fantasy*

————— *Catalog numbers are subject to change without notice.* —————

Stern, Rose, Istomin, Ormandy, Philadelphia Orchestra. Sony Essential
Classics 46549 [ADD] + Piano Concerto No. 5; or in boxed set 48397 with all
five piano concertos (3 CDs)

Zimmermann, Cohen, Manz, Saraste, English Chamber Orchestra. Classics
for Pleasure Silver Doubles 4775 (2) [ADD/DDD] + Dvořák: Cello Concerto;
Elgar: Cello Concerto; Tchaikovsky: *Rococo* Variations

Overtures

Beethoven wrote several overtures for ballets, plays, or operas. One or two are not
known to have been written for any event in particular. He wrote four different overtures,
all still in the repertoire, for his only opera; the *Fidelio* overture is good, but the one called
Leonore No. 3 (reflecting his original choice of title) is the most famous, and is often heard
separately as a concert piece. It and the overture to *Egmont* (a patriotic play by Goethe) are
among Beethoven's most stirringly dramatic works. Many of these overtures appear as
"fillers" on Beethoven symphony recordings, as you will see below; the discs listed here are
exclusively collections of the overtures.

C. Davis, Bavarian Radio Symphony Orchestra. (Omits *Leonore* Overture No.
2) CBS [Sony] 44790 [DDD]

Karajan, Berlin Philharmonic Orchestra. Deutsche Grammophon Galleria
427256 (2) [ADD]

Masur, Leipzig Gewandhaus Orchestra. Philips Duo 438706 (2) [ADD] +
Contredanses, German Dances, Minuets (with Marriner, Academy of St. Martin-
in-the-Fields)

Quartets for Strings

The 16 string quartets are among the greatest chamber works ever written, and provide an interesting chronological picture of Beethoven's evolution as a composer. They are
traditionally divided into three groups referred to as Early, Middle, and Late, correspond-
ing to distinct phases in his stylistic development. You can begin sampling with single discs
that contain a couple of the more famous quartets, or perhaps get a box set of the Middle
Quartets (Nos. 7-11), which are meatier than the Early Quartets (Nos. 1-6) but easier to
digest than the Late ones (Nos. 12-16).

Alban Berg Quartet. Middle Quartets (nos. 7-11), EMI 47130 (3) [DDD]
Cleveland Quartet. Nos. 6, 7, Telarc 80229 [DDD]
Cleveland Quartet. Nos. 8, 9, Telarc 80268 [DDD]
Cleveland Quartet. Nos. 10, 11, Telarc 80351 [DDD]

——— *Since CDs can change label and number, use artists as main reference.* ———

Emerson Quartet. No. 11, Deutsche Grammophon 423398 [DDD] + Schubert: Quartet No. 14 "Death and the Maiden"
Lindsay Quartet. Middle Quartets (nos. 7-11), ASV 207 (2) [DDD]
Talich Quartet. Nos. 9, 14, Calliope 9638
Tokyo String Quartet. Middle Quartets (nos. 7-11), RCA Victor Red Seal 60462 (3) [DDD]
Végh Quartet. Nos. 8, 9, Valois 4404 [AAD]

Sonatas (32) for Piano

These are core works for understanding Beethoven. Their composition spanned his entire life, and they reveal virtually every facet of his imagination and experimentation with his favorite instrument. It is an enormous amount of music, and the beginner will usually want to start with the three most beloved sonatas: No. 8 in C Minor, Op. 13, "Pathétique;" No. 14 in C-sharp Minor Op. 27, No. 2, "Moonlight" and No. 23 in F Minor, Op. 57, "Appassionata." All albums listed contain at least all three.

Arrau. Philips 422970 [ADD]
Brendel. Philips 411470 [ADD]
Jandó. Naxos 8.550045 [DDD]
Rubinstein. RCA Victor Red Seal 61443 [ADD] + Sonata No. 26
R. Serkin. CBS [Sony] 37219 [ADD]

Sonatas for Violin and Piano No. 5 in F, Op. 24, "Spring;" No. 9 in A, Op. 47, "Kreutzer"

Of the ten sonatas for violin and piano, these two are the best known, and the beginning collector will surely want to start with them, especially the "Kreutzer" (named for the violinist who was to have played it, but never did), with its combination of brilliance and profundity, which first took the violin sonata out of the parlor and into the concert auditorium. Listed are only great performances that have both these works on a single disc.

Nishizaki, Jandó. Naxos 8.550283 [DDD]
Perlman, Ashkenazy. London [Decca] 410554 [ADD]
Szeryng, Rubinstein. RCA Victor Gold Seal 61861 [ADD]
Zukerman, Barenboim. EMI 64631 [ADD] + Sonata No. 8

——— *Artists are listed alphabetically, not in order by critical ranking.* ———

Symphonies

As a body, these are the most famous and beloved symphonies ever written, and for many people they are the first and most essential classical works to which they are exposed. For many later Romantic composers, they were the summit of musical art and the object of almost religious veneration, a phenomenon which had an unfortunate inhibiting effect (Brahms, for instance, dithered over his great first symphony for more than 20 years, troubled by "hearing Beethoven's footsteps" close behind him).

This exaggerated adulation is what many of today's Beethoven detractors are reacting against. Perhaps we should clear our minds of preconceptions and received opinion, and just enjoy the symphonies for the exciting, dramatic paeans to Beethoven's revolutionary ideals that they are.

Many people like to buy all nine symphonies in one convenient set. There have been many such compendia and they often contain bonuses of miscellaneous fillers such as the overtures, at a savings over buying them all separately. But be aware that no set has ever had total consensus from the critics, which is to be expected since it is asking too much for any one conductor to produce the best performances of all nine symphonies.

Complete Symphonies

Brüggen, Orchestra of the 18th Century. Philips 442156 (5) [DDD] + *Egmont* and *Coriolan* Overutres

Gardiner, Orchestre Révolutionnaire et Romantique. Archiv 439900 (5) [DDD]

Harnoncourt, Chamber Orchestra of Europe. Teldec 46452 (5) [DDD]

Karajan, Berlin Philharmonic Orchestra. Deutsche Grammophon 429036 (5) [ADD]

Klemperer, Philharmonia Orchestra. EMI 68057 (7) [ADD]

Norrington, London Classical Players. EMI 49852 (6) [DDD] + 3 overtures

Szell, Cleveland Orchestra. Sony Essential Classics 48396 (5) [ADD] + 3 overtures

Toscanini, NBC Symphony Orchestra. RCA Victor Gold Seal 60324 (5) [ADD] + *Leonore* Overture No. 3

Wand, North German Radio Symphony Orchestra. RCA Victor Red Seal 60090 (6) [DDD]

Weller, City of Birmingham Symphony Orchestra. Chandos 7042 (5) + "Symphony No. 10"

——— *[DDD] indicates newest recordings; [ADD] or [AAD] are reissues.* ———

The really dedicated Beethoven symphony fan, especially one on a less restricted budget, will want to collect these works individually, as follows:

No. 1 in C, Op. 21; No. 2 in D, Op. 36

Although less remote from Mozart than the later symphonies, these first two are still unquestionably by Beethoven. Nevertheless, they stand apart from the others, and since they fit perfectly together on one disc that is how you will usually find them.

Dohnányi, Cleveland Orchestra. Telarc 80187 [DDD]
Tilson Thomas, English Chamber Orchestra. Sony 44905 [DDD]
Ferencsik, Hungarian State Orchestra. Hungaroton White Label 110 [ADD]
Walter, Columbia Symphony Orchestra. Sony 64460 [ADD] + *Coriolan*
Overture

No. 3 in E-flat, Op. 55, "Eroica"

No doubt the story will never stop being told that Beethoven wrote this symphony to honor Napoleon, then crossed out the dedication when that supposed champion of democracy proclaimed himself emperor. It is a beloved, even believable, story, but there is not a shred of evidence that it is true, and the music is quite dramatic enough without it. In fact, what is significant is that the "Eroica" truly represents a revolution, not in politics, but in music: a vast expansion of symphonic thought, contained within a highly intellectual and logical design. This symphony is usually taken as the real beginning of the Romantic era, much as Wagner's *Tristan und Isolde* represents for many the beginning of the Modern period.

Bernstein, Vienna Philharmonic Orchestra. Deutsche Grammophon 431024
[ADD] + overtures
Drahos, Nicolaus Esterházy Sinfonia. Naxos 8.553475 [DDD] + Symphony
No. 8
Harnoncourt, Chamber Orchestra of Europe. Teldec 75708 [DDD] +
Symphony No. 1
Levine, Metropolitan Opera Orchestra. Deutsche Grammophon 439862
[DDD] + Schubert: Symphony No. 8 "Unfinished"
Sawallisch, Royal Concertgebouw Orchestra. EMI 54501 [DDD] + Symphony
No. 1
Tennstedt, London Philharmonic Orchestra. EMI 55186 [DDD] +
Mussorgsky: *The Night on Bare Mountain*
B. Walter, Columbia Symphony Orchestra. Sony 64461 [ADD] + Symphony
No. 8

——— *CDs go in and out of print; availability of all listed items is not assured.* ———

Wand, North German Radio Symphony Orchestra. RCA Victor Red Seal
60755 [DDD] + overtures

No. 4 in B-flat, Op. 60

Dismissed by many critics, especially in the 19th century, as a lightweight, this symphony abounds in wild alterations of rhythm and mood. There is no "program," no nickname, no explanation, no pat way to characterize what is going on, so the Fourth remains
one of Beethoven's least known and discussed works. Yet the second movement contains
one of Beethoven's most beautiful melodies: Berlioz likened it to the Archangel Michael
singing at the gates of heaven.

> **Hogwood, Academy of Ancient Music.** L'Oiseau-Lyre 417615 [DDD] +
> Symphony No. 5
> **Solti, Chicago Symphony Orchestra.** London [Decca] 421580 [DDD] +
> Symphony No. 5
> **Szell, Cleveland Orchestra.** Sony Essential Classics 48158 [ADD] + Symphony
> No. 7
> **B. Walter, Columbia Symphony Orchestra.** Sony 64462 [ADD] + Symphony
> No. 6

No. 5 in C Minor, Op. 67

Amazingly, the most famous of all symphonies has never acquired a nickname. It is
just "Beethoven's Fifth." Indeed many people know what you mean if you just refer to
"The Fifth," without mentioning the composer. Everybody agrees that this exceptionally
dramatic, and in the end, joyful symphony "means" something special, that it implies some
kind of "program." But what that might be, most listeners seem to prefer to imagine for
themselves. Perhaps that is why this tends to be one of the works that people most treasure
as a personal possession. Beethoven himself gave a clue when he pointed to the famous four
opening notes and said "Thus Fate knocks at the door!"

> **Böhm, Vienna Philharmonic Orchestra.** Deutsche Grammophon Originals
> 447433 [ADD] + Symphony No. 6
> **Furtwängler, Vienna Philharmonic Orchestra.** EMI 69803 [ADD] (mono) +
> Symphony No. 7
> **Giulini, Los Angeles Philharmonic Orchestra.** Deutsche Grammophon
> 445502 [DDD] + Schumann: Symphony No. 3
> **Harnoncourt, Chamber Orchestra of Europe.** Teldec 75712 [DDD] +
> Symphony No. 2

———— *Some CDs may be available only through importers.* ————

Hogwood, Academy of Ancient Music. L'Oiseau-Lyre 417615 [DDD] + Symphony No. 4

Karajan, Berlin Philharmonic Orchestra. Deutsche Grammophon 419051 [ADD] + Symphony No. 8, *Fidelio* Overture

C. Kleiber, Vienna Philharmonic Orchestra. Deutsche Grammophon 447400 [ADD] + Symphony No. 7

Mackerras, Royal Liverpool Philharmonic Orchestra. Classics for Pleasure Eminence 2212 [DDD] + Symphony No. 7

Solti, Chicago Symphony Orchestra. London [Decca] 421580 [DDD] + Symphony No. 4

B. Walter, Columbia Symphony Orchestra. Sony 64463 [ADD] + Symphony No. 7

Wand, North German Radio Symphony Orchestra. RCA Victor Red Seal 61930 [ADD] + Symphony No. 6

No. 6 in F, Op. 68, "Pastorale"

'The antisocial Beethoven is reported to have once said "I love a tree more than a man." He put his money where his mouth was in this symphony, for which he provided an explicit program. The movements are marked "Awakening of happy feelings upon reaching the countryside," "Scene at the brook," "Cheerful gathering of country folk," "Thunderstorm," and finally, "Shepherd's song: Happy, grateful feelings after the storm." Here, for once, those stern musicologists who are always warning us against reading pictorial meanings into music maintain a red-faced silence.

Böhm, Vienna Philharmonic Orchestra. Deutsche Grammophon Originals 447433 [ADD] + Schubert: Symphony No. 5

Böhm, Vienna Philharmonic Orchestra. Deutsche Grammophon 437928 (2) [ADD] + Symphonies 7, 8, *Leonore* Overture No. 3, *Fidelio* Overture (Dresden State Orchestra in the overtures)

Harnoncourt, Chamber Orchestra of Europe. Teldec 75709 [DDD] + Symphony No. 8

Tennstedt, London Philharmonic Orchestra. EMI Studio 63891 [DDD] + Symphony No. 8

B. Walter, Columbia Symphony Orchestra. Sony 64462 [ADD] + Symphony No. 4

Wand, North German Radio Symphony Orchestra. RCA Victor Red Seal 61930 [ADD] + Symphony No. 5

―――― *U.S. labels and numbers are given first, U.K. in [brackets] when needed.* ――――

No. 7 in A, Op. 92

Beethoven here indulges himself in rhythmic experimentation to create an abandoned outpouring of pure kinetic energy. Wagner called this symphony "the apotheosis of the dance." Beethoven himself called it "one of my best works." But it has remained problematical for some listeners who miss the nobility or thoughtfulness they find in the other symphonies. Some contemporary critics thought the feverish final movement was proof Beethoven was going insane. The late conductor Sir Thomas Beecham hated the Seventh: "It sounds," he said, "like a bunch of yaks jumping about." Certainly Beethoven was in high spirits when he wrote it!

Abbado, Vienna Philharmonic Orchestra. Deutsche Grammophon 423364 [DDD] + Symphony No. 8

Böhm, Vienna Philharmonic Orchestra. Deutsche Grammophon 437928 (2) [ADD] + Symphonies 6, 8, *Leonore* Overture No. 3, *Fidelio* Overture (Dresden State Orchestra in overtures)

C. Davis, Royal Philharmonic Orchestra. EMI Doubleforte 69364 (2) [ADD] + Schubert: Symphony No. 9; Rossini: Overtures

Furtwängler, Vienna Philharmonic Orchestra. EMI 69803 [ADD] (mono) + Symphony No. 5

C. Kleiber, Vienna Philharmonic Orchestra. Deutsche Grammophon 447400 [ADD] + Symphony No. 5

Mackerras, Royal Liverpool Philharmonic Orchestra. Classics for Pleasure Eminence 2212 [DDD] + Symphony No. 5

Szell, Cleveland Orchestra. Sony Essential Classics 48158 [ADD] + Symphony No. 4, overtures

B. Walter, Columbia Symphony Orchestra. Sony 64463 [ADD] + Symphony No. 5

No. 8 in F, Op. 93

Beethoven wrote this symphony at the same time as No. 7, and it has been seen as a more relaxed exercise in rhythmic devices. Sir George Grove suggested the nickname "Humorous" for No. 8, and certainly there are plenty of outlandish moments that one might take for Beethovenian "raspberries"; the second movement, for example, would seem to make comic reference to the recently invented metronome, concluding with a mechanical breakdown.

Abbado, Vienna Philharmonic Orchestra. Deutsche Grammophon 423364 [DDD] + Symphony No. 7

——— *All CDs listed are considered approximately equal in (high) merit.* ———

Böhm, Vienna Philharmonic Orchestra. Deutsche Grammophon 437928 (2) [ADD] + Symphonies 6, 7, *Leonore* Overture No. 3, *Fidelio* Overture (Dresden State Orchestra in the overtures)

Drahos, Nicolaus Esterházy Sinfonia. Naxos. 8.553475 [DDD] + Symphony No. 3

Harnoncourt, Chamber Orchestra of Europe. Teldec 75709 [DDD] + Symphony No. 6

Karajan, Berlin Philharmonic Orchestra. Deutsche Grammophon 419051 [ADD] + Symphony No. 5

Tennstedt, London Philharmonic Orchestra. EMI Studio 63891 [DDD] + Symphony No. 6

B. Walter, Columbia Symphony Orchestra. Sony 64461 [ADD] _ Symphony No. 3

No. 9 in d, Op. 125, "Choral"

Beethoven's final symphony was also his largest in scale, and, until the colossi of Bruckner and Mahler, the longest. More than 30 years before he finished the Ninth, Beethoven had confided to a friend that he wanted to set Friedrich Schiller's Ode "To Joy" to music. He decided to incorporate it as the last movement of his last symphony only after much soul-searching. Early audiences found it puzzling or embarrassing. Beethoven's fellow composer Ludwig Spohr, usually an admirer, called it "tasteless and monstrous;" and a modern critic, Norman Suckling, has referred to it as "Beethoven's celebrated misfire."

This is not to denigrate the creative imagination and iron control which produced this mighty work, but to indicate how unnecessary it is to bow meekly before masterpieces as if they were gods. We ought to approach them as friends; none perhaps without fault, but all with something to love, though never demanding our worship. Beethoven, an apostle of democracy, a man who denounced Napoleon when he turned tyrant, would not stand for such an attitude.

It is fair to question whether words are needed to drive home a message that might have been more subtly conveyed by musical means alone—especially when the words are so fulsome as Schiller's (least favorite line: "Wollust ward dem Wurm gegeben," or "Even to a worm ecstasy is granted"). But Beethoven apparently wanted to be sure no one missed the poem's message of universal brotherhood, and the surging rapture of the last movement seldom fails to enthrall an audience. One is hard-pressed not to be moved at the line "Seid umschlungen, Millionen." It is difficult not to believe that the bitter, lonely Beethoven is writing, as he once said, "From the heart, to the heart," when the chorus cries "O you millions, let me embrace you."

--- *CDs listed are solid, central choices, not necessarily "the greatest."* ---

Bernstein, members of various orchestras. *Ode to Freedom*, Deutsche Grammophon 429861 [DDD]

Bernstein, Vienna Philharmonic Orchestra. Deutsche Grammophon 410859 [ADD]

Böhm, Vienna Philharmonic Orchestra. Deutsche Grammophon 445503 [DDD]

Gardiner, Orchestra Révolutionnaire et Romantique. Archiv 447074 [DDD]

Giulini, London Symphony Orchestra. EMI Encore 67763

Karajan, Berlin Philharmonic Orchestra. Deutsche Grammophon Originals 447401 [ADD] + Coriolan Overture

Mackerras, Royal Liverpool Philharmonic Orchestra. Classics for Pleasure Eminence 2186 [DDD]

Reiner, Chicago Symphony Orchestra. RCA Victor Gold Seal 6532 [ADD]

B. Walter, Columbia Symphony Orchestra. Sony 64464 [ADD]

Trio No. 6 in Bb, Op. 97, "Archduke"

The clear champion among Beethoven's 11 trios for piano, violin and cello, the "Archduke" is named for one of the composer's most generous patrons. It is distinguished by melodic beauty and wide-ranging vision.

Beaux Arts Trio. Philips Solo 412891 [ADD] + Trio No. 4 "Ghost"

Oistrakh, Knushevitsky, Oborin. EMI Doublefforte 69367 + Schubert: Piano Trio No. 1; Brahms: Violin Sonatas; encores

Perlman, Harrell, Ashkenazy. EMI 47010 [DDD] + Trio No. 10

Solomon Trio. Carlton Classics Double 6600107 [30366 00107] (2) [DDD] + Trios Nos. 5, 6; *Kakadu* Variations, Allegretto in E-flat

Thibaud, Casals, Cortot. EMI 61024 (mono) + Schubert Piano Trio No. 1

[The above is the oldest recording listed in this book. It was recorded in 1924, but still sounds excellent, and in any case is one of the greatest records of chamber music ever made. Nevertheless, at this writing it is not being distributed in the U.S. because Americans will not buy anything this old unless it is marked down to 29¢. It is available in the U.K., or in the U.S. through the Internet or import services. I said in the Foreword that I would list "historical" recordings only when they are truly exceptional. This is the best example I could give.]

Luigi Boccherini (1743-1805)

Boccherini wrote about 500 works, but is remembered today mainly for one cello concerto and a famous minuet so tiny we cannot give it space here. Boccherini's admirers are growing in number, however, and his stock continues to rise. One of his earliest fans was, in

——— *Some famous CDs are not listed because currently out of print.* ———

fact, Franz Joseph Haydn, who called him "a genius." Their styles were so interrelated that a contemporary musician in a famous phrase called Boccherini "the wife of Haydn."

At age 13 he was already an accomplished cellist, and in his mid-20s he settled in to a lucrative position at the Spanish court. Alas, after a few years of wealth and fame, he fell out with the new monarch, Charles IV, who prohibited not only the performance of Boccherini's music, but even the mention of his name. By 1803, he was living with his wife and five children in a single room where he eventually died, we are told, of sickness and starvation.

Boccherini has tremendous historical importance as the true inventor of the modern string trio, quartet, and quintet. His compositions, while they may fall short of Beethoven's and Mozart's in stature, are tuneful, graceful, suavely harmonized, inventive, and virtuosic. While not sublime, they are very far above the ordinary, and they make exceedingly pleasurable listening.

Concerto in B-flat for Cello and Orchestra (arr. Grützmacher)

The most popular of Boccherini's 12 known cello concertos has in the 20th century become one of the staples of the cello repertoire. It is idiomatically written for the instrument, so any competent cellist can do well with it.

Kanta, Breiner, Capella Istropolitana. Naxos 8.550059 [DDD] + Haydn: Cello Concerti Nos. 1 and 2

Ma, Zukerman, St. Paul Chamber Orchestra. Sony 39964 + J. C. Bach: Sinfonias Concertante

Christoph Willibald von Gluck (1714-1787)

Gluck was almost exclusively an opera composer, and in the course of it became one of the most significant figures in the history of the opera form. He composed some 40 works for the lyric stage, of which only six comprise the "reform operas" for which he became famous, and of which only one, *Orfeo ed Euridice*, is still regularly performed. There are few composers who have been held in higher regard yet have a smaller public.

He was born of German and Bohemian stock, his father being a huntsman and forest ranger to various aristocrats. Christoph, musically talented, grew up playing chamber music in noble households. He studied with Sammartini in Milan for three years and then began producing his first operas in several cities, where picking up along the way an eclectic view of style. Indeed, although he was of Teutonic blood, he wrote all his operas in Italian or French, and eventually was looked upon as an internationalist.

By the age of 40 he had written about 20 operas, married a rich banker's daughter, and been engaged as musical director of the Imperial court in Vienna, where he fell in with a faction who wanted to modernize opera by getting rid of the *castrati* (male sopranos), making the drama more realistic and unified, and balancing the roles of music and words. Up to this time opera was usually a rather stilted affair of mythological allegories with a heavy tilt towards vocal display.

Gluck was more or less selected by the reform faction at court to implement their theories, which he first did in the opera *Alceste*. To it he affixed a famous written preface laying down the manifesto of the new movement. Despite this, Gluck was a true composer of his era, trained to compose on command, and he continued to write operas in the old style even after causing a sensation with his greatest "reform" opera, *Orfeo ed Euridice*.

In his last years, partially paralyzed by a stroke, Gluck was befriended by both Salieri and Mozart, and the latter honored him by improvising a set of variations on Gluck's comic *opera La Rencontre imprévue*. Ironically, while the ideals of "reform opera" were much trumpeted later on by Wagner, they actually influenced mainly the French school, especially Berlioz. Today the general public is familiar only with the haunting aria "Che faro" and the *Dance of the Blessed Spirits*, both from *Orfeo ed Euridice*; but an investigation into his other operas, especially Alceste and *Iphigénie en Tauride*, can be a revelation. This is often music of great beauty and nobility.

Orfeo ed Euridice

The most famous of Gluck's operas reworks the old Greek legend of the god of music who goes down to the Elysian Fields to retrieve his beloved wife from the land of death, but he invests it with the innovations of the reform faction at the Viennese court: the music outlines and underlines the words and the scenes are composed straight through. Everything is subservient to the dramatic conception, instead of being the slave of some artist or fashion.

Gardiner, McNair, English Baroque Soloists. (1762 Vienna version) Philips 434093 (2) [DDD]

Leppard, Baker, London Philharmonic Orchestra. (1774 Paris version, sung in Italian) Erato Libretto 45864 (2) [DDD]

Franz Joseph Haydn (1732-1809)

Haydn was born of a humble but musical rural Austrian family, and early revealed a beautiful singing voice. He was sent off as a lad to St. Stephen's Cathedral in the big city of

Vienna, where he picked up the rudiments of theory, and got himself thrashed by the Empress herself when she caught him clambering about the church scaffolding.

"I never had real teachers," he confessed towards the end of his life. Thrown on his own resources at age 16, when his choirboy's voice broke, he taught himself the scores of C. P. E. Bach's sonatas on a broken-down old spinet in an unheated garret. He survived by playing evening serenades and giving lessons.

He was not a child prodigy in the manner of Mozart, who has for generations over-shadowed him. He plodded away at his work 16 to 18 hours a day. He was past 40 when he wrote the works for which he is most admired today. In the course of a well-ordered, industrious life he became known as the "father" of the symphony and the string quartet. Although he did not actually invent these forms, he was the first to develop them to an eminence which would provide a standard for later composers.

When Haydn was 49 he first met the 25-year-old Mozart and recognized in him a genius even greater than his own. Without a trace of jealousy, and never too smug to keep learning, Haydn studied the younger man's work and enriched his own compositions with its lessons. The two became dear friends, and Haydn was crushed by Mozart's death in 1791.

Haydn lived on for another 18 years, to the age of 77, renowned for his wisdom, piety, patience, honesty, and modesty; yet there were those who said they had never seen him laugh, and that even when he was joking there was a certain sadness in his eyes.

He died full of honors during the French occupation of Vienna. It was not his countrymen alone who mourned him. Napoleon himself ordered a guard of honor to accompany the corpse. At the memorial service, Mozart's *Requiem* was sung.

Concerto in E-flat for Trumpet

This is the most famous of all trumpet concertos. Strangely, it dropped from view after Hadyn's death until 1928, when it was revived on a radio broadcast. Then it became a hit, and it has stayed at the top of the brass charts ever since.

Bennett, Pinnock, The English Concert. Archiv 431678 [DDD] + Oboe Concerto in C, Keyboard Concerto in D

Hardenberger, Marriner, Academy of St. Martin-in-the-Fields. Philips 420203 [DDD] + Trumpet concerti by Hummel, Stamitz, Hertel

Marsalis, Leppard, National Philharmonic Orchestra (Washington, DC). Sony 39310 [DDD] + Violin Concerto No. 1 (with Lin, Marriner, Minnesota Orchestra), Cello Concerto No. 2 (with Ma, Garcia, English Chamber Orchestra)

———— *Artists are listed alphabetically, not in order by critical ranking.* ————

The Creation

This is the best known and most beloved oratorio after Handel's *Messiah*. Written near the end of the composer's long life, it is a moving testimony to his gentle faith. The most famous moments are the thrilling burst of sound at the words "And there was light"; and the magnificent chorus "The heavens are telling the glory of God," which only Handel's "Hallelujah" chorus exceeds in popularity.

Gardiner, English Baroque Soloists. (Sung in German) Archiv 449217 (2) [DDD]

Hogwood, Academy of Ancient Music, Oxford New College Choir. (Sung in English) L'Oiseau-Lyre 430397 (2) [DDD]

Karajan, Vienna Philharmonic Orchestra. (Sung in German) Deutsche Grammophon Galleria 435077 (2) [ADD]

Rattle, City of Birmingham Symphony Orchestra and Chorus. (Sung in English) EMI 54159 (2) [DDD]

Weil, Tafelmusik. (Sung in German) Sony Vivarte 57965 [DDD]

Mass No.11 in D Minor, "Nelson"

If you are averse to religious music, fear not. Had Haydn lived two centuries longer this might have been his film score for *Raiders of the Lost Ark*. It was actually written just as Admiral Nelson had defeated Napoleon in the Battle of the Nile, and its Latin subtitle means "Mass in Time of Fear." Its rumbling of drums, pealing of trumpets, and choral pleadings and rejoicings would knock the shingles off a church.

Bernstein, New York Philharmonic Orchestra, Westminster Choir. Sony 47563 (2) [ADD] + Mass No. 10, Symphony No. 88

Marriner, Academy of St. Martin-in-the-Fields, King's College Choir, Cambridge. London [Decca] Jubilee 421146 [ADD] + Vivaldi: *Gloria*

Pinnock, The English Concert. Archiv 423097 [ADD] + *Te Deum*

Willcocks, London Symphony Orchestra, Choir of King's College, Cambridge. London [Decca] 421146 [ADD] + Vivaldi: *Gloria*

Quartet in C, Op. 76, No. 3, "Emperor"

This is only the most familiar string quartet out of dozens by Haydn, scarcely a one of which fails to deliver for the aficionado of chamber music. The nickname comes from the second, or slow, movement, which is a set of four variations on an original (and noble) melody which has served as both the German and Austrian national anthems.

——— *[DDD] indicates newest recordings; [ADD] or [AAD] are reissues.* ———

Kodály Quartet. Naxos 8.550129 [DDD] + Quartets Op. 76/1, 2
Takács Quartet. London [Decca] 421360 [DDD] + Quartets Op. 76/1, 2

Symphonies

Officially, Haydn wrote 104 symphonies, though we now know that one more is lost, and two others are disguised in his catalog as "divertimenti." There truly is not one that is not melodious, infectious, and well-built. We may sense that they are not on quite the same level as Mozart's and Beethoven's—we feel happiness and sadness rather than joy and tragedy—but no composer other than Haydn produced such a quantity of symphonic music at such a consistently high level. Perhaps the most amazing thing is that we are not talking about a fumbling search from primitive beginnings to later mastery, but a steady, confident progression from the first little masterwork right up the ladder to the top, scarcely ever missing a rung.

If there is any composer who made it to Heaven, it would have to be Haydn, who inscribed each of his scores "In the name of the Lord," and "Praise to God," who had no enemies and committed no sins worth mentioning.

You can easily recognize which Haydn symphonies are the most popular because virtually all of them have nicknames, given not by the composer but by his grateful publishers and listeners. The earliest one that still appears frequently on orchestra programs is No. 45, the "Farewell" symphony, so named because Haydn wrote the last movement to allow groups of players to conclude their parts and leave the stage one after another until no one is left!

Other famous symphonic nicknames include "The Bear" (No. 82), "The Hen" (83), "Oxford" (92), "Surprise" (94), "Miracle" (96), "Military" (100), "Clock" (101), "Drum Roll" (103), and "London" (104). On top of that, Nos. 93 through 104 are known collectively as the "London" or "Salomon" Symphonies, and Nos. 82-87 as the "Paris" Symphonies. Perhaps we would do better to call Haydn the "Father of the Nickname" instead of "Father of the Symphony."

Beecham, Royal Philharmonic Orchestra. Nos. 93-98, EMI 64389 (2) [AAD]
Bernstein, New York Philharmonic Orchestra. Nos. 94-99, Sony 47553 (3) [ADD]
C. Davis, Concertgebouw Orchestra. Nos. 93-104, Philips Duo Vol. 1, 442611 (2) [ADD]; Vol. 2, 442614 (4) [ADD]
Fischer, Austro-Hungarian Haydn Orchestra. Nos. 82-87, Nimbus 5419/20 (2) [DDD]
Glover, Royal Philharmonic Orchestra. Nos. 101, 103, RPO [Tring] 053 [DDD]

——— *CDs go in and out of print; availability of all listed items is not assured.* ———

Goodman, Hanover Band. Nos. 90-92, Hyperion 66521 [DDD]

Harnoncourt, Vienna Concentus Musicus. Nos. 31, 59, 73, Teldec 90843 [DDD]

Hogwood, Academy of Ancient Music. Nos. 94, 96, L'Oiseau-Lyre 414330 [DDD]

Kuijken, Orchestra of the Age of Enlightenment. Nos. 82-84, Virgin Classics 59537 [DDD]

Kuijken, Orchestra of the Age of Enlightenment. Nos. 85-87, Virgin Classics 59557 [DDD]

Marriner, Academy of St. Martin-in-the-Fields. Nos. 82-87, Philips Duo 438727 (2) [ADD]

Szell, Cleveland Orchestra. Nos. 92, 94, 96, Sony 46332 [ADD]

Szell, Cleveland Orchestra. Nos. 93-98, Sony 45673 (2) [ADD]

Ward, Northern Chamber Orchestra. Nos. 6-8, Naxos 8.550722 [DDD]

Weil, Tafelmusik. Nos. 45-47, Sony Vivarte 53986 [DDD]

Wolfgang Amadeus Mozart (1756-1791)

Mozart is the finest all-time example of a Wunderkind with staying power. There were other child prodigies who became composers: Mendelssohn, Bizet, Boccherini, Arriaga, Lekeu come to mind—but you see how quickly the list fades into obscurity. Most infant geniuses burn out by their 20s. What kept Mozart's flame burning ever brighter, from his first compositions at age five, to his 626th masterpiece at age 35? No one knows.

It is fashionable nowadays to sniff at the traditional epithet "Divine" applied to Mozart, to belittle or doubt his reported ability to compose great works in his head while playing billiards and to write them down at his later convenience, to emphasize his scatalogical language and love of roistering as if to prove he was scarcely different from you or I.

It won't wash. There is too much evidence that his talents and perceptions and intuitions were light years beyond the ordinary. He seemed to know most of the basics of music by the age most of us are just learning to tell the big hand from the little hand. Melody, gorgeous melody, flowed from him like sparkling waters from an artesian well. At every turn in his works there are little subtleties and details about which critics have written whole books of analysis; if Mozart had taken time to ponder each of them he would have needed to live another 35 years—but he didn't. He music sounds effortless. With almost any other composer (Beethoven is a good example) composition is a result of long, deep thinking, and numberless revisions, "art concealing art." With Mozart it is different. It *is* effortless!

No other composer is so resistant to being taken apart and exposed as a set of cogs and gears, his accomplishments shown to be nothing more than the result of preordained chemical reactions. I am not exaggerating when I say that there are pages of his music

——— *Some CDs may be available only through importers.* ———

which to the experienced eye look clumsy, or impossible to play, but when heard sound smooth as silk. No one knows how Mozart's mind made the leap of intuition from page to stage. There are hours upon hours of pieces that sound "pretty" on the surface, but carry some nameless undercurrent that unsettles or moves the soul. No one is able to explain just what Mozart has done, musically, to produce this effect, which on paper looks identical to the genial, untroubled music of Haydn.

Perhaps we should simply let Haydn say what he thought: "If I could tell every music lover...what I feel about the inimitable works of Mozart, their depth of emotion and their unique musical quality, every nation would compete to possess such a great person within its boundaries." This from a composer 25 years older, far more famous and successful at the time, and considered the genius of his era. Haydn did not need to say this—he simply had no choice. I like also the way British actor Tom Courtenay has put it. In an interview in the *New Yorker* (Oct 23, 1995, p. 37) he said of a favorite Mozart piece that it "seems to take in everything—the sadness, the beauty, the fun in spite of it all. He gets to the heart of the matter."

Though Mozart's life was short, it was full of incident, and we can only touch on the highlights here. He was born in Salzburg, Austria to a musical family. His proud and parsimonious father, Leopold, trotted him out as a sideshow wonder at the age of five, eager to burnish the family name and make a fortune. Dressed in lace jabeau and buckled shoes little Wolfgang played the harpsichord before the Empress herself. By his late teens he had toured much of Europe and along the way picked up the styles and techniques of many contemporary composers.

For several years he suffered employment in the oppressive music establishment of the Archbishop of Salzburg, being released in 1781 "with a kick," as he said, "on my ass." He was soon happier in Vienna, where he married, had children, and enjoyed his first public recognition. As time passed, however, he experienced increasing difficulties in health and finances. His brief moment in the sun clouded over, and he was reduced to contant borrowing to support his family.

One day an ominous stranger appeared at his door, offering to pay Mozart to write a Requiem Mass. The man was anonymously representing an eccentric nobleman who bought works from indigent talents and passed them off as his own; but the ailing Mozart imagined this visitor to have come from the Beyond, to warn him of his own death. And die he did, in the middle of the winter, with the great Requiem incomplete. His wife was too ill to attend the funeral. He was buried in an unmarked pauper's grave, whose exact location was soon forgotten.

It was only a few years before romantic fantasies began to embellish Mozart's image. One of the most macabre was that he had not died of natural causes but had been poisoned by a rival composer, Antonio Salieri. This theory inspired several fictional works, most notably in our time Peter Shaffer's play *Amadeus*, and the popular film based on it. Historians justly complain about distorting and fictionalizing a life that is already dramatic

——— *U.S. labels and numbers are given first, U.K. in [brackets] when needed.* ———

and unbelievable enough. But what can you expect? Mozart, like Alexander the Great or Charlemagne, was bigger than life. When people or events surpass our comprehension we mythologize them. And thus have we done with the Divine Mozart, for whom we can find no parallel among our brethren.

Concerto in A for Clarinet, K.622

Mozart wrote this work of "greatness and transcendent beauty" (Alfred Einstein) for his good friend, the great clarinetist Anton Stadler. It is one of his very last works, and is one of those that speaks most poignantly of a sadness underlying the surface calm.

Hosford, Schneider, Chamber Orchestra of Europe. ASV 814 [DDD] + Oboe Concerto, Sinfonia Concertante, K.297b

Johnson, Leppard, English Chamber Orchestra. ASV 532 [DDD] + Flute and Harp Concerto

King, Tate, English Chamber Orchestra. Hyperion 66199 [DDD] + Clarinet Quintet

Marcellus, Szell, Cleveland Orchestra. CBS [Sony] 37810 [AAD] + *Sinfonia Concertante*, K.364

Pay, Hogwood, Academy of Ancient Music. L'Oiseau-Lyre 414339 [DDD] + Oboe Concerto, K.314

Prinz, Böhm, Vienna Philharmonic Orchestra. Deutsche Grammophon 429816 [ADD] + Oboe Concerto, K.314, Bassoon Concerto, K.191

Shifrin, Schwarz, Mostly Mozart Orchestra. Delos 3020 [DDD] + Clarinet Quintet

Concertos for Flute: No. 1 in G, K.313; No. 2 in D, K.314

Mozart claimed to hate the flute. After hearing these sparkling works one might wonder: with an enemy like this, who needs friends? They were commissioned by a wealthy Dutch sea captain who was an amateur flutist on the side. Weird, but true.

Galway (flutist and conductor), Chamber Orchestra of Europe. RCA Victor Red Seal 7861 (2) [DDD] + other Mozart selections

Hall, Thomas, Philharmonia Orchestra. IMP [Carlton Classics] PCD 2036

Milan, Leppard, English Chamber Orchestra. Chandos 8613 [DDD] + other Mozart selections

Rampal, Mehta, Israel Philharmonic Orchestra. CBS 44919 [DDD] + other Mozart selections

——— *All CDs listed are considered approximately equal in (high) merit.* ———

Concertos (4) for Horn, K.412, 417, 447, 495

Like the Clarinet Concerto, the French Horn Concertos were written for a close friend—this time, horn player Joseph Leutgeb, "ass, ox, and fool" as Mozart described him, à la Don Rickles. This quartet of genial pieces remains at the pinnacle of French horn literature.

Brain, Karajan, Philharmonia Orchestra. EMI 56321 (mono) + Quintet for Piano and Winds, K.452

Halstead, Goodman, Hanover Band. Nimbus 5104

Koster, Weil, Tafelmusik. Sony 53369 [DDD] + Concert Rondo in E-flat

Pyatt, Marriner, Academy of St. Martin-in-the-Fields. Erato 17074 [DDD] + Horn Quintet

Tuckwell (horn and conductor), Philharmonia Orchestra. Collins Classics 1153 [DDD] + other short pieces

Tuckwell, Marriner, Academy of St. Martin-in-the-Fields. EMI 69569 + other Mozart selections

Concertos for Piano and Orchestra (27)

Mozart was the first great composer to prefer the piano over the harpsichord, and his enthusiasm shows. These represent the largest body of great concerted piano music by any composer, and Mozart's highest overall achievement in instrumental music.

The first eight have their youthful charms, but it is with No. 9, written when Mozart was 21, that he hits his stride. It is perhaps a bit unusual that the most famous of the set is No. 20, rather than the seven which come after it. Regardless of individual merits, all the piano concertos are significant and one might well wish to opt for a complete boxed set. As for individual concertos, I have tried to condense the hundreds of available recordings to a representation of the most famous ones.

Complete sets:

Brendel, Marriner, Academy of St. Martin-in-the-Fields. Complete Mozart Edition, Vol. 7, Philips 422507 (12) [ADD]

Immerseel (fortepiano), Anima Eterna. Channel Classics CCS Box 10 (10) [DDD]

Perahia (piano and conductor), English Chamber Orchestra. Sony 46441 (12) [ADD, DDD]

Uchida, Tate, English Chamber Orchestra. Philips 438207 (9) [DDD]

——— *CDs listed are solid, central choices, not necessarily "the greatest."* ———

Single discs:

Ashkenazy (piano and conductor), Philharmonia Orchestra. Nos. 20, 21, 23, 27, London [Decca] Double 436383 [ADD] + Piano Sonata No. 17, Rondo in A Minor, K.511

Ashkenazy (piano and conductor), Philharmonia Orchestra. Nos. 25, 26, London [Decca] 411810 [DDD]

Ashkenazy, Kertész, London Symphony Orchestra. Nos. 8, 9, London [Decca] 443576 [ADD] + Concert Rondo No. 2

Barenboim (piano and conductor), Berlin Philharmonic Orchestra. Nos. 24, 25, Teldec 75715 [DDD]

Bilson (fortepiano), Gardiner, English Baroque Soloists. Nos., 20, 21, Archiv 419609 [DDD]

Brendel, Marriner, Academy of St. Martin-in-the-Fields. Nos. 9, 15, 22, 25, 27, Philips Duo 442571 (2) [ADD/DDD]

Brendel, Marriner, Academy of St. Martin-in-the-Fields. Nos. 19-21, 23, 24, , Philips Duo 442269 (2) [ADD/DDD] + Concert Rondos Nos. 1, 2

Casadesus, Szell, Cleveland Orchestra. Nos. 21, 24, Sony 38523 [AAD]

Jandó, Ligeti, Concentus Hungaricus. Nos. 12, 14, 21, Naxos 8.550202 [DDD]

Jandó, Ligeti, Concentus Hungaricus. Nos. 16, 26, Naxos 8.550207 [DDD] + Rondo in A, K.386

Kempff, Leitner, Berlin Philharmonic Orchestra, Bamberg Symphony Orchestra. Nos. 8, 23, 24, 27, Deutsche Grammophon Double 439699 (2) [ADD]

Lipatti, Karajan, Lucerne Festival Orchestra. No. 21, EMI 69792 (mono) [ADD] + Schumann: Piano Concerto in A Minor

Moravec, Vlach, Czech Philharmonic Orchestra. Nos. 23, 25, Supraphon 11-0271 [AAD]

Perahia, English Chamber Orchestra. Nos. 9, 21, Sony 34562 [ADD]

Perahia, English Chamber Orchestra. Nos. 11, 12, 14, Sony 42243 [ADD]

Perahia, English Chamber Orchestra. Nos. 17, 18, Sony 36686 [ADD]

Perahia, English Chamber Orchestra. Nos. 19, 23, Sony 39064 [DDD]

Perahia, English Chamber Orchestra. Nos. 20, 27, Sony 42241 [ADD]

Pires, Abbado, Chamber Orchestra of Europe. Nos. 17, 21, Deutsche Grammophon 439941 [DDD]

Shelley (piano and conductor), London Mozart Players. Nos. 9, 17, Chandos 9068 [DDD]

R. Serkin, Szell, Cleveland Orchestra. Nos. 19, 20, CBS 37236 [ADD]

Uchida, Tate, English Chamber Orchestra. Nos. 26, 27, Philips 420951 [DDD]

———— *Some famous CDs are not listed because currently out of print.* ————

Concerto No. 5 in A for Violin, K.219

Mozart wrote just five violin concertos, all as a youth of 19. The last three are much the best, and the fifth is the most popular for its final movement in "Turkish" style.

Huggett (violin and conductor), Orchestra of the Age of Enlightenment. Virgin Classics 45010 [DDD] + Violin Concertos 1, 2

Menuhin (violinist and conductor), Bath Festival Orchestra. EMI Encore 67779 [ADD] + Violin Concertos 1, 3

Nishizaki, Gunzenhauser, Capella Istropolitana. Naxos 8.550063 [DDD] + Violin Concerto No. 3

Perlman, Levine, Vienna Philharmonic Orchestra. (Complete) Deutsche Grammophon Masters 445535 (2) [DDD]

Schneiderhan, Jochum, Berlin Philharmonic Orchestra. Deutsche Grammophon 447403 [ADD] + Beethoven: Violin Concerto

Shumsky, Tortelier, Scottish Chamber Orchestra. Nimbus 5009 [DDD] + Violin Concerto No. 4

Tetlaff, German Chamber Philharmonic. (Complete) Virgin Classics 45214 (2) [DDD] + short violin works

Don Giovanni, K.527

This is the greatest opera ever written. At least that is the opinion of a large number of critics and just plain opera lovers. It may not be the most popular, or the most historically significant, but there is something about it that makes it seem somehow, well, greater. Maybe it is the ambiguous tone, neither really comic nor tragic, combined with the wonderful melodies, and the excellent text by the greatest of all opera librettists Lorenzo da Ponte, and...

One evening long ago, little Charles Gounod, the composer-to-be of another great opera, *Faust*, was taken by his mother to the Paris Opera to see *Don Giovanni*. When the solemn trombones intoned the theme of the Commendatore in the overture, the wide-eyed lad scrunched down in his seat. "Mama," he whispered, "this is real music!" That is all anyone needs to know.

C. Davis, Wixell, Royal Opera House, Covent Garden Chorus and Orchestra. Philips 422541 (3) [ADD]

Giulini, Wächter, Philharmonia Orchestra and Chorus. EMI 56232 (3) [ADD]

Gardiner, Gilfry, Monteverdi Choir, English Baroque Soloists. Archiv 445870 (3) [DDD]

——— *Catalog numbers are subject to change without notice.* ———

Haitink, Allen, London Philharmonic Orchestra, Glyndebourne Chorus.
EMI 47037 [DDD]

Harnoncourt, Hampson, Concertgebouw Orchestra. Teldec 44184 (3) [DDD]

Karajan, Ramey, Berlin Philharmonic Orchestra. Deutsche Grammophon
419179 (3) [DDD]

Krips, Siepi, Vienna Philharmonic Orchestra and State Opera Chorus.
London [Decca] 411626 (3) [ADD]

Mackerras, Skovhus, Scottish Chamber Orchestra and Chorus. Telarc 80420
(3) [DDD]

Norrington, Schmidt, London Classical Players. EMI 54859 (3) [DDD]

Exsultate, Jubilate, K.165

This short motet (under 15 minutes) might serve as an introduction to Mozart's
sacred choral music, which includes other motets (e.g. the lovely *Ave, Verum Corpus*,
K.618); two settings of the vespers, or evening, service; four litanies; 18 masses, of which
the best known are those nicknamed "Credo," "Coronation," and "The Great"; and the
famous Requiem, listed separately below. The *Exsultate, Jubilate* is, as you might guess even
if you have no Latin, a joyful effusion, and concludes with a coloratura "Alleluia" which has
long been the joy of sopranos.

Te Kanawa, C. Davis, London Symphony Orchestra and Chorus. Philips
412873 [ADD] + other short choral works

The Magic Flute (Die Zauberflöte), K.620

"Magic" is indeed the word to describe this funny, joyful, moving, fantastic opera from
the end of Mozart's life, a children's adventure on one level and an adult allegory on another. This is the opera to try on opera-haters; if they don't catch on, they are hopeless. From
the glorious overture to the final chorus, there is hardly a page of this score that does not
enchant the ear and the imagination.

Böhm, Janowitz, Berlin Philharmonic Orchestra. Deutsche Grammophon
449728 (3) [ADD]

Christie, Mannion, Les Arts Florissants. Erato 12705 (2) [DDD]

Haitink, Popp, Bavarian Radio Symphony Orchestra and Chorus. EMI
47951 (3) [DDD]

Halász, Soloists, Failoni Orchestra, Budapest. Naxos 8.660030 [DDD]

Klemperer, Janowitz, Philharmonia Orchestra and Chorus. EMI Studio
69971 [55173] (2) [ADD]

———— *Since CDs can change label and number, use artists as main reference.* ————

Marriner, Te Kanawa, Academy of St. Martin-in-the-Fields, Ambrosian Opera Chorus. Philips 426276 (2) [DDD]
Solti, Lorengar, Vienna Philharmonic Orchestra and State Opera Chorus. London [Decca] 433210 (2) [DDD]

The Marriage of Figaro (Le Nozze di Figaro), K.492

This is Mozart's greatest comedy, and one of the masterpieces of all comic opera. The unsophisticated listener is swept along by the delightful story and the endless profusion of beautiful melodies, while the more experienced hand is amazed by the complexity and unerring skill of the architecture and orchestration, and the perfectly balanced blend of farce and warm humanity. It is a work that demands both affection and reverence.

Böhm, Prey, Berlin German Opera Orchestra and chorus. Deutsche Grammophon 449728 [ADD]
C. Davis, Ganzarolli, BBC Chorus and Symphony Orchestra. Philips 422540 (3) [ADD]
Gardiner, Terfel, English Baroque Soloists. Archiv 439871 (3) [DDD]
Giulini, Taddei, Philharmonia Orchestra and Chorus. EMI Studio 63266 (2) [ADD]
Gui, Bruscantini, Glylndebourne Chorus and Festival Orchestra. Classics for Pleasure 4724 (2) [ADD]
Solti, Ramey, London Philharmonic Orchestra. London [Decca] 410150 (3) [DDD]

Mass No. 18 in C Minor, K.427/417a "The Great Mass"

Mozart wrote nearly 20 Masses, of which this is the last and greatest, rivalled only by the *Requiem* in his sacred music.

Abbado, Augér, Berlin Radio Chorus, Berlin Philharmonic Orchestra. Sony 46671 [DDD]
Gardiner, McNair, Monteverdi Choir, English Baroque Soloists. Philips 420210 [DDD]
Karajan, Hendricks, Vienna Singverein, Berlin Philharmonic Orchestra. Deutsche Grammophon "Karajan Gold" 439012 [DDD]
Marriner, Te Kanawa, Academy of St. Martin-in-the-Fields. Philips 438999 [DDD] + *Ave Verum Corpus*

———— *Artists are listed alphabetically, not in order by critical ranking.* ————

Overtures

Mozart was one of the very greatest opera composers and even if you are not an opera fan you will still enjoy the brilliant, tuneful overtures to his vocal works. Even some of the obscure operas have preludes equal to those from the more famous ones.

Marriner, Academy of St. Martin-in-the-Fields. EMI 47014 [DDD]
B. Walter, Columbia Symphony Orchestra. CBS [Sony] 37774 + *Eine kleine
    Nachtmusik, Masonic Funeral Music*
Weil, Tafelmusik. Sony Vivarte 46695 [DDD]
Wordsworth, Capella Istropolitana. Naxos 8.550185 [DDD]

Quartets Nos. 14-19, "Haydn Quartets"

Mozart wrote 23 string quartets in all, but this integrated set of six probably represents the summit of his writing in the chamber music category. It was inspired by the quartets of his teacher and friend, Franz Joseph Haydn, but goes beyond anything the older master composed, a fact which Haydn ackowledged with respect and affection. In turn Mozart dedicated the set to Haydn in a famous letter.

Alban Berg Quartet. Nos. 17, 19 only, Teldec 43037
Chilingirian Quartet. All 6, CRD 3362, 3363, 3364 [DDD]
Emerson Quartet. All 6, Deutsche Grammophon 431797 (3) [DDD]
Melos Quartet. Nos. 17, 19 only, Deutsche Grammophon 429818 [ADD]
Salomon Quartet. All 6, Hyperion 44001/3 (3) [DDD]

Quintet in A for Clarinet and Strings, K.581

Like the Clarinet Concerto (see above) this smaller-scaled work was written for Mozart's friend Anton Stadler. The composer's love for the clarinet—his favorite wind instrument—is obvious here in the warm, expressive writing.

De Peyer, Melos Ensemble. EMI 63116 [ADD] + Brahms: Clarinet Quintet
Hacker, Salomon Quartet. Saydisc 17 [DDD] + 2 fragments for clarinet quintet
    (arr. Druce)
King, Gabrieli String Quartet. Hyperion 66199 [DDD] + Clarinet Concerto
Leister, Berlin Soloists. Teldec 46429 [DDD] + Brahms: Clarinet Quintet
Meyer, Quatuor Mosaïques. Astrée Auvidis 8736 + "Kegelstatt" Trio
Shifrin, Chamber Music Northwest. Delos 3020 [DDD] + Clarinet Concerto
Wright, Marlboro Ensemble. Sony 46252 [ADD] + Schubert: *Trout* Quintet

———— *[DDD] indicates newest recordings; [ADD] or [AAD] are reissues.* ————

Requiem, K.626

The well-known story of how this work came to be written is told above in the biography of Mozart. Since he died before its completion, his wife authorized one of his students, Franz Süssmayr, to finish it using Mozart's sketches. This version has prevailed until recent years, when some scholars began trying to reconstruct Mozart's intentions. I regret to report that so far no Ph.D. professors have managed to fool me into thinking they were Mozart (and by the way, Bach and Beethoven didn't go to college either).

Barenboim, Orchestre de Paris, Paris Opera Chorus. EMI 47342 [DDD]

Gardiner, English Baroque Soloists. Philips 420197 [DDD] + *Kyrie* in D Minor, K.341

Herreweghe, La Chapelle Royale, Collegium Vocale, Orchestre des Champs-Elysées. Harmonia Mundi 901620

Hickox, Northern Sinfonia, London Symphony Chorus. Virgin Ultraviolet 61260 [DDD]

Karajan, Vienna Singverein, Vienna Philharmonic Orchestra. Deutsche Grammophon "Karajan Gold" 439023 [DDD]

Schreier, Dresden State Orchestra. Philips 411420 [DDD]

Serenade No. 13 in G, K.525, "Eine kleine Nachtmusik"

Mozart wrote a dozen or more serenades on commission from various nobles as a kind of background music for elegant soirees. Most of them have five movements. It would seem one movement is missing from the most famous of them, the "Little Night Music." Nevertheless, what is left is the most enchanting of all Mozart's lighter orchestral works, which include also the Divertimenti and Cassations, along with assorted marches and country dances.

Hogwood, Academy of Ancient Music. L'Oiseau-Lyre 411720 [DDD] + Serenade No. 6 "Serenata Notturno"

I Musici. Philips Digital Classics 410606 [DDD] + Albinoni: Adagio; Pachelbel: Canon in D; Boccherini: Minuet, *et al.*

Mackerras, Prague Chamber Orchestra. Telarc 80108 [DDD] + Serenade No. 9 "Posthorn"

Serenata of London. Carlton IMP PCD 861 [DDD] + Serenade No. 6 "Serenata Notturna"; Elgar: Serenade for Strings; Grieg: *Holberg* Suite

Stamp, Academy of London. Virgin Classics 59533 [DDD] + Prokofiev: *Peter and the Wolf;* Saint-Saëns: *Carnival of the Animals*

——— *CDs go in and out of print; availability of all listed items is not assured.* ———

B. Walter, Columbia Symphony Orchestra. CBS 37774 [AAD] + 4 overtures, *Masonic Funeral Music*

Sinfonia Concertante in E-flat for Violin and Viola, K.364

This is the greater of two works bearing this description, which means "a symphony in the nature of a concerto." It is an 18th-century form, giving two or more instrumentalists the chance to show off, which has pretty much become extinct nowadays. This Mozart work is considered by all critics the best such piece ever written.

Brainin/Schidlof, Gibson, Scottish National Orchestra. Chandos 6506 [DDD] + Symphony No. 39

Druian/Skernick, Szell, Cleveland Orchestra. CBS 37810 [AAD] + Clarinet Concerto

Lin/Laredo, Leppard, English Chamber Orchestra. Sony 47693 [DDD] + Concertone, K.190

Perlman/Zukerman, Mehta, Israel Philharmonic Orchestra. Deutsche Grammophon 415486 [DDD] + *Concertone*, K.190

Sonata No. 11 in A for Piano, K.331

Mozart wrote 17 sonatas for solo piano. They have not been as popular with audiences as Beethoven's sonatas, or indeed as Mozart's own piano concertos. They are splendid works nonetheless, and if you are doubtful start with this one, whose final infectious movement is often heard separately as the "Rondo alla Turca."

Klien. Vox/Turnabout 7194 [ADD] + Sonata No. 8, 5 other pieces
Perahia. Sony 48233 [DDD[+ Sonatas Nos. 8, 15
Uchida. Philips 412123 [DDD] + Sonata No. 12, Fantasia in D Minor, K.397

Symphonies (41)

Abbado, Berlin Philharmonic Orchestra. Nos. 28, 29, 35, Sony 48063 [DDD]
Bernstein, Vienna Philharmonic Orchestra. Nos. 40, 41, Deutsche Grammophon 431040 or 445548 [DDD]
Gardiner, English Baroque Soloists. Philips 426315 [DDD]
Gibson, Scottish National Orchestra. No. 39, Chandos 6506 [DDD] + Sinfonia Concertante, K.364
Glover, London Mozart Players. Nos. 31, 36, 38, ASV 647 [DDD]

─────── *Some CDs may be available only through importers.* ───────

Klemperer, Philharmonia Orchestra. Nos. 25, 29, 31, 33-36, 38-41, EMI Studio 63272 (4) [ADD]

Kubelik, Bavarian Radio Symphony Orchestra. Nos. 35, 36, Sony 44647 [DDD] + Violin Rondo, K.269 (with Zukerman)

Mackerras, Prague Chamber Orchestra. Nos. 25, 28, 29, Telarc 80165 [DDD]

Mackerras, Prague Chamber Orchestra. Nos. 36, 38, Telarc 80148 [DDD]

Marriner, Academy of St. Martin-in-the-Fields. Nos. 24-27, 32, EMI Red Line 69818 (2) [DDD]

Marriner, Academy of St. Martin-in-the-Fields. "The Last Five Symphonies", Philips Duo 438332 (2) [ADD]

Szell, Cleveland Orchestra. Nos. 35, 39, CBS 38472 [ADD]

Szell, Cleveland Orchestra. Nos. 35, 40, 41, Sony Essential Classics 46333 [ADD]

B. Walter, Columbia Symphony Orchestra. Nos. 35-36, 38-41, Sony 45676 (2)

Wordsworth, Capella Istropolitana. Nos. 25, 27-36, 38-41, Naxos 8.505004 (4) [DDD]

[A final word on Mozart recordings: the most monumental CD project yet is the Complete Mozart Edition from Philips, comprising virtually everything the composer ever wrote: over 220 hours of music on 180 digital discs in 45 boxed sets. The list price is $2,336.]

—— U.S. labels and numbers are given first, U.K. in [brackets] when needed. ——

The Early Romantics
(ca. 1820-1850)

Individualism and emotional expression were not characteristics that suddenly appeared in the Romantic era—we have noted previously that they already had taken root in the Classical period of music history—but by about 1820, they had evolved from being important elements to becoming the dominant aspects of musical esthetics.

The Germans led the Romantic charge in literature as well as in music. Just as Beethoven's *Eroica* Symphony is generally taken as a marker for the beginning of musical Romanticism, Goethe's *The Sorrows of Young Werther* can be considered the cornerstone of Romantic fiction. The rest of the Western world fell into line in short order. Soon, each of the fine arts was feeding Romantic ideals and techniques to the others: Schopenhauer and Nietzsche in philosophy; Byron, Poe, and Lamartine in literature; Manet and Whistler in art. All of them succumbed to Romantic principles, then served as models and inspirations for each other.

The Romantic idea of personal expression was reinforced by an increasing nationalism and competition between cultures, which in turn were fostered by the Industrial Revolution, the rapid development of science and invention, and the bitter rivalries of wars from those of Napoleon to the Franco-Prussian conflict of 1870. This is, of course, a grossly simplified scenario, but it is not false.

In music, an emphasis on subjectivity resulted in a cult of instrumental virtuosity, a warmer and more rhapsodic type of melody, a search for colorful and dramatic effects, an expansion of musical forms, and a frequent reliance on fanciful or even grotesque subject matter for programmatic works. These goals were achieved with the aid of several technical innovations, including an increase in the use of chromatic harmonies, a gradual obscuring of the rules of tonality and modulation, the virtual abandonment of counterpoint, and the introduction of entirely new musical instruments or mechanical improvements to the old ones.

The important composers of the "early" Romantic period, generally acknowledged as extending from about 1820 to about 1850, share a general feeling of fresh, youthful lightness and spontaneity. There is no mistaking the refreshing breeze that blows through Schumann's *Spring* Symphony, or the "fairy music" of Mendelssohn. The pulse of impetuous youth is irresistibly apparent in the primary colors of Rossini's surging crescendos, or the *Roman Carnival* and *Fantastic Symphony* of Berlioz. The easygoing Romanticism of this early period could sometimes devolve into mere parlor sweetness or bourgeois sentimentality; we can sense things veering perilously in this direction occasionally in the music of .

Chopin and Schubert, though their superior genius almost always saves them from the crudities of their lesser contemporaries.

Perhaps another way of defining the "early Romantics" is to specify what they were not. They were not the cool, objective formalists of the Classical period, nor were they the fierce nationalists or ponderous philosophizers of the later 19th century. Their forms were loose: analysts often refer politely to Schubert's as "discursive," and those of Berlioz usually defy definition. Their melodies floated in the airy realms of *Scenes from Childhood*, or an Invitation to the Dance. Their themes were as evanescent as a scherzo of Queen Mab, a trout tumbling down a country brook, or an enchanting dream of a midsummer night.

Vincenzo Bellini (1801-1835)

Bellini was the flashing meteor among Italian opera composers. Showing talent at an early age, he was successful with a lyrical stage work while still a student at the Naples Conservatory. Shortly after, his second opera was hailed by his generous older contemporary, Gaetano Donizetti as "our Bellini—bella! bella! bella!"

And "Bellini" ("little beautiful one") he was, in both his exquisite long-breathed melodies (the joy and inspiration of Chopin), and in his angelic countenance (the joy and inspiration of numerous women). He never married, preferring liaisons such as the one he had with a Milanese woman who had a rich but accommodating husband. Bellini expressed his thanks to her for "protecting me from marriage."

Bellini never became much of an orchestrator, but he was no facile tune-spinner either. His melodies had integrity as well as beauty. Bellini shunned the pyrotechnics of Rossini, and was the first opera composer to insist that his works actually be performed as written. This dismayed many a singer of this day, but set the standard for his later compatriot, Giuseppe Verdi.

After his initial successes in Italy, Bellini found himself the toast first of London, and then of Paris, where he became the intimate of Chopin, Rossini, and other luminaries—including, much to his detriment, the poet Heinrich Heine. Bellini, not only angelic but positively childlike, was much attracted by magic and superstition. Heine, who once described Bellini as "a sigh in ballroom slippers," loved to tease him. One evening at a seance at the home of the Princess Belgioioso, the poet said since Bellini was a genius he should expect to die young like Mozart. A few days later, at the tender age of 34, he succumbed to a stomach infection.

Norma

The supreme masterpiece among Bellini's ten operas contains the aria "Casta Diva," a moonlit invocation of a Druid priestess, and one of the sublimely beautiful creations for the human voice.

———— *CDs listed are solid, central choices, not necessarily "the greatest."* ————

Serafin, Callas, La Scala Orchestra and Chorus. EMI 47303 (3) (mono)
Serafin, Callas, La Scala Orchestra and Chorus. EMI 63000 (3) [ADD]
[The older, monophonic recording finds Callas in better voice. The later, stereo version shows vocal deterioration, but has better sound and a better supporting cast, while the star's dramatic qualities are undiminished. In any case, one of these is unquestionably the first (if not last) *Norma* to put in your collection.]

Hector Berlioz (1803-1869)

With his tousled hair and avant-garde ideas, Berlioz was the wild man of the early Romantics. His father, a cultured country doctor, instilled in him a love of the classics, especially Virgil. He failed, however, to convince Hector to become a physician like himself. Cut off from parental support, young Berlioz lived the bohemian life for several years.

In 1827 he attended his first performance of Shakespeare. Although he knew virtually no English, he fell passionately in love with both *Hamlet* and Harriet Smithson, the actress who played Ophelia. He pursued her for several years, idolized her in his programmatic *Symphonie fantastique*, and in 1833 actually married her. Reality, alas, did not measure up to the Romantic ideal; after a while, they drifted apart.

More than any composer up to his time, he was interested in creating a synthesis of music and literature. He looked to Shakespeare (*Romeo and Juliet*), Byron (*Harold in Italy*), Goethe (*The Damnation of Faust*), Scott (*Rob Roy, Waverley*), and even the American James Fenimore Cooper (*Le corsaire*), for his subjects. His early exposure to Virgil led to what many consider his masterpiece, the gigantic epic opera *The Trojans*.

He became a master of orchestration, enlarging the orchestra to unheard-of dimensions in order to depict his vast conceptions. He paid little attention to the conventional rules of form. His structures were dictated by the literary or poetic exigencies of his imagination instead of rules from some handbook of composition. He ended up writing his own text on orchestration, and the first theoretical work on the art of conducting.

It was as a conductor, in fact, that he was better known than a composer. In his day his music was considered "ear-splitting." And most of his income was actually derived from his journalistic career, as a critic writing about the music of other composers. In later years he had some success abroad, but at home in France he was always considered something of an amusing eccentric. He became progressively more embittered and spent his last years obsessed with thoughts of death.

Berlioz was to become for many later composers, especially Wagner, the archetype of the Romantic in music. His stubborn commitment to his artistic ideals and his passionate self-absorption inspired even those who did not agree with him on every detail. Critical opinion varied widely on the intrinsic worth of his music, and the argument is by no means settled today. Until the conductor Colin Davis began championing his works in the

———— Some famous CDs are not listed because currently out of print. ————

1960s I believe a majority of musicologists still wrote Berlioz off as a composer who was historically important, but whose music one needed not actually to hear.

Berlioz assuredly had his weaknesses. Among all the great composers he seemed to have the most trouble coming up with memorable melodies, and those that work often seem too short, or after a promising beginning trail off into the ether. His stentorian gestures sometimes degenerate into bombast. Listeners who love to follow musical logic had better leave him alone; the great critic Tovey, while acknowledging his genius, once irritably complained that he simply did not have time to follow "the butterfly vagaries" of Berlioz's mind.

In the last generation or so, however, there has been a considerable explosion of interest in this music. Perhaps it is no accident that the works of an iconoclastic, free-thinking, opium-smoking, bohemian radical caught on in the 1960s; but don't expect to hear rock 'n' roll! What we can wallow in today is the colorful, almost cinematic, unfolding of musical images so vivid that they seem to tell a story without the aid of words. Berlioz was indeed the creator of program music as we think of it, and his best works are brilliant records of a fevered and fertile imagination.

The Damnation of Faust, Op. 24 (selections)

This "dramatic legend," sometimes performed as an opera, is really a loosely connected series of scenes from the Faust story, some with vocal parts, some without. Three purely orchestral selections are often heard separately at concerts.

Zinman, Baltimore Symphony Orchestra. Telarc 80164 [DDD] + selections from *Roméo et Juliette* and *Les Troyens*, two overtures, *Hymne des Marseillais*

Harold in Italy, for Viola and Orchestra, Op. 16

The great violin virtuoso Paganini asked Berlioz to write him a concerto to show off his new instrument, a Stradivarius viola. Not surprisingly, Berlioz found himself unable to write a conventional, three-movement concerto. Instead he created a four-movement symphony with pictorial associations based on a drama by Byron, and featuring the viola as a rather reticent commentator. Also not surprisingly, the flashy Paganini begged off playing the piece, complaining that the viola part had "too many rests." It has become far more popular nowadays, being considered one of the composer's more lyrically poetic tone-pictures.

Caussé, Gardiner, Orchestre Révolutionnaire et Romantique. Philips 446676 [DDD] + *Tristia*

Imai, C. Davis, London Symphony Orchestra. Philips 416431 [ADD] + *Tristia*, Prelude to Act II of *Les Troyens*

Imai, C. Davis, London Symphony Orchestra. Philips Duo 442290 (2) [ADD] + *Symphonie fantastique, Symphonie funèbre et triomphale, Roman Carnival* and *Le Corsaire* Overtures
McInnes, Bernstein, French National Orchestra. EMI 64745 [ADD] + 2 Overtures (with Previn, London Symphony Orchestra)
Zukerman, Dutoit, Montreal Symphony Orchestra. London [Decca] 421193 [DDD]

Roméo et Juliette, Op. 17

Another Berlioz hybrid form, this "dramatic symphony" is neither a symphony nor an opera, but a series of 12 numbers grouped in three sections, depicting episodes in Shakespeare's play. The composer himself considered the love music in Part II to be his greatest inspiration; also famous are the diaphanous "Queen Mab Scherzo," and the final scene in the tomb.

Zinman, Baltimore Symphony Orchestra. Telarc 80164 [DDD] + selections from *Damnation of Faust* and *Les Troyens*, two overtures, *Hymne des Marseillais*

Symphonie fantastique, Op. 14

By far the best known work of Berlioz, the "Fantastic Symphony" was inspired by his passion for Harriet Smithson (see biography). Naturally, being by Berlioz, it departs somewhat from convention. It has five movements instead of four, and each bears a programmatic title: "Visions and Passions," "The Ball," "Scenes in the Country," "March to the Gallows," and "Dream of a Witches' Sabbath." The work's pictorial associations had a profound influence on Franz Liszt, and later Richard Strauss, both of whom carried forward the development of the "tone poem." The striking and innovative orchestration was also influential; and Wagner's use of the *Leitmotif* can be traced, at least in part, to the introduction here of a recurrent theme—the *idée fixe*—as a unifying device.

Argenta, Paris Conservatory Orchestra, Suisse Romande Orchestra. London [Decca] 452305 [ADD] + Liszt: *Les Préludes*
Beecham, French National Radio Orchestra. EMI 64032 (mono) + *Le Corsaire* Overture, *Royal Hunt and Storm* from *Les Troyens*
C. Davis, London Symphony Orchestra. Philips Duo 442290 (2) [ADD] + *Harold in Italy, Symphonie funèbre et triomphale, Roman Carnival* and *Le Corsaire* Overtures
C. Davis, Royal Concergebouw Orchestra. Philips 411425 [ADD]

Since CDs can change label and number, use artists as main reference.

Fournet, Tokyo Metropolitan Symphony Orchestra. Denon 8097 [DDD] +
Saint-Saëns: *Danse macabre*
Gardiner, Orchestre Révolutionnaire et Romantique. Philips 434402 [DDD]
Norrington, London Classical Players. EMI 49541 [DDD]

Frédéric Chopin (1810-1849)

For a century and a half, Chopin has been generally accepted by both critics and people (there is a distinction) as the greatest composer of music *for the piano*. Despite his fame and familiarity, however, there is scarcely another composer whose image has been more distorted by the media, then and now.

Chopin's father was a Frenchman who emigrated to Poland, married a Polish woman, and became an ardent Polish patriot. He had lived in his adopted land more than 20 years by the time Fryderyk—to give his un-Frenchified name—was born. The child swiftly developed as a piano prodigy and in short order was performing before the rich and the royal.

Poland was under one of its many foreign dominations at the time, and the expanding ranks of nationalists and revolutionaries turned to the young pianist as one of their symbols of hope for independence. He was not to disappoint them, even though he moved more or less permanently to Paris at age 21 in search of wider recognition and greater fortune. He stayed in close touch with Polish expatriates in Paris, and generously supported Polish artists and musicians.

This he could well afford, since he was one of the earliest composers to get rich through his music. The Parisian nobility fawned over him as giddily as had the Polish— especially aristocratic ladies, who found the gaunt, dreamy-eyed Chopin the paragon of Romantic idealism. He, in turn, charged them enormous fees for private lessons.

Despite the availability of countless countesses, Chopin chose for his one passionate love an older woman who dressed like a man, smoked cigars, and professed socialism. Aurore Dudevant—known to literature and posterity as "George Sand"—was a novelist of dumpy figure and limber mind. In addition to a husband, she was known to have several lovers besides Chopin, including Prosper Merimée (who wrote the novelette *Carmen*), the poet Alfred de Musset (whose texts several French composers set to music), and probably Franz Liszt. Not surprisingly, one of the principal themes of her novels was a disdain for the institution of marriage.

The peculiar affair lasted for nine years, until constant bickering, much of it involving wrangles with "George's" two adult children, drove them apart. Meanwhile Chopin had ruined his always delicate health; what was intended for a romantic idyll on Majorca in the winter of 1838-39 turned into a miserable ordeal of damp weather that dangerously weakened his lungs. He was not yet 40 when he died of tuberculosis. He was buried in France,

——— Artists are listed alphabetically, not in order by critical ranking. ———

but accompanying his body was a silver urn containing Polish soil which Chopin had brought with him from his native land two decades before. The incidents of his life have proved irresistible to novelists and filmmakers of sentimental tendencies. Through them much of the public has received an image of the dainty, swooning pianist of the glittering salon, succumbing to the Freudian lure of an androgynous woman, and paying for his neurotic obsession by dying a tragic early death, clutching a couple of crumpled polonaises in one withered hand. This is an exaggerated picture. His body was indeed frail, and his pianism delicately refined, but he had a hard business head as his publishers learned to their dismay. He may have seemed effeminate, but he had no homosexual liaisons, and before taking up with the mannish but man-eating George Sand he had had several physical relations with attractive young women. And though he was sincerely patriotic, he did not hesitate to take up residence in Paris for half of his life in order to live in luxury.

But the most significant distortion that needs correcting is that Chopin's music is insubstantial. A few decades ago it was fashionable on Tin Pan Alley to arrange Chopin's most striking melodies into syrupy popular songs or backgrounds for tearjerker movies. True, Chopin wrote dozens of suave melodies, strongly influenced by early Italian opera, which he loved. But he also loved Bach, and underpinning these gorgeous tunes there is a solid and sophisticated harmonic and rhythmic structure that almost never fails to save them from triviality. The "pop" versions, stripped of the composer's rich textures, give a falsely cloying impression of the music. But even in Chopin's day many did not see beneath the deceptive prettiness of his work's surface. It took another great composer, Robert Schumann, to characterize it perfectly: "Cannon—buried in flowers."

Concerto No. 1 in E Minor for Piano, Op. 11
Concerto No. 2 in F Minor for Piano, Op. 21

As a genius in smaller forms, Chopin struggled with these larger structrues and soon abandoned the effort. They are not very well orchestrated, but they have survived because the solo piano parts are so attractive. The Concerto "No. 2" is actually the earlier, more compact, and fresher of the pair. Recommendations for a first purchase are here limited to recordings that have both these concertos on one disc (or set).

Arrau, Inbal, London Philharmonic Orchestra. *Complete Works for Piano and Orchestra*, Philips 438338 (2) [ADD]
Perahia, Mehta, Israel Philharmonic Orchestra. Sony 44922 [DDD]
Rubinstein, Skrowaczewski (in No. 1), Wallenstein (in No. 2), New Symphony Orchestra of London. RCA Victor Red Seal 5612 [ADD]
Székely, Németh, Budapest Symphony Orchestra. Naxos 8.550123 [DDD]
Tirimo, Glushchenko, Philharmonia Orchestra. Conifer 51247 [DDD]

——— *[DDD] indicates newest recordings; [ADD] or [AAD] are reissues.* ———

Vásáry, Northern Sinfonia. ASV Quicksilva 6141 [DDD]
Zimerman, Giulini, Los Angeles Philharmonic Orchestra. Deutsche Grammophon 415970 [ADD]

Piano Anthologies

Ashkenazy. _Favourite Chopin_, London [Decca] Jubilee 417798 [DDD]
Perahia. _Piano Music_, Sony 64399 [DDD]
Rubinstein. Selections from _The Chopin Collection_, RCA Victor Red Seal 7725 [ADD]

Sonata No. 2 in B-flat Minor for Piano, Op. 35

Best known of the three sonatas, No. 2 displays the greatest unity: its theme is Death, highlighted by the famous Funeral March in the third movement. No other piece of music has become so identified with the Grim Reaper; Chopin is reported to have composed it while dressed in a shroud and clutching a real skeleton in one arm. (Debunkers vigorously deny such a thing could have happened, but this may be giving the Romantics too much credit for rationality.)

Andsnes. Virgin Classics 59072 (2) [DDD] + Sonatas Nos. 1, 3; Sel. etudes and mazurkas
Perahia. Sony 32780 [ADD] + Sonata No. 3
Pollini. Deutsche Grammophon 415346 [DDD] + Sonata No. 3
Rubinstein. RCA Victor Red Seal 5616 [ADD] + Sonatas No. 1, 3, _Fantaisie_ in F Minor, Op. 49

Gaetano Donizetti (1797-1848)

Donizetti was born in Bergamo, Italy, of humble parentage, in a cellar apartment where "no ray of light," as Donizetti later wrote, "ever penetrated." The best job his father ever had was janitor in a pawnshop. Little Gaetano showed musical talent at an early age, enrolling in the local music school at nine. When he was only 13 his music teacher wrote a miniature opera for his students and cast Gaetano in the title role of "The Little Composer." One of his prophetic lines was: "I have a vast mind, swift talent, ready fantasy—and I'm a thunderbolt at composing."

In a career spanning only 30 years Donizetti wrote some 70 operas, sometimes as many as four in a single year. Unlike most Italian opera composers he wrote hundreds of other works as well, including 16 symphonies, 19 string quartets, 28 cantatas, and three oratorios. Such prodigality was accompanied, unfortunately, by considerable unevenness of quality, and it undermined his health.

As early as 1829 he was showing symptoms of the syphilis that was to kill him almost 20 years later, after spending his last year and a half in excruciating suffering in a madhouse. "While his melodies," wrote Heinrich Heine, "ravish the world with their happy accents and are sung and trilled everywhere, he himself sits, a frightening image of insanity, in a sanatorium not far from Paris...he recognizes no one. Such is the fortune of poor mankind."

He wrote his first opera at the age of 19, but was 25 before he had a significant success—with what was already his ninth stage work. He had to wait for Rossini's retirement before being crowned king of Italian opera with *Anna Bolena* in 1830. (A dubious but wonderful story has someone asking Donizetti if he believed the reports that Rossini wrote *The Barber of Seville* in only 13 days, with the younger composer snapping back: "Why not? He's so lazy!") One triumph then followed another, peaking with *Lucia di Lammermoor* in 1835. He was named director of the prestigious Naples Conservatory in 1837, but after a short tenure became disgusted with various irritations and moved to France, where he composed some of his best works including *La fille du régiment* and a comic opera, *Don Pasquale*, which is perhaps surpassed only by Rossini's *Barber of Seville*.

Lucia di Lammermoor

"Bel canto," literally "beautiful singing," was a specific style of Italian opera that flourished in the early 19th century. As one might readily deduce, its focus was not on logical plots or philosophical profundity, but on providing opportunities for vocal display. Lucia is easily the most representative of bel canto operas, with its florid mad scene and its stupendous sextet. It became a cultural icon in its own time; Tolstoy in *Anna Karenina* and Flaubert in *Madame Bovary* both used it almost as a character, as a symbol of the Romantic sensibility.

Bonynge, Sutherland, Royal Opera House Orchestra. London [Decca] 410193 (3) [ADD]

Karajan, Callas, RIAS Symphony Orchestra. EMI Studio 63631 (2) [ADD]

[I have been an opera fan for nearly 50 years, and if there is any recording more exciting than the Sextet from *Lucia* as sung by Maria Callas, Giuseppe di Stefano, Rolando Panerai, and three other singers, I have missed it. A recent catalog lists 10 complete recordings of *Lucia* with Maria Callas on various labels with suspiciously similar-looking casts. These are indeed each slightly different "takes" from around the same period, but be careful to buy only the exact performance listed above, Angel 63631, from 1955, conducted by Herbert von Karajan. For years this was a best-seller as an illegal pirate recording, until EMI got smart and decided to keep the money for themselves.]

Pritchard, Sutherland, Santa Cecilia Academy Orchestra. London [Decca] 411622 (2) [ADD]

——— *Some CDs may be available only through importers.* ———

Mikhail Glinka (1804-1857)

Glinka is the acknowledged founder of the nationalist school of Russian composition, although his historical position is perhaps more significant than the works themselves. Not one of music history's more prepossessing characters, Glinka was a spoiled rich kid and a mama's boy. Though admittedly of a delicate constitution, he exaggerated his health problems as an excuse to take vacations in Spain. His requirements in women were that they be extremely young and extremely stupid. Eventually he married one of these bimbos, then proceeded to be constantly unfaithful to her. She, in turn, despised music, and complained that he spent too much money on staff paper.

Glinka came along at a time when musical culture in Russia was barely discernible. He was largely self-taught, and his influences came more from Bellini and Donizetti than from Beethoven or Mozart. And yet years later Tchaikovsky dared to equate Glinka with Mozart, whom he worshipped above all other composers.

Few of Glinka's works are regularly heard today except in the Russia. They sound pleasant enough, but there is certainly nothing greatly remarkable, let alone revolutionary, about them. Glinka's good fortune was to decide, in the mid-1830s, to write a Russian opera starring the peasants instead of the nobility, and spiced with beloved native folk songs. In a country that did not even have a music conservatory until 1850, *A Life for the Tsar* (later renamed *Ivan Susanin* by the Bolsheviks) seemed like a burst of creative genius. He gave Russian composers a hero to look up to, and a new respect in greater Europe. Glinka's influence is obvious in the masterpieces of Tchaikovsky, Rimsky-Korsakov, and Mussorgsky, all of whom surpassed him in quality, but might never have existed without him.

Russlan and Ludmila: Overture

This was the first truly Russian opera. Although the whole work is seldom heard outside Russia, the whirling, stamping overture remains Glinka's top hit.

Reiner, Chicago Symphony Orchestra. RCA Victor Gold Seal 60176 [ADD] + Prokofiev: *Alexander Nevsky; Lt. Kijé* Suite

Slatkin, St. Louis Symphony Orchestra. Telarc 80072 [DDD] + Borodin: *In the Steppes of Central Asia*; Rimsky-Korsakov: *Russian Easter* Overture; Tchaikovsky: *Marche slave*

———— *U.S. labels and numbers are given first, U.K. in [brackets] when needed.* ————

Felix Mendelssohn (1809-1847)

Unlike Glinka, Mendelssohn is one of the *most* attractive figures in the history of music. Handsome and hard-working, gentle and genteel, he impressed men at the chessboard, and women on the dance floor. Born into a wealthy, cultured family, he wore his inheritance so lightly that it aroused little resentment. He had a touchingly close relationship with his sister Fanny, herself a talented musician and composer, and a happy marriage that produced five children (one of the latter-day descendants was George Mendelssohn, founder and president for many years of Vox Records).

After Mozart, with whom he has been favorably compared by Schumann and many others since, Mendelssohn was perhaps the most astonishing child prodigy of music, not so much because of his young age, but for the high quality of what he wrote. No teenager—perhaps not even Mozart—ever wrote pieces more melodically memorable, stylish and energetic, refined and finished than the Octet in E-flat, or the overture to *A Midsummer Night's Dream*. It is true that many of his later works seemed to decline in freshness and spontaneity, but the common impression that Mendelssohn "burned out" at an early age is exaggerated.

In his day, Mendelssohn was as important a scholar and conductor as he was a composer. Almost singlehandedly—and at the age of 20!—he revived the long-neglected music of Bach by leading a performance of the *St. Matthew Passion* from a manuscript copy. He founded the Leipzig Conservatory of Music, and conducted its orchestra, which is still alive and prominent today. He raised the standards of orchestral playing in Europe and offered generous assistance to struggling young composers. Although extremely popular in his native Germany, he achieved even more success in England, which he visited numerous times as the favorite composer of Queen Victoria.

Unquestionably over-rated in its time, Mendelssohn's music came in for compensatory contempt in the mid-20th century. Many treated it as facile, lightweight, and overly sentimental. Nowadays a better balance has been struck. Most critics and historians, while admitting that the music plumbs no great depths, rightly point out that it does not intend to do so; and that to despise its fresh lyricism, poise, and youthful poetry is to take a very cheap shot indeed.

Concerto in E Minor for Violin, Op. 64

This is probably the most popular of all violin concertos. A recent record catalog showed nearly 50 performances in print. The reason in obvious: it overflows with enchantingly beautiful melodies, never letting down for a moment, and while eschewing profundity it manages to delight the novice and the connoisseur at once.

——— *All CDs listed are considered approximately equal in (high) merit.* ———

Chee-Yun, López-Cobos, London Philharmonic Orchestra. Denon 78913 [DDD] + Vieuxtemps: Violin Concerto No. 5

Chung, Dutoit, Montreal Symphony Orchestra. London [Decca] 410011 [DDD] + Tchaikovsky: Violin Concerto

Francescatti, Mitropoulos, New York Philharmonic Orchestra; Ormandy, Philadelphia Orchestra. Sony Masterworks Heritage 62339 (2) (mono) [ADD] + Bruch: Violin Concerto No. 1; Saint-Saëns: Violin Concerto No. 3; Tchaikovsky: Violin Concerto; Prokofiev: Violin Concerto No. 2; Chausson: *Poème*

Heifetz, Munch, Boston Symphony Orchestra. RCA Victor Red Seal 5933 [ADD] + Tchaikovsky: Violin Concerto (with Reiner Chicago Symphony Orchestra), *Sérénade Mélancolique*, Waltz from *Serenade for Strings*

Kennedy, Tate, English Chamber Orchestra. EMI 49663 [DDD] + Bruch: Violin Concerto No. 1; Schubert: Rondo

Menuhin, Frühbeck de Burgos, London Symphony Orchestra. EMI Seraphim 68524 (2) [ADD] + Symphony No. 4, *Hebrides* Overture, *A Midsummer Night's Dream* Overture, *Ruy Blas* Overture (with Previn conducting); Bruch: Violin Concerto No. 1 (with Menuhin, Frühbeck de Burgos)

Menuhin, Furtwängler, Berlin Philharmonic Orchestra. EMI 69799 [ADD] (mono) + Beethoven: Violin Concerto

Mullova, Marriner, Academy of St. Martin-in-the-Fields. Philips 432077 [DDD] + Violin Concerto in D Minor

Mutter, Karajan, Berlin Philharmonic Orchestra. Deutsche Grammophon 445515 [DDD] + Brahms: Violin Concerto

Nishizaki, Jean, Slovak Philharmonic Orchestra. Naxos 8.550153 [DDD] + Tchaikovsky: Violin Concerto

Sitkovetsky, Marriner, Academy of St. Martin-in-the-Fields. Hänssler Classic 98.934 [DDD] + Brahms: Violin Concerto

A Midsummer Night's Dream: Incidental Music, Op. 21, 61

The magical overture was written when Mendelssohn was 17, a feat not equalled in quality even by Mozart. Many years later he was commissioned to write additional music illustrating Shakespeare's comedy and he produced 13 more numbers, of which the best known are the Nocturne, the Scherzo, and the famous Wedding March, which in an organ transcription has sent millions of newlyweds out the church door.

Kovács, Budapest Symphony Orchestra. LaserLight 15526 [DDD] + Symphony No. 4 (with Sándor, Philharmonia Orchestra)

———— *CDs listed are solid, central choices, not necessarily "the greatest."* ————

Litton, London Philharmonic Orchestra and Chorus. Classics for Pleasure 4593 [DDD]

Mackerras, Orchestra of the Age of Enlightenment. Virgin Classics 59135 [DDD] + Symphony No. 4

Previn, London Symphony Orchestra. EMI 47163 [ADD]

Szell, Cleveland Orchestra. Sony Essential Classics 48264 [ADD] + Smetana: *The Moldau*; Bizet: Symphony in C (with Stokowski conducting National Philharmonic)

Szell, Cleveland Orchestra. CBS [Sony] 37760 [ADD] + Symphony No. 4

Octet in E-flat Major for Strings, Op. 20

Mendelssohn was even younger (16) when he wrote this miraculously beautiful and delicate chamber piece than when he composed the *Midsummer Night's Dream* Overture. But then, he had been writing chamber works since he was 11, so he had plenty of practice. Most famous is the fleet Scherzo movement, the very distillation in tones of innocent youth.

Academy of St. Martin-in-the-Fields Chamber Ensemble. Philips 420400 [ADD] + String Quintet No. 2

Cleveland Quartet, Meliora String Quartet. Telarc 80142 [DDD] + String Quartet No. 2

Overtures

Aside from the wonderful overture to *A Midsummer Night's Dream*, Mendelssohn wrote several others, most famous of which is the lovely landscape painting called the *Hebrides*, or *Fingal's Cave*, Overture. It was inspired by a visit to the Scottish Highlands. Consciously or not, Richard Wagner seems to have adapted its opening theme as his *leitmotif* for the three Rhinemaidens in *The Ring of the Nibelung*. Other Mendelssohn overtures include *Calm Sea and Prosperous Voyage*, *Ruy Blas*, *The Fair Melusina*, and *Athalia*.

Abbado, London Symphony Orchestra. Deutsche Grammophon 423104 [DDD]

Flor, Bamberg Symphony Orchestra. RCA Victor Red Seal 7905 [DDD]

Previn, London Symphony Orchestra. EMI Seraphim 68524 (2) [ADD] + Symphony No. 4; Violin Concerto in E Minor; Bruch: Violin Concerto No. 1 (with Menuhin, Frühbeck de Burgos)

Reiner, Chicago Symphony Orchestra. (*Hebrides* only) RCA Victor Gold Seal 61793 [ADD] + Brahms: Symphony No. 3; Schubert: Symphony No. 5

——— *Some famous CDs are not listed because currently out of print.* ———

Symphony No. 4 in A Major, Op. 90 "Italian"

Only the last movement of the most popular of Mendelssohn's five symphonies offers anything identifiably "Italian," but we can say that the entire work is gloriously sunny. It is a bundle of happy memories of the composer's trip to italy at age 21 when, already a famous composer, and rich and handsome to boot, he was mobbed by enamored ladies at the Roman Carnival, who pelted him with sugar candies. Sweet! And so is this delicious symphony.

Abbado, London Symphony Orchestra. Deutsche Grammophon 427810 [DDD] + Symphony No. 3

Chernaik, Apollo Chamber Orchestra. Meridian 84261 [DDD] + Symphony No. 3

Lubbock, Orchestra of St. John's. ASV 6004 [ADD] + Symphony No. 3

Mackerras, Orchestra of the Age of Enlightenment. Virgin Classics 59135 [DDD] + Exc. from *A Midsummer Night's Dream*

Previn, London Symphony Orchestra. EMI Seraphim 68524 (2) [ADD] + *Hebrides* Overture, *A Midsummer Night's Dream* Overture, *Ruy Blas* Overture; Violin Concerto in E Minor; Bruch: Violin Concerto No. 1 (with Menuhin, Frühbeck de Burgos)

Sándor, Philharmonia Orchestra. LaserLight 15526 [DDD] + Incidental Music to *A Midsummer Night's Dream* (with Kovács, Budapest Symphony Orchestra

Sinopoli, Philharmonia Orchestra. Deutsche Grammophon Masters 445514 [DDD] + Schubert: Symphony No. 8 "Unfinished"

Szell, Cleveland Orchestra. CBS [Sony] 37760 [ADD] + *Midsummer Night's Dream* sel.

Niccolò Paganini (1782-1840)

Paganini is remembered principally as the all-time wizard of the violin. That's wizard, not genius. Before he was born, it is said, his mother had a dream that her son would become the world's greatest violinist. Papa Paganini took the prophecy seriously and drove the boy to practice day and night. By age 11, Niccolò was a master virtuoso. By his mid-teens, he was wealthy, and he had already begun the endless round of gambling, drinking, and womanizing which was to mark his lifestyle to the end.

Paganini revolutionized violin-playing. He added one astounding new technique after another, until his performances were so amazing that many believed the rumor that he had signed over his soul to the Devil. This, of course, only made the audiences larger and more fanatical. The artist, capitalizing on his cadaverous frame and sunken cheeks, did nothing to discourage the idea.

——— Catalog numbers are subject to change without notice. ———

The bulk of his compositions were for the violin (although he also wrote for the viola and guitar), and were designed for his personal use. Many of them he carried only in his head so that no other violinist could try to outdo him, and they are now lost to us. Of his six surviving violin concerti, the manuscripts of four came to light only in recent years. Also noteworthy is the set of 24 Caprices, one of which has held a curious fascination for a number of later composers; Rachmaninov, for instance, used it as the basis for his great *Rhapsody on a Theme of Paganini*.

In the hands of a master violinist, Paganini's works provide hours of kinetic thrills. Lightning bolts flash, sparks fly, hearts leap into throats; this was how people entertained themselves before the roller coaster was invented. Of course, there is not a single bar of his music which touches the soul. Perhaps Paganini *was* in league with the Devil, after all.

Concerto No. 1 in D Major for Violin, Op. 6

Paganini deliberately withheld many of his works from publication in order to monopolize the virtuoso circuit. No. 1, whose publication he allowed, remains by far the most popular to this day. It has been recorded both in the full-length original version, and in tightened-up editions by both Fritz Kreisler and August Wilhelmj.

Accardo, Dutoit, London Philharmonic Orchestra. Deutsche Grammophon 415378 [ADD] + Violin Concerto No. 2

Kaler, Gunzenhauser, Polish National Radio Symphony Orchestra. Naxos 8.550649 [DDD] + Violin Concerto No. 2

Kantorow (violin and conductor), Auvergne Orchestra. Denon 77611 [DDD] + Violin Concerto No. 2

Menuhin, Erede, Royal Philharmonic Orchestra. EMI 47088 + Violin Concerto No. 2

Perlman, Foster, Royal Philharmonic Orchestra. EMI 47101 + Sarasate: *Carmen Fantasy*

Shaham, Sinopoli, New York Philharmonic Orchestra. Deutsche Grammophon 429786 [DDD] + Saint-Saëns: Violin Concerto No. 3

Vengerov, Mehta, Israel Philharmonic Orchestra. Teldec 73266 [DDD] + Saint-Saëns: *Introduction and Rondo Capriccioso, Havanaise*; Waxman: *Carmen Fantasy*

Gioacchino Rossini (1792-1868)

Rossini was the first opera composer to become a wealthy international superstar, a feat he accomplished partly by piling one thrilling effect upon another. For example, his technique of ending an overture or a scene with an exciting buildup of repeated runs on the strings

——— Since CDs can change label and number, use artists as main reference. ———

was virtually patented: to this day it is known as the "Rossini crescendo," and no one would dare to copy it. To this extent he paralleled Paganini—but in truth, he was a far better composer. Paganini wrote slick, superficially brilliant scores to cover up his deficiencies; Rossini deliberately suppressed his grounding in Haydn and Mozart to play to the galleries, and thus make more money.

At first glance this seems reprehensible, but reading Rossini's life and becoming familiar with his magnificent sense of humor almost forces one to wink at his artistic peccadilloes. He was prodigally gifted: sunny, robust Italianate melody seemed to gush from him as from a Roman fountain. He was also blessed, or cursed, with a prodigal appetite, and by middle age he had become an enormous mass of mirthful flesh. He claimed to have wept only three times in his life: when his mother died, when his first opera failed, and when once, on a cruise, he accidentally dropped a truffled turkey overboard.

Rossini wrote about three dozen operas, both serious and comic, but only one, *The Barber of Seville*, got the formula exactly right. So right, in fact, that hardly anyone would dispute to this day that it is the most perfect comic opera ever written. In the early 19th century, however, almost all of Rossini's operas were successful, conquering stages in one country after another (the novelist Stendhal called Rossini the "Napoleon of Music").

Suddenly, at the age of 37, at the height of his fame, Rossini virtually stopped composing. Although he lived almost 40 more years, the once prolific genius now wrote nothing beyond a *Stabat Mater* and some short songs and piano pieces, a situation unique in the history of music. Reams of theory have been written about this "great renunciation," but no one explanation seems totally satisfactory. It is clear that Rossini suffered for the first 25 years of his retirement from some kind of mental or emotional problem: he could not sleep, he could not digest, he experienced panic attacks, he fell into long depressions.

It is pleasant to report, however, that by 1855 his symptoms seemed to abate, and he was able to spend his last 13 years in good spirits, living the good life in Paris, entertaining lavishly, delighting one and all with his mordant wit—to wit: when Rossini's great operatic rival Meyerbeer died, an aspiring young musician approached Rossini with a projected elegy for the funeral. The aged maestro listened uncomfortably as the youth hammered out his lugubrious and uninspired opus at the keyboard. At length the budding composer concluded and looked up hopefully. "Not bad," Rossini coughed, "not bad. But, don't you think it would have been better if you had died, and Meyerbeer had written the music..."

The Barber of Seville

The premiere, in 1816, of the greatest comic opera ever written was almost as comical as the opera itself. An anti-Rossini clique came to boo, a cat ran across the stage, one of the main characters tripped and fell flat on his face. As the mishaps piled up the audience grew more and more derisive. One observer said it seemed that all the whistlers in Italy had rendezvoused at the theater. But later that night when Rossini's friends stopped by to console

—————— *Artists are listed alphabetically, not in order by critical ranking.* ——————

him, they found him sleeping like a baby. His confidence was vindicated: by the second performance *The Barber of Seville* was a hit.

Galliera, Callas, Philharmonia Orchestra. EMI 56310 (2) [ADD]
Gui, de los Angeles, Royal Philharmonic Orchestra. EMI 64162 (2) [ADD]
Humburg, Ganassi, Failoni Chamber Orchestra. Naxos 8.660027/29 (3) [DDD]
López-Cobos, Larmore, Lausanne Chamber Orchestra. Teldec 74885 (2) [DDD]
Patané, Bartoli, Bologna Teatro Comunale. London [Decca] 425520 (3) [DDD]

Overtures

Except for *The Barber of Seville,* Rossini's operas are known today principally through their sprightly overtures. The most famous of them are *William Tell, Semiramide, La gazza ladra, La Cenerentola, L'Italiana in Algeri, La scala di seta,* and, of course, *The Barber of Seville.* Every one of the recommended recordings contains the *William Tell* Overture, and many, if not all, of the others.

Abbado, London Symphony Orchestra. *Basic 100,* Vol. 13, RCA 61554 + Verdi: overtures
Chailly, National Philharmonic Orchestra (London). 14 overtures, London [Decca[Double 443850 (2) [ADD]
C. Davis, Royal Philharmonic Orchestra. 5 overtures, EMI Doublefforte 69364 (2) [ADD] + Beethoven: Symphony No. 7; Schubert: Symphony No. 9
Giulini, Philharmonia Orchestra. EMI Studio 69042
Goodman, Hanover Band. RCA Victor Red Seal 68139 [DDD]
Levi, Atlanta Symphony Orchestra. Telarc 80334 [DDD]
Norrington, London Classical Players (on period instruments). EMI 54091 [DDD]

Franz Schubert (1797-1828)

Schubert was surely the greatest of the early Romantics. In nearly a thousand compositions, completed in his brief 31 years (a life even shorter, you will note, than Mozart's), he frequently touches the most ineffable depths of human emotion. Yet except to a close circle of devoted friends, Schubert remained virtually unknown until years after his tragic death. His brief life, spent entirely in Vienna, was remarkably uneventful. His father, though no Leopold Mozart, was a schoolmaster and musician, and gave young Franz his first lessons.

——— *[DDD] indicates newest recordings; [ADD] or [AAD] are reissues.* ———

The boy showed considerable precocity. By age 21 he had already written hundreds of songs, and most of his symphonies. He followed in his father's footsteps for a while, but soon tired of school-teaching and attempted to make his way as a composer; that is, he became a habitué of beer gardens and late-night parties.

Many were the evenings he spent among his Bohemian friends, quaffing tankards and accompanying vocalists in his songs. Apparently, even though he was short, pudgy, and unkempt, he was the center of these events, for even then they were known affectionately as "Schubertiades." These carefree days, alas, were numbered. By his mid-20s Schubert had contracted syphilis, and soon afterwards his circle of companions began to break apart. He suffered gradually increasing bouts of depression, yet in his final precious few years he wrote some of the most lyrical and lovable chamber, symphonic, and vocal music in the history of music.

In May of 1827 Schubert visited the dying Beethoven, and in a few days was serving as a torch-bearer in the funeral procession. The next year, he himself was dead, but was mourned only by a handful of family and friends. The world quickly forgot him and his music gathered dust for some 40 years. But long before the inevitable revival, the poet Grillparzer had contributed these lines to Schubert's tombstone, as wrenching as any of the composer's melodies: "Music has here entombed a rich treasure—but still fairer hopes."

Moments Musicaux, Op. 94 (D.780)

These six little pieces, with their passing shadows and glints of sunshine, are characteristic examples of a genre that has been called "bourgeois classicism." They also charmingly display Schubert's winning manner. There is a lovably bumpkinish quality even about the original title page which reads in peddler's French: *Moments Musicals*. No. 3 in F minor is the best known, with its staccato notes in the left hand and its delicious quasi-Russian melody in the right.

O'Conor. Telarc 80369 [DDD] + Piano Sonata No. 20
Tan. Virgin Veritas 61161 [DDD] + 3 Klavierstücke; Beethoven: Allegretto in C Minor, *et al.*

Quartet No. 14 in D minor, D.810 "Death and the Maiden"

"Each night, on going to bed, I hope I may not wake up again, and each morning only recalls yesterday's grief." So wrote Schubert in 1823 when he had begun to realize that his health would never again be robust. Several works from this and his few succeeding years are unabashedly morbid in tone, none more so than this famous string quartet whose slow movement is based on the theme from an earlier song about Death coming for a young person. As if to underscore the point, Schubert quotes another of his songs about death, "The Erl-King," in the last movement.

Alban Berg Quartet. EMI 47333 [DDD] + Quartet No. 13
Brandis Quartet. Nimbus 5438 [DDD] + Quartet No. 13
Chilingirian Quartet. Nimbus 5048/9 (2) [DDD] + Quartets Nos. 13, 15
Curzon, Vienna Philharmonic String Quartet. London [Decca] 417459 [ADD] + *Trout* Quintet
Emerson Quartet. Deutsche Grammophon 423398 [DDD] + Beethoven: Quartet No. 11
Gabrieli String Quartet. Classics for Pleasure Silver Double 4772 (2) [ADD] + Borodin: Quartet No. 2; Brahms: Clarinet Quintet; Dvořák: Quartet No. 12 "American"
Lindsay Quartet. ASV 560 [DDD] + Quartet No. 12
Melos Quartet. Harmonia Mundi 901408/09 (2) [DDD] + Quartets 12, 13, 15
Prague Quartet. Denon 8005 + Quartet No. 13
Quartetto Italiano. Philips Duo 446163 (2) [ADD] + Quartets Nos. 12, 13, 15
Talich Quartet. Calliope 9234 [DDD] + Quartet No. 10
Tokyo Quartet. RCA Victor Red Seal 7990 [DDD] + Quartet No. 4

Quintet in A, D.667 "Trout"

Once again Schubert uses one of his songs ("Die Forelle"— "The Trout") as a theme for a chamber composition, this time in the fourth movement. The work is structurally odd in two respects: it has five movements instead of four, and replaces one of the standard two violins of the ensemble with a viola. The profuse lyricism which flows from the pages of this score has assured its place as the most beloved chamber work by Schubert.

Brendel, Zehetmair, Zimmermann, Duven, Riegelbauer. Philips 446001 [DDD] + Mozart: Piano Quartet No. 1
Curzon, Vienna Octet members. London [Decca] 417459 [ADD] + Quartet No. 14 "Death and the Maiden"
O'Conor, Cleveland Quartet. Telarc 80225 [DDD] + String Quartet No. 13
A. Schiff, Hagen Quartet. London [Decca] 411975 [DDD]
R. Serkin, J. Laredo, Naegele, Parnas, J. Levine. Sony 46252 [ADD] + Mozart: Clarinet Quintet

———— *Some CDs may be available only through importers.* ————

Rosamunde: Incidental Music, Op. 26 (D.797)

Rosamunde was a play by a dotty middle-aged lady named Wilhelmina (or Helmine) von Chézy. By being simultaneously rich, dowdy, and supremely self-confident, she had managed to draw around her a circle of devoted dilettantes. Mme. von Chézy was able to force several of her abominable stage works upon desperate and impecunious composers— such as Schubert, who wrote about an hour's worth of music to accompany *Rosamunde*. The play had exactly one performance, on 20 December 1823. Generally, the critics praised the score, or what they could hear of it, for the restless audience chattered loudly throughout. The author thundered that her play had been ruined by insufficient rehearsal, by a poor prompter, and so on. But to her everlasting credit, she did not dare to blame Schubert's music; it was, she stoutly insisted, "magnificent." As far as is known, this was the only correct artistic judgment she ever made.

Most recordings offer highlights from the full score. Albums listed feature the full score only if noted as "complete."

Abbado, von Otter, Chamber Orchestra of Europe. (Complete) Deutsche Grammophon 431655 [DDD]
Abbado, Chamber Orchestra of Europe. (Overture only) Deutsche Grammophon 423656 [DDD] + Symphony No. 9
Groves, English Sinfonia. Carlton Classics 6700872 [3306 700872] [DDD] + Symphony No. 8 "Unfinished"
Harnoncourt, Royal Concertgebouw Orchestra. Teldec 74785 [DDD] + Symphony No. 8 "Unfinished"
Mackerras, Orchestra of the Age of Enlightenment. Virgin Veritas 61305 [DDD] + Symphonies Nos. 5, 8 "Unfinished"

Sonata No. 21 in B-flat Major for Piano, Op. Posth. (D.960)

This last of Schubert's 22 piano sonatas, of which some are incomplete, is generally agreed to be his best. One may understandably wonder what even greater heights he might have reached had he lived beyond his 31 years. Some critics fault Schubert for not following the rules of sonata form as perfected by Beethoven (Schubert often favors his melodies at the expense of working them out in development sections). This may horrify Prussian musicologists, but many will prefer the view that Schubert was an avant-gardist among the early Romantics, creating a synthesis of classical form with the Romantic spirit. Both elements, incidentally, are admirably balanced in this sonata.

Curzon. London [Decca] 448578 [ADD] + Brahms: Piano Sonata No. 3
Kovacevich. EMI 55359 [DDD] + Allegretto in C minor, 12 *Ländler*, D.790

—— *U.S. labels and numbers are given first, U.K. in [brackets] when needed.* ——

Lupu. London [Decca] 440295 [DDD] + Sonata in A, D.664
Rubinstein. RCA Victor Red Seal 6257 [ADD] + 2 Impromptus, *Wanderer Fantasy*
A. Schiff. London [Decca] 440310 [DDD] + Sonatas Nos. 2, 11

Songs (Lieder)

Schubert is acknowledged as the greatest of all classical song composers, period. He wrote some 600 songs in his three decades, and even the very first ones, written in his teens, sound like the polished works of a master of the medium. There was something in a poem that inspired Schubert to re-create it melodically and harmonically in a way that almost always made a bad poem seem good, and a good poem even better.

Although they may occasionally indulge in both, most classical singers specialize in opera while others concentrate on what is called in the trade "art song," that is, short solo vocal works set to a poem and composed with all the accoutrements of classical music, as opposed to folk or popular songs. This is one of the genres most difficult to introduce to people with no classical music background, partly because most of it is in non-English languages, partly because the idiom is so unfamiliar and formal in comparison to pop music. It helps to take Lieder in short doses at the beginning and invest in a little study, including making the effort to follow along with a translation when listening. If an art song is good, its words will be crucial to enjoying it.

Ameling, Baldwin. Philips Silver Line 420870 [ADD]
Baker, Moore, Parsons. *A Schubert Evening*, EMI Doublefforte 69389 (2) [ADD]
Battle, Levine. Deutsche Grammophon 419237 [DDD]
Bostridge, Johnson, Fischer-Dieskau (narrator). *Die Schöne Müllerin: Complete Songs*, Vol. 25, Hyperion 33025 [DDD]
Fischer-Dieskau, Moore. EMI Studio 69503 [ADD]
Hampson, McLaughlin, Johnson. *Complete Songs*, Vol. 14, Hyperion 33014 [DDD]
M. Price, Johnson. *Complete Songs*, Vol. 15, Hyperion 33015 [DDD]
Schwarzkopf, Fischer. EMI 64026 (mono) [ADD]
Terfel, Martineau. Deutsche Grammophon 445294 [DDD]
Various singers, Johnson. *A Voyage of Discovery*, Hyperion 200 [DDD]

Symphony No. 5 in B-flat Major, D.485

Schubert was only 19 when he wrote this enchanting, rather Mozartian symphony of chamber-orchestra proportions (sorry, no trumpets, no drums). All four movements have graceful, dancelike qualities—and of course, lovely melodies.

————— *All CDs listed are considered approximately equal in (high) merit.* —————

Beecham, Royal Philharmonic Orchestra. EMI 69750 [ADD] + Symphony
   Nos. 3, 6
Böhm, Vienna Philharmonic Orchestra. Deutsche Grammophon Originals
   447433 [ADD] + Beethoven: Symphony No. 6
Mackerras, Orchestra of the Age of Enlightenment. Virgin Veritas 61305
   [DDD] + Symphony No. 8 "Unfinished", Incidental Music to *Rosamunde*
Reiner, Chicago Symphony Orchestra. RCA Victor Gold Seal 61793 [ADD] +
   Brahms: Symphony No. 3; Mendelssohn: *Hebrides* Overture
B. Walter, Columbia Symphony Orchestra. Sony 64487 [ADD] + Symphony
   Nos. "7," 8 "Unfinished"; Beethoven: *Leonore* Overture No. 3

Symphony No. 8 in B Minor, D.759 "Unfinished"

There are other famous unfinished symphonies (Bruckner's No. 9 and Mahler's No.
10, for example), left incomplete at their composers' deaths. But it was not death that
caused Schubert to stop after writing only two movements (and a few bars of a third) of his
most famous symphony, which is also one of the most beloved symphonies ever written by
anybody. No one knows why he laid this score aside, going on later to compose the much
longer (and complete) Symphony No. 9.

It seems clear that he had no intention of proceeding beyond the second movement,
for several months after writing it he sent the half-torso score to a music society as a gift for
electing him a member. The most satisfying theory is that, following these two incompara-
bly sad and mysterious movements, Schubert just could not think of a way to top them;
rather than write an anti-climax, he simply let the tantalizing question mark stand. Our
astonishment is only increased by learning that this strange, towering work lay for 43 years
in a drawer of one of Schubert's friends before having its first public performance.

Groves, English Sinfonia. Carlton Classics 6700872 [3306 700872] [DDD] +
   Incidental Music to *Rosamunde*
Harnoncourt, Royal Concertgebouw Orchestra. Teldec 74785 [DDD] +
   Rosamunde (sel.)
Karajan, Berlin Philharmonic Orchestra. EMI 64628 [ADD] + Symphony
   No. 9
Levine, Metropolitan Opera Orchestra. Deutsche Grammophon 439862
   [DDD] + Beethoven: Symphony No. 3
Mackerras, Orchestra of the Age of Enlightenment. Virgin Veritas 61305
   [DDD] + Symphony No. 5, Incidental Music to *Rosamunde*
Sinopoli, Philharmonia Orchestra. Deutsche Grammophon Masters 445514
   [DDD] + Mendelssohn: Symphony No. 4

———— *CDs listed are solid, central choices, not necessarily "the greatest."* ————

B. **Walter, Columbia Symphony Orchestra.** Sony 64487 [ADD] + Symphonies
Nos. 5, "7"; Beethoven: *Leonore* Overture No. 3
Wand, Berlin Philharmonic Orchestra. RCA Victor Red Seal (2) 68314
[DDD] + Symphony No. 9

Symphony No. 9 in C, D.944 "The Great"

Schubert's last symphony had a slightly better fate than his Unfinished: at least there
was an attempt to have it performed before he died. But the Vienna Philharmonic decided
it was too difficult. Some 11 years after the composer's death, the same orchestra did put
the first two movements on a program—but with an aria from Donizetti's *Lucia di
Lammermoor* inserted between them to keep the audience awake! Both Schumann and
Mendelssohn championed the work, to little avail. Mendelssohn tried to include it in an
1844 concert he conducted, but had to withdraw it after his players kept cracking up over
passages they found ridiculous.

Today, audiences are at a loss to decide what is more wonderful, this symphony's beautiful melodies, its magical harmonic transitions, or its magnificent structural development
concluding with one of the most joyful outbursts of sunshine in all music. "In originality
of harmony and modulation, and in his gift of orchestral coloring," wrote Antonín Dvořák
in 1894, "Schubert has had no superior...I do not hesitate to place him next to Beethoven,
far above Mendelssohn, as well as above Schumann." Take that!

Abbado, Chamber Orchestra of Europe. Deutsche Grammophon 423656
[DDD] + *Rosamunde* Overture
C. Davis, Royal Philharmonic Orchestra. EMI Doublefforte 69364 (2) [ADD]
+ Beethoven: Symphony No. 7; Rossini: Overtures
Karajan, Berlin Philharmonic Orchestra. EMI 64628 [ADD] + Symphony No.
8 "Unfinished"
Mackerras, Orchestra of the Age of Enlightenment. Virgin Veritas 61245
[DDD]
B. **Walter, Columbia Symphony Orchestra.** CBS [Sony] Odyssey 44828
[ADD]
Wand, Berlin Philharmonic Orchestra. RCA Victor Red Seal 68314 (2)
[DDD] + Symphony No. 8 "Unfinished"

Trio No. 1 in B-flat Major, Op. 99 (D.898)

This wonderful chamber piece gives us Schubert in his most untrammeled happy
mood, than which, little in music can be more pleasing. A feeling of bliss prevails virtually
from the first bar to the last, even in the nocturnal slow movement.

——— *Some famous CDs are not listed because currently out of print.* ———

Beaux Arts Trio, Grumiaux Trio. Philips Duo 438700 (2) [ADD] + Trio No. 2, other works for piano trio

Golub, Kaplan, Carr. Arabesque 6580 (2) [DDD] + Trio No. 2, *Notturno* in E-flat, Sonata Movement in B-flat, D.28

London Mozart Trio. IMP [Carlton Classics] PCD 1006 [DDD] + Dvořák: Trio No. 4 "Dumky"

Oistrakh, Knushevitsky, Oborin. EMI Doubleforte 69367 [ADD] + Beethoven: Trio No. 6 "Archduke"; Brahms: Violin Sonatas; encores

Thibaud, Casals, Cortot. EMI 61024 (mono) + Beethoven: Trio No. 6 "Archduke"

"Wanderer" Fantasy for Piano in C Major, Op. 15 (D.760)

The title is not a wry comment on Schubert's reputation for desultory writing, but yet another reference to a song which provides thematic material ("Der Wanderer"). This piece looks forward, structurally, to the rhapsodic view of sonata form embraced by Franz Liszt. It is one of Schubert's most dramatic keyboard works.

Perahia. Sony 42124 [DDD] + Schumann: *Fantasia* in C

Pollini. Deutsche Grammophon 447451 [ADD] + Schumann: *Fantasia* in C

Rubinstein. RCA Victor Red Seal 6257 [ADD] + 2 Impromptus, Sonata in B-flat, D.960

Winterreise, Op. 89 (D.911)

This cycle of 24 songs could be considered the diametric opposite of the Piano Trio No. 1, as there is scarcely a cheerful moment in it. It is a powerfully eloquent, heartrending diary of the winter journey of a rejected lover, whose unquenchable pain leads him to quiet madness and a longing for death.

The effect is akin to seeing a series of snapshots of a person gradually disintegrating over time. The piano accompaniment is often vividly wrenching, suggesting falling leaves, growling dogs rattling their chains, or the ominous beating of the wings of a crow, yet Schubert's pure harmonies keep the music well away from the edge of melodramatic hysteria. There are few works of vocal music more convincing in their tragedy.

Allen, Vignoles. Virgin Classics 59036 [DDD]

Fischer-Dieskau, Moore. Deutsche Grammophon 415187 [ADD]

Holzmair, Cooper. Philips 446407 [DDD]

Hotter, Moore. EMI 61002 (m)

——— *Catalog numbers are subject to change without notice.* ———

Robert Schumann (1810-1856)

Schumann was nothing if not methodical. With a self-discipline unique among composers he confined himself first to piano pieces, then moved on to songs, orchestral works, and chamber music. Despite this—or possibly because of it—he died in a madhouse, the tragic victim of an utterly disordered brain.

Ironic no doubt, but then Schumann was no stranger to paradox. He expounded the most fantastic and fanciful aspects of the Romantic credo, yet in his private life was considered to be conservative and dull. He spoke and wrote constantly about the "music of the future," but had minimal appreciation for his two contemporaries, Liszt and Wagner, who were its embodiments.

Even his fabled love affair with Clara Wieck seems far less ideal, upon close scrutiny, than legend would have it. True, their long courtship in defiance of her father's wishes did result in lifelong marriage and several children; but before the courtship Schumann contracted syphilis, during it he was briefly engaged to another woman, and after it the relationship suffered from both Robert's jealous resentment of Clara's own considerable musical talents, and her driving him to the point of exhaustion in a quest for greater financial reward, insisting that he write the large symphonic works for which he was ill-suited by temperament.

It was in the smaller forms, the piano pieces and songs, that Schumann seemed most comfortable. Indeed his successful longer works, such as *Carnaval*, are frequently really a series of short pieces strung together. The chamber works, though graced with lovely ideas, are sometimes clumsily structured; and the fresh poetry of the four symphonies is hobbled here and there by awkward orchestration.

Yet there may have been no composer better than Schumann in overcoming technical deficiencies by sheer force of inspiration. His innate sensitivity to the portrayal of shifting moods almost never fails him, and in his best works one is struck over and over by the impression that each scene or emotion is colored in just the right way.

Schumann has literary aspirations, but it was in his music that he created true poetry. He was the favorite composer of another miniaturist, the Venezuelan composer Reynaldo Hahn (1875-1947), who once wrote of Schumann: "There is no emotion that he has not experienced: all the phenomena of nature are familiar to him—moonlight, bright or hazy, sunrise and sunset, confused shadows, dull weather, radiant weather, fresh scents, the majesty of evening, swirling mists, powdery snow—he has known them all and can impart to us the thousand and one emotions associated with them."

———— *Since CDs can change label and number, use artists as main reference.* ————

Carnaval, Op. 9

Of all the early Romantics, Schumann was the most effective at injecting playful wit into his music, and there is no more delightful display of it than in this kaleidoscopic keyboard picture of carnival characters. Among the numerous portraits are two that reveal Schumann's "split personality": "Eusebius" represents his poetic, dreamy side, while "Florestan" refers to the fiery crusader within him. Schumann continued to use these pseudonyms when writing reviews and articles about music, indicating he was aware of his paradoxical nature.

> **Barenboim.** Deutsche Grammophon 431167 [ADD] + *Kinderscenen, Faschingsschwank aus Wien*
> **Jandó.** Naxos 8.550784 [DDD] + *Kinderscenen, Papillons*
> **Rubinstein.** RCA Victor Red Seal 5667 [ADD] + "The Prophet Bird" from *Waldscenen, Phantasiestücke*
> **Shelley.** Chandos 8814 [DDD] + *Kinderscenen*, Toccata in C

Chamber Music (Miscellaneous)

> **Fuller, Helicon Foundation artists.** *A Schumann Salon Concert*, Helicon 1018 [DDD]
> **Kliegel (cello), Merscher (piano).** *Phantasiestücke*, op. 73, *Stücke im Volkston*, Op. 102, Adagio and Allegro, Op. 70, Naxos 8.550654 [DDD] + Schubert: "Arpeggione" Sonata, D.821
> **Zukerman (violin, viola), Neikrug (piano).** Violin sonatas 1, 2; *Phantasiestücke*, Op. 73; *Drei Romanzen*, Op. 94; *Märchenbilder*, Op. 113, RCA Victor Red Seal 68052 (2) [DDD]

Concerto in A minor for Piano, Op. 54

Now one of the most beloved Romantic piano concertos, this work was unsuccessful at its premiere in 1845 and for many years thereafter. The starched-shirt critics of those days were mightily offended by its rhapsodic, free nature, not to mention its lack of virtuoso display. Both traditional sonata form and showiness were inimical to Schumann's spirit; once, years before he actually wrote the Piano Concerto, he predicted it would be "a compromise between a symphony, a concerto and a huge sonata." It is. And it is (mostly) ravishingly tender rather than thunderous or brilliant.

> **Cliburn, Reiner, Chicago Symphony Orchestra.** RCA Living Stereo 62691 [ADD] + Prokofiev: Piano Concerto No. 3 (with Hendl conducting)

—————*Artists are listed alphabetically, not in order by critical ranking.* —————

Jandó, Ligeti, Budapest SO. Naxos 8.550118 [DDD] + Grieg: Piano Concerto
Lipatti, Karajan, Philharmonia Orchestra. EMI 69792 (mono) [ADD] +
Mozart: Piano Concerto No. 21
Perahia, C. Davis, Bavarian Radio Symphony Orchestra. Sony 44899 [DDD]
+ Grieg: Piano Concerto
R. Serkin, Ormandy, Philadelphia Orchestra. Sony 37256 + Piano Quintet,
Op. 44 (with Budapest String Quartet)

Dichterliebe, Op. 48

Schumann is second only to Schubert in the realm of art songs—in number (about 140 compared with Schubert's 600), and in familiarity, if not in inspiration. At least in variety of style and expression, Schumann may be Schubert's superior. While the vast majority of Schubert's songs are lyrical romances, Schumann ranges freely from those all the way to such unexpected things as the terrifying ballad "Die beiden Grenadiere" ("The Two Grenadiers"). Perhaps the best known of all Schumann songs is "Ich grolle nicht" ("I'll not complain"), a song with a penetrating idea, an unforgettable melody, and a highly original declamatory structure. "Ich grolle nicht" is, however, only one of 16 marvelous songs making up the cycle *Dichterliebe*—"Poet's Love."

Fischer-Dieskau, Brendel. Philips 416352 [DDD] + *Liederkreis*
Holzmair, Cooper. Philips 446086 [DDD] + *Liederkreis, Lieder nach Heinrich Heine*
Partridge (Ian), Partridge (Jennifer). Classics for Pleasure 4651 [ADD] +
Liederkreis

Kinderscenen, Op. 15

This baker's dozen of short pieces are Schumann's touching and amusing recollections of childhood. Although he intended them for adults to play, there actually were some children who could play them before the invention of television. People who have never heard, or perhaps even wanted to hear, "classical music" are often startled to find they can hum the tunes from "Scenes of Childhood," so pervasive have they become in our culture, turning up everywhere from elevators to Laurel and Hardy movies.

Argerich. Deutsche Grammophon 410653 + *Kreisleriana*
Brendel. Philips 434732 [DDD] + *Fantasiestücke, Kreisleriana*
Barenboim. Deutsche Grammophon 431167 [ADD] + *Carnaval, Faschingsschwank aus Wien*
Jandó. Naxos 8.550784 [DDD] + *Carnaval, Papillons*

——— *[DDD] indicates newest recordings; [ADD] or [AAD] are reissues.* ———

Lupu. London [Decca] 440496 [DDD] + *Humoreske, Kreisleriana*
Shelley. Chandos 8814 [DDD] + *Carnaval,* Toccata in C

Quintet in E-flat for Piano and Strings, Op. 44

A richly Romantic work, jammed with delicious melodies and sweeping to a thrilling conclusion.

Ax, Cleveland Quartet. RCA Victor Red Seal 6498 [DDD] + Piano Quartet, Op. 47
Beaux Arts Trio, Rhodes, Bettelheim. Philips 420791 [ADD] + Piano Quartet, Op. 47
Kodály Quartet, Jandó. Naxos 8.550406 [DDD] + Brahms: Quintet, Op. 34
R. Serkin, Budapest Quartet. CBS [Sony] 37256 + Piano Concerto in A Minor (with Ormandy conducting)

Complete Symphonies

Goodman, Hanover Band. RCA Victor Red Seal 61931 (2) [DDD] + *Overture, Sherzo and Finale*, Op. 52
Karajan, Berlin Philharmonic Orchestra. Deutsche Grammophon 429672 (2) [ADD]
Szell, Cleveland Orchestra. Sony Classics Masterworks Heritage 62349 (2) [ADD] + *Manfred* Overture

Symphony No. 1 in B-flat Major, Op. 38 "Spring"

The "Spring" Symphony, in which Clara professed to hear clearly "the buds, the scent of violets, the fresh green leaves, the birds in the air," was written in the dead of winter, 1840/1. The "Spring" in it was not meant to be the season of the year so much as the beginning of Robert's career, and his honeymoon with Clara. There are no literal nature-paintings in it, but if doesn't lighten your step, you may need to get out more.

Janowski, Royal Liverpool Philharmonic Orchestra. ASV Quicksilva 6073 [DDD] + Symphony No. 3
Karajan, Berlin Philharmonic Orchestra. Deutsche Grammophon Originals 447408 [ADD] + Brahms: Symphony No. 1
Kubelik, Bavarian Radio Symphony Orchestra. Sony Essential Classics 48269 [ADD] + Symphony No. 2

——— *CDs go in and out of print; availability of all listed items is not assured.* ———

Levine, Berlin Philharmonic Orchestra. Deutsche Grammophon 435856
[DDD] + Symphony No. 4, *Manfred* Overture
Masur, London Philharmonic Orchestra. Teldec 95501 [DDD] + Symphony
No. 3

Symphony No. 2 in C Major, Op. 61

This is the least known of Schumann's symphonies, but it has many beauties often
overlooked. The second movement, a Scherzo, is as exhilarating an orchestral romp as anyone has written.

Kubelik, Bavarian Radio Symphony Orchestra. Sony Essential Classics 48269
[ADD] + Symphony No. 1

Symphony No. 3 in E-flat Major, Op. 97 "Rhenish"

Inspired by scenes of life along the Rhine river, the "Rhenish" is both the most original
and most popular of Schumann's symphonies. Two of the five (!) movements are inspired
by the then-unfinished Cathedral of Cologne, where Schumann witnessed the majestic
enthronement of an archbishop. Other parts of the symphony suggest peasant dances,
morning sunrises, and so on.

Giulini, Los Angeles Philharmonic Orchestra. Deutsche Grammophon
445502 [DDD] + Beethoven: Symphony No. 5
Janowski, Royal Liverpool Philharmonic Orchestra. ASV Quicksilva 6073
[DDD] + Symphony No. 1
Kubelik, Bavarian Radio Symphony Orchestra. Sony Essential Classics 48270
[ADD] + Symphony No. 4, *Manfred* Overture
Masur, London Philharmonic Orchestra. Teldec 95501 [DDD] + Symphony
No. 1

Symphony No. 4 in D Minor, Op. 120

This was originally Schumann's Symphony No. 2, written shortly after the "Spring"
Symphony. Its premiere was not well received, and even the composer had second
thoughts. He laid the score aside for ten years, then revised it extensively and brought it out
as Symphony No. 4, which it has remained. The four movements are continuous, that is,
distinct from each other but linked by bridge materials, without full stops between them.
The work could almost be described as a tone poem constructed on symphonic principles.

——— *Some CDs may be available only through importers.* ———

Kubelik, Bavarian Radio Symphony Orchestra. Sony Essential Classics 48270
[ADD] + Symphony No. 3, *Manfred* Overture
Levine, Berlin Philharmonic Orchestra. Deutsche Grammophon 435856
[DDD] + Symphony No. 1, *Manfred* Overture

Carl Maria von Weber (1786-1826)

The earliest of the early Romantics, Weber deserves much credit for establishing and popu-larizing the whole Romantic movement in music. Sadly, he has fallen on hard times in our century; his works are the least played and known of all his contemporaries, and several attempts to start revivals have fallen flat. This is partly because of his short career (he died at age 39), partly because his music is so thoroughly, almost provincially, German that it doesn't "travel" well. But mostly it is because his style was soon subsumed under that of his spiritual descendant, Richard Wagner, whose works were longer, louder, and better market-ed. They quite drowned poor Weber out.

Weber was the most talented member of a musical family with ambition. A grandfa-ther added the honorific "von" to the family name; his father was a small-town Kapellmeister, his mother a talented singer; and his two cousins, Aloysia and Constanze, were both involved with Mozart: the former was his great love, the latter became his wife.

As a child, despite being crippled by a hip deformity, Carl Maria was dragged around Europe as a child prodigy by his father, who wanted him to be seen as another Mozart. The boy was able to study with Haydn's younger brother Michael (who was Mozart's friend), and published his first compositions at age 11. He became a concert pianist at 12, had his first opera produced at 14, and by 15 won the post of Kapellmeister at Breslau. A frail con-stitution and a grinding schedule wore him down, and he died while in London, where he was buried. 18 years later his remains were returned to Germany. In the harbor, ships of many nations dipped their flags in homage, and at the re-interment the graveside eulogy was delivered by the one man who owed the most to Weber: Richard Wagner.

Invitation to the Dance, Op. 65

Originally written for piano solo, this piece is most familiar in a brilliant orchestral transcription by Berlioz. Another Weber innovation, it is the first symphonic waltz, the direct ancestor of all those wonderful waltzes by the Strauss family, and every bit their equal.

Goodman, Hanover Band. Nimbus 5154 [DDD] + Overtures
Reiner, Chicago Symphony Orchestra. RCA Living Stereo 68160 [ADD] + J.
Strauss, Jr.: Waltzes

———— *U.S. labels and numbers are given first, U.K. in [brackets] when needed.* ————

Overtures

Except for *Der Freischütz,* most of Weber's operas no longer hold the stage, but their dramatic and melodious overtures survive.

Goodman, Hanover Band. Nimbus 5154 [DDD] + *Invitation to the Dance*
Järvi, Philharmonia Orchestra. Chandos 9066 [DDD]

All CDs listed are considered approximately equal in (high) merit.

The Mainstream Romantics
(ca. 1850-1890)

The Early Romantics were given dates of about 1820 to 1850. Mainstream Romanticism, however, is not so much defined by dates as by a state of mind. The composers whom we think of as the "central" composers of the Romantic era in music definitely did not do their work on the first half of the 19th century, but some of them overlapped with those we can distinguish as Late Romantics towards the end of that era.

We can often identify the Mainstreamers by their strong tendency to emphasize ethnicity and nationality; by the greater weight and seriousness of their vision as compared to the Early Romantics; and most of all by the full-blooded rhapsodic manner of their expression, which obliterated all traces of those ties to the Classical period that we can still always hear in the works of Mendelssohn or Schubert or even Rossini.

Until about 1960 they were, with the exception of Beethoven, the composers who heavily dominated orchestral concert programs. For the better part of a century it was Brahms and Tchaikovsky who were played most often, with Mozart thrown in occasionally almost as a sop to historians, and Haydn was a distinct oddity on a program.

The same situation prevailed in opera. Mozart's masterpieces were heard only sporadically, and all but a handful of the once wildly popular operas of Bellini, Donizetti, and Rossini vanished from the stage. The lyrical theater scene belonged to Verdi and Wagner.

Although the most famous of the Mainstream Romantics are still doing perfectly well at the box office, they have had to learn to share with composers earlier and later than they. The great revival of interest in Baroque music, especially in the 1960s, threatened for a while to block them out, and renewed respect and love for Haydn and Mozart further diluted their hegemony, creating a growing suspicion that their vast heavings and stentorian pronouncements were perhaps more hot air than true profundities. And the assault continued from the other side, from a growing appreciation of the modern composers for whom the Mainstream Romantic approach so often seemed to be anathema.

The Mainstreamers were thus squeezed for a generation or more between the simpler, clearer lines of earlier music, and the non-sentimental esthetic of the modernists. But by the 1990s it was clear that the Mainstream Romantics were being rapidly rehabilitated. Not only was Tchaikovsky chic again, there was even a deluge of recordings of works by totally forgotten Mainstreamers such as Joachim Raff, Anton Rubinstein, and Alexis de Castillon.

The secret of this renaissance was simple: once listeners stopped believing Mainstream Romantic music was sacred writ, and purged its dogmatisms from their systems, they could take it again to their hearts on a new basis. One no longer had to worship at the shrine of

Wagner, or brood darkly on his half-baked theories on Man and His Destiny; as soon as one realized Wagner was a magnificent entertainer who misread himself as a prophet, his music became available again as a source of delight. But from that point on, it would be understood as more sensuous than intellectual.

Georges Bizet (1838-1875)

Bizet must turn every day in his grave, frustrated that although he was nearly as great a child prodigy as Mozart or Meldelssohn, and that his opera *Carmen* is the most-performed opera in the world, beloved of audiences and critics alike, he is never mentioned as one of the five or even ten greatest composers, let alone greatest opera composer. At least many music lovers know about this paradox; few, however, are aware that Bizet was a virtuoso pianist, called by Liszt one of the three best in Europe, though he chose not to follow a keyboard career.

He was an only child in a musical family, entered the Paris Conservatory at the early age of nine, and wrote his ever-fresh Symphony in C at age 17. A student of Gounod, and later his good friend, he won the Prix de Rome in 1857 and immediately embarked on his chosen career as an opera composer. Though praised by Berlioz, among others, Bizet suffered one artistic disaster after another and was often reduced to turning out hack dance music to stay alive.

He persisted, carried along by his modesty, common sense, and faith in his abilities. Though he was no great innovator, and founded no school, he was a master of orchestration, and one of the finest of all French melodists. His ability to make his cahracters come alive, to portray their conflicts with intenstiy and convincing realism, enabled him to practically finish off the old French Grand Opera.

He worked rapidly. Like Mozart he composed most of his works in his head before writing them down. He felt, in fact, a strong affinity with Mozart as a similarly "natural" and "balanced" musician. The two men died at nearly the same ages. But of course the sounds they produced were very different: Bizet, though he liked to say his heart was really German, or Italian, and who set every one of his operas in countries other than France, was French to the bone. Not however the French of Debussy, of moonlit waves and medieval forests, but of the sunlit Mediterranean and the passionate tempers of modern men and women.

Carmen

One of the few operas to appeal equally to audiences and critics (belatedly), *Carmen* is a compelling story of the tragic love of a Spanish officer for a gypsy cigarette girl, set to music that is constantly ablaze with inner or outer passion. It teems with memorable

——— *Some famous CDs are not listed because currently out of print.* ———

melodies and moves right along to a suspenseful and shocking ending. It was more or less a flop at its premiere in 1875, and Bizet did not live to see it become perhaps the most popular opera ever written. Early critics mocked its "degrading" libretto and its "obscure, colorless" music; once again, critics struck out—within a few years Friedrich Nietzsche was writing "How elevating is such a work! It makes the listener feel like a masterpiece himself."

Beecham, de los Angeles, French National Orchestra and Chorus. Angel 56214 (3) [ADD]
Karajan, Baltsa, Berlin Philharmonic Orchestra. Deutsche Grammophon 410088 (3)
Karajan, L. Price, Vienna Philharmonia Orchestra and State Opera Chorus. RCA Gold Seal 6199 (3) [ADD]
Prêtre, Callas, Paris National Opera Theater Orchestra, René Duclos Choir. EMI 54368 (2) [ADD]
Reiner, Stevens, RCA Victor Orchestra. RCA Victor Gold Seal 7981 (3) (mono)
Solti, Troyanos, London Symphony Orchestra. London [Decca] 414489 (3) [ADD]

L'Arlésienne Suites; Carmen Suites

Three years before *Carmen*, Bizet accepted a commission to write incidental music for Alphonse Daudet's play about rustic love in Provence called *L'Arlésienne* ("The Maid from Arles"). Best known in two suites for concert performance, the most famous piece is the breathless *Farandole* from Suite No. 2. Bizet also arranged two suites from *Carmen* for concert hall use. These suites happen to fit conveniently on one disc and make the most natural possible pairing, so there is little reason not to purchase them so, especially when there are several fine versions to choose from.

Dutoit, Montreal Symphony Orchestra. London [Decca] 417839 [DDD]
López-Cobos, Cincinnati Symphony Orchestra. (*L'Arlésienne* Suite No. 2 not included) Telarc 80224 [DDD] + Symphony in C
Munch, New Philharmonia Orchestra. London [Decca] 443033 (2) [ADD] + Offenbach: *Gaité Parisienne*; Chabrier: *España, Joyeuse marche* (with Ansermet, Suisse Romande Orchestra); Saint-Saëns: *Danse macabre, La rouet d'Omphale*; Bizet: *Jeux d'enfants* (with Martinon, Paris Conservatory Orchestra); Dukas: *The Sorcerer's Apprentice* (with Solti, Israel Philharmonic Orchestra);
Stokowski, National Philharmonic Orchestra. CBS [Sony] 37260 [ADD]

—— *Catalog numbers are subject to change without notice.* ——

Symphony No. 1 in C

Bizet was but a stripling of 17 when he wrote this symphony as a test piece for the Paris Conservatory. It was never played in his lifetime, and was forgotten until the 1920s. Even then it waited another decade for its premiere. No one was prepared to believe it could be very good. They were wrong. It is extremely well written, and there is hardly another symphony that breathes more naturally the fresh air of youth.

Johanos, New Zealand Symphony Orchestra. Naxos 8.553027 [DDD] + _Jeux d'enfants, Scènes bohémiennes_ from _La jolie fille de Perth_

López-Cobos, Cincinnati Symphony Orchestra. Telarc 80224 [DDD] + _Carmen_ Suites; _L'Arlésienne_ Suite No. 1

Orpheus Chamber Orchestra. Deutsche Grammophon 423624 [DDD] + Prokofiev: Symphony No. 1; Britten: Simple Symphony

Stokowski, National Philharmonic Orchestra. Sony Essential Classics 48264 [ADD] + Mendelssohn: _A Midsummer Night's Dream_ (sel.); Smetana: _The Moldau_ (with Szell, Cleveland Orchestra)

Alexander Borodin (1833-1887)

Borodin was one of the most appealing characters among the composers. Beginning life with a severe handicap, as the illegitimate son of a Russian nobleman, who farmed the child out to one of his serfs, Borodin nevertheless showed talent in both music and science at an early age, and managed to secure an excellent education.

He spent his entire professional life as a chemist, teacher, and administrator of the St. Petersburg Medico-Surgical Academy, where he took a leading role in establishing medical education for Russian women, and wrote such yawners as _The Solidification of Aldehydes_ and _Researches on the Fluoride of Benzol_. His beloved hobby of composing was relegated to his few spare hours, mostly during vacations, and even then he was subject to endless inter-ruptions from family and friends (and sometimes from his pet cats as they walked across the keys of his piano).

Despite this he was recognized early on as a major talent and was readily included in the group later known as the "Mighty Five." These were the great Russian nationalist com-posers including Mussorgsky, Cui, Balakirev, and Rimsky-Korsakov. Many of Borodin's works remained incomplete, or needed orchestration which was usually contributed by Rimsky-Korsakov or Alexander Glazunov. Yet of all these professional composers, Borodin wrote the best-integrated forms, had the strongest grasp of symphonic development, and showed the most consistent employment of thematic material. And his strikingly beautiful melodies, though fewer in number, are as distinctive as Tchaikovsky's.

——— _Since CDs can change label and number, use artists as main reference._ ———

Plagued by numerous health problems, including cholera and several heart attacks, Borodin was only 54 when he died at a masquerade ball. He was wearing a red peasant shirt and boots, laughing and joking, we are told, when just at the stroke of midnight he collapsed and was gone—fulfilling the desirable end envisioned by Keats:

> *"To cease upon the midnight,*
> *With no pain."*

Prince Igor: Overture; Polovtsian Dances

Borodin's opera *Prince Igor* is one of the most colorful in the Russian repertoire and it is a wonder it is not heard more often in the West, especially since a number of its great melodies have long since become familiar through the American musical *Kismet*. The overture was actually sewn together by Glinka and Rimsky-Korsakov after Borodin's death, based on remembrances of his playing them on the piano. The spectacular *Polovtsian Dances* occur as part of Khan Konchak's victory celebration in Act II, and contain choral parts often omitted in concert performance.

Bátiz, Mexico State Symphony Orchestra. ASV Quicksilva 6018 [DDD] + Symphony No. 2

Beecham, Royal Philharmonic Orchestra. EMI 47717 [ADD] + Rimsky-Korsakov: *Scheherazade*

Dorati, London Symphony Orchestra. (*Prince Igor* Overture omitted) Mercury 434308 [ADD] + Rimsky-Korsakov: *Capriccio espagnol, Le Coq d'or* Suite, *Russian Easter* Overture

Karajan, Berlin Philharmonic Orchestra. (*Prince Igor* Overture omitted) Deutsche Grammophon 419063 [ADD] + Rimsky-Korsakov: *Scheherazade*

Järvi, Gothenburg Symphony Orchestra. (*Prince Igor* Overture omitted) Deutsche Grammophon 429984 [DDD] + *In the Steppes of Central Asia*; Tchaikovsky: *1812* Overture, *Marche slave*; Rimsky-Korsakov: *Russian Easter* Overture, *Capriccio espagnol*,

Shaw, Atlanta Symphony Orchestra and Chorus. Telarc 80039 [DDD] + Stravinsky: *Firebird* Suite

Tjeknavorian, National Philharmonic Orchestra (London). (*Dances* only) RCA Victrola 60535 [ADD] + *In the Steppes of Central Asia*, Symphony No. 2

Quartet No. 2 in D

One of the few works Borodin actually completed, the Quartet No. 2 like Prince Igor contains themes which found a wider audience in the musical *Kismet*. It was dedicated to

──── *Artists are listed alphabetically, not in order by critical ranking.* ────

the composer's wife, probably as a 20th anniversary gift, and sustains a happy mood throughout.

> **Borodin Quartet.** EMI 47795 [DDD] + Quartet No. 1
> **Gabrieli String Quartet.** Classics for Pleasure Silver Double 4772 (2) [ADD] +
> Dvořák: Quartet No. 12 "American"; Brahms: Clarinet Quintet; Schubert:
> Quartet No. 14 "Death and the Maiden"

Symphony No. 2 in B Minor

This symphony is so ultra-Russian it makes Tchaikovsky sound Danish. In fact it is probably the best Russian Romantic symphony outside of Tchaikovsky's. And when was the last you heard it on *your* orchestra's program?

> **Ashkenazy, Royal Philharmonic Orchestra.** London [Decca] 436651 [DDD] +
> Symphony No. 1, *In the Steppes of Central Asia*
> **Bátiz, Mexico State Symphony Orchestra.** ASV Quicksilva 6018 [DDD] +
> *Prince Igor*: Overture and *Polovtsian Dances*
> **Tjeknavorian, National Philharmonic Orchestra (London).** (Dances only)
> RCA Victrola 60535 [ADD] + *In the Steppes of Central Asia, Polovtsian Dances*
> from *Prince Igor*

Johannes Brahms (1833-1897)

If Brahms did not have a "split personality," he certainly had a double nature. Born into humble circumstances, he grew up in a cramped three-room apartment, and earned money as a youth by playing the paino in taverns and brothels. We may not be surprised, then, to discover that he developed a lifelong obsession for settled, respectable, bourgeois comfort— yet this was in constant conflict with the demands of his genius.

Although he became immensely successful both artistically and financially, he continued all his life to live in a modest house, wear rumpled old clothes, and eat in the cheapest restaurants. He was parsimonious in acquiring money, but prodigal in giving it away. He was preoccupied with trying to secure a permanent conducting post, yet turned down most offers he received; and when he did get a position, he soon found some lame excuse to give it up.

He fell in love several times, most famously with Robert Schumann's wife Clara. He never married, and was apparently never able to tell Clara his feelings, even long after Robert had died. Always shy by nature, he became morose and even rude in later years. The story was current that when Brahms left a gathering he was apt to say "If there is any-

--- ***[DDD]** indicates newest recordings; **[ADD]** or **[AAD]** are reissues.* ---

one here whom I have forgotten to insult, I beg his forgiveness." Yet there was no one more likely to rush to the aid of a needy friend, nor to make gifts and loans of money without fanfare, and without demand for repayment.

He was a native of Hamburg, but spent his most productive years in Vienna, where his shaggy beard and mane of hair, fuming cigar, and ill-fitting suit hugging his portly frame became legendary fixtures of the local scene. With his prickly temperament, perhaps it was not entirely coincidental that one of his favorite taverns was named The Red Hedgehog.

Brahms's musical career began in the shadow of his heroes: Schubert, Schumann, and especially Beethoven. Although he appreciated the fantasy elements of some of the early Romantics, he was repulsed by the free and rhapsodic constructions of contemporaries such as Liszt; nor did he have any aptitude for opera or dramatic music as did Wagner. Much was made of the rivalry between Brahms and Wagner, and indeed they were living symbols of antithetical artistic ideals, but the controversy was more accurately between their followers, not between the men themselves.

Brahms stayed true to the last to the traditional formal bounds of composition, developing an antiquarian interest in later life which led him to collect, and sometimes edit, works of numerous Renaissance and Baroque composers. He was a scholarly intellectual who collected not only old music manuscripts, but books on religion, philosophy, history, and poetry.

In his own music he kept his personality in the background, emphasizing structure and rich harmony. There is a gentle but dark solemnity about much of his output which las led inevitably to the adjective "autumnal" being applied to it. Not for Brahms the sparkling cascades of Saint-Saëns, the lightning brilliance of Liszt, or the blinding colors of Wagner. His was a serious and austere art, and in its magnificent execution it brought to a full cadence, just as Bach had done long before, the entire tendency of an age. As his biographer Karl Geiringer wrote, "The musical output of five hundred years is summarized in Brahms's works."

Academic Festival Overture, Op. 80

The title perfectly mirrors the union here of the scholarly and the festive, a trick known to few other than Brahms. It was written in thanks to the University of Breslau for conferring on him a Doctorate of Philosophy in 1880. Four traditional student songs are woven into the brilliant textures, culminating in a joyful outburst of the Latin song *Gaudeamus igitur* ("Therefore let us rejoice"). The overture is easily obtainable as "filler" on any number of Brahms discs of larger works, of which the following may be mentioned as recommendable under the major titles.

Barenboim, Chicago Symphony Orchestra. Erato 94817 (4) [DDD] + *Haydn Variations*, *Tragic* Overture, Symphonies Nos. 1-4

———— *CDs go in and out of print; availability of all listed items is not assured.* ————

Haitink, Royal Concertgebouw Orchestra. Philips 438320 (2) + Piano Concertos Nos. 1, 2 (with Arrau), *Tragic* Overture, *Haydn Variations*

Klemperer, Philharmonia Orchestra. EMI Studio 69651 [ADD] + Symphony No. 1, *Tragic* Overture

Loughran, Hallé Orchestra. Classics for Pleasure Silver Double 4766 (2) [ADD] + *Haydn Variations*; Piano Concertos Nos. 1, 2 (with Tirimo, Sanderling, Levi, London Philharmonic Orchestra)

Masur, New York Philharmonic Orchestra. Teldec 77291 [DDD] + Symphony No. 2

Previn, Royal Philharmonic Orchestra. Telarc 82006 [DDD] + Symphony No. 4

Skrowaczewski, Hallé Orchestra. IMP [Carlton Classics] PCD 2014 [DDD] + Symphony No. 1

Szell, Cleveland Orchestra. Sony Essential Classics 46330 [ADD] + Symphony No. 4, *Tragic* Overture

Szell, Cleveland Orchestra. Sony Essential Classics 48398 (3) [ADD] + Symphonies 1-4, *Hungarian Dances, Tragic* Overture, *Haydn Variations*

Concerto No. 1 in D Minor for Piano, Op. 15

This was Brahms's first major orchestral work, written when he was in his early 20s. It is one of the longest concertos ever written, partly because it evolved from a projected symphony which Brahms abandoned after sketching it out in a two-piano version. The whole concerto can be interpreted as a struggle between the majestic opening theme of the first movement and other materials, with the original theme triumphant at the end.

Arrau, Haitink, Royal Concertgebouw Orchestra. Philips 438320 (2) + Piano Concerto No. 2, *Academic Festival* Overture, *Tragic* Overture, *Haydn Variations*

Curzon, Szell, London Symphony Orchestra. London [Decca] Classic Sound 425082 [ADD] + Franck: *Symphonic Variations*; Litolff: *Scherzo*

Gilels, Jochum, Berlin Philharmonic Orchestra. Deutsche Grammophon 447446 (2) [ADD] + Concerto No. 2, Fantasias, Op. 116

Kempff, Dresden State Orchestra, Konwitschny. Deutsche Grammophon Double 437374 (2) [ADD] + solo piano pieces

R. Serkin, Szell, Cleveland Orchestra. Sony 37803 [ADD]

Tirimo, Sanderling, London Philharmonic Orchestra. Classics for Pleasure Silver Double 4766 (2) [ADD] + Piano Concertos No. 2 (with Levi conducting); *Academic Festival* Overture, *Haydn Variations* (with Loughran, Hallé Orchestra)

───── *Some CDs may be available only through importers.* ─────

Concerto No. 2 in B-flat for Piano, Op. 83

A frequent candidate for greatest piano concerto ever written, this work is unusual in its four-movement form, massive scale, and relatively subdued role for the solo instrument. The Viennese critic Eduard Hanslick called it "a symphony with piano obbligato." Brahms impishly referred to it as "a tiny, tiny piano concerto, with a tiny, tiny wisp of a scherzo."

Arrau, Haitink, Royal Concertgebouw Orchestra. Philips 438320 (2) + Piano Concerto No. 1, *Academic Festival* Overture, *Tragic* Overture, *Haydn Variations*
Ashkenazy, Haitink, Vienna Philharmonic Orchestra. London [Decca] 410199 [DDD]
Brendel, Abbado, Berlin Philharmonic Orchestra. Philips 432975
Gilels, Jochum, Berlin Philharmonic Orchestra. Deutsche Grammophon 447446 (2) [ADD] + Concerto No. 1, Fantasias, Op. 116
Rubinstein, Krips, RCA Victor Symphony Orchestra. RCA Victor Gold Seal 61442 [ADD] + solo piano pieces
R. Serkin, Szell, Cleveland Orchestra. Sony 37258 [ADD]
Tirimo, Levi, London Philharmonic Orchestra. Classics for Pleasure Silver Double 4766 (2) [ADD] + Piano Concertos No. 1 (with Sanderling conducting); *Academic Festival* Overture, *Haydn Variations* (with Loughran, Hallé Orchestra)

Concerto in D for Violin, Op. 77

Like the two piano concertos, Brahms's single violin concerto is symphonic in scope and style. It was written for, and dedicated to, the composer's friend Joseph Joachim, one of the great violinists of that era. It was premiered on New Year's Day, 1879, to a reception as chilly as the weather. One reviewer called it "a concerto against the violin." In time, nevertheless, it became the chief rival of Beethoven's violin concerto in eminence.

Bell, Dohnányi, Cleveland Orchestra. London [Decca] 444811 [DDD] + Schumann: Violin Concerto
Heifetz, Reiner, Chicago Symphony Orchestra. RCA Victor Red Seal 5402 [ADD] + Beethoven: Violin Concerto
Heifetz, Reiner, Chicago Symphony Orchestra. RCA Victor Gold Seal 61495 [ADD] + Tchaikovsky: Violin Concerto
Kremer, Bernstein, Vienna Philharmonic Orchestra. Deutsche Grammophon 431031 [DDD] + Double Concerto (with Maisky)

——— *U.S. labels and numbers are given first, U.K. in [brackets] when needed.* ———

Little, Handley, Royal Liverpool Philharmonic Orchestra. Classics for Pleasure
Eminence 2203 [DDD] + Sibelius: Violin Concerto

Menuhin, Kempe, Berlin Philharmonic Orchestra. EMI Seraphim 68256 (2)
[ADD] + *Hungarian Dances* (sel.) (with Kubelik, Royal Philharmonic
Orchestra); Symphony No. 4 (with Giulini, New Philharmonia Orchestra);
Haydn Variations (with Giulini, Philharmonia Orchestra)

Mutter, Karajan, Berlin Philharmonic Orchestra. Deutsche Grammophon
445515 [DDD] + Mendelssohn: Violin Concerto in E Minor

Perlman, Barenboim, Berlin Philharmonic Orchestra. EMI 54580 [DDD]

Perlman, Giulini, Chicago Symphony Orchestra. EMI 47166 [ADD]

Sitkovetsky, Marriner, Academy of St. Martin-in-the-Fields. Hänssler Classic
98.934 [DDD] + Mendelssohn: Violin Concerto in E Minor

Udagawa, Mackerras, London Symphony Orchestra. Chandos 8974 [DDD] +
Bruch: Violin Concerto No. 1

Zukerman, Mehta, Los Angeles Philharmonic Orchestra. RCA Victor Red Seal
68046 [DDD] + Bruch: Violin Concerto No. 1 (with London Philharmonic
Orchestra)

Concerto in A for Violin and Cello, Op. 102

This too was written for Joachim, but also for the cellist Robert Hausmann. And like
the violin concerto it had a dismal premiere, being denounced as "unplayable," "joyless,"
and "autumnal." Autumnal it surely is; the composer's final orchestral work, it is resigned
and reflective in tone throughout. Most modern audiences find it poignantly beautiful
rather than joyless.

Francescatti, Fournier, B. Walter, Columbia Symphony Orchestra. CBS
37237 [ADD] + *Tragic* Overture

Kaler, Kliegel, Constantine, National Symphony Orchestra of Ireland. Naxos
8.550938 [DDD] + Scumann: Cello Concerto

Kremer, Maisky, Bernstein, Vienna Philharmonic Orchestra. Deutsche
Grammophon 431031 [DDD] + Violin Concerto

Oistrakh, Fournier, Galliera, Philharmonia Orchestra. EMI Doublefforte
69331 [ADD] + Beethoven: Triple Concerto, Mozart: Violin Concerto No. 3,
Prokofiev: Violin Concerto No. 2

Oistrakh, Rostropovich, Szell, Cleveland Orchestra. EMI 66219 [ADD] +
Beethoven: Triple Concerto (plus Sviatoslav Richter, with Karajan conducting)

Stern, Ma, Abbado, Chicago Symphony Orchestra. Sony 42387 [DDD] +
Piano Quartet No. 3

——— *All CDs listed are considered approximately equal in (high) merit.* ———

German Requiem, Op. 45 (Ein Deutsches Requiem)

Inspired, if that is the word, by the death of his mother, this unique choral work established Brahms's fame at age 35. Unlike all other Requiems, this one is a prayer for the living instead of the dead. It eschews the traditional Latin Catholic text for sections of the Luther Bible chosen by Brahms himself; faith and consolation are the keynotes.

Gardiner, Orchestre Révolutionnaire et Romantique, Monteverdi Choir. Philips 432140 [DDD]
Herreweghe, La Chapelle Royale, Collegium Vocale, Orchestre des Champs Elysées. Harmonia Mundi 901608
Klemperer, Philharmonia Orchestra and Chorus. EMI 56218 [ADD]
Previn, Royal Philharmonic Orchestra, Ambrosian Singers. Teldec 75862 [DDD]

Hungarian Dances (orchestral versions)

Originally written for piano four-hands (i.e., piano duet, two pianists sitting at one instrument), these have become among the most familiar short works by Brahms in their orchestral transcriptions—sometimes by the composer, sometimes by others. They are perhaps not ideal for continuous listening, but they are essential to have around the house; play two or three every so often to get yourself going.

Bernstein, New York Philharmonic Orchestra. (Sel.) Sony 47572 [ADD] + Liszt: *Les Préludes, Hungarian Rhapsodies*; Enesco: *Romanian Rhapsody* No. 1
Bogár, Budapest Symphony Orchestra. (Complete) Naxos 8.550110 [DDD]
Karajan, Berlin Philharmonic Orchestra. (sel.) Deutsche Grammophon 447434 [ADD] + Dvořák: *Slavonic Dances* (sel.), *Scherzo capriccioso*
Kubelik, Royal Philharmonic Orchestra. (Sel.) EMI Seraphim 68256 (2) [ADD] + Violin Concerto (with Menuhin, Kempe, Berlin Philharmonic Orchestra); Symphony No. 4 (with Giulini, New Philharmonia Orchestra); *Haydn Variations* (with Giulini, Philharmonia Orchestra)
Ormandy, Philadelphia Orchestra. Nos. 17-21 only. Sony Essential Classics 48398 (3) [ADD] + Symphonies 1-4, *Academic Festival Overture*, *Tragic Overture*, *Haydn Variations* (Szell, Cleveland Orchestra)
Skrowaczewski, Hallé Orchestra. (sel.) Carlton Classics 6700272 [30367 00272] [DDD] + Symphony No. 4

———— CDs listed are solid, central choices, not necessarily "the greatest." ————

Quintet in B Minor for Clarinet and Strings, Op. 115

Among Brahms's last works are four inspired by his acquaintance with the clarinetist Mühlfeld. This quintet is among the composer's most sonorous and satisfying chamber works; the ecstatically trance-like slow movement is quintessentially "autumnal" Brahms.

De Peyer, Melos Ensemble. EMI 63116 [ADD] + Mozart: Clarinet Quintet
King, Gabrieli String Quartet. Classics for Pleasure Silver Double 4772 (2) [ADD] + Dvořák: Quartet No. 12 "American"; Borodin: Quartet No. 2; Schubert: Quartet No. 14 "Death and the Maiden"
Leister, Berlin Soloists. Teldec 48429 [DDD] + Mozart: Clarinet Quintet
Neidich, Juilliard String Quartet. Sony 66285 (2) [DDD] + String Quartets 1-3
Puddy, Delmé Quartet. Carlton Classics 6700972 [3036 700972] [DDD] + Dvořák: String Quartet No. 12 "American"
Shifrin, Chamber Music Northwest. Delos 3066 [DDD] + String Quintet in G, Op. 111
Stoltzman, Tokyo String Quartet. RCA Victor Red Seal 68033 [DDD] + Weber: Clarinet Quintet

Symphonies (4)

Nowhere is Brahms more successful than in his four famous symphonies in achieving his ideal of uniting 19th-century Romantic ideals with 18th-century Classical form. His speech is clearly post-Beethoven, yet his orchestration is far more restrained than Bruckner or Mahler, or even, much earlier, Berlioz. There are no Romantic "programs" in the Brahms symphonies, only "absolute" music. They rely on grand architecture, rich harmonization, dramatic force, and poetic melodies to achieve the synthesis that makes them the most admired of all Mainstream Romantic symphonies.

Complete Symphonies

Barenboim, Chicago Symphony Orchestra. Erato 94817 (4) [DDD] + *Haydn Variations, Tragic* Overture, *Academic Festival* Overture
Karajan, Berlin Philharmonic Orchestra. Deutsche Grammophon 427602 (3) [DDD] + *Tragic* Overture, *Haydn Variations*
Szell, Cleveland Orchestra. Sony Essential Classics 48398 (3) [ADD] + *Academic Festival* Overture, *Hungarian Dances, Tragic* Overture, *Haydn Variations*

——— *Some famous CDs are not listed because currently out of print.* ———

Wand, North German Radio Symphony Orchestra. RCA Victor Gold Seal 60085 (3) [DDD]

Symphony No. 1 in C Minor, Op. 68

Haunted by the imaginary tread of Beethoven behind him, Brahms was 43 when he got brave enough to try out a first symphony. To those who tried to hurry him he snapped: "A symphony is no joke." His fears were validated when the 1876 premiere was tepid. Critics harped on the similarity of the main theme of the last movement to that of the finale of Beethoven's Ninth. "Any fool," glowered Brahms, "can see that." Obviously he intended the resemblance as a symbolic launching point. Today its grandeur and nobility make it the most popular of his symphonies.

Karajan, Berlin Philharmonic Orchestra. Deutsche Grammophon Originals 447408 [ADD] + Schumann: Symphony No. 1
Klemperer, Philharmonia Orchestra. EMI Studio 69651 [ADD] + *Academic Festival* Overture, *Tragic* Overture
Norrington, London Classical Players. EMI 54286 [DDD] + *Haydn Variations*
Skrowaczewski, Hallé Orchestra. IMP [Carlton Classics] PCD 2014 [DDD] + *Academic Festival* Overture
B. Walter, Columbia Symphony Orchestra. CBS Odyssey 44827 [ADD]

Symphony No. 2 in D, Op. 73

Unusually genial for Brahms, the second symphony followed hard upon the long-delayed first, written just a year later at a holiday resort where presumably the sun-drenched waters contributed to its warm inspiration. Its premiere, unlike that of Symphony No. 1, was a complete success.

Abbado, Berlin Philharmonic Orchestra. Deutsche Grammophon 427643 [DDD] + *Alto Rhapsody*
Karajan, Berlin Philharmonic Orchestra. Deutsche Grammophon 429153 [ADD] + Symphony No. 3
Klemperer, Philharmonia Orchestra. EMI Studio 69650 [ADD] + *Alto Rhapsody*
Masur, New York Philharmonic Orchestra. Teldec 77291 [DDD] + *Academic Festival Overture*
B. Walter, Columbia Symphony Orchestra. Sony 64471 [ADD] + Symphony No. 3

———— Catalog numbers are subject to change without notice. ————

Symphony No. 3 in F, Op. 90

Several years passed before Brahms resumed his symphonic activity. He was now 50, and even commentators not given to reading things in have suggested that its subject is the struggle between youth and age. The premiere in 1883 was tumultuous, far beyond anything for the previous two symphonies, despite attempts by a Wagner clique to disrupt the performance. The mostly-stormy final movement is unusual in ending with a peaceful rainbow of sound.

Abbado, Berlin Philharmonic Orchestra. Deutsche Grammophon 429765 [DDD] + *Tragic* Overture, *Song of Destiny*
Haitink, Boston Symphony Orchestra. Philips 442120 + *Alto Rhapsody* (with Nes, Tanglewood Festival Chorus)
Karajan, Berlin Philharmonic Orchestra. Deutsche Grammophon 429153 [ADD] + Symphony No. 2
Karajan, Berlin Philharmonic Orchestra. Deutsche Grammophon Galleria 437645 [ADD] + Symphony No. 4
Klemperer, Philharmonia Orchestra. EMI Studio 69649 [ADD] + Symphony No. 4
Reiner, Chicago Symphony Orchestra. RCA Victor Gold Seal 61793 [ADD] + Schubert: Symphony No. 5; Mendelssohn: *Hebrides* Overture
Skrowaczewski, Hallé Orchestra. IMP [Carlton Classics] PCD 2039 [DDD] + *Haydn Variations*
B. Walter, Columbia Symphony Orchestra. Sony 64471 [ADD] + Symphony No. 2

Symphony No. 4 in E Minor, Op. 98

The final Brahms symphony is his most austere and Classical, often melancholy in mood, but never tragic. The last movement, a set of 30 variations with a magnificent conclusion, is a deliberate slap in the faces of some of Brahms's more loosely Romantic fellow-composers. Brahms himself conducted the first performance in 1885.

Abbado, Berlin Philharmonic Orchestra. Deutsche Grammophon 435349 [DDD] + *Haydn Variations, Nänie*
Bernstein, Vienna Philharmonic Orchestra. Deutsche Grammophon 445508 [DDD] + *Tragic* Overture
C. Davis, Bavarian Radio Symphony Orchestra. RCA Victor Red Seal 60383 [DDD]

───── *Since CDs can change label and number, use artists as main reference.* ─────

Giulini, New Philharmonia Orchestra. EMI Seraphim 68256 (2) [ADD] + Violin Concerto (with Menuhin, Kempe, Berlin Philharmonic Orchestra); *Haydn Variations* (with Giulini, Philharmonia Orchestra); *Hungarian Dances* (sel.) (with Kubelik, Royal Philharmonic Orchestra)

Karajan, Berlin Philharmonic Orchestra. Deutsche Gammophon Galleria 437645 [ADD] + Symphony No. 3

C. Kleiber, Vienna Philharmonic Orchestra. Deutsche Grammophon 400037 [DDD]

Klemperer, Philharmonia Orchestra. EMI Studio 69649 [ADD] + Symphony No. 3

Previn, Royal Philharmonic Orchestra. Telarc 82006 [DDD] + *Academic Festival* Overture

Skrowaczewski, Hallé Orchestra. Carlton Classics 6700272 [30367 00272] [DDD] + *Hungarian Dances* (sel.)

Szell, Cleveland Orchestra. Sony Essential Classics 46330 [ADD] + *Academic Festival* Overture, *Tragic* Overture

B. Walter, Columbia Symphony Orchestra. Sony 64472 [ADD] + *Tragic* Overture, *Song of Destiny*

Tragic Overture, Op. 81

Which tragedy? Oh, none in particular. Who else but morose old Brahms would think to write a generically tragic overture just for the fun of it? Actually, it was conceived as a more serious companion piece to the ebullient *Academic Festival* Overture, which Brahms may have worried was altogether too jocular for a man of his reputation.

Abbado, Berlin Philharmonic Orchestra. Deutsche Grammophon 429765 [DDD] + Symphony No. 3, *Song of Destiny*

Abbado, Berlin Philharmonic Orchestra. Deutsche Grammophon 435349 [DDD] + *Haydn Variations, Nänie*

Barenboim, Chicago Symphony Orchestra. Erato 94817 (4) [DDD] + Symphonies 1-4, *Haydn Variations, Academic Festival* Overture

Bernstein, Vienna Philharmonic Orchestra. Deutsche Grammophon 445508 [DDD] + Symphony No. 4

Haitink, Royal Concertgebouw Orchestra. Philips 438320 (2) + Piano Concertos Nos. 1, 2 (with Arrau), *Academic Festival* Overture, *Haydn Variations*

Karajan, Berlin Philharmonic Orchestra. Deutsche Grammophon 427602 (3) [DDD] + Symphonies Nos. 1-4, *Haydn Variations*

Klemperer, Philharmonia Orchestra. EMI 69651 [ADD] + Symphony No. 1, *Academic Festival* Overture

————— *Artists are listed alphabetically, not in order by critical ranking.* —————

Szell, Cleveland Orchestra. Sony Essential Classics 46330 [ADD] + *Academic Festival* Overture, Symphony No. 4

Szell, Cleveland Orchestra. Sony Essential Classics 48398 (3) [ADD] + Symphonies 1-4, *Academic Festival Overture, Hungarian Dances, Haydn Variations*

B. Walter, Columbia Symphony Orchestra. Sony 37237 [ADD] + Double Concerto

B. Walter, Columbia Symphony Orchestra. Sony 64472 [ADD] + Symphony No. 4, *Song of Destiny*

Trio in E-flat for Horn, Violin, and Piano, Op. 40

One of Brahms's most expressive chamber works, this unusual trio relies on the intrinsic nature of the French horn to create the desired atmosphere of Romantic nature-painting, tinged with gentle melancholy.

M. Thompson, Dubinsky, Edlina. Chandos 8606 [DDD] + Clarinet Trio

Tuckwell, Perlman, Ashkenazy. London [Decca] 414128 [ADD] + Franck: Violin Sonata

Variations on a Theme by Haydn, Op. 56a

This brilliant orchestral tour de force is far more entertaining than its dustily academic title portends. The theme, as modern muckrakers have discovered, isn't even by Haydn anyway, so forget about scholarship and just listen while Brahms takes this attractive (anonymous) melody and tosses it up and down and around the orchestra until it finally bounces joyfully into the blue.

Abbado, Berlin Philharmonic Orchestra. Deutsche Grammophon 435349 [DDD] + Symphony No. 4, *Nänie*

Barenboim, Chicago Symphony Orchestra. Erato 94817 (4) [DDD] + Symphonies 1-4, *Tragic* Overture, *Academic Festival* Overture

Giulini, Philharmonia Orchestra. EMI Seraphim 68256 (2) [ADD] + Violin Concerto (with Menuhin, Kempe, Berlin Philharmonic Orchestra); *Hungarian Dances* (sel.) (with Kubelik, Royal Philharmonic Orchestra); Symphony No. 4 (with Giulini, New Philharmonia Orchestra)

Haitink, Royal Concertgebouw Orchestra. Philips 438320 (2) + Piano Concertos Nos. 1, 2 (with Arrau), *Academic Festival* Overture, *Tragic* Overture

Karajan, Berlin Philharmonic Orchestra. Deutsche Grammophon 427602 (3) [DDD] + Symphonies Nos. 1-4, *Tragic* Overture

───── *[DDD] indicates newest recordings; [ADD] or [AAD] are reissues.* ─────

Loughran, Hallé Orchestra. Classics for Pleasure Silver Double 4766 (2) [ADD] + *Academic Festival* Overture; Piano Concertos Nos. 1, 2 (with Tirimo, Sanderling, Levi, London Philharmonic Orchestra)
Norrington, London Classical Players. EMI 54286 [DDD] + Symphony No. 1
Skrowaczewski, Hallé Orchestra. IMP [Carlton Classics] PCD 2039 [DDD] + Symphony No. 3
Szell, Cleveland Orchestra. Sony Essential Classics 48398 [ADD] + Symphonies 1-4, *Academic Festival* Overture, *Hungarian Dances, Tragic* Overture

Max Bruch (1838-1920)

Bruch seems, on paper, about as stuffy and conservative as a 19th-century German composer could get. Writing once about a new opera by his contemporary Hans Pfitzner—not exactly a liberal himself—Bruch called it "unspeakably despicable...the sad product of...a sick brain—of a super-aesthetic," adding that it was nothing more than "dismaying fantastic nonsense."

We might expect the music of such a backward-looking composer to be plodding and dull, yet he wrote two of the sprightliest works in the violin repertoire, and took an abiding interest in the national music of several cultures and incorporated elements of them into his own works. Not bad for a fuddy-duddy.

Bruch had a career as both conductor and conservatory teacher, but composing was his meat. In his long life of 82 years he wrote operas, symphonies, choral and chamber works, piano pieces. His best works are enlivened by a warmly ingratiating melodic style. He was also a skillful illusionist: those who hear his snappy Scottish Fantasy or his deeply soulful *Kol Nidrei* for the first time are equally surprised to learn that he was neither Scottish nor Jewish.

Concerto No. 1 in G Minor for Violin, Op. 26

Neither profound nor tightly organized, this beloved concerto gets by on enormous charm and surface beauty. If you stick up your nose at this sort of thing, stranger, pass by.

Chung, Tennstedt, Concertgebouw Orchestra. EMI 54072 + Beethoven: Violin Concerto
Francescatti, Mitropoulos, New York Philharmonic Orchestra; Ormandy, Philadelphia Orchestra. Sony Masterworks Heritage 62339 (2) (mono) [ADD] + Mendelssohn: Violin Concerto in E Minor; Saint-Saëns: Violin Concerto No. 3; Tchaikovsky: Violin Concerto; Prokofiev: Violin Concerto No. 2; Chausson: *Poème*

——— *CDs go in and out of print; availability of all listed items is not assured.* ———

Kennedy, Tate, English Chamber Orchestra. EMI 49663 [DDD] + Mendelssohn: Violin Concerto in E Minor; Schubert: Rondo

Menuhin, Frühbeck de Burgos, London Symphony Orchestra. EMI Seraphim 68524 (2) [ADD] + Mendelssohn: Violin Concerto in E Minor; Symphony No. 4, *Hebrides* Overture, *A Midsummer Night's Dream* Overture, *Ruy Blas* Overture (with Previn conducting)

Stern, Ormandy, Philadelphia Orchestra. CBS [Sony] 37811 [ADD] + Lalo: *Symphonie espagnole*

Udagawa, Mackerras, London Symphony Orchestra. Chandos 8974 [DDD] + Brahms: Violin Concerto

Wei, Bakels, Philharmonia Orchestra. ASV 680 [DDD] + Saint-Saëns: Violin Concerto No. 3

Zukerman, Mehta, London Philharmonic Orchestra. RCA Victor Red Seal 68046 [DDD] + Brahms: Violin Concerto (with Los Angeles Philharmonic Orchestra)

Anton Bruckner (1824-1896)

Bruckner was one of those people who make others cough, fidget, and leave the room when they enter. Possibly today we would label him an idiot savant. He barged around Vienna in rumpled clothes and mismatched socks, a shapeless figure with a shaved head, speaking in a rough rustic dialect.

He either did not know how to act, or simply never grew up. His manners were atrocious. He frequently proposed marriage to teenage girls, sometimes immediately after meeting them. When he met his hero, Richard Wagner, he fell on his knees before him and kissed his hand. When he was pleased with the rehearsal of one of his symphonies, he tipped the conductor a dollar. And when the Austrian Emperor asked if he could do anything for him, Bruckner nervously suggested that perhaps he could "take care of" the critic Hanslick, who made such merciless fun of his music.

Occasionally one of these inappropriate actions or remarks transcended itself, as when after the rehearsal of another of his symphonies, Bruckner ran up excitedly to the bored conductor and asked how he had liked it. The maestro coughed and fidgeted. "Very nice, Anton, very nice...but don't you think it's a little too long?" The composer's face turned livid. "No!" he shot back, "my symphony is not too long. You are too short!"

Bruckner came from the countryside in Upper Austria. His father, a schoolmaster and organist, died when Anton was 12. The boy was educated at a nearby monastery. He was a slow but determined learner, especially in music. When assigned to write an exercise in counterpoint, he would stay up all night and the next day turn in sheets full of examples.

Eventually he moved to Vienna, where he was able to secure a professorship at the Conservatory. He spent the rest of his life teaching, and trying, with limited success, to get

——— *Some CDs may be available only through importers.* ———

his music performed. He wrote a few fine choral works, but his focus was on the symphony. He wrote 11 of those altogether (the last imcomplete at his death), although they have such clear family resemblances that one of Bruckner's more withering critics claimed he had actually written only one symphony—nine times. (He said nine because that is how many are officially numbered. There were two very early works which Bruckner never meant to publish; they have been retrieved, revived, and re-numbered as the "Student" Symphony and Symphony No. "0.")

Once considered clumsily and ineptly written, the symphonies are more often now seen as uniquely original. Audiences and critics, as ploddingly slow as Bruckner himself, have gradually come to find in them a noble, even mystical, beauty. Those whose visual imaginations are stimulated by music generally interpret Bruckner's symphonic world as one of dark forests and mysteriously murmuring streams, which are now and then bathed in bursts of overwhelming radiance. Whether this is the light of the morning sun striking the peaks of Bruckner's beloved Alps, or the glory of the Catholic God in whom he so simply and devoutly believed, it is hard to say. Perhaps it is both.

Symphony No. 4 in E-flat, "Romantic"

Surely the nickname is redundant, but this is the shortest and most immediately accessible of Bruckner's symphonies: its sonorities are radiant, its structure compact, its mood joyful.

Abbado, Vienna Philharmonic Orchestra. Deutsche Grammophon 431719 [DDD]
Blomstedt, San Francisco Symphony. London [Decca] 443327 [DDD]
Jochum, Berlin Philadelphia Orchestra. Deutsche Grammophon 449718 [ADD] + Sibelius: *Night Ride and Sunrise*
Sawallisch, Philadelphia Orchestra. EMI 55119 [DDD]

Symphony No. 7 in E

Bruckner spent two years writing this symphony, the first composition by anyone to use a quartet of "Wagner tubas" outside of Wagner's own stage works. Well over an hour long, it is structurally complex but easy to listen to based on its beautiful melodic material. Bruckner claimed the principal theme was whistled to him in a dream by his friend Ignaz Dorn; he immediately woke up, lit a candle, and wrote it down!

Abbado, Vienna Philharmonic Orchestra. Deutsche Grammophon 437518 [DDD]
Barenboim, Berlin Philharmonic Orchestra. Teldec 77118 [DDD]

———— *U.S. labels and numbers are given first, U.K. in [brackets] when needed.* ————

Jochum, Dresden State Orchestra. EMI Doublefforte 68652 (2) [ADD] + Symphony No. 3

Karajan, Vienna Philharmonic Orchestra. Deutsche Grammophon "Karajan Gold" 439037 [DDD]

Masur, New York Philharmonic Orchestra. Teldec 97467 [DDD]

B. Walter, Columbia Symphony Orchestra. CBS [Sony] Odyssey 45669 (2) [ADD] + Symphony No. 5 (conducted by Eugene Ormandy)

Symphony No. 8 in C Minor

The composer took not two, but six years to work on this, his own choice for his greatest symphony. In its first revised version, both audience and critics greeted warmly the first performance on 18 December 1892. His fellow composer Hugo Wolf wrote that "this symphony is the creation of a giant." Even longer than No. 7, it concludes with one of the truly overpowering symphonic finales—a gradual and ever more splendiferous sunrise over the Alps. Or so it is in *my* dreams.

Giulini, Vienna Philharmonic Orchestra. Deutsche Grammophon Masters 445529 (2) [DDD]

Karajan, Vienna Philharmonic Orchestra. Deutsche Grammophon 427611 (2) [DDD]

Tennstedt, London Philharmonic Orchestra. EMI 64849 [DDD]

Wand, North German Radio Symphony Orchestra. RCA Victor Red Seal 68047 (2) [DDD]

Symphony No. 9 in D Minor

Bruckner died before completing this mystical, sometimes harsh and terrifying symphony, so that it concludes with an adagio movement. Its tonal structure is Bruckner's most forward-looking. Its premiere took place in 1903, several years after the composer's death, and even then it was considered necessary to revise the orchestration to make it more palatable. Today it is usually played unvarnished, in all its craggy grandeur.

Barenboim, Berlin Philharmonic Orchestra. Teldec 72140 [DDD]

Giulini, Vienna Philharmonic Orchestra. Deutsche Grammophon 427345 [DDD]

B. Walter, Columbia Symphony Orchestra. Sony 64483 [ADD]

———— *All CDs listed are considered approximately equal in (high) merit.* ————

Emmanuel Chabrier (1841-1894)

In his day, Chabrier was considered a talented amateur. He was, indeed, a civil servant, an employee of the Ministry of the Interior in Paris, but music was his true love, and at the age of 38, after seeing a performance of Wanger's *Tristan und Isolde*, he quit his job and devoted himself to composing.

And, to playing the piano—if "playing" is not too weak a word. Aflred Cortot called him "demolisher of pianos." Performing "à la Chabrier" came to mean indulging in what Vincent d'Indy described as "contrasting accents: pianissimi that became inaudible, then sudden explosions in the midst of the most exquisite softness." After a Chabrier recital, the corners of the keys were lilkely to be broken, and the lid scratched and gashed. "In his native town," Cortot reminisced, "they still remember his last visit, after which all the local pianos had to be repaired."

Enormously fat, Chabrier was equally expansive in wit and drollery. He was once accosted by Benjamin Godard, a composer of little talent whose sentimental pieces had some currency at the time. Said Godard, "What a pity, my dear Emmanuel, that you took to music so late." Replied Chabrier, "It is much more annoying, my dear Benjamin, that you took to it so early."

Chabrier's piano music was harmonically in advance of its time. Erik Satie and the members of *Les Six* acknowledged their debt to Chabrier, Ravel vastly admired him, and Poulenc called him "my spiritual grandfather." It is ironic, but perhaps not surprising, that Chabrier is most remembered today for one of his few orchestral works, *España*.

España

About a year after a stimulating trip to Spain, Chabrier concocted this brew of *jotas* and *malagueñas* which has become a mainstay of the light orchestral repertoire. British composer Constant Lambert went so far as to call *España* "the most perfectly orchestrated composition of the last century." Such a judgment is even more amazing when one knows that Chabrier had to teach himself orchestration by copying out Wagner's *Tannhäuser*!

Ansermet, Suisse Romande Orchestra. London [Decca] 443033 (2) [ADD] + Joyeuse marche; Saint-Saëns: *Danse macabre, La rouet d'Omphale*; Bizet: *Jeux d'enfants* (with Martinon, Paris Conservatory Orchestra); *L'Arlèsienne* Suites, *Carmen* Suites, Offenbach: *Gaité Parisienne* (with Munch, New Philharmonia Orchestra); Dukas: *The Sorcerer's Apprentice* (with Solti, Israel Philharmonic Orchestra)

———— CDs listed are solid, central choices, not necessarily "the greatest." ————

Ansermet, Suisse Romande Orchestra. London [Decca] Classic Sound 448576 [ADD] + Dukas: *The Sorcerer's Apprentice*; Debussy: *La Mer*; Honegger: *Pacific 231*; Ravel: *Boléro, La Valse*

Bernstein, New York Philharmonic Orchestra. CBS [Sony] 37769 [ADD] + Dukas: *Sorcerer's Apprentice*; Saint-Saëns: *Danse macabre*, Bacchanale from *Samson et Dalila*; Ravel: *Pavane for a Dead Princess*; Offenbach: Overture to *Orpheus in the Underworld*

Paray, Detroit Symphony Orchestra. Mercury 434303 [ADD] + other Chabrier pieces; Roussel: Suite in F

Tortelier, Ulster Orchestra. Chandos 8852 [DDD] + *Suite Pastorale*; Dukas: *La Péri, Sorcerer's Apprentice*

Ernest Chausson (1855-1899)

Chausson was the son of a wealthy construction contractor named (appropriately, perhaps) Prosper Chausson, who was prominent in the remodelling and reconstruction of Paris as advocated by Mayor Haussman in the mid-19th century. Ernest's two brothers died young and he was doted on, being educated at home by private tutors and introduced into the most fashionable salons by age 15.

He quickly developed a taste for all the fine arts. At first he divided his attention among music, painting, and literature, but by age 24 he entered the Paris Conservatory and settled on a career as composer. He studied with Massenet and attended lectures given by Franck. But it was the then-new and exciting music of Wagner that gripped his imagination. Chausson's few surviving compositions bear the marks of all these influences, and yet have a distinctive sound of their own.

He was just beginning to hit his stride when an accident took his life. He was riding a bicycle down a hill when he lost control and hit a brick wall. He was only 44 years old. Many years later, in 1936, his widow auctioned off some of his collection of paintings. There were major works by Gauguin, Manet, Degas, Corot, and Delacroix which today would sell for many millions of dollars. This composer's life was tragically short, but at least he did not suffer like so many others the shame and agony of poverty.

Poème for Violin and Orchestra, Op. 25

Inspired by his teacher Franck's theories of cyclical form, the haunting *Poème* is Chausson's best-known work and has been danced as a ballet.

Francescatti, Mitropoulos, New York Philharmonic Orchestra; Ormandy, Philadelphia Orchestra. Sony Masterworks Heritage 62339 (2) (mono)

——— *Some famous CDs are not listed because currently out of print.* ———

[ADD] + Mendelssohn: Violin Concerto in E Minor; Bruch: Violin Concerto No. 1; Saint-Saëns: Violin Concerto No. 3; Tchaikovsky: Violin Concerto; Prokofiev: Violin Concerto No. 2

Perlman, Martinon, Orchestre de Paris. EMI 47725 [DDD] + Ravel: *Tzigane*; Saint-Saëns: *Havanaise, Rondo and Introduction Capriccioso*

Perlman, Mehta, New York Philharmonic Orchestra. Deutsche Grammophon 423063 [DDD] + Saint-Saëns: *Havanaise, Introduction and Rondo Capriccioso*; Ravel: *Tzigane*; Sarasate: *Carmen Fantasy*

Tortelier (violin and conductor), Ulster Orchestra. Chandos 8952 [DDD] + *Poème de l'amour et de la mer*; Fauré: *Pelléas et Mélisande, Pavane*

Symphony in B-flat, Op. 20

While picking up where Franck's only symphony leaves off, Chausson's only symphony is spiced with Wagnerisms yet highly individual. It is both melodious and dramatic.

Fournet, Netherlands Symphony Orchestra. Denon 73675 [DDD] + Faure: *Pelléas et Mélisande*

Mata, Dallas Symphony Orchestra. Dorian 90181 [DDD] + Ibert: *Escales, Divertissement*

Munch, Boston Symphony Orchestra. RCA Victor Gold Seal 60683 [ADD] + Saint-Saëns: *Introduction and Rondo Capriccioso* (with D. Oistrakh)

Léo Delibes (1836-1891)

Delibes was a star pupil at the Paris Conservatory, winning a first prize at the age of 14. At 17 he secured the first of several appointments as church organist which supported him, along with accompanying on the piano at the Théâtre Lyrique opera house, until 1871, when he was at last able to live off the revenues of his compositions.

His first breakthrough was the ballet *Coppélia* (1870). Another few years brought success with the ballet *Sylvia*, and the opera *Lakme*. His charming music plumbs no depths, but shows a talent beyond the routine as well as a masterly grasp of orchestration, albeit conventional. His ballets had an enormous influence on Tchaikovsky, who in fact expressed a preference for the music of Delibes over that of Brahms; and years later, that other great Russian ballet composer, Igor Stravinsky, rated Delibes higher than Beethoven on a list of great melodists! (Nowadays it is a struggle to get a music critic to rate Delibes over Gounod.)

Catalog numbers are subject to change without notice.

Coppélia Suite; Sylvia Suite

Coppélia and *Sylvia* are very high peaks in the 19th-century range of ballets, with ravishing melodies ravishingly scored. Suites from either or both of them make a concentrated case for their beauties.

Karajan, Berlin Philharmonic Orchestra. Deutsche Grammophon Galleria 429163 [ADD] + Offenbach: *Gaité Parisienne*; Chopin: *Les Sylphides*
Ormandy, Philadelphia Orchestra. Sony Essential Classics 46550 [ADD] + Tchaikovsky: *Nutcracker* Suite; Chopin: *Les Sylphides*

Antonín Dvořák (1841-1904)

Dvořák was the eldest of eight children born to the innkeeper and sausage-maker František Dvořák and his wife Anna, a former servingmaid in a lord's castle, in the picturesque town of Nelahozeves, 30 miles north of Prague. His family were socially humble, but intelligent, loving, and hardworking—qualities the musically talented Antonín inherited and never lost.

"I would gladly give all my symphonies," he once said, "had I been able to invent the locomotive!" He was a railroad buff, a pigeon breeder, a nature lover, a card player, a connoisseur of sausages, and a devoted family man. He almost did give away his symphonies, but not for a train; he was so absent-minded he forgot his first four symphonies. They were rediscovered one by one, beginning as late as 1923, and until very recent years even the enormously popular "New World" Symphony, now known as No. 9, was listed as No. 5.

Dvořák began playing the fiddle as a small boy, and sang in the church choir. Soon he was picking up the viola, piano, and organ too. His doting father hoped against hope that Antonín would become a butcher, and by age 15 he had indeed advanced from apprentice to journeyman in that trade; but at last, prodded by the boy's admiring teacher, František conceded that music was his son's true calling, and let him go off to the capital to study.

Slowly Antonín made his methodical way up the musical ladder, playing in orchestras throughout his 20s, and trying his hand at composing. Many of these early works ended up in the fireplace—or like those first four symphonies, in the closet. By his 30s he had won the admiration of several influential musicians, most notably Johannes Brahms, who remained a lifelong friend and supporter. Until recent years Dvořák was often characterized as a kind of "peasant Brahms," as if he were forever condemned to be second-rate. Brahms himself never thought any such thing. "I'd be delighted," he said to a Dvořák detractor, "to think up a main theme as good as those that Dvořák has discarded."

Dvořák's essentially gentle life was marred now and then by tragedy. The worst year was 1876, when his first three children all died of various diseases within a few months of each other. Stunned by grief, Dvořák worked through his feelings in a moving setting of the *Stabat Mater,* the medieval poem in which Mary contemplates the sacrifice of her son on the cross. The work is a testimony to the composer's emotional stability and deep faith.

He was 50 years old before he was fully recognized even in his native Bohemia, and he had had to pave the way in the previous decade with six trips to England, where his warm personality and rich melodic gift were more readily appreciated. Better known to Americans are the three years he spent in the U.S., beginning in 1892, as director of the (now defunct) New York National Conservatory of Music.

His summer vacations were spent in the hamlet of Spillville, Iowa, where a band of immigrants had created a charming slice of Bohemia in America. The town is still on the map, and a day's side trip to visit the Dvořák museum and other quaint attractions is well worth a music lover's time. After 20 years, I still fondly remember consuming corn fritters served on red-and-white-checked oilcloth-covered tables at the Czech Inn, while outside in the town square a uniformed band played in the gazebo.

I felt Dvořák's spirit very much alive in the New World.

Carnival Overture, Op. 92

Although programmatic music was not Dvořák's forte, he attempted a few overtures with story lines. The only one that has won wide popularity is *Carnival,* an irresistibly boisterous picture of a Slavic fair.

Farrer, Royal Philharmonic Orchestra. ASV 794 [DDD] + *In Nature's Realm, Othello, Scherzo capriccioso, Symphonic Variations*
Reiner, Chicago Symphony Orchestra. RCA Living Stereo 62587 [ADD] + Symphony No. 9; Smetana: *Bartered Bride* Overture; Weinberger: *Polka and Fugue* from *Schwanda the Bagpiper*
Szell, Cleveland Orchestra. CBS [Sony] 36716 + Smetana: Dances from *The Bartered Bride, The Moldau*

Concerto in B Minor for Cello, Op. 104

Had he written nothing else, Dvořák would be considered a genius for this greatest of all cello concerti. Brahms is said to have given up an idea to write a similar work after hearing this one. Not only is its melodic material exquisite, but at every turn Dvořák has ingeniously sidestepped or conquered the inherent problem of hearing the solo cello over a full orchestra.

——— *Artists are listed alphabetically, not in order by critical ranking.* ———

Cohen, Macal, London Philharmonic Orchestra. Classics for Pleasure Silver
Doubles 4775 (2) [ADD/DDD] + Beethoven: Triple Concerto; Elgar: Cello
Concerto; Tchaikovsky: *Rococo Variations*

P. Fournier, Szell, Berlin Philharmonic Orchestra. Deutsche Grammophon
Resonance 429155 [ADD] + Bloch: *Schelomo*; Bruch: *Kol Nidrei*

Ma, Maazel, Berlin Philharmonic Orchestra. CBS 42206 [DDD] + *Rondo
Capriccioso, Silent Woods*

Rostropovich, Karajan, Berlin Philharmonic Orchestra. Deutsche
Grammophon Originals 447413 [ADD] + Tchaikovsky: *Rococo Variations*

H. Schiff, C. Davis, Congertgebouw Orchestra. Philips Solo 442401 [ADD] +
Symphony No. 9 (with Dorati conducting)

Quartet No. 12 in F, Op. 96, "American"

It took Dvořák only two weeks to write the most popular of his 14 string quartets,
during one of his summers in Spillville. He is said to have taken great interest in the music
of a band of American Indians visiting the town, and may have incorporated some features
into this and others of his works written in the U.S., although one is hard-pressed to make
much distinction between Indian folk scales or rhythms and those of Bohemia, or anywhere else. Only direct quotations of specific melodies would prove the case, and this
Dvořák did not provide.

Alban Berg Quartet. EMI 54215 + Smetana: String Quartet No. 1

Delmé Quartet. Carlton Classics 6700972 [3036 700972] [DDD] + Brahms:
Clarinet Quintet

Gabrieli String Quartet. Classics for Pleasure Silver Double 4772 (2) [ADD] +
Borodin: Quartet No. 2; Brahms: Clarinet Quintet; Schubert: Quartet No. 14
"Death and the Maiden"

Guarneri Quartet. RCA Gold Seal 6263 [ADD] + Piano Quintet in A, Op. 81
(with Artur Rubinstein)

Lindsay Quartet. ASV 797 [DDD] + Quartet No. 13

Slavonic Dances, Opp. 46, 72

Dvořák's two sets of *Slavonic Dances*, written first for piano duet and then orchestrated, were directly inspired by the similar *Hungarian Dances* of Brahms. Success of the first
set was directly responsible for establishing Dvořák's fame outside of Bohemia. Eight years
passed before he got around to satisfying his salivating publisher with the second group.

—— [DDD] indicates newest recordings; [ADD] or [AAD] are reissues. ——

Dohnányi, Cleveland Orchestra. London [Decca] 430171 [DDD]
Karajan, Berlin Philharmonic Orchestra. (sel.) Deutsche Grammophon 447434 [ADD] + *Scherzo capriccioso;* Brahms: *Hungarian Dances* (sel.)
Szell, Cleveland Orchestra. (4) CBS [Sony] 36716 [ADD] + *Carnival* Overture; Smetana: *The Moldau,* Dances from *The Bartered Bride*
Szell, Cleveland Orchestra. (2) EMI Doublefforte 69509 (2) [ADD] + Symphony No. 8; Beethoven: Piano Concerto No. 5 (with Gilels), Variations

Symphony No. 7 in D Minor, Op. 70

This is the first of Dvořák's nine symphonies to achieve unquestioned parity with the great masters, and many critics still consider it his best, although Nos. 8 and 9 are more popular with the public. Dvořák was consciously working here to be serious and to employ strict symphonic logic; what the less intellectual listener misses is the customary profusion of Bohemian folk-like melodies.

Dohnányi, Cleveland Orchestra. London [Decca] 430728 [DDD] + Symphony No. 8
Dorati, London Symphony Orchestra. Mercury Living Presence 434312 [ADD] + Symphony No. 8
Jansons, Oslo Philharmonic Orchestra. EMI 54663 [DDD] + Symphony No. 8
Pešek, Royal Liverpool Philharmonic Orchestra. Virgin Classics 59516 [DDD] + Symphony No. 8
Previn, Los Angeles Philharmonic Orchestra. Telarc 80173 [DDD] + My Home overture

Symphony No. 8 in G, Op. 88

After the critical success of No. 7, Dvořák seems to relax and write a more folksy symphony for his own enjoyment. Infused throughout with Bohemian rustic idioms, No. 8 is the sunniest and most lovable of them all.

Barbirolli, Hallé Orchestra. EMI 64193 [ADD] + *Scherzo capriccioso, Legends* (3)
Dohnányi, Cleveland Orchestra. London [Decca] 430728 [DDD] + Symphony No. 7
Dorati, London Symphony Orchestra. Mercury Living Presence 434312 [ADD] + Symphony No. 7

Jansons, Oslo Philharmonic Orchestra. EMI 54663 [DDD] + Symphony No. 7

Neumann, Czech Philharmonic Orchestra. Supraphon 7703 [DDD]

Pešek, Royal Liverpool Philharmonic Orchestra. Virgin Classics 59516 [DDD] + Symphony No. 7

Szell, Cleveland Orchestra. EMI Doublefforte 69509 (2) [ADD] + 2 *Slavonic Dances*; Beethoven: Piano Concerto No. 5 (with Gilels), Variations

B. Walter, Columbia Symphony Orchestra. Sony 64484 [ADD] + Symphony No. 9

Symphony No. 9 in E Minor, Op. 95, "From the New World"

Musicologists have shouted themselves hoarse reminding us that the only thing truly New Worldish about Dvořák's best-known symphony is its title, and the fact that it was written in Spillville, Iowa. Dvořák himself warned an early note-writer: "Leave out all that nonsense about my having made use of original American melodies. I have only composed in the spirit of such melodies."

None of this has stopped American audiences from feeling strongly that there is something uniquely native about this music, and uncountable listeners still believe the haunting theme of the second movement is an authentic Negro spiritual called "Goin' Home," although it was first published as such 18 years after Dvořák's death!

Dorati, Congertgebouw Orchestra. Philips Solo 442401 [ADD] + Cello Concerto (with H. Schiff, C. Davis)

Kertész, Vienna Philharmonic Orchestra. London [Decca] Weekend Classics 417678 [AAD] + Smetana: *The Moldau*

Macal, London Philharmonic Orchestra. Classics for Pleasure 9006 [DDD] + *Symphonic Variations*

Reiner, Chicago Symphony Orchestra. RCA Living Stereo 62587 [ADD] + *Carnival* Overture; Smetana: *Bartered Bride* Overture; Weinberger: *Polka and Fugue* from *Schwanda the Bagpiper*

B. Walter, Columbia Symphony Orchestra. Sony 64484 [ADD] + Symphony No. 8

Symphonies 7, 8, 9

In addition to the above, the last three Dvořák symphonies are often available in one handy two-disc set. For example:

——— Some CDs may be available only through importers. ———

C. Davis, Amsterdam Concertgebouw Orchestra. Philips Duo 438347 (2)
[ADD] + *Symphonic Variations*
Dohnányi, Cleveland Orchestra. London [Decca] 421082 (2) [DDD]
Neumann, Czech Philharmonic Orchestra. Supraphon 11-0559 (2) [DDD]

César Franck (1822-1890)

As the spelling of his surname hints, Franck was a Walloon–a French-speaking Belgian, an ethnic group traditionally mocked, if not despised, by pedigreed French. Nevertheless, Franck made his career in Paris playing the organ, teaching, and composing. Condescendingly tolerated by the musical establishment as a naively pious "pater seraphicus," he exerted an almost mystical hold over a small but significant band of devotees including d'Indy, Chausson, and Duparc.

The unpleasant French habit of lampooning Belgians was actually abetted by Franck's serene imperviousness to criticism, and resulted in an unusually large number of spiteful remarks being directed at this gentle soul. His fellow composer Charles Gounod pronounced Franck's Symphony in D Minor to be "the affirmation of impotence pushed to dogma." Another rival, Saint-Saëns, sniped of his *Prelude, Chorale and Fugue* that "the chorale is not a chorale, and the fugue not a fugue." Disregarding all this, Franck calmly went about his work, following his own muse, and saying nothing derogatory about anybody, including his detractors.

He was born in Liège (now in Belgium, then in the Netherlands) and showed musical talent early, especially on the piano. His father pushed him to become a virtuoso, but his studies at the Paris Conservatory led him to a lifelong love of the organ. This instrument thereafter dominated his life: he loved nothing more than sitting in the loft, dreaming over the keys, or quietly discussing it with, or teaching it to, his students. His composing was limited to spare moments, and even his orchestral works, like Bruckner's, often betray the influence of his devotion to organ technique.

He was a bit like Bruckner in other ways as well: his clothes were ill-fitting, he grimaced to himself as he hurried nervously down the street, he was absent-minded and sometimes embarrassingly childlike. If no one showed up for his classes at the Conservatory he might stop by Massenet's classroom, pop his head in the door and plaintively ask "Isn't there anyone for me?" All of this only made him more lovable to his clique of followers. Known as *la bande à Franck*, they believed in him as a musical prophet, based primarily on his development of "cyclic form," and thought of him as a saintly father.

Philip Hale once wrote of Franck that he "went through this life as a dreamer, seeing little or nothing of that which passed about him, thinking only of his art, and living only for it." Perhaps this contributed to his death, for one April day in 1890 Franck was struck by a bus while he was scurrying to the house of a student to give a lesson. He picked himself up and went on with the lesson, but his health began to deteriorate and several months later he died of complications from the accident. In his last days, with his devoted students around him, the ever-solicitous "angelic father" murmured "My children! My poor children!"

Sonata in A for Violin and Piano

In his time Franck was best known for his organ music, and indeed his compositions for organ are ranked next to those of Bach. All the stranger then that his lone sonata for violin and piano should outshadow in fame everything but his notorious symphony. Written in 1886, it is always melodically memorable, often rhythmically exciting, and occasionally structurally innovative.

Chung, Lupu. London [Decca] 421154 [ADD] + pieces by Debussy and Ravel
Grumiaux, Hajdu. *The Best of César Franck*, Philips Duo 442296 (2) [ADD] + Symphony in D Minor, *Symphonic Variations, Les Eolides*, organ works
Perlman, Ashkenazy. London [Decca] 414128 [ADD] + Brahms: Horn Trio, short works by Saint-Saëns and Schumann

Symphony in D Minor

Few beloved symphonies have been more maligned than this one. Beginning with the premiere in 1889, critics have carped that the opening theme is a ripoff of either Beethoven's String Quartet No. 16 or (!) Liszt's *Les Préludes*, the themes are too chromatic (too many sharps and flats), the spaces between the notes in the themes are too close together, the themes are too similar to each other, there are only three movements instead of the usual four, the cyclical structure is awkward and artificial, the orchestration is too thick and unimaginative, and worst of all for those at the first performance: an English horn is used in the second movement! Such an unthinkable thing had never been done. The critics shouted during the music, the audience booed, even the players in the orchestra booed. Leaving the concert hall, Franck (who was nothing if not placid) commented only: "It sounded just as I thought it would."

In the papers the next day the symphony was variously described as dismal, morose, graceless, and even immoral. Critics still make fun of it, but audiences have come to love it for reasons critics seem incapable of understanding: most people listen to what the composer is saying, not the mechanics of how he is saying it. Once audiences got the point, that it is a symphony analogous to a bud which slowly but inexorably uncoils until it blossoms into a sun-drenched rose, they found it beautiful. So may you, if you don't over-analyze it.

Dutoit, Montreal Symphony Orchestra. London [Decca] 430278 [DDD] + d'Indy: *Symphony on a French Mountain Air*

———— *All CDs listed are considered approximately equal in (high) merit.* ————

Maazel, Berlin Radio Symphony Orchestra. Deutsche Grammophon 449720
[ADD} + Mendelssohn: Symphony No. 5
Monteux, Chicago Symphony Orchestra. RCA Victor Gold Seal 6805 [ADD]
+ d'Indy: *Symphony on a French Mountain Air*; Berlioz: Overture to *Béatrice et
Bénedict* (with Munch, Boston Symphony Orchestra)
Otterloo, Amsterdam Concertgebouw Orchestra. *The Best of César Franck*,
Philips Duo 442296 (2) [ADD] + Violin Sonata, *Symphonic Variations, Les
Eolides*, organ works
Paray, Detroit Symphony Orchestra. Mercury Living Presence 434368 [ADD]
+ Rachmaninov: Symphony No. 2

Edvard Grieg (1843-1907)

Grieg is the most famous Norwegian nationalist composer. Ironically, he was of half-Scottish descent, found his principal musical inspiration in Denmark, and employed only a handful of genuine folk tunes in the hundreds of pieces that audiences assume are ethnically authentic. It was Grieg's genius to create a musical fingerprint that signified the Norwegian spirit–minus jingoism—to all the world, while remaining almost wholly original.

His mother, an accomplished pianist, began training him from the age of six, and he wrote his first piece at age nine. Later he studied at the Leipzig Conservatory, where Arthur Sullivan, the future collaborator with Gilbert, was a classmate. After a few years going back and forth to Denmark, where Copenhagen's leading composer, Niels Gade, encouraged him, he settled down once and for all in Norway.

He was all of 23 years old when he founded the Norwegian Academy of Music. Only two years later, with 39 years of life ahead of him, he wrote his masterpiece, the Piano Concerto in A Minor. Subsequently he largely restricted himself to the smaller forms, principally songs and short piano pieces, which gained him his permanent, if not entirely accurate, reputation as a miniaturist, as well as the even less appropriate nickname of "the Chopin of the North."

Although his incidental music for Ibsen's play *Peer Gynt* is his other best-known work, connoisseurs would point to his exquisitely crafted, poetically expressive Norwegian songs as perhaps his most significant achievement. Unfortunately, these have little currency outside of Norway.

Despite frail health he made frequent tours abroad to promote Norwegian music, including that of other composers. A man of principle and courage, he was the only famous musician to speak out publicly in defense of Alfred Dreyfus when that military officer was being railroaded by French anti-Semites. A letter of support from Grieg was printed in newspapers across Europe, and he himself became an object of ugly prejudice: one piece of hate mail arrived marked "To the Composer of Jewish music, Edvard Grieg."

——— *CDs listed are solid, central choices, not necessarily "the greatest."* ———

He suffered also from critical barbs. In his time, and even to this day, a large portion of the critical establishment gave Grieg's music short shrift. George Bernard Shaw dismissed *Peer Gynt* as "two or three catchpenny phrases served up with plenty of orchestral sugar." Claude Debussy said Grieg's music had the taste of "a pink bonbon filled with snow." But if his works sometimes lent themselves to sentimental exploitation, it was not the composer's intention. "It is surely no fault of mine," Grieg once snapped, "that my music is heard in third-rate restaurants, and from schoolgirls."

For the most part however, Grieg lived a quiet and uneventful life with his beloved wife Nina, a talented singer for whom most of his songs were written, at their idyllic home, Troldhaugen ("Hill of the Trolls") a few miles from Bergen, until his death at age 64. By then he had written a large body of quintessentially Romantic pieces in a warmly lyrical style, accumulated countless awards and honors, and won the love of both his countrymen and the world. His was a life devoid of grandiose theatrics, exhibiting instead an even temper, a becoming modesty, and a noble humanity.

Concerto in A Minor for Piano, Op. 16

Grieg was but 25 when he wrote his only piano concerto, and it shows. Its structure is partly cribbed from Schumann's concerto (in the same key), the various sections are awkwardly joined together, repeats and restatements are reproduced verbatim without even minimal alterations to increase interest. But nobody cares about such academic concerns (except, of course, academics); what people hear are the fresh melodies and the enchantment of their poetry. It has become the very prototype of the Romantic Piano Concerto, and Sergei Rachmaninov, for one, considered it the greatest ever written.

Andsnes, Kitaenko, Bergen Philharmonic Orchestra. Virgin Classics 59613 [DDD] + 6 Lyric Pieces, Op. 65; Liszt: Piano Concerto No. 2
Derwinger, Hirokami, Norrköping Symphony Orchestra. (Original version) BIS 585 [DDD] + solo piano pieces
Jandó, Ligeti, Budapest Symphony Orchestra. Naxos 8.550118 [DDD] + Schumann: Piano Concerto
Perahia, C. Davis, Bavarian Radio Symphony Orchestra. Sony 44899 [DDD] + Schumann: Piano Concerto
Vogt, Rattle, City of Birmingham Symphony Orchestra. EMI 54746 [DDD] + Schumann: Piano Concerto

Peer Gynt Suites Nos. 1, 2, Opp. 46, 55

Henrik Ibsen himself invited Grieg, then aged 31, to write the incidental music for his folk drama *Peer Gynt*. Intimidated at first, Grieg gradually warmed to the commission, pro-

—— *Some famous CDs are not listed because currently out of print.* ——

ducing 22 musical numbers. Most people become familiar with the score through the two suites Grieg made for concert hall use. Although "Solvejg's Song" and "Ase's Death" were the composer's favorite excerpts, the public has chosen "Morning" and "In the Hall of the Mountain King."

> **Beecham, Royal Philharmonic Orchestra.** EMI 64751 + Symphonic Dance No. 2, Overture "In Autumn"
> **Gunzenhauser, CSSR State Philharmonic Orchestra of Kosicke.** Naxos 8.550140 [DDD] + 2 Lyric Pieces, *Sigurd Jorsalfar* Suite, *Wedding Day at Troldhaugen*
> **Järvi, Gothenburg Symphony Orchestra.** Deutsche Grammophon 427807 [DDD] + Sigurd *Jorsalfar* Suite, *Lyric* Suite
> **Karajan, Berlin Philharmonic Orchestra.** Deutsche Grammophon 419474 [DDD] + *Holberg* Suite, *Sigurd Jorsalfar* Suite

Edouard Lalo (1823-1892)

Lalo is today considered one of the least of "the great composers," not because he wrote bad music, but because he was never quite in step with fashion, and seldom made the most practical decisions as to what direction to take in his career. At age 16, determined to make music his life, and defying his military father, he ran off to Paris and enrolled at the Conservatory. Poverty, disillusion with the formalism of his lessons, and inability to get his compositions published led to years of despair. He was 43 when he fell in love with one of his students, an excellent singer who inspired him to try, try again. After another seven years he finally had his first success, and three years still later became widely known for his *Symphonie espagnole*, which was admired greatly by Tchaikovsky.

Almost at once he was awarded the Legion of Honor (Chevalier, and a few years later, Officer) and became a respected figure in the French music world, known for his great air of dignity which was enhanced by a gravely handsome face, snowy hair and beard, and natty apparel. It was not long, however, before an attack of paralysis led to a gradual decline in his health, aggravated by bouts of depression and a conviction that his art was being unjustly neglected.

Known as a progressive in his time–brief as that was—he was a man of almost ascetic artistic idealism who tried to avoid the routine and the merely eccentric with equal determination. His musical expression was delicate, tasteful, and beautifully orchestrated. He repeatedly refused to take the easy path to fame and fortune; urged by a friend to turn out boilerplate ballet music (wildly popular in the France of his time), he snapped that he had no interest in "concocting bonbons." And yet the music he did write, brilliantly colored and rhythmically "exotic," seems thoroughly conservative, sometimes even conventional, in hindsight. Everyone agrees it is "pretty," but in the world of the arts that is a damning

——— *Catalog numbers are subject to change without notice.* ———

adjective. More than a century after his death, Lalo is still without the wide recognition he so deeply desired.

Symphonie espagnole for Violin and Orchestra, Op. 21

The one work that has kept Lalo's name alive reflects, perhaps, some of the Spanish blood that was flowing in his veins. It is a highly colored, melodious work in five movements–not really a symphony, but a sort of hybrid between a concerto and an orchestral suite.

Chang, Dutoit, Concertgebouw Orchestra. EMI 55292 [DDD] + Vieuxtemps: Violin Concerto No. 5

Chee-Yun, López-Cobos, London Philharmonic Orchestra. Denon 18017 [DDD] + Saint-Saëns: Violin Concerto No. 3

Little, Handley, Royal Scottish National Orchestra. EMI Eminence 2277 [DDD] + Bruch: *Scottish Fantasy*

Perlman, Barenboim, Orchestre de Paris. Deutsche Grammophon 445549 [DDD] + Saint-Saëns: Violin Concerto No. 3; Berlioz: *Rêverie et Caprice*

Stern, Ormandy, Philadelphia Orchestra. CBS [Sony] 37811 [ADD] + Bruch: Violin Concerto No. 1

Franz Liszt (1811-1886)

Liszt was about seven or eight people rolled into one: piano virtuoso, composer, conductor, music teacher, author, man of the cloth, notorious lover, and all-around unforgettable character. No one else in the history of classical music was more rabidly Romantic, more outrageous, more controversial, more energetic, more downright amazing. Asked late in life if he had written his memoirs, Liszt replied "It is enough to have lived such a life as mine."

He invented the "tone poem," a short orchestral form of liberal construction meant to picture or apostrophize a poetic, literary, or historical subject. He originated a type of composition based on "transformation of themes" which went against the established dogmas and influenced dozens of composers after him. He was the first to give solo piano recitals (in fact, the term "recital" probably was his coinage), and the first to perform at the piano in "profile position."

Despite his many notorious liaisons with high-titled women, accompanied by duels, attempted poisonings, and grotesque adventures outlandish enough to fill a dozen purple novels, Liszt's significance to history is principally as a pianist. He was said by everyone who heard him—and that was half of Europe—to be the greatest pianist who ever lived, and although there are no recordings to document that claim, most scholars are still convinced of

——— Since CDs can change label and number, use artists as main reference. ———

it. With his long hair and demonic good looks, he had women swooning at his concerts, but despite an excess of showmanship there was real substance to his musical style. He was apparently able to sight-read almost anything, playing it on a read-through with a mixture of spontaneity and depth, chatting the while to ladies right and left of the piano.

Born in Hungary of German parents but French in taste and upbringing, Liszt became a man of the world, yet with yearnings toward spirituality. A fantastic pastiche of colorful contradictions, he was a cosmopolite and sybarite in whose music we find the wildness of the gypsy, the solemnity of the abbé, and sometimes an astonishing avant-gardism that points far down the road of musical evolution.

One of his most admirable traits was a genuine interest in encouraging young musical talent. He gave unstintingly of money and moral support to a host of other developing musicians, most famously Richard Wagner, who was to become his son-in-law by marrying his daughter Cosima (after stealing her from her rightful husband, but that is another story).

More than a hundred years after his death, Liszt has yet to take an unassailable place in the pantheon of greatest composers. Much of his music—that, unfortunately, which is best known—is marred by bombast, yet there are pages of the most refined delicacy which are far less often heard. Looking back, there still seem to be several Franz Liszts, and few are prepared even now to say which one, if any, is the one whom a more distant posterity will honor.

Concertos (2) for Piano and Orchestra

Although the Piano Concerto No. 1 in E-flat is dramatic in tone, and No. 2 in A is moody and reflective, both of them have so many other features in common that they are often spoken of almost as twins. Each is cast in a single continuous movement and is developed through Liszt's principle of the "transformation of themes." Both were sketched in the 1830s, but not finished and premiered until 1855 and 1857 respectively, Liszt soloing in the first, then conducting in the second. Although they were frankly designed to show off Liszt's virtuosity, they contain poetry as well, if the performer and listener will both pay attention. The following listings are restricted to recordings that have both concertos on one album:

Ax, Salonen, Philharmonia Orchestra. Sony 53289 [DDD] +Schoenberg: Piano Concerto

Richter, Kondrashin, London Symphony Orchestra. Philips Solo 446200 (2) [ADD] + Sonata in B Minor

Zimerman, Ozawa, Boston Symphony Orchestra. Deutsche Grammophon 423571 [DDD] + *Totentanz*

——— *Artists are listed alphabetically, not in order by critical ranking.* ———

Hungarian Rhapsodies (orchestral versions) (6)

After making a serious study of Hungarian folk music for several years, Liszt undertook to write 19 piano rhapsodies based on his understanding of gypsy idioms, characteristically alternating between the poles of *lassan* (slow voluptuous music) and *friskan* (fast voluptuous music). Subsequently he (and Franz Doppler) orchestrated six of these; only beware, the numbers attached to the orchestral versions are not the same as the piano versions. By far the most famous is (orchestral) No. 2, a masterpiece of fiery abandon.

Bernstein, New York Philharmonic Orchestra. (Sel.) Sony 47572 [ADD] + *Les Préludes*; Brahms: *Hungarian Dances* (sel.); Enesco: *Romanian Rhapsody* No. 1
Boskovsky, Philharmonia Hungarica, London Philharmonic Orchestra. EMI Studio Plus 64627 [ADD] + *Rákóczy* March; *Hungarian Battle* March
Dorati, London Symphony Orchestra. Mercury Living Presence 432015 [ADD] + Enesco: *Romanian Rhapsody* No. 1
Mehta, Israel Philharmonic Orchestra. (6 sel.) CBS [Sony] 44926 [DDD]

Les Préludes (Symphonic Poem No. 3)

Far and away the most famous of Liszt's 13 tone poems, *Les Préludes* was inspired by a bit of tortured poetry by Alphone de Lamartine characterizing life as a series of preludes to the afterlife. The spirit of the piece, then, is man's struggle to the stars. In many minds, however, its association is with the Lone Ranger, since parts of it were used as bridge music on the classic radio and television show; few people are aware of this, however, believing it all to be part of Rossini's *William Tell Overture* and getting frustrated when they can't find it therein.

Argenta, Suisse Romande Orchestra, Paris Conservatory Orchestra. London [Decca] 452305 [ADD] + Berlioz: *Symphonie fantastique*
Bernstein, New York Philharmonic Orchestra. Sony 47572 [ADD] + other *Hungarian Rhapsodies*; Brahms: *Hungarian Dances* (sel.); Enesco: *Romanian Rhapsody* No. 1
Halász, Polish National Radio Symphony Orchestra (Katowice). Naxos 8.550487 [DDD] + *Mazeppa*; *Prometheus*; *Tasso, lamento e trionfo*

Sonata in B Minor for Piano

If the pieces described above are a bit tawdry and crass in places, no such catering to the galleries will be found in Liszt's great piano sonata, surprisingly the only one he wrote.

———— *[DDD] indicates newest recordings; [ADD] or [AAD] are reissues.* ————

Although it is written in accord with his usual theories, it is altogether more tasteful and noble: it even contains a fugue! At the same time, it has plenty of drama.

Brendel. Philips 434078 [DDD] + encores
Curzon. London [Decca] 452306 [ADD] + *Liebestraum* No. 3, other short pieces; Schubert: Impromptu in A-flat, D.935/2
Gilels. RCA Living Stereo 61614 [ADD] + Schubert: Piano Sonata No. 17, D.850
Pizarro. Collins Classics 1357 [DDD] + other short pieces
Pollini. Deutsche Grammophon 427322 [DDD] + short pieces
Richter. Philips Solo 446200 (2) [ADD] + Piano Concertos 1, 2 (with Kondrashin, London Symphony Orchestra)

Modest Mussorgsky (1839-1881)

Mussorgsky was at once among the most original and least polished of all the great composers. His ideal was not Beauty, but Truth, and in the course of his idealistic quest he created a sound and style so distinctive that hardly anyone has dared to follow it for fear of being accused of plagiarism. He is the great primitive of classical music, who like Grandma Moses in painting managed to overwhelm the senses (and ultimately the critics) by sheer force of personality and inspiration.

He was born to wealth, growing up carefree on a large estate. He showed an early propensity for music, and was able to perform a large piano concerto by age 11. Although his father loved music and encouraged the boy, he thought music was no more than a pastime and packed him off to military school. The director there was puzzled by the youth's studious demeanor. He tried to get him to drink wine and chase women like any proper officer (Tailhook, we see, is nothing new), but he preferred to study German philosophy and read classical literature.

After graduation he became a fixture in St. Petersburg salons, playing inconsequential piano ditties in his uniform for adoring society ladies, affecting aristocratic manners. Soon however he became a student of Mily Balakirev, founder of the Russian nationalist movement which culminated in the group, of which Mussorgsky was a member, called "The Five," or "The Mighty Handful."

Within two years he had decided to forsake military service for music, traveling the countryside and imbuing himself with Russian folk influences so immoderately that he suffered a temporary breakdown. A tendency to dabble in drugs and drink was exacerbated by his impoverishment in 1861, when the family fortune was lost in the abolishment of serfdom, and by the death of his beloved mother in 1865. His health steadily deteriorated, but his creative powers only increased. He shed his artistic inhibitions and let his natural idealism flower wherever and however it might, leaving many of his works incomplete as his restless mind turned from one project to another. All the while he was forced to support himself with a miserable clerical job in the Ministry of Transport, which left only the odd hour for his real vocation.

The death of a close friend in 1873, the scorn he suffered from "professional" composers, the drudgery and loneliness of his daily life, led irrevocably to spiraling dissolution. By the time of the unforgettable, unforgiving portrait by Repin, he had sold his furniture to pay for liquor, dressed in rags, and was often homeless. He died a week after his 42nd birthday, pleading pitifully for a bottle of cognac.

Only gradually over the decades has his music taken its rightful place-at first, usually in orchestrations or revisions by other composers, later in the original versions when their rough power was finally understood to need no fussy fixing to be valid. In his last stupefied days, no one would have been more amazed than Mussorgsky to foresee that *Boris Godunov* would one day by considered one of the handful of greatest operas ever written, *Pictures at an Exhibition* would be one of the handful of most performed and recorded orchestral works of all time, and *A Night on Bald Mountain* would be immortalized by Walt Disney. Patronized by his colleagues, it was Mussorgsky who, ironically, was to justify more than any of the others the epithet of "Mighty Handful."

Boris Godunov

I will pass over here the complicated story of the various versions of this great and unique opera; suffice it to say that there are basically two–Mussorgsky's original, and Rimsky-Korsakov's revision (although there are variants of these, and revisions by other parties altogether, including Shostakovich). Until recent years the Rimsky-Korsakov orchestration was the only one allowed on stage; but gradually it became clear that Mussorgsky's original, once thought to be technically crude, had a power and integrity of its own which made Rimsky's well-meaning wax job look altogether too slick.

That the supposedly amateurish and untutored Mussorgsky could create one of the towering masterpieces of opera is astonishing, but no more so than that a small-town commoner with apparently only a village school education could write *Hamlet* and *King Lear*. Perhaps a couple of centuries from now someone will "prove" that Mussorgsky's works were actually written by someone else (Rimsky-Korsakov, perhaps?).

Abbado, Kotcherga, Ramey, Berlin Philharmonic Orchestra. Sony 58977 (3) [DDD]

Dobrowen, Christoff, French National Radio Orchestra. EMI 65192 (3) (mono) [ADD]

[The classic complete performance, despite its 1952 monophonic sound, which is admirably clear nonetheless. Not available in the U.S. at this writing, but can be obtained in the U.K. or via Internet and some import shops.]

———— *Some CDs may be available only through importers.* ————

A Night on Bald Mountain

Originally written for *Salammbô* an uncompleted opera, and later incorporated into another opera, *The Fair at Sorochinsk*, this musical picture of a witches' sabbath finally became famous as an independent tone poem, and served for one of the most memorable episodes in Walt Disney's animated film *Fantasia.*

Bernstein, New York Philharmonic Orchestra. CBS 36726 [ADD] + *Pictures at an Exhibition*
Dorati, London Symphony Orchestra. Mercury Living Presence 432004 [ADD] + Prokofiev: *Romeo and Juliet* Suites
Maazel, Cleveland Orchestra. Telarc 80042 [DDD] + *Pictures at an Exhibition*
Reiner, Chicago Symphony Orchestra. RCA Living Stereo 61958 [ADD] + *Pictures at an Exhibition*
Sinopoli, New York Philharmonic Orchestra. Deutsche Grammophon 429785 [DDD] + *Pictures at an Exhibition*; Ravel: *Valses nobles et sentimentales*
Tennstedt, London Philharmonic Orchestra. EMI 55186 [DDD] + Beethoven: Symphony No. 3

Pictures at an Exhibition (orch. Ravel)

Now one of the most universally loved "orchestral spectaculars," Mussorgsky's original is for piano solo. At least a dozen other musicians have arranged it for orchestra, but by far the most famous was Maurice Ravel, and the recommended recordings are all of his version.
The piece is a tribute to Mussorgsky's friend Victor Hartmann, a painter, who had recently died. Each of the twelve main sections is a musical impression of an actual painting, linked by a theme marked "Promenade" which represents Mussorgsky walking from one exhibit to another. There is not a weak "picture" in the entire gallery, and all are crowned by the overwhelmingly majestic finale "The Great Gate at Kiev," possibly the noblest loud music ever written.

Bernstein, New York Philharmonic Orchestra. CBS [Sony] 36726 [ADD] + *A Night on Bald Mountain*
Karajan, Berlin Philharmonic Orchestra. Deutsche Grammophon 429162 [ADD] + Stravinsky: *Rite of Spring*
Karajan, Berlin Philharmonic Orchestra. Deutsche Grammophon "Karajan Gold" 439013 [DDD] + Ravel: *Boléro, Rapsodie espagnole*
Karajan, Berlin Philharmonic Orchestra. Deutsche Grammophon Originals 447426 [ADD] + Debussy: *La Mer;* Ravel: *Boléro*

——— *U.S. labels and numbers are given first, U.K. in [brackets] when needed.* ———

Maazel, Cleveland Orchestra. Telarc 80042 [DDD] + *A Night on Bald Mountain*

Maazel, New Philharmonia Orchestra. EMI Seraphim 68539 (2) [ADD] + *Alborada del gracioso, Boléro, Pavane for a Dead Princess, La valse*//Ravel: *Valses nobles et sentimentales*; Debussy: *La mer, Nocturnes* (with Previn, Royal Philharmonic Orchestra)

Muti, Philadelphia Orchestra. EMI 64516 + Stravinsky: *Rite of Spring*

Reiner, Chicago Symphony Orchestra. RCA Living Stereo 61958 [ADD] + *A Night on Bald Mountain*

Sinopoli, New York Philharmonic Orchestra. Deutsche Grammophon 429785 [DDD] + *A Night on Bald Mountain*; Ravel: *Valses nobles et sentimentales*

Solti, Chicago Symphony Orchestra. London [Decca] 417754 [DDD] + Bartók: Concerto for Orchestra

Solti, Chicago Symphony Orchestra. London [Decca] 430446 [DDD] + Tchaikovsky: *Overture 1812*; Prokofiev: Symphony No. 1

Szell, Cleveland Orchestra. Sony Essential Classics 48162 [ADD] + Kodály: *Háry János* Suite; Prokofiev: *Lt. Kijé* Suite

Toscanini, NBC Symphony Orchestra. *The Toscanini Collection*, Vol. 44, RCA Victor Gold Seal 60321 (mono) [ADD] + Tchaikovsky: Piano Concerto No. 1 (with Horowitz)

Jacques Offenbach (1819-1880)

Born Isaac Juda Eberst, Offenbach was the son of a synagogue cantor who was also a bookbinder and music teacher. He later changed his name, using his native village of Offenbach for the latter half. Since Offenbach was near Cologne, he sometimes referred to himself also as "O. de Cologne."

Wit, sometimes of the rapier variety, was the most memorable feature of his persona, and it informed the dozens of satirical operettas he composed over a very successful theatrical career, including *La Périchole, La belle Hélène,* and *Orphée aux enfers* (*Orpheus in the Underworld*), a parody on Greek mythology, and source of the naughty but immortal *Can-Can*. "Offenbach's music," said George Bernard Shaw, "is wicked...Every accent is a snap of the fingers in the face of moral responsibility."

He was but a teenager when he moved to Paris and began his career as a cellist; in fact he wrote several notable works for cello, but these continue to be overshadowed by his infectious stage works. Despite the light nature of his subject matter, Offenbach was a composer with finely honed skills and considerable grace, earning him Rossini's accolade as "the Mozart of the Champs-Elysées."

Offenbach's artistic side was overlooked by most of his contemporaries, friends or foes. He accepted an invitation to make an American tour in 1876, the centennial of the United

States, to perform his own works. Many orchestras honored him by featuring his music on their programs, but the ultra-Teuton Theodore Thomas, then director of the Philadelphia Centennial Exposition, pointedly refused to have anything to do with such Gallic frippery. A yellow journalist tried to egg Offenbach on by asking him what he thought of the shocking snub. "Tell Mr. Thomas," he calmly replied, "that I shall be delighted to conduct his compositions, when he achieves the dignity of becoming a composer." Despite the fortune he made from his comedies, Offenbach did have a burning need to write something "serious" that would assure him that same dignity for posterity. He succeeded, but just barely; he died four months before the premiere of *The Tales of Hoffmann*, an opera unique in its haunting blend of tragedy, comedy, and grotesquerie.

Gaité Parisienne (arr. Rosenthal)

Oddly enough, Offenbach's most famous work was written 57 years after his death. In 1937 the great American impresario Sol Hurok was in need of a new ballet to launch the reorganized Ballet Russe de Monte Carlo, and commissioned Manuel Rosenthal to raid Offenbach's numerous operettas for their most delectable quadrilles and can-cans, waltzes and galops. The result is a perfect, pre-digested Offenbach "sampler."

Fiedler, Boston Pops Orchestra. RCA Living Stereo 61847 [ADD] + Rossini, arr. Respighi: *La boutique fantasque*

Karajan, Berlin Philharmonic Orchestra. Deutsche Grammophon Galleria 429163 [ADD] + Delibes: *Coppélia* Suite; Chopin: *Les Sylphides*

Karajan, Berlin Philharmonic Orchestra. *Famous Ballets*, London [Decca] Double 437404 (2) [ADD] + Chopin: *Les Sylphides*, Delibes: *Coppélia* Suite, Gounod: *Faust* ballet music, Ravel: *Boléro*, Tchaikovsky: *Sleeping Beauty* Suite

Munch, New Philharmonia Orchestra. London [Decca] 443033 (2) [ADD] + Bizet: *L'Arlésienne* Suites, *Carmen* Suites; *Jeux d'enfants*, Saint-Saëns: *Danse macabre*, *La rouet d'Omphale* (with Martinon, Paris Conservatory Orchestra); Chabrier: *España*, *Joyeuse marche* (with Ansermet, Suisse Romande Orchestra); Dukas: *The Sorcerer's Apprentice* (with Solti, Israel Philharmonic Orchestra)

Previn, Pittsburgh Symphony Orchestra. Philips Solo 442403 [ADD] + Overtures and suites (with Almeida conducting)

Nikolai Rimsky-Korsakov (1844-1908)

Rimsky-Korsakov stands as a beacon for those who imagine they can never learn enough to comprehend classical music; he began his career as a naval officer and ended up being one of the greatest orhestrators of all time, and the teacher of Igor Stravinsky, considered by many the greatest 20th-century composer.

——— *CDs listed are solid, central choices, not necessarily "the greatest."* ———

Despite intending throughout his youth to follow a family tradition in the Navy, he showed considerable musical talent. His study was sporadic at best until he fell in with Mily Balakirev, father of the Russian nationalist school of composition later known as "The Five," or "The Mighty Handful." Balakirev saw in the young enthusiast for Russian folk songs, native opera, and Orthodox chant a ripe convert for own theories designed to establish a native musical culture second to none.

Rimsky had a public triumph with his first symphony at age 21, receiving a standing ovation dressed in his crisp naval uniform. Still essentially an amateur, he went from one success to another, barely keeping ahead of the game by studying harmony and theory on his own in the most slapdash way, often discovering basic principles of composition simply through trial-and-error. His talent was so great that despite his shaky credentials he was invited in 1871 to become a professor or composition and instrumentation at the prestigious St. Petersburg Conservatory. Always becomingly modest, he wrote in his delightful autobiography that "At the time I could not harmonize a chorale propery, had never written a single contrapuntal exercise in my life, and had only the haziest understanding of strict fugue. I didn't even know the names of the augmented and diminished intervals or the chords!"

Eventually Rimsky became so obsessed with mastering the techniques of music that he partially alienated those of his early supporters who thought he was betraying their ideals of a music rooted in the Russian people. He mollified them by producing the most monumental collection of Russian folk songs ever compiled. But the "Mighty Handful" was breaking up: by 1887, Mussorgsky and Borodin were dead, and Balakirev and Cui had drifted into other interests. Rimsky became by default the leader of his own group of nationalist composers, including Glazunov (his favorite), Liadov, Arensky, Ippolitov-Ivanov, and Stravinsky, whose ballet *The Firebird* owes very much to his teacher's influence.

Rimsky himself then blossomed as a significant composer, creating his greatest works over a 20-year period, interrupted only by a two-year depression. He gave generously to other composers in encouragement, and in helping them with their work; he actually contributed the orchestrations for several works by Borodin and Mussorgsky. Towards the end of his life he was dismissed from the Conservatory for supporting the revolutionary activities of the students, but public outrage forced his reinstatement. By this time, he was a national icon.

Capriccio espagnol, Op. 34

Rimsky-Korsakov was brutally frank about his motive in writing this piece that glitters with dazzling orchestral color. The reason, he says in his autobiography, was to create a work that "glitters with dazzling orchestral color." And there we could leave the matter, to be chewed upon as by a mangy dog or music critic. But that would ignore the fact that under the guise of a warhorse or chestnut Rimsky was here reviving the Baroque technique

——— *Some famous CDs are not listed because currently out of print.* ———

of concertante playing, featuring solos by different instruments or groups of instruments. And it would pass over his concept, brilliantly implemented in this piece, that the melodies and rhythms and structures of a piece must relate organically to the inherent qualities of the instruments used, a concept which had a direct influence on Stravinsky and his followers. If you wish, however, you may simply accept the standard view that the *Capriccio espagnol* is nothing more than a hackneyed dray-horse of the pops repertoire. It's your life!

Bernstein, New York Philharmonic Orchestra. CBS [Sony] 36728 [AAD] + Tchaikovsky: *Capriccio italien*
Dorati, London Symphony Orchestra. Mercury Living Presence 434308 [ADD] + *Russian Easter* Overture, *Le Coq d'or* Suite; Borodin: *Polovtsian Dances* from *Prince Igor*
Järvi, Gothenburg Symphony Orchestra. Deutsche Grammophon 429984 [DDD] + *Russian Easter* Overture; Tchaikovsky: *1812* Overture, *Marche slave*; Borodin: *Polovtsian Dances* from *Prince Igor*, *In the Steppes of Central Asia*
Mackerras, London Symphony Orchestra. Telarc 80208 [DDD] + *Scheherazade*

Russian Easter Overture, Op. 36

It's a long, long way from "Christ the Lord is Risen Today" to the feverish sustained crescendo that is the *Russian Easter Overture*. In my many years in classical broadcasting I loved nothing more than to play this work without introduction on Easter Sunday and have people call up to complain that the music was totally inappropriate. The piece seems to have a lot more to do with pagan spring festivals of Old Russia than the Christian holiday, but whatever it is, it's exciting!

Dorati, London Symphony Orchestra. Mercury 434308 [ADD] + *Capriccio espagnol, Le Coq d'or Suite*; Borodin: *Polovtsian Dances* from *Prince Igor*
Järvi, Gothenburg Symphony Orchestra. Deutsche Grammophon 429984 [DDD] + *Capriccio espagnol*; Tchaikovsky: *1812* Overture, *Marche slave*; Borodin: *Polovtsian Dances* from *Prince Igor*, *In the Steppes of Central Asia*
Slatkin, St. Louis Symphony Orchestra. Telarc 80072 [DDD] + Glinka: *Russlan and Ludmila* Overture; Borodin: *In the Steppes of Central Asia*; Tchaikovsky: *Marche slave*

Scheherazade, Op. 35

Inspired by the *Arabian Nights*, this huge tone poem disguised as a four-movement symphony is among the most colorfully orchestrated works in the repertoire, outstripping

———— Catalog numbers are subject to change without notice. ————

even most other pieces by Rimsky-Korsakov. There is an entire strain of quasi-Oriental compositions in classical music, and this is the king of them all. Or, shall we say, queen. For such *Scheherazade* becomes by mellowing her scimitar-happy husband with her fascinating stories.

Beecham, Royal Philharmonic Orchestra. EMI 47717 [ADD] + Borodin: *Polovtsian Dances* from *Prince Igor*

Chung, Paris Opera-Bastille Orchestra. Deutsche Grammophon 437818 [DDD] + Stravinsky: *Firebird* Suite

Karajan, Berlin Philharmonic Orchestra. Deutsche Grammophon 419063 [ADD] + Borodin: *Polovtsian Dances* from *Prince Igor*

Maazel, Berlin Radio Symphony Orchestra. Deutsche Grammophon Originals 447414 [ADD] + Falla: *El amor brujo*; Exc. from *The Three-Cornered Hat*

Mackerras, London Symphony Orchestra. Telarc 80208 [DDD] + *Capriccio espagnol*

Reiner, Chicago Symphony Orchestra. RCA Victor Gold Seal 60875 [ADD] + Debussy: *La Mer*

Yuasa, London Philharmonic Orchestra. Classics for Pleasure 2214 [DDD] + Prokofiev: *Lt. Kijé* Suite

Camille Saint-Saëns (1835-1921)

Saint-Saëns had relatively easy sailing as an all-around musician throughout his life, but he paid for it posthumously. He began as an incredible prodigy on the piano, composing his first piece at three and playing in Beethoven chamber music before he was five. He was a star pupil at the Paris Conservatory and soon developed into one of the greatest piano and organ virtuosos in Europe, securing a 20-year tenure as organist at the great Church of the Madeleine.

His enormous energy and almost dizzying intellect expressed themselves in wide-ranging interests. He was a talented amateur astronomer and archaeologist. He learned several languages, was an excellent caricaturist, wrote poetry and plays. He wrote articles and books on literature, painting, hypnotism and philosophy. He was one of the first important 19th-century scholars of Renaissance music, and composed the first important film score, for the 1908 silent picture *The Assassination of the Duc de Guise*.

He was, in fact, the most highly and widely cultured composer known to history; yet today his music is often conversely considered among the least profound. During most of his lifetime he was adulated; statues of him were erected, streets named after him, and a museum of his memorabilia was even opened while he was still living. He made stacks of money and was regularly mentioned in the same breath with Mozart and Beethoven.

——— *Since CDs can change label and number, use artists as main reference.* ———

Then he did the worst possible thing: he died. Almost at once a reaction set in. Typed as "the greatest talent who was not a genius," he was redefined as one whose enormous intelligence was spread too thin to achieve true greatness. His works, it was said, were facile and slick rather than substantive. (He himself justified his work by saying "The artist who does not feel completely satisfied by elegant lines, by harmonious colors, and by a beautiful succession of chords does not understand the art of music.")

Despite the critical sniffing, a surprising number of his works continue to hold their place because of their melodic beauty and suave orchestration, political correctness be damned. Saint-Saëns followed his own muse without too much concern for fashions. His heart was never fully in the 19th century anyway; over and over in his works we hear echoes of the Baroque. What seemed in his time to be stiff formality can be heard today as a touching nostalgia for an earlier era. Perhaps we can appreciate his preference for absolute music without comparing it unfavorably with his confreres, by enjoying it on his terms rather than just ours—that is, by savoring its elegance, proportion, and good taste on its own merits.

Carnival of the Animals

Tossed off as a joke for a Mardi Gras concert, *Carnival of the Animals* was never intended for publication, and Saint-Saëns would be mortified to discover it is today better known than all his other works. That doesn't mean it is bad, however. It is actually a piece of enormous wit, charm, and verve—far better than its composer apparently realized.

Bernstein, New York Philharmonic Orchestra. CBS 37765 + Prokofiev: *Peter and the Wolf*
DePreist, Royal Stockholm Philharmonic Orchestra. BIS 555 [DDD] + Symphony No. 3; *Bacchanale* from *Samson et Dalila, et al.*
Dutoit, Montreal Symphony Orchestra. London 430720 [DDD] + Symphony No. 3
Fournet, Tokyo Metropolitan Symphony Orchestra. Denon 8097 [DDD] + Berlioz: *Symphonie fantastique*
Janowski, French Radio Philharmonic Orchestra. Teldec 46155 [DDD] + Poulenc: Double Piano Concerto
Licata, Royal Philharmonic Orchestra. RPO [Tring] 046 [DDD] + Prokofiev: Peter and the Wolf (with Gielgud); Bizet: *Jeux d'enfants*
Ormandy, Philadelphia Orchestra. Sony Essential Classics 47655 [ADD] + Symphony No. 3, *Danse Macabre, Bacchanale* from *Samson et Dalila, French Military March* from *Suite Algérienne*
Previn, Pittsburgh Symphony Orchestra. Philips 400016 [DDD] + Ravel: *Ma mère l'oye*

———— *Artists are listed alphabetically, not in order by critical ranking.* ————

Stamp, Academy of London. Virgin Classics 59533 [DDD] + Prokofiev: *Peter and the Wolf* (with Gielgud); Mozart: *Eine kleine Nachtmusik*

Concerto No. 1 in A Minor for Cello, Op. 33

An ingratiating example of one of the most difficult types of concerto, the first cello concerto dates from 1872 and was a lifelong favorite of Pablo Casals, who played it at his debut in 1905. Ostensibly in one movement, it is actually in three sections with a charming neo-Baroque minuet like a big cherry in the center.

Harnoy, Freeman, Victoria Symphony Orchestra. *Ofra Harnoy Collection*, Vol. 3, RCA Victor Gold Seal 68373 [DDD] + *Le Cygne* from *Carnival of the Animals*; Tchaikovsky: *Rococo* Variations, *et al.*
Ma, Maazel, French National Orchestra. Sony 46506 or 66935 [DDD] + Piano Concerto No. 2, Violin Concerto No. 3
Rolland, Varga, BBC Philharmonic Orchestra. ASV 867 [DDD] Lalo: Cello Concerto; Massenet: *Fantaisie*
Starker, Dorati, London Symphony Orchestra. Mercury Living Presence 432010 [ADD] + Lalo: Cello Concerto; Schumann: Cello Concerto

Concerto No. 2 in G Minor for Piano, Op. 22

Anton Rubinstein gave the premiere of this, the most popular of the five Saint-Saëns piano concertos, in 1868. Years later it became a mainstay of the repertoire of Artur Rubinstein (no relation to Anton!). The first movement begins with a very Bach-like prelude. The second movement contains one of the composer's most famous and memorable melodies. The final movement is a sort of "perpetual motion" that sweeps to a conclusion more akin to Offenbach than to Bach (a witty observation often attributed to Oscar Levant, but actually originated by the pianist Sigismund Stojowski. As long as I'm at it, let me point out that the famous quip "I laughed all the way to the bank" was not first said by Liberace but by the great coloratura soprano Amelita Galli-Curci).

Collard, Previn, Royal Philharmonic Orchestra. EMI 47816 + Piano Concerto No. 4
Licad, Previn, London Philharmonic Orchestra. Sony 46506 or 66935 [DDD] + Cello Concerto No. 1, Violin Concerto No. 3
Rubinstein, Ormandy, Philadelphia Orchestra. RCA Victor Gold Seal 61863 [ADD] + Falla: *Nights in the Gardens of Spain;* Franck: *Symphonic Variations*

———— *[DDD] indicates newest recordings; [ADD] or [AAD] are reissues.* ————

Concerto No. 3 in B Minor for Violin, Op. 61

Saint-Saëns's last violin concerto was written in 1881 for the great virtuoso Pablo de Sarasate, who contributed suggestions that were incorporated into it. It is surprisingly dramatic and symphonic for a composer supposedly so cavalier and facile, which seems to have made it a little less popular than some of his other great concertos. (Why do I get the feeling that people listen avidly to the worst pieces by Saint-Saëns and then complain that they are inferior?)

Chee-Yun, López-Cobos, London Philharmonic Orchestra. Denon 18017 [DDD] + Lalo: *Symphonie espagnole*
Francescatti, Mitropoulos, New York Philharmonic Orchestra; Ormandy, Philadelphia Orchestra. Sony Masterworks Heritage 62339 (2) (mono) [ADD] + Mendelssohn: Violin Concerto in E Minor; Bruch: Violin Concerto No. 1; Tchaikovsky: Violin Concerto; Prokofiev: Violin Concerto No. 2; Chausson: *Poème*
Lin, Tilson Thomas, Philharmonia Orchestra. Sony 46506 or 66935 [DDD] + Cello Concerto No. 1, Piano Concerto No. 2
Perlman, Barenboim, Orchestre de Paris. Deutsche Grammophon 445549 [DDD] + Lalo: *Symphonie espagnole*; Berlioz: *Rêverie et Caprice*
Rachlin, Mehta, Israel Philharmonic Orchestra. Sony 48373 [DDD] + Wieniawski: Violin Concerto No. 2
Shaham, Sinopoli, New York Philharmonic Orchestra. Deutsche Grammophon 429786 [DDD] + Paganini: Violin Concerto No. 1
Wei, Bakels, Philharmonia Orchestra. ASV 680 [DDD] + Bruch: Violin Concerto No. 1

Danse Macabre, Op. 40

Along with Mussorgsky's *A Night on Bald Mountain*, this is the best-known piece of "Hallowe'en music." It is the most successful of four tone poems by Saint-Saëns, famous for its rattling "bones" which the composer self-quoted humorously as "Fossils" in *Carnival of the Animals*. It was the first concert work to employ a xylophone, and you may play it for your children with impunity as it is only about as scary as *Abbott and Costello Meet the Wolf Man*.

Bernstein, New York Philharmonic Orchestra. CBS [Sony] 37769 [ADD] + Dukas: *Sorcerer's Apprentice*; Ravel: *Pavane for a Dead Princess*; *Bacchanale* from *Samson et Dalila*; Chabrier: *España*; Offenbach: Overture to *Orpheus in the Underworld*

——— *CDs go in and out of print; availability of all listed items is not assured.* ———

DePreist, Royal Stockholm Philharmonic Orchestra. BIS 555 [DDD] + Symphony No. 3, *Bacchanale* from *Samson et Dalila, et al.*

Dutoit, Philharmonia Orchestra. London [Decca] Jubilee 425021 [ADD] + *Havanaise, Introduction and Rondo Capriccioso, Marche héroique,* three tone poems

Fournet, Tokyo Metropolitan Symphony Orchestra. Denon 8097 [DDD] + Berlioz: *Symphonie fantastique*

Maazel, Pittsburgh Symphony Orchestra. Sony 53979 [DDD] + Symphony No. 3, *Phaéton, Bacchanale* from *Samson et Dalila*

Martinon, Paris Conservatory Orchestra. London [Decca] 443033 (2) [ADD] + *La rouet d'Omphale,* Bizet: *Jeux d'enfants; L'Arlèsienne* Suites, *Carmen* Suites, Offenbach: *Gaité Parisienne* (with Munch, New Philharmonia Orchestra); Chabrier: *España, Joyeuse marche* (with Ansermet, Suisse Romande Orchestra); Dukas: *The Sorcerer's Apprentice* (with Solti, Israel Philharmonic Orchestra);

Ormandy, Philadelphia Orchestra. Sony Essential Classics 47655 [ADD] + *Carnival of the Animals,* Symphony No. 3, *Bacchanale* from *Samson et Dalila,* *French Military March* from *Suite Algérienne*

Havanaise; Introduction and Rondo Capriccioso

These are two separate pieces, but they are almost inseparable on recordings. They need no explanation as they are self-evident vehicles for the display of violinistic virtuosity. The *Havanaise* has a Cuban flavor. Unless noted otherwise, all recordings listed contain both works. If separate, it is because the rest of the recording is highly desirable otherwise.

Chung, Dutoit, Royal Philharmonic Orchestra. London [Decca] Jubilee 425021 [ADD] + *Danse macabre, Marche héroique,* three tone poems

Oistrakh, Munch, Boston Symphony Orchestra. (*Havanaise* omitted) RCA Victor Gold Seal 60683 [ADD] + Chausson: Symphony in B-flat

Perlman, Martinon, Orchestre de Paris. EMI 47725 [DDD] + Ravel: *Tzigane;* Chausson: *Poème*

Perlman, Mehta, New York Philharmonic Orchestra. Deutsche Grammophon 423063 [DDD] + Chausson: *Poème;* Ravel: *Tzigane;* Sarasate: *Carmen Fantasy*

Vengerov, Mehta, Israel Philharmonic Orchestra. Teldec 73266 [DDD] + Paganini: Violin Concerto No. 1; Waxman: *Carmen Fantasy*

Symphony No. 3 in C Minor, Op. 78, "Organ"

The huge orchestra for which this symphony is scored is augmented further by an organ. Had it been practical, Saint-Saëns would have added a herd of trumpeting elephants. It has long been a favorite for demonstrating great recorded sound, especially now on digital compact discs. The stupendous organ chorale which launches the final section is based on the melody of an *Ave Maria* by the Flemish Renaissance composer Jacob Arcadelt (a fact which I have not seen mentioned elsewhere, so I shall accept credit for the discovery until proved wrong. This same tune shows up in an *Ave Maria* for organ solo by Saint-Saëns's good friend, Franz Liszt).

DePreist, Royal Stockholm Philharmonic Orchestra. BIS 555 [DDD] + *Danse macabre*, *Bacchanale* from *Samson et Dalila, et al.*
Dutoit, Montreal Symphony Orchestra. London [Decca] 430720 [DDD] + *Carnival of the Animals*
Levine, Berlin Philharmonic Orchestra. Deutsche Grammophon 419617 [DDD] + Dukas: *The Sorcerer's Apprentice*
Maazel, Pittsburgh Symphony Orchestra. Sony 53979 [DDD] + *Danse macabre*, *Phaéton*, *Bacchanale* from *Samson et Dalila*
Munch, Boston Symphony Orchestra. RCA Living Stereo 61500 [ADD] + Debussy: *La Mer*; Ibert: *Escales*
Ormandy, Philadelphia Orchestra. Sony Essential Classics 47655 [ADD] + *Carnival of the Animals, Danse Macabre, Bacchanale* from *Samson et Dalila,* French Military March from *Suite Algérienne*
Tortelier, Ulster Orchestra. Chandos 8822 [DDD] + Symphony No. 2

Bedřich Smetana (1824-1884)

A splendid musician, Smetana had the misfortune to be only the second greatest Czech (or more precisely, Bohemian) composer. Had Antonín Dvořák not existed his star would surely be higher; as it turns out, he has at least held on to world fame through his stirring tone poem *The Moldau*, though he wrote a great deal of excellent music that patiently awaits discovery by the international public.

Largely self-taught as a child, Smetana was playing Haydn quartets by age five and composing by eight. Later on he got some formal training, came to the attention of Franz Liszt who became his friend, and at age 24 founded the first important music school in Prague. Overcoming the tragedies of the deaths of his four-year-old daughter and the childhood sweetheart who had become his wife, he remarried and redoubled his efforts to promote Czech musical culture, writing musical criticism, and founding or directing theaters, orchestras, and schools. Ironically, this great patriot was in his mid-20s before he even began to learn the Czech language; his first tongue was German, the official language of the country when he was born.

At age 50, tragedy struck again when he became stone deaf. But he overcame this handicap too, writing the great cycle of six tone poems *Ma Vlast* ("My Country"), which includes *The Moldau*, long after he could not hear a note of it. Worn down by care and work, and by disappointment at flagging public interest in his music, he gradually fell prey to depressions. He spent the last year of his life in a mental institution. Belatedly, his countrymen hailed him as the father of Czech music, and after the creation of the free republic of Czechoslovakia in 1924 Paul Stefan euologized Smetana as "the standard bearer and symbol of the history and liberation of his people."

The Bartered Bride: Overture and Dances

Few "ethnic" operas find success outside their native lands, but this one does. You don't have to comprehend every nuance of rustic Bohemian folk customs to enjoy the open humor and vivacious spirits of *The Bartered Bride*. The Overture and three famous dances—Polka, Furiant, and *Dance of the Comedians*—give a fair preview of the work.

Bělohlávek, Prague Symphony Orchestra. *Smetana Festival*, Supraphon 11-0037 [DDD] + *The Moldau, From Bohemian Fields and Groves, Libuse* Overture, *Triumphal* Symphony

Szell, Cleveland Orchestra. CBS [Sony] 36716 [ADD] + *The Moldau*; Dvořák: *Carnival* Overture

The Moldau (Vltava)

Bohemia's principal river is the subject of this beloved tone poem, second of the six making up the cycle "My Fatherland" (*Ma Vlast*). Delicately rippling strings represent the tiny stream where the river originates; the orchestra continues vividly to suggest the course of the river and sights along its banks, such as old castles; and finally it roars over St.John's rapids as Prague, the "golden city," comes into view. If there is any piece with "sweep," this is it.

Bělohlávek, Prague Symphony Orchestra. *Smetana Festival*, Supraphon 11-0037 [DDD] + Overture and dances from *The Bartered Bride*; *From Bohemian Fields and Groves, Libuše* Overture, *Triumphal* Symphony

Kertész, Vienna Philharmonic Orchestra. London [Decca] Weekend Classics 417678 [ADD] + Dvořák: Symphony No. 9

Szell, Cleveland Orchestra. CBS [Sony] 36716 [ADD] + Dances from *The Bartered Bride*; Dvořák: *Carnival* Overture

Szell, Cleveland Orchestra. Sony Essential Classics 48264 [ADD] + Mendelssohn: *A Midsummer Night's Dream* (sel.); Bizet: Symphony in C (conducted by Stokowski)

———— *All CDs listed are considered approximately equal in (high) merit.* ————

Johann Strauss II (1825-1899)

Johann Strauss II will forever be known as the Waltz King for his more than 400 irresistible Viennese waltzes, polkas, operettas, and so on, but he must also share honors with his father and two younger brothers, all of whom were part of the unique family who have become synonymous with concert dance music. Although Johann, Jr., was the greatest and most prolific of them, it is sometimes startling to realize that some marvelous piece one thought was surely his is actually by Johann, Sr., Josef, or Edouard. None of these, by the way, was related to another famous composer, Richard Strauss (*q.v.*).

Johann, Jr. took over his father's famous dance orchestra upon his death in 1849 and began a long series of tours all over Europe. By 1863 he was appointed director of the Imperial Court Balls, and in the next few years wrote most of his best works, including the world's greatest waltz, *The Blue Danube*, and the world's greatest operetta, *Die Fledermaus* ("The Bat"). Although his music was "light," Strauss's accomplishments are nothing to sneeze at. They were greatly admired by Johannes Brahms, who is said once to have autographed Mme. Strauss's fan by inscribing a few bars of *The Blue Danube* and adding "Unfortunately, not by me."

After a career of extraordinary vigor and success, Johann Strauss II died of pneumonia in 1899, bringing to a close a century and an era. His music, so full of optimism, charm, camaraderie, and rich sentiment, still stands as the symbol of nostalgia for a golden age of Viennese Romanticism that can never come again.

Waltzes, Polkas, Overtures

All anthologies contain *The Blue Danube* Waltz, at the very least, with a good helping of other most famous Strauss Family hits.

Boskovsky, Vienna Philharmonic Orchestra. *Weekend in Vienna: Strauss Favourites*, London [Decca] Weekend Classics 417885 [ADD]

Boskovsky, Vienna Philharmonic Orchestra. London [Decca] Double Decker 443473 (2) [AAD]

Karajan, Battle, Vienna Philharmonic Orchestra. *1987 New Year Concert in Vienna*, Deutsche Grammophon 419616 [DDD]

Kunzel, Cincinnati Pops Orchestra and Chorale. *Straussfest*, Telarc 80098 [DDD]

Reiner, Chicago Symphony Orchestra. RCA Living Stereo 68160 [ADD] + Weber: *Invitation to the Dance*; R. Strauss: *Rosenkavalier* Waltzes

———— *CDs listed are solid, central choices, not necessarily "the greatest."* ————

Peter Ilyich Tchaikovsky (1840-1893)

Tchaikovsky was to become for many the apotheosis of the Russian Romantic—wild as a Cossack, palpitating with larger-than-life emotion, dripping with hyperinflated sentimentality—yet his inmost thoughts were entirely opposite: "I am so much in love with the music of *Don Giovanni* that, even as I write to you, I could shed tears of agitation and emotion. In his chamber music, Mozart charms me by his purity and distinction of style and his exquisite handling of the parts. No one else has ever known as well how to interpret so exquisitely in music the sense of resigned and inconsolable sorrow. It is thanks to Mozart that I have devoted my life to music."

The quotation is from a letter written in 1878 to Tchaikovsky's platonic friend and patroness Nadezhda von Meck, who like most music lovers in that era thought Mozart to be very weak tea next to Beethoven or Wagner. It may surprise us to find the composer of such lushly Romantic works as the *Romeo and Juliet* Fantasy Overture and *The Nutcracker* ballet rhapsodizing over purity of style and exquisite interpretation, when critics have been telling us for decades that Tchaikovsky is unsubtle, unintellectual, even downright crude. At the same time, of course, the public has been gorging itself on his music.

Who is right? Maybe all of the above. Tchaikovsky had little patience with the classic German rules of composition, preferring loose and free forms as vehicles for his passionately colored inspirations. Under adademic analysis his music reveals countless "faults" for critics to pounce upon; but in the concert hall, or on records, the vitality of rhythm, the astounding range of orchestral color, and the ravishing beauty of melody sweep everything and everybody before them.

Neurotic from childhood, Tchaikovsky led a tortured emotional life. He suffered alternately from hallucinations, hypochondria, colitis, hysteria, and self-pity. Much has been written (and filmed) about his obsessions, his sex life, his morbidity, but none of that has anything to do with enjoying his art except to make a little clearer the sources of his intensely poetic expression.

Tchaikovsky stood apart from the ultra-nationalist Russian school typified by such composers as Rimsky-Korsakov and Mussorgsky. Like them, he did use a certain amount of native folk idioms in his works, but he preferred the cosmopolitan musical language of Western Europe, particularly France. It was this cross-fertilization, in large part, that gave his music its distinctive blend of elegance and earthy passion.

His artistic credo was founded on a deep sense of destiny, of a cruel and relentless Fate which one can never overcome, but can only accept with (as he had gleaned from Mozart) "a sense of resigned and inconsolable sorrow." Even his death seemed an inevitable consequence of his anguished lifestyle: drinking a glass of unboiled water (which some believe was a deliberate suicide), he quickly contracted cholera and perished in unspeakable agony.

——— *Some famous CDs are not listed because currently out of print.* ———

Capriccio italien, Op. 45

Similar in vein to Rimsky-Korsakov's *Capriccio espagnol*, with an obvious geographical difference, the Tchaikovsky piece was written seven years earlier and is less sophisticated in construction. It makes a similarly brilliant effect, however, and truth to tell I have never heard anyone cry out at a performance "Long live Rimsky-Korsakov's more complex structure!"

Bernstein, New York Philharmonic Orchestra. CBS 36728 [AAD] + Rimsky-Korsakov: *Capriccio espagnol*

Dorati, Minneapolis Symphony Orchestra. Mercury Living Presence 434360 [ADD] + Overture *1812*; Beethoven: *Wellington's Victory*

Dudarova, Symphony Orchestra of Russia. Olympia 512 [DDD] + Overture *1812, Romeo and Juliet*, 5 other orchestral pieces

Dutoit, Montreal Symphony Orchestra. London [Decca] 417300 [DDD] + *Marche slave, Nutcracker* Suite, Overture *1812*

Leaper, Royal Philharmonic Orchestra. Naxos 8.550500 [DDD] + Overture *1812, Marche slave, Romeo and Juliet*

Concerto No. 1 in B-flat for Piano, Op. 23

"Utterly worthless...absolutely unplayable...bad, trivial, vulgar," said Nicholas Rubinstein after hearing the first play-through of what was to become the most popular piano concerto of all time. And he was the composer's friend! But Tchaikovsky fixed the problem: he turned the piece over to a different pianist, who gave the premiere in Boston in 1875. The audience went wild, and so they have remained ever since.

Argerich, Dutoit, Royal Philharmonic Orchestra. Deutsche Grammophon 415062 [ADD] + Prokofiev: Piano Concerto No. 3 (with Abbado conducting)

Argerich, Kondrashin, Bavarian Radio Symphony Orchestra. Philips 446673 [ADD] + Rachmaninov: Piano Concerto No. 3

Cliburn, Kondrashin, RCA Symphony Orchestra. RCA Victor Red Seal 55912 [ADD] + Rachmaninov: Piano Concerto No. 2

Gilels, Mehta, New York Philharmonic Orchestra. Sony Essential Classics 46339 [ADD] + Violin Concerto (with Oistrakh, Ormandy, Philadelphia Orchestra)

Horowitz, Toscanini, NBC Symphony Orchestra. *The Toscanini Collection*, Vol. 44, RCA Victor Gold Seal 60321 (mono) [ADD] + Mussorgsky: *Pictures at an Exhibition*

Pletnev, Fedoseyev, Philharmonia Orchestra. Virgin Classics 59612 [DDD] + Concert Fantasy, Op. 56

———— *Catalog numbers are subject to change without notice.* ————

Concerto in D for Violin, Op. 35

Technically one of the most demanding violin concertos (as well as one of the half dozen most loved), Tchaikovsky's is no mere flashy display piece. In fact it is one of his soberer works. Nevertheless the critic Hanslick wrote that "the Andante begins pleasantly but soon plunges into the atmosphere of a Russian feast, where everybody is drunk and the faces of the people are brutal and revolting."

Bell, Ashkenazy, Cleveland Orchestra. London [Decca] 421716 [DDD] + Wieniawski: Violin Concerto No. 2

Chang, C. Davis, London Symphony Orchestra. EMI 54753 [DDD] + Brahms: *Hungarian Dances* (sel.)

Chung, Dutoit, Montreal Symphony Orchestra. London [Decca] 410011 [DDD] + Mendelssohn: Violin Concerto

Chung, Previn, London Symphony Orchestra. London [Decca] Classic Sound 425080 [ADD] + Sibelius: Violin Concerto

Francescatti, Mitropoulos, New York Philharmonic Orchestra; Ormandy, Philadelphia Orchestra. Sony Masterworks Heritage 62339 (2) (mono) [ADD] + Mendelssohn: Violin Concerto in E Minor; Bruch: Violin Concerto No. 1; Saint-Saëns: Violin Concerto No. 3; Prokofiev: Violin Concerto No. 2; Chausson: *Poème*

Heifetz, Reiner, Chicago Symphony Orchestra. RCA Victor Red Seal 5933 [ADD] + Mendelssohn: Violin Concerto (with Munch, Boston Symphony Orchestra), *Sérénade Mélancolique*, Waltz from *Serenade for Strings*

Heifetz, Reiner, Chicago Symphony Orchestra. RCA Victor Gold Seal 61495 [ADD] + Brahms: Violin Concerto

Nishizaki, Jean, Slovak Philharmonic Orchestra. Naxos 8.550153 [DDD] + Mendelssohn: Violin Concerto

Oistrakh, Ormandy, Philadelphia Orchestra. Sony Essential Classics 46339 [ADD] + Piano Concerto No. 1 (with Gilels, Mehta, New York Philharmonic Orchestra)

Repin, Krivine, London Symphony Orchestra. Erato 98537 [DDD] + Sibelius: Violin Concerto

Stern, Ormandy, Philadelphia Orchestra. Sony 66829 [ADD] + Sibelius: Violin Concerto

Marche slave, Op. 31

The Serbs, with Russian support, were fighting the Muslims. Bosnia in the 1990s? No, Serbia vs. Turkey, 1876. Tchaikovsky wrote this orchestral march as part of a benefit for

——— Since CDs can change label and number, use artists as main reference. ———

wounded Serbian soldiers. The opening funeral march is transformed into a victory hymn at the end.

Dutoit, Montreal Symphony Orchestra. London [Decca] 417300 [DDD] + *Capriccio italien, Nutcracker* Suite, Overture *1812*
Edwards, Royal Liverpool Philharmonic Orchestra. Classics for Pleasure Eminence 2152 [DDD] + Overture *1812, Romeo and Juliet, Francesca da Rimini*
Järvi, Gothenburg Symphony Orchestra. Deutsche Grammophon 429984 [DDD] + *1812* Overture; Rimsky-Korsakov: *Russian Easter* Overture, *Capriccio espagnol*, Borodin: *Polovtsian Dances* from *Prince Igor*, *In the Steppes of Central Asia*
Leaper, Royal Philharmonic Orchestra. Naxos 8.550500 [DDD] + *Capriccio italien*, Overture *1812, Romeo and Juliet*
Pletnev, Russian National Orchestra. Virgin Classics 59661 [DDD] + Symphony No. 6
Slatkin, St. Louis Symphony Orchestra. Telarc 80072 [DDD] + Glinka: *Russlan and Ludmila* Overture; Rimsky-Korsakov: *Russian Easter* Overture; Borodin: *In the Steppes of Central Asia*

Nutcracker Suite, Op. 71a

Only a modest success at its premiere in 1892, *The Nutcracker* has gone on to become one of the handful of most familiar classical works around the world. In some ways it is inferior musically to *Swan Lake* and *Sleeping Beauty*, and its wider fame can be attributed to the success of the suite the composer made for concert hall use, which was actually performed prior to the complete ballet! (It brought down the house.)

Dutoit, Montreal Symphony Orchestra. London [Decca] 417300 [DDD] + *Capriccio italien, Marche slave*, Overture *1812*
Dutoit, Montreal Symphony Orchestra. London [Decca] 443555 [DDD] + *Sleeping Beauty* (sel.), *Swan Lake* (sel.)
Kurtz, Philharmonia Orchestra. EMI Seraphim 68537 (2) [ADD] + Exc. from *Sleeping Beauty, Swan Lake*; Symphony No. 6, *Romeo and Juliet* (with Giulini conducting)
Levine, Vienna Philharmonic Orchestra. Deutsche Grammophon 437806 [DDD] + *Sleeping Beauty* Suite, *Swan Lake* Suite
Rostropovich, Berlin Philharmonic Orchestra. Deutsche Grammophon 449726 [ADD] + *Sleeping Beauty* Suite, *Swan Lake* Suite
Ormandy, Philadelphia Orchestra. Sony Essential Classics 46550 [ADD] + Delibes: *Coppélia* and *Sylvia* Suites

——— *Artists are listed alphabetically, not in order by critical ranking.* ———

Overture 1812, Op. 49

Like the *Marche slave*, the Overture *1812* is an occasional piece, designed to be played in a public square to commemmorate the defeat of Napoleon in Russia. Despite the unmistakable and dominating quotations of the Tsarist national anthem and the French *Marseillaise* which trumpet forth every few seconds, American audiences cheer and applaud when the overture is played, as it so often is, for Independence Day fireworks displays. Inexplicably, when at one of these I once cried out "Long live the Tsar!" I was severely reprimanded.

Dorati, Minneapolis Symphony Orchestra. Mercury Living Presence 434360 [ADD] + *Capriccio italien*; Beethoven: *Wellington's Victory*

Dudarova, Symphony Orchestra of Russia. Olympia 512 [DDD] + *Capriccio italien, Romeo and Juliet,* 5 other orchestral pieces

Dutoit, Montreal Symphony Orchestra. London [Decca] 417300 [DDD] + *Capriccio italien, Marche slave, Nutcracker* Suite

Edwards, Royal Liverpool Philharmonic Orchestra. Classics for Pleasure Eminence 2152 [DDD] + *Marche slave, Romeo and Juliet, Francesca da Rimini*

Järvi, Gothenburg Symphony Orchestra. Deutsche Grammophon 429984 [DDD] + *Marche slave*; Rimsky-Korsakov: *Russian Easter* Overture, *Capriccio espagnol,* Borodin: *Polovtsian Dances* from *Prince Igor, In the Steppes of Central Asia*

Leaper, Royal Philharmonic Orchestra. Naxos 8.550500 [DDD] + *Capriccio italien, Marche slave, Romeo and Juliet*

Solti, Chicago Symphony Orchestra. London [Decca] Jubilee 430446 [DDD] + Mussorgsky: *Pictures at an Exhibition*; Prokofiev: Symphony No. 1

Romeo and Juliet Fantasy Overture

Tchaikovsky chose the unusual designation "fantasy-overture" to indicate that he did not intend a conventional tone poem with a specific narrative program, but an open-ended form that would suggest elements of the immortal story, thoroughly Russianized as it is in the composer's hands. It contains some of Tchaikovsky's most heart-rending melodies, and has perhaps his most hair-raising conclusion.

Dudarova, Symphony Orchestra of Russia. Olympia 512 [DDD] + *Capriccio italien,* Overture *1812,* 5 other orchestral pieces

Edwards, Royal Liverpool Philharmonic Orchestra. Classics for Pleasure Eminence 2152 [DDD] + *Marche slave,* Overture *1812, Francesca da Rimini*

Giulini, Philharmonia Orchestra. EMI Seraphim 68537 (2) [ADD] + Symphony No. 6; Exc. from *Nutcracker, Sleeping Beauty, Swan Lake* (with Kurtz conducting)

——— *[DDD] indicates newest recordings; [ADD] or [AAD] are reissues.* ———

Leaper, Royal Philharmonic Orchestra. Naxos 8.550500 [DDD] + *Capriccio italien, Marche slave,* Overture *1812*
Litton, Bournemouth Symphony Orchestra. Virgin Ultraviolet 61267 + Symphony No. 6
Maazel, Cleveland Orchestra. Telarc 82002 [DDD] + Symphony No. 4
Ormandy, Philadelphia Orchestra. RCA Silver Seal 60908 [ADD] + Symphony No. 6

Sleeping Beauty Suite, Op. 66a

Instead of being, like most ballets, a string of more or less independent pieces, *Sleeping Beauty* has an integrated symphonic structure. By any measure it is one of Tchaikovsky's finest scores. He gave much credit for his inspiration to fellow ballet composer Léo Delibes (*q.v.*).

Dutoit, Montreal Symphony Orchestra. London [Decca] 443555 [DDD] + *Nutcracker* (sel.), *Swan Lake* (sel.)
Kurtz, Philharmonia Orchestra. EMI Seraphim 68537 (2) [ADD] + Exc. from *The Nutcracker, Swan Lake*; Symphony No. 6, *Romeo and Juliet* (with Giulini conducting)
Levine, Vienna Philharmonic Orchestra. Deutsche Grammophon 437806 [DDD] + *Nutcracker* Suite, *Swan Lake* Suite
Rostropovich, Berlin Philharmonic Orchestra. Deutsche Grammophon 449726 [ADD] + *Nutcracker* Suite, *Swan Lake* Suite

Swan Lake Suite, Op. 20a

The first of Tchaikovsky's three great ballets was unsuccessful at first (1877) and was withdrawn. The composer intended to revise it but never had time. After his death it was better received and has long since become a staple of the repertory, having actually had more performances than the other two. It was a favorite mine for early film scores; *Swan Lake* even shows up as the title music for the 1931 *Dracula* with Bela Lugosi.

Dutoit, Montreal Symphony Orchestra. London [Decca] 443555 [DDD] + Nutcracker (sel.), *Sleeping Beauty* (sel.)
Kurtz, Philharmonia Orchestra. EMI Seraphim 68537 (2) [ADD] + Exc. from *The Nutcracker, Sleeping Beauty*; Symphony No. 6, *Romeo and Juliet* (with Giulini conducting)
Levine, Vienna Philharmonic Orchestra. Deutsche Grammophon 437806 [DDD] + *Nutcracker* Suite, *Sleeping Beauty* Suite

———— *CDs go in and out of print; availability of all listed items is not assured.* ————

Rostropovich, Berlin Philharmonic Orchestra. Deutsche Grammophon 449726 [ADD] + *Nutcracker* Suite, *Sleeping Beauty* Suite

Symphonies (6)

The first three of Tchaikovsky's symphonies have value, but are not unquestioned masterpieces. The finales of Nos. 1 and 2 are among my favorite subjects for "conducting calisthenics" when I need a little arm-waving to get going on a groggy day; nevertheless I will confine myself to detailed recommendations of just the three later symphonies. Get those under your belt and you can indulge in the earlier ones.

Symphony No. 4 in F Minor, Op. 36

"Our symphony," Tchaikovsky called No. 4 in typical ambiguously suggestive correspondence with his arms-length patroness Madame von Meck, who proceeded to shell out even more rubles. Untypically, Tchaikovsky steadfastly maintained that this was his best symphony, even years later (normally his favorite work was the one he had just written). The whole structure revolves around a "Destiny" motive introduced in the first movement on horns and trumpets.

Bernstein, New York Philharmonic Orchestra. Sony 47633 [ADD] + *Francesca da Rimini*
Jansons, Oslo Philharmonic Orchestra. Chandos 8361 [DDD]
Maazel, Cleveland Orchestra. Telarc 82002 [DDD] + *Romeo and Juliet*

Symphony No. 5 in E Minor, Op. 64

The idea of the "Destiny" motive having worked so well in Symphony No. 4, Tchaikovsky turned to the gimmick again in No. 5, where it intrudes even more frequently. Although I generally love Tchaikovsky, this has annoyed me from childhood; nevertheless it is impossible not to be won over by the beautiful melody in the slow movement.

Abbado, Chicago Symphony Orchestra. CBS 42094 [DDD] + *The Voyevoda*
Edwards, London Philharmonic Orchestra. Classics for Pleasure Eminence 2187 [DDD] + Exc. from *Eugene Onegin* (with Hannan)
Jansons, Oslo Philharmonic Orchestra. Chandos 8351 [DDD]
Previn, Royal Philharmonic Orchestra. Telarc 80107 [DDD] + Rimsky-Korsakov: *Tsar Saltan* Suite

——— *Some CDs may be available only through importers.* ———

Symphony No. 6 in B Minor, Op. 74, "Pathètique"

Tchaikovsky's most unconventional symphony is his most original and convincing. The nickname "pathetic" was given by the composer's brother after the first performance, where the audience was a-pathetic. Traditionally symphonies end in triumph or at least quiet affirmation, but this one concludes in heart-wrenching despair. Although Tchaikovsky attached no program to the work, it seems obvious that it means to suggest the descent of a soul. A mix of emotions in the first movement yields to a brief idyll of happiness in the second; the third movement begins as a jolly march-along, but evolves almost imperceptibly into a terrifying army whose boots crush everything in their path, followed by the utter desolation of the final movement.

An upsetting experience I often have in classical music is when uncomprehending audiences, as they regularly do, applaud vigorously at the end of the march; I can't help thinking these are the same kind of people who packed picnic lunches and spent their Sundays watching the guillotinings during the French Revolution.

Giulini, Philharmonia Orchestra. EMI Seraphim 68537 (2) [ADD] + *Romeo and Juliet*; Exc. from *Nutcracker, Sleeping Beauty, Swan Lake* (with Kurtz conducting)
Jansons, Oslo Philharmonic Orchestra. Chandos 8446 [DDD]
Litton, Bournemouth Symphony Orchestra. Virgin Ultraviolet 61267 + *Romeo and Juliet*
Ormandy, Philadelphia Orchestra. RCA Silver Seal 60908 [ADD] + *Romeo and Juliet*
Pletnev, Russian National Orchestra. Virgin Classics 59661 [DDD] + *Marche slave*
Wand, North German Radio Symphony Orchestra. RCA Victor Red Seal 61190 [DDD] + Stravinsky: *Pulcinella* Suite

Symphonies 4, 5, 6

In addition to the above, there are excellent boxed sets of all three of the "great" Tchaikovsky symphonies, as follows:

Karajan, Berlin Philharmonic Orchestra. Deutsche Grammophon 453088 (2) [ADD]
Masur, Leipzig Gewandhaus Orchestra. Teldec 95981 [DDD]
Mravinsky, Leningrad Philharmonic Orchestra. Deutsche Grammophon 419745 (2) [ADD]

——— *U.S. labels and numbers are given first, U.K. in [brackets] when needed.* ———

Giuseppe Verdi (1813-1901)

Verdi is acknowledged as the greatest of all the Italian opera composers. With the possible exception of Monteverdi (no relation) centuries before, he is the greatest Italian composer, opera or no. He started inauspiciously enough, as the son of an innkeeper in an obscure village. In love with music from an early age, he tried to enter the Milan Conservatory at age 19 but was rejected as too old, too uncouth, too untrained.

He continued to study privately and by 1839 wrote his first opera, *Oberto*. It was a fair success, but shortly afterwards Verdi's young wife and a daughter both died, and his second opera, a comedy, was a fiasco. The feckless composer was understandably plunged into gloom and for months secluded himself in an attic.

The director of the famed La Scala Opera House, Merelli, believed in Verdi's talent however, and finally induced him to write a work based on the story of Nebuchadnezzar in the Bible. *Nabucco* was a triumph, and established Verdi as Italy's rising star of the lyric stage. Its moving chorus, "Va, pensiero, sull'ali dorate" ("Fly, my thought, on golden wings"), became almost a national anthem for those who sought freedom for Italy, then divided and under Austrian domination.

Verdi soon became a political as well as musical figure. He deliberately inserted patriotic allusions into his operas in order to express solidarity with Italian nationalists. His great *Requiem* was written to honor the freedom fighter Alessandro Manzoni. During a long period of political ferment, the initials V.E.R.D.I were scrawled on walls everywhere (*graffiti* is, we recall, an Italian word), ostensibly to honor the composer, but understood by all to stand for the revolutionary motto: "Vittorio Emmanuele, Re d'Italia" (Victor Emmanuel, King of Italy).

After *Nabucco*, Verdi enjoyed a steady progression to wealth and world fame with a string of some three dozen operas, and hardly a failure among them. He became so beloved that even his weak operas would be quickly forgiven, and the public would move on with relief to another masterpiece.

But Verdi never rested on his laurels, and there are few composers in whom one can trace such a clear development of continuous improvement from the first work to the last. There is nothing more astonishing in music than Verdi's composition in his 80th year of *Falstaff*, a comedy of Shakespearian scope, written with supreme effortless sophistication. 60 years earlier, Verdi had been chugging out cheap marches for a provincial band. His very life was one long opera, with a glorious finale.

It came in January of 1901, when he died in Milan of a stroke at the age of 87. All Italy was plunged into grief. The Roman Senate was called into special session to hear eulogies, and on the day of the funeral all schools were closed. The streets of Milan were clogged with some 250,000 mourners as the horse-drawn cortège made its way slowly, majestically to the Musicians Home, which Verdi had helped found with his own money, and where he had asked to be buried. Someone in the crowd began to sing. Gradually, soft-

———— All CDs listed are considered approximately equal in (high) merit. ————

ly, the melody was passed along, until a quarter of a million people, tears in their eyes, had joined in the largest chorus of all human history:

> *Va, pensiero—*
> *Fly, my thought, on golden wings....*

Aida

One of the most exotically colored operas in the repertoire, *Aida* is Verdi's most truly "grand" opera in the dictionary sense of the word. (The vernacular habit of calling all opera "grand" is sloppy at best; the term is properly limited to four- or five-act musical epics on heroic subjects, with elaborate scenery and plenty of spectacle.) Verdi here fills the bill, yet manages to invest this rather remote story of ancient Egyptian political maneuverings with some real characterization and human feeling.

It was commissioned by the Khedive of Egypt to help celebrate the planned opening of the Suez Canal in 1869. The Khedive, a generous sort, paid Verdi three times his normal fee. Nevertheless, the composer got behind schedule and the premiere took place two years late. Not long afterwards, Egypt went bankrupt and the Khedive was tossed out on his ear. The opera, however, is still raking it in at the box office.

Abbado, Ricciarelli, La Scala Orchestra and Chorus. Deusche Grammophon 410092 (3) [DDD]

Karajan, Freni, Vienna Philharmonic Orchestra. EMI Studio 69300 (3) [ADD]

Karajan, Tebaldi, Vienna Philharmonic Orchestra. London [Decca] 414087 (3) [ADD]

Levine, Millo, Metropolitan Opera Orchestra and Chorus. Sony 45973 (3) [DDD]

Leinsdorf, L. Price, London Symphony Orchestra. RCA Victor Gold Seal 6198 (3) [ADD]

Muti, Caballé, New Philharmonic Orchestra. EMI 56246 (3) [ADD]

Perlea, Milanov, Rome Opera House Orchestra and Chorus. RCA Victor Gold Seal 6652 (3) (mono) [ADD]

Solti, L. Price, Rome Opera Orchestra and Chorus. London [Decca] 417416 (3) [ADD]

Otello

Verdi was in his 70s and long retired when his young friend Arrigo Boito tempted him with a splendid adaptation of Shakespeare's play. He pretended indifference for a long time,

——— *CDs listed are solid, central choices, not necessarily "the greatest."* ———

but finally couldn't control himself: the libretto was too good, his love of the Bard too deep to let the opportunity slip by. When the work premiered in 1887, after a 15-year hiatus in Verdi operas, the world was stunned to find the composer had been maturing in silence. His technique and authority were beyond anything that had gone before, and even more was to come a few years later in *Falstaff*. The newcomer to Verdi, however, will likely find *Otello* more immediately satisfying.

> **Chung, Domingo, Bastille Opera Chorus and Orchestra.** Deutsche Grammophon 439805 [DDD]
> **Levine, Domingo, National Philharmonic Orchestra, London, Ambrosian Opera Chorus.** RCA Victor Red Seal 2951 (2) [ADD]
> **Serafin, Vickers, Rome Opera House Orchestra and Chorus.** RCA Victor Gold Seal 1969 (2) [ADD]
> **Solti, Pavarotti, Chicago Symphony Orchestra and Chorus.** London [Decca] 433669 (2) [DDD]

Requiem

Despite the enduring greatness of his operas, there are many who would say Verdi's best monument is his magnificent *Requiem,* written to commemorate the death of the Italian patriot Alessandro Manzoni. Written on a breathtakingly vast musical canvas, it is not so much a liturgical work as it is "Verdi's greatest opera." The depiction of the Day of Judgment, with menacing brass seeming to gradually approach from first one corner of the cosmos, then another, is one of the most unforgettably vivid moments in all Romantic music.

> **Abbado, Vienna Philharmonic Orchestra, Vienna State Opera Chorus.** Deutsche Grammophon 435884 (2) [DDD]
> **Fricsay, Berlin RIAS Symphony Orchestra and Chamber Choir, St. Hedwig Cathedral Choir.** Deutsche Grammophon Originals 447442 (2) [ADD]
> **Gardiner, Orchestre Révolutionnaire et Romantique, Monteverdi Choir.** Philips 442142 (2) [DDD] + 4 *Sacred Pieces*
> **Giulini, Philharmonia Orchestra and Chorus.** EMI 56250 (2) [ADD] + *4 Sacred Pieces*
> **Muti, Philharmonia Orchestra, Ambrosian Chorus.** EMI Doublefforte 68613 (2) [ADD] + Cherubini: Requiem in C Minor
> **Shaw, Atlanta Symphony Orchestra and Chorus.** Telarc 80152 (2) [DDD] + Verdi opera choruses
> **Solti, Chicago Symphony Orchestra and Chorus.** RCA Victor Gold Seal 61403 (2) [ADD]

——— *Some famous CDs are not listed because currently out of print.* ———

Toscanini, NBC Symphony Orchestra, Robert Shaw Chorale. *The Toscanini*
Collection, Vol. 63, RCA Victor Gold Seal 60299 (2) (mono) [ADD]

Rigoletto

The story concerns a vicious humpback whose obsession to protect his beautiful
daughter backfires. The original play was by Victor Hugo, who until just a few years ago
was widely considered to be a Great Author. With his customary skill Verdi does make it a
great opera, and it was the first one to bring him international fame. The most famous aria
in all his operas, "La donna è mobile," comes from Act III.

Giulini, Cappucilli, Vienna Philharmonic Orchestra. Deutsche Grammophon
415288 (2) [ADD]
Bonynge, Milnes, London Symphony Orchestra. London [Decca] 414269 (2)
[ADD]
Serafin, Gobbi, Callas, La Scala Orchestra and Chorus. EMI 56327 (2)
(mono) [ADD]
Sinopoli, Bruson, Santa Cecilia Academy Orchestra and Chorus. Philips
412592 (2) [DDD]
Solti, Merrill, RCA Italiana Opera Orchestra and Chorus. RCA Gold Seal
6506 (2) [ADD]

La Traviata

Alexander Dumas, Jr.'s once-popular play *The Lady of the Camellias* was the source for
Verdi's ever-popular opera. It is the classic treatment of the "fallen woman" theme. On
paper it all looks hopelessly hokey, but such is Verdi's commitment that the opera is deeply
convincing and moving. It has been made into a commercially successful film, a singular
feat for an opera.

Bonynge, Sutherland, National Philharmonic Orchestra, London, London
Opera Chorus. London [Decca] 430491 (2) [DDD]
C. Kleiber, Cotrubas, Bavarian Radio Symphony Orchestra and Chorus.
Deutsche Grammophon 415132 (2) [ADD]
Rizzi, Gruberova, Ambrosian Singers, London Symphony Orchestra. Teldec
76348 (2) [DDD]
Serafin, de los Angeles, Rome Opera House Orchestra and Chorus. Classics
for Pleasure 4450 (2) [ADD]
Solti, Gheorghiu, Royal Opera House, Covent Garden, Chorus and
Orchestra. London [Decca] 448119 (2) [DDD]

——— *Catalog numbers are subject to change without notice.* ———

Richard Wagner (1813-1883)

Wagner became not just a composer, but a phenomenon. One of the great self-promoters of history, he was the barker, ringmaster, and center attraction of his own one-man circus. By sheer force of personality, if not character, he dominated the musical headlines in the late 19th century and beyond. He was a driven man who could not stand to not get his way.

People didn't like his operas? He would re-name them "music dramas" and write books denouncing his detractors. Theaters wouldn't put them on? He would build his own theater and orchestra and create a cult of performing his works. He literally established a religion with himself as the savior of music: it was called Wagnerism, and his devotees were known as Wagnerites. People wouldn't join the religion? They must be evil Jews.

The parallels with a vicious Austrian paperhanger were obvious to the architects of the Third Reich, who adopted Wagner as their composer laureate, further complicating history's assessment of an already complex issue. The music of Wagner was not heard in Israel until great Jewish musicians such as Leonard Bernstein and Daniel Barenboim pleaded for it, holding that the music itself should not be condemned for the sins of the man who wrote it.

In all fairness, Wagner's notorious anti-Semitism was nothing near the doctrinaire system espoused by the Nazis, and he was as likely to forget all about it if someone he needed to play or conduct his music was Jewish. Everything in his life had to be subservient to his artistic goals, and if anti-Semitism got in the way, it went out the window like anything else. Ironically, it has been fairly well established that Wagner was not the son of his putative father Carl Wagner, but the natural child of his mother's lover and later second husband, a Jewish actor named Ludwig Geyer.

In his early school days in Dresden, Wagner showed far more aptitude for literature than for music. Partly under the influence of a scholarly uncle he imbibed the ancient classics, Shakespeare, and Goethe. Not until the relatively late age (for a musician) of 14 did he decide, after hearing a Beethoven symphony for the first time, that he would devote himself to music. With the energy typical of a fanatic he plunged into a study of music theory and was soon composing. Amazingly, the man who would for a time be proclaimed a greater composer than Bach, Mozart, or Beethoven was largely self-taught and tutored.

At first he concentrated on symphonic music, but by the end of his university days at Leipzig he had turned to opera and taken the job of director of a small company in Magdeburg. He married one of the singers there, Minna Planer. With her he was soon migrating all over Europe, pursued by creditors. Wagner's appetites were enormous, not least for clothes and luxuries, and he considered being asked to pay for them an affront to his artistic divinity.

The Wagners were near starvation when his opera *Rienzi* was finally a success. From then on it was a fairly steady climb upwards, assisted by the patronage of King Ludwig II of Bavaria (who turned his fairy-tale castle Neuschwanstein into a Wagner theme park) and the growing army of Wagnerites who fanned out across Europe to promote the theories and works of their Master (as they called him). There were interruptions, as when Wagner had to flee for his life after supporting the Revolution of 1848, and another exile after he stole the wife of one of his closest friends, the conductor Hans von Bülow (further complicated by the fact that the woman was Franz Liszt's daughter Cosima—Liszt also had been a Wagner supporter).

Never one to think small, Wagner had in mind for years a magnum opus that would be based on the old German sagas and Norse eddas. The result, after many years of sporadic work, was *The Ring of the Nibelung*, a continuous epic which required four evenings to perform and led Wagner to build his own theater, the Bayreuth Festspielhaus, to stage it. Like the man himself, his greatest work was bigger than life.

Wagner's theories of opera as a synthesis of all the arts; his method of composition, involving liberal use of the thematic device which he called the *Leitmotif* and a through-composed style of "endless melody" without set pieces and arias; and his vision of a "music of the future," which was little more than an expanded reliance on chromaticism (more sharps and flats!), created about him a cachet of almost supernatural authority. Not everyone fell for it, however, and there was always a vigorous anti-Wagner faction, with Johannes Brahms elevated somewhat reluctantly to its symbolic head.

Today, when Wagner has receded to the status of an enormously talented, if rather unpleasant, human, most people can listen to his music without bowing under its pseudo-philosophical baggage. It is music of stupendous force, color, and drama. (Some would say too much so—"I like Wagner's music better than any other music," wrote Oscar Wilde. "It is so loud that one can talk the whole time without people hearing what one says."). Its harmonic innovations made possible a new direction in music from Bruckner and Debussy to the present. It stirred up the world of the arts and made people think more than they ever had about the role of music and the musician in life. Despite its many faults, it is a mighty legacy.

Orchestral Selections

Most Wagnerites are first seduced by orchestral arrangements, minus the singing, of large sections (commonly called "bleeding chunks") of the operas. Almost all of these have had to have some surgery to extricate them from the original contexts. There are some overtures and preludes, and truncations with identifying labels such as "Forest Murmurs," "Ride of the Valkyries," and "Siegfried's Rhine Journey." Many people have heard only these Reader's Digest versions and are positively shocked to find out that there are words that go with them. Nevertheless, they are a legitimate way to enter Wagner's world, so let us hack away.

Furtwängler, Philharmonia Orchestra. EMI 64935 (mono) [ADD]
Handley, Royal Philharmonic Orchestra. RPO [Tring] 008 [DDD] + *Siegfried Idyll*

——— *Artists are listed alphabetically, not in order by critical ranking.* ———

Jansons, Oslo Philharmonic Orchestra. EMI 54583 [DDD]
Karajan, Berlin Philharmonic Orchestra. EMI Studio Plus 64334 [ADD]
Levine, Metropolitan Opera Orchestra. Deutsche Grammophon 435874
   [DDD]
López-Cobos, Cincinnati Symphony Orchestra. Telarc 80379 [DDD]
Reiner, Chicago Symphony Orchestra, RCA Victor Orchestra. RCA Gold Seal
   61792 [ADD] + Humperdinck: *Dream Pantomime* from *Hansel und Gretel*
Szell, Cleveland Orchestra. *Ring* hlts, CBS [Sony] 36715 [ADD]
Szell, Cleveland Orchestra. CBS [Sony] 38486 [ADD]
Solti, Vienna Philharmonic Orchestra. *Ring* hlts., London [Decca] 410137
   [DDD]
Solti, Vienna Philharmonic Orchestra. London [Decca] 440107 [ADD/DDD]
Tennstedt, Berlin Philharmonic Orchestra. EMI Doubleforte 68616 [DDD]
Various conductors and orchestras. *Overtures and Preludes*, Deutsche
   Grammophon Double 439687 (2) [ADD] + *Siegfried Idyll*

The Flying Dutchman (Der fliegende Holländer)

This is Wagner's earliest opera to still hold the boards, and one of the easiest to slide
into if you are ready to try the Whole Thing. He wrote it originally in one continuous long
act; being a living god he had of course forgotten that mortals need to go to the rest room,
and eventually under pressure he divided it up into three acts.

It is a mildly horrific Gothic tale of a ghostly sea captain who sails the oceans eter-
nally with a spectral crew, seeking release from his curse through the pure love of a maid.
The music positively reeks of the salt spray and the howling wind in the topsail, with more
chain-rattling and bone-clanking than in *Spook Chasers with the Bowery Boys* (it is quite cinematic, come to think of it).

Dohnányi, Hale, Vienna Philharmonic Orchestra. London [Decca] 436418
   (2) [DDD]
Dorati, London, Royal Opera House, Covent Garden, Orchestra and
   Chorus. London [Decca] 417319 (2) [ADD]
Karajan, van Dam, Berlin Philharmonic Orchestra. EMI 64650 (2) [DDD]
Nelsson, Estes, Bayreuth Festival Orchestra and Chorus. Philips 434599 (2)
   [DDD]
P. Steinberg, Muff, Vienna ORF Symphony Orchestra, Budapest Radio
   Choir. Naxos 8.660025/26 (2) [DDD]

———— *[DDD] indicates newest recordings; [ADD] or [AAD] are reissues.* ————

Der Ring des Nibelungen

The Ring, as it is familiarly called, is to a normal-sized opera (let's say *Rigoletto*) as the Pyramid of Cheops is to a summer cabin: very impressive, much bigger, but not necessarily better. I say that with all love, because the *Ring* is one of the great experiences a person can have in music. You can't very well ignore it. You can waste time walking around it, but it would be better just to climb up and explore it.

Wagner certainly had a sense of the epic, and he wisely chose the myths of his own culture on which to build his greatest monument. It took 28 years of work from the first sketches in 1848 to the premiere in 1876, at the theater Wagner had to have built to accomodate it. Although some aspects of the story are of limited interest to non-Teutons, most of it has universal resonance, and Wagner has poured into it the best of his considerable talent.

Once you have succumbed to the various bleeding chunks offered on highlights albums, there is a good possibility you will want to have the whole *Ring*; just remember you will have to set aside some 15 or 16 hours of listening time, and don't spread it too thin or you may forget the story and have to start over, despite the numerous recaps Wagner thoughtfully works into the text as it goes along. (Some listeners hate these as holding up the action.)

Solti, Flagstad, Vienna Philharmonic Orchestra. London [Decca] 414100 (15) [ADD]

[There are other estimable *Ring* recordings, particularly those conducted by Böhm, Barenboim, and (historically) Furtwängler; but this is the inevitable "first" *Ring*, and if you mean to collect Wagner no one will take you seriously if you don't have it. Similarly, if you can only have one *Ring*, this is the one to have.]

Tristan und Isolde

No one but Wagner would have written this stupendous five-hour drama as a diversion when he needed a break from the *Ring!* It stands apart from his other compositions as an experiment in structure and especially harmony, and is often considered the seminal work which made 20th-century music possible. Its roots, like the *Ring's*, are mythical, but in its treatment it explores depths of psychology which were never dreamed of in opera before Wagner's time. Whole books have been written on its significance, but if you can master the *Ring*, you should be able to toss this one off on a Friday night.

Böhm, Nilsson, Bayreuth Festival Orchestra and Chorus. Deutsche Grammophon 434425 (3) [ADD]
Furtwängler, Flagstad, Philharmonia Orchestra, Covent Garden Chorus. EMI 56254 (4) (mono) [ADD]

——— *CDs go in and out of print; availability of all listed items is not assured.* ———

Karajan, Dernesch, Berlin Philharmonic Orchestra, German Opera Chorus.
EMI Studio 69319 (4) [ADD]

Die Walküre

"The Valkyrie" is the second of the four operas, or "evenings" as Wagner called them, that make up the *Ring,* and the one most often called on to stand alone. It does work quite well as a self-contained unit, and of the four probably offers the most for your money and time. If you aren't sure you want to invest in the complete *Ring* you could start with *Die Walküre* and decide whether to pick up on the rest later. And remember: it's only four hours long!

Solti, Nilsson, Vienna Philharmonic Orchestra. London [Decca] 414105 (4)
[ADD]

The Late Romantics
(ca. 1890-1915)

The composers of this period, or sub-period if you will, were all born between 1845 and 1865. That places them chronologically, but they generally share more than dates. They share the fact that their most important work came after Liszt and Wagner, who with their rhapsodic forms and widening sense of tonality had confused, if not revolutionized, the art of composition.

Many of these composers were not sure which way to turn. No one could go back to the pre-Wagnerian days, which were now considered a closed book at best, utterly passé at worst. But whither? No one was prepared to abandon everything overnight, although that is how many felt standing in Wagner's intimidating shadow, hearing the Master's disciples telling them that all they had learned of music theory was superseded by the Music of the Future—whatever, and whenever, that was.

All of the Late Romantic composers chose to remain within the confines of the major-minor tonal system, even though some, like Debussy, stretched it to the limit. But they all sensed that the old system was somehow coming to an end. In Elgar and Delius we hear nostalgia for the long-ago-and-far-away; in Mahler the anxiety and angst of facing the unknown; in Richard Strauss and Humperdinck an attempt to keep the old Wagnerian juggernaut rolling along. Mascagni and Leoncavallo, and to a lesser extent Puccini, sought release from the old restraints through extremes of sensation. Fauré tried to stop the disintegration by binding modern tendencies with the glue of classicism. D'Indy called on his students to have faith in the midst of artistic crisis, to rise above despair through reason; and Dukas simply gave up and tore most of his music into shreds.

Whatever their response, all were seeking an answer to a nagging question: What future had Western music, after the old scaffolding was removed? None of them came up with a perfect solution, but most of them, each in his individual way, helped form a bridge to the future. It was a period of ferment and experimentation, alternating between hope and frustration, but no definite break with the past had yet come. That will be a story for the next chapter.

Claude Debussy (1862-1918)

Acknowledged today as not only one of the most original and seminal composers at the beginning of the 20th century, Debussy was a popular success as well–a combination seldom to be noted. Here is a man who could turn harmony upside down and use it to write *Clair de lune,* a piece that has almost become Muzak. "A century of airplanes," he once said, "deserves its own music. As there are no precedents, I must create anew."

He was a talented child who entered the prestigious Paris Conservatory at only ten years of age. Except for four years of study in Italy, he remained in his beloved Paris all his life. His favorite description of himself was simply "musicien française."

His artistic path was determined by exposure to the Symbolist poets, whose theories he wished to apply to music. Although he later repudiated Wagnerism, it was an early influence on him, and he took something away also from the Paris Exhibition of 1889, where he became fascinated by Javanese gamelan music. The result was a musical "school" known as Impressionism, of which Debussy became the chief (and frankly, almost only) composer. His goal was not, like his German contemporary Richard Strauss, to literally depict extramusical subjects in tones, but to suggest them.

He hit on a style which leaned heavily on the whole-tone scale, which has six notes instead of the conventional eight, with different intervals between them. With this device he was able to create unique melodies, chords, and harmonies that seemed earthy and sensual, yet at the same time exquisitely delicate and fragile. It was a fascinating sound, richly capable of evoking subtle sensations.

For its day, however, around the turn of the century, it was puzzling and upsetting to many listeners. Gone were the comfortable black and white rules and forms of musical composition, replaced by fleeting allusions, splashes of color, and hints of forbidden perfumes. It all smacked of subversiveness.

When Debussy's great opera was being rehearsed in 1902, the arch-conservative composer Camille Saint-Saëns was spotted in the street by a friend. "Maestro," he exclaimed, "I thought you were out of town." The old man glowered. "I have thtayed in Parith," he spat, in his notorious lisp, "to thpeak ill of *Pelléath et Mélithande!*" Debussy paid no attention to such criticism. Even as a student at the Conservatory he ignored the old rules. One of his professors, hearing him practicing bizarre chord progressions on the piano, barked at him "What rule do you follow?" Debussy quietly replied: "Mon plaisir."

Images pour orchestre

Written between 1908 and 1912 and later put together out of order, the three *Images* are "Gigues" (jigs), "Iberia" (Spain), and "Rondes de printemps" (Spring round dance). "Ibéria," the longest section, is the most popular and is often heard separately. Manuel de Falla, the greatest composer of Spain, said Debussy had spent only a few hours in his country, but had caught its musical character more accurately than many native composers had done. "Ibéria" itself divides into three sections: "In the Streets and Byways," "Fragrances of the Night," and "Morning of a Festival Day."

Dutoit, Montreal Symphony Orchestra. London [Decca] 425502 [DDD] +
   Nocturnes

———— *All CDs listed are considered approximately equal in (high) merit.* ————

Haitink, Concertgebouw Orchestra. Philips Duo 438742 (2) [ADD] + *Nocturnes, La mer, Prelude to the Afternoon of a Faun, Jeux,* more

Paray, Detroit Symphony Orchestra. (*Ibéria* only) Mercury Living Presence 434343 [ADD] + *La mer, Nocturnes, Prelude to the Afternoon of a Faun*

Reiner, Chicago Symphony Orchestra. (*Ibéria* only) RCA Victor Gold Seal 60179 [ADD] + Ravel: *Alborada del gracioso, Pavane for a Dead Princess, Rapsodie espagnole, Valses nobles et sentimentales*

Salonen, Los Angeles Philharmonic Orchestra. Sony 62599 [DDD] + *La mer, Prelude to the Afternoon of a Faun*

Tortelier, Ulster Orchestra. Chandos 8850 [DDD] + Ravel: *Alborada del gracioso, Rapsodie espagnole*

La Mer

Debussy loved the sea as much as any composer ever has: "She has shown me all her moods," he told his publisher. *La mer* ("The Sea"), completed in 1905, is the composer's largest tone poem, and the one of his works more than any other which fully represents what he meant by Impressionism. The three movements are marked "From Dawn till Noon on the Sea," "Play of the Waves," and "Dialog of the Wind and the Sea."

Ansermet, Suisse Romande Orchestra. London [Decca] Classic Sound 448576 [ADD] + Dukas: *The Sorcerer's Apprentice*; Chabrier: *España*; Honegger: *Pacific 231*; Ravel: *Boléro, La valse*

Baudo, London Philharmonic Orchestra. Classics for Pleasure Eminence 9502 [ADD] + *Prelude to the Afternoon of a Faun*

Dutoit, Montreal Symphony Orchestra. London [Decca] 430240 [DDD] + *Prelude to the Afternoon of a Faun, Jeux, Martyrdom of St. Sebastian* (sel.)

Frühbeck de Burgos, London Symphony Orchestra. IMP [Carlton Classics] PCD 915 [DDD] + *Nocturnes, Prelude to the Afternoon of a Faun*

Haitink, Concertgebouw Orchestra. Philips Duo 438742 (2) [ADD] + *Images pour orchestre, Nocturnes, Prelude to the Afternoon of a Faun, Jeux,* etc.

Karajan, Berlin Philharmonic Orchestra. Deutsche Grammophon Galleria 427250 [ADD] + *Prelude to the Afternoon of a Faun*; Ravel: *Boléro, Daphnis et Chloé* Suite No. 2

Karajan, Berlin Philharmonic Orchestra. Deutsche Grammophon Originals 447426 [ADD] + Mussorgsky: *Pictures at an Exhibition*; Ravel: *Boléro*

Karajan, Berlin Philharmonic Orchestra. EMI 64357 [ADD] + Ravel: *Boléro, La valse, Alborada del gracioso* (with Orchestre de paris)

Martinon, ORTF Orchestra. EMI 69587 [ADD] + *Nocturnes, Prelude to the Afternoon of a Faun*

——— *CDs listed are solid, central choices, not necessarily "the greatest."* ———

Munch, Boston Symphony Orchestra. RCA Living Stereo 61500 [ADD] + Saint-Saëns: Symphony No. 3; Ibert: *Escales*

Ormandy, Philadelphia Orchestra. *The Debussy Album*, CBS [Sony] 30950 (2) [ADD] + *Danses sacrées et profanes, Nocturnes, Prelude to the Afternoon of a Faun, Clair de lune*

Paray, Detroit Symphony Orchestra. Mercury Living Presence 434343 [ADD] + *Ibéria* from *Images pour orchestre, Nocturnes, Prelude to the Afternoon of a Faun*

Previn Royal Philharmonic Orchestra. EMI Seraphim 68539 (2) [ADD] + *Nocturnes*; Ravel: *Valses nobles et sentimentales, Alborada del gracioso, Boléro, Pavane for a Dead Princess*; Mussorgsky: *Pictures at an Exhibition* (with Maazel, New Philharmonia Orchestra)

Reiner, Chicago Symphony Orchestra. RCA Living Stereo 68079 [ADD] + Respighi: *Pines of Rome, Fountains of Rome*

Reiner, Chicago Symphony Orchestra. RCA Gold Seal 60875 [ADD] + Rimsky-Korsakov: *Scheherazade*

Salonen, Los Angeles Philharmonic Orchestra. Sony 62599 [DDD] + *Images pour orchestre, Prelude to the Afternoon of a Faun*

Simon, Philharmonia Orchestra. Cala 1001 [DDD] + *Clair de lune* (orch. Caplet), other short orchestral pieces

Nocturnes

"The title 'Nocturnes,'" Debussy wrote, "is to be interpreted…in a decorative sense." It is meant to designate, he explained, "all the various impressions and the special effects of light that the word suggests." Again the work is in three sections: "Nuages" (clouds), "Fêtes" (festivals), and "Sirènes" (sirens, that is, of the feminine kind). Written 1897-99, the *Nocturnes* are heard much less often than they deserve due to the extra expense of a female chorus in the last movement only.

Dutoit, Montreal Symphony Orchestra. London [Decca] 425502 [DDD] + *Images pour orchestre*

Frühbeck de Burgos, London Symphony Orchestra and Chorus. IMP [Carlton Classics] PCD 915 [DDD] + *La mer, Prelude to the Afternoon of a Faun*

Haitink, Concertgebouw Orchestra. Philips Duo 438742 (2) [ADD] + *Images pour orchestre, La mer, Prelude to the Afternoon of a Faun, Jeux*, etc.

Martinon, ORTF Orchestra. EMI 69587 [ADD] + *La mer, Prelude to the Afternoon of a Faun*

Ormandy, Philadelphia Orchestra. *The Debussy Album*, CBS [Sony] 30950 (2) [ADD] + *Danses sacrées et profanes, La mer, Prelude to the Afternoon of a Faun, Clair de lune*

———— *Some famous CDs are not listed because currently out of print.* ————

Paray, Detroit Symphony Orchestra. Mercury Living Presence 434343 [ADD] + *Ibéria* from *Images pour orchestre, La mer, Prelude to the Afternoon of a Faun*
Previn Royal Philharmonic Orchestra. EMI Seraphim 68539 (2) [ADD] + *La mer*; Ravel: *Valses nobles et sentimentales// Alborada del gracioso, Boléro, Pavane for a Dead Princess*; Mussorgsky: *Pictures at an Exhibition* (with Maazel, New Philharmonia Orchestra)

Piano Music

Debussy wrote a considerable body of significant music for one and two pianos, including two books of Preludes, but the one piece that everyone knows him by is *Clair de lune* ("Moonlight"), which is actually one movement of the *Suite Bergamasque.*

One of comedian Victor Borge's standard lines was pretending to misunderstand the title as "Clear the Saloon." That's good, but even better was the real-life incident when I once asked a very confused young music-seeker whether she liked Debussy, and with a perplexed expression she responded: "Fields?"

Each collection listed is guaranteed to contain at least *Clair de lune.*

[For the orchestral version, get Cala 1001 [DDD] with Geoffrey Simon conducting the Philharmonia Orchestra in *Clair de lune* and other fascinating orchestral transcriptions, plus *La mer*; or, the double CBS [Sony] set 30950 [ADD] titled *The Debussy Album*, which contains also *La mer*, the *Nocturnes, Danses sacrées et profanes*, and *Prelude to the Afternoon of a Faun.*]

Kocsis. Philips 412118 [DDD]
Ortiz. IMP [Carlton Classics] PCD 846 [DDD] + works by Chabrier, Ibert, Milhaud, Poulenc, Ravel
Rogé. London [Decca] Double 443021 (2) [ADD]

Prélude à l'après-midi d'un faune

Inspired by a poem of the same name by the symbolist Stephane Mallarmé, *Prelude to the Afternoon of a Faun* was Debussy's first hit. It describes a mythical faun drowsing in the afternoon sun, dreaming of two nymphs. In diaphonous music of magical haziness, Debussy creates a perfect picture of dreamlike sensuality which has never been surpassed.

Baudo, London Philharmonic Orchestra. Classics for Pleasure Eminence 9502 [ADD] + *La mer*
Dutoit, Montreal Symphony Orchestra. London [Decca] 430240 [DDD] + *La mer, Jeux, Martyrdom of St. Sebastian* (sel.)
Frühbeck de Burgos, London Symphony Orchestra. IMP [Carlton Classics] PCD 915 [DDD] + *La mer, Nocturnes*

———— *Catalog numbers are subject to change without notice.* ————

Haitink, Concertgebouw Orchestra. Philips Duo 438742 (2) [ADD] + *Images pour orchestre, La mer, Nocturnes, Jeux,* etc.

Karajan, Berlin Philharmonic Orchestra. Deutsche Grammophon Galleria 427250 [ADD] + *La mer;* Ravel: *Boléro, Daphnis et Chloé* No. 2

Martinon, ORTF Orchestra. EMI 69587 [ADD] + *Nocturnes, La mer*

Ormandy, Philadelphia Orchestra. *The Debussy Album,* CBS [Sony] 30950 (2) [ADD] + *Danses sacrées et profanes, Nocturnes, La Mer, Clair de lune*

Paray, Detroit Symphony Orchestra. Mercury Living Presence 434343 [ADD] + *Ibéria* from *Images pour orchestre, La mer, Nocturnes*

Salonen, Los Angeles Philharmonic Orchestra. Sony 62599 [DDD] + *Images pour orchestre, La mer*

Tortelier, Ulster Orchestra. Chandos 8893 [DDD] + Ravel: *Daphnis et Chloé* (complete)

Quartet in G Minor, Op. 10

Debussy's only string quartet is actually one of his least characteristic works, having no program explicit or implied. It is experimental in form and style, but has become a standard of the chamber music repertoire nonetheless. Listed here are only exceptional recordings that also include the Ravel Quartet in F (the most common and natural coupling).

Alban Berg Quartet. EMI 47347 [DDD] + Ravel: Quartet in F

Carmina Quartet. Denon 75164 [DDD] + Ravel: Quartet in F

Hagen Quartet. Deutsche Grammophon 437836 [DDD] + Ravel: Quartet in F; Webern: String Quartet

Juilliard Quartet. Sony 52554 [DDD] + Ravel: Quartet in F; Dutilleux: Quartet

Orpheus Quartet. Channel Classics 3892 [DDD] + Ravel: Quartet in F; Dutilleux: *Ainsi la nuit*

Quartetto Italiano. Philips Silver Line 420894 [ADD] + Ravel: Quartet in F

Frederick Delius (1862-1934)

Henry James said that the two most beautiful words in the English language are "summer afternoon." The spirit of that thought inhabits the music of Delius, who is remembered mainly for a number of small pieces—exquisitely serene tone poems with delicious titles such as *On Hearing the First Cuckoo in Spring, A Song Before Sunrise,* and *In a Summer Garden.* The opulent harmonies of these works lend themselves ideally to their subject matter, and are part and parcel of the Late Romantic style.

Sir Thomas Beecham, the conductor who more than anyone championed Delius and brought the music of this recluse to public attention, called him "the last great apostle in

———— Since CDs can change label and number, use artists as main reference. ————

our time of romance, beauty and emotion in music." His sound is absolutely unique. Both rapturous and elegant, sensuous and refined, it is the sound of evanescent landscapes. The melodies are magically beautiful, but they are not the kind that are easy to remember and hum after you hear them; they evaporate into the twilight of the imagination, and the uncertain memory of them pulls you back to Delius with a desire to hear them again.

Delius was the son of a wealthy English wool merchant who did everything in his power to keep Frederick away from foolishness such as music; who, in fact, refused to admit his son was a composer even after he was famous. The young Delius was packed off to Florida where he tried in vain for two years to manage some orange groves his father had bought as an investment. He spent most of his time studying theory with the organist of a church in Jacksonville, and taking notes on the music of the freed slaves, while the oranges rotted on the ground.

His father was finally willing to pay his way to the Leipzig Conservatory just to get rid of him. He studied there three years, then moved to Paris where he married. The couple eventually decided to make their permanent home in the lovely small French town of Grez-sur-Loing outside of Fontainebleu; here they lived quietly for the remainder of his life, another 37 years, and here Delius wrote most of the works for which he is remembered, becoming more and more withdrawn from the world.

In his final years he was incapacitated by blindness, but a young musician who was one of his admirers, Eric Fenby, made an offer unique in the history of composing: he would live with the couple and take dictation. Thus Delius "wrote" his last works, composing them in his head and then telling Fenby how to write them down, note by note, chord by chord.

Tone poems

As mentioned above, Sir Thomas Beecham, one of the greatest conductors on records, almost singlehandedly championed Delius right out of obscurity into the limelight. He once said of this music "I found it as alluring as a wayward woman, and determined to tame it. And it wasn't done in a day!" His definitive (stereo) recordings, although they date back a few years, have been well remastered and sound quite fresh. They will be classics in every sense forever, and are joined here only by those of comparable stature in even better sound.

Beecham, Royal Philharmonic Orchestra. EMI 47509 (2) [ADD]
A. Davis, BBC Symphony Orchestra. Teldec 90845 [DDD]
Del Mar, Bournemouth Sinfonietta. Chandos 6502 [ADD]
Hickox, Northern Sinfonia. EMI 65067 [DDD]

——— *Artists are listed alphabetically, not in order by critical ranking.* ———

Paul Dukas (1865-1935)

Dukas is remembered almost exclusively for one tone poem, *L'Apprenti sorcier*. It is one of only a handful of works that survived his obsessive perfectionism, for he either abandoned or destroyed most of his compositions out of dissatisfaction.

Born in Paris of a mother who was an accomplished pianist, Dukas showed that early talent for music so common among composers. He later claimed that as a baby he had "given suck in 9/8 time." He entered the Paris Conservatory at age 17 and stayed there for eight years, immersing himself in counterpoint and fugue.

His first public work, an overture, was succesful in 1892, but it was the orchestral scherzo, *The Sorcerer's Apprentice*, which made him suddenly a sensation in 1897. Dukas was mortified, since he had only written the piece as an example to his students (he was now a professor at the Conservatory) of how *not* to write a scherzo!

The piece was indeed unrepresentative of its composer. Dukas was greatly influenced by Debussy, and his opera *Ariane et Barbe-bleue* is esteemed by connoisseurs as the greatest successor to *Pelléas et Mélisande*. What of Dukas's music survives is distinguished by great delicacy of expression—not the rumbunctious cavortings of his greatest hit!

The Sorcerer's Apprentice (L'Apprenti sorcier)

Written long before Mickey Mouse was even thought of, the tone poem depicts the story precisely as Walt Disney told it. (It is the only music in *Fantasia* of which that can be said.) A young student of magic decides to try his hand when the master is away. He manages to get a broom to come to life and draw water for him, but he doesn't know to undo the spell and soon the house is flooded. Chopping the broom in half only creates two brooms to bring twice as much water. The apprentice's despairing cries bring the master back. He calms the waters, removes the spell, and gives the errant lad a kick in the pants.

Ansermet, Suisse Romande Orchestra. London [Decca] Classic Sound 448576 [ADD] + Chabrier: *España*; Debussy: *La Mer*; Honegger: *Pacific 231*; Ravel: *Boléro, La Valse*

Bernstein, New York Philharmonic Orchestra. CBS [Sony] 37769 [AAD] + Saint-Saëns: *Danse Macabre*, Bacchanale from *Samson et Dalila*; Chabrier: *España*; Ravel: *Pavane for a Dead Princess*; Offenbach: Overture *to Orpheus in the Underworld*

Levine, Berlin Philharmonic Orchestra. Deutsche Grammophon 419617 [DDD] + Saint-Saëns: Symphony No. 3

——— *[DDD] indicates newest recordings; [ADD] or [AAD] are reissues.* ———

Solti, Israel Philharmonic Orchestra. London [Decca] 443033 (2) [ADD] + Saint-Saëns: *Danse macabre, La rouet d'Omphale* Bizet: *Jeux d'enfants* (with Martinon, Paris Conservatory Orchestra); *L'Arlèsienne* Suites, *Carmen* Suites, Offenbach: *Gaité Parisienne* (with Munch, New Philharmonia Orchestra); Chabrier: *España, Joyeuse marche* (with Ansermet, Suisse Romande Orchestra); **Tortelier, Ulster Orchestra.** Chandos 8852 [DDD] + *La Péri*; Chabrier: *España, Suite Pastorale*

Edward Elgar (1857-1934)

Dressed like any English squire in his vest and cravat, smiling benignly over a bushy mustachio, composing *Pomp and Circumstance* marches and a Coronation Ode for Edward VII, Elgar could easily have become a caricature of the establishment British composer-laureate. But there was another side to him, sensitive and intimate, which gives depth even to his "public" works, and which is all the more fascinating because he was so reluctant to show it.

The young Elgar learned music mostly from his father, an organist and piano-tuner, and on his own. He had no university or professional training in music, but set himself up at age 16 teaching piano and violin. He took what part he could in local musical life, but living in Worcester the best job he could get was conducting the orchestra at a mental hospital. He credited his experience arranging for wildly unlikely instrumental combinations at the County Lunatic Asylum in helping him become a brilliant orchestrator later in life.

It was love that finally released his creative genius. In 1889 he married one of his piano students, Caroline Alice Roberts, eight years his senior. She believed firmly that Elgar was a genius, something he apparently had never considered. Thereafter music poured from him and his fame increased, until he was knighted in 1904. No matter how public he became, however, he held his private life and thoughts as tenaciously secret as he could.

Recent biographers have tried to prove that some earlier love still lurked in his psyche, as hinted in the inscription to his Violin Concerto: "A qui esta encerrada el alma de...." ("Herein is enshrined the soul of..."), a quotation from LeSage's *Gil Blas*. But Elgar was ever fond of puzzles and mysteries, as evidenced by his famous *Enigma Variations*, and may have simply liked to tease.

Whatever other loves he may have had, the fact remains that his muse flourished only as long as Caroline lived. When she died in 1920, after a brief illness, Elgar placed in her coffin symbols of all the honors she had inspired him to win. From that day until his own death 14 years later, he wrote no music at all, spending his time instead chopping wood or wandering the countryside.

Talking to a friend during his final illness, Elgar suddenly began humming a tune from his last work, the Cello Concerto. "If ever after I'm dead," he whispered, "you hear someone whistling this tune on the Malvern Hills, don't be alarmed. It's only me."

—— *CDs go in and out of print; availability of all listed items is not assured.* ——

Concerto for Cello in E Minor, Op. 85

Elgar's more popular concerto (he wrote only two, the other for violin) was given its premiere in 1919 by Felix Salmond, for whom it was written, with the composer conducting. It is unusually intimate for Elgar, a kind of expression of sorrow from someone very shy. Its only major flaw is a tacked-on happy ending that nobody could possibly believe. Despite that, the work has taken its place beside the Dvořák as one of the great cello concertos.

> **Cohen, Del Mar, London Philharmonic Orchestra.** Classics for Pleasure Silver Doubles 4775 (2) [ADD/DDD] + Beethoven: Triple Concerto; Dvořák: Cello Concerto; Tchaikovsky: *Rococo Variations*
> **Du Pré, Barbirolli, London Symphony Orchestra.** EMI 56219 + *Sea Pictures*
> **Isserlis, Hickox, London Symphony Orchestra.** Virgin Ultraviolet 61125 [DDD] + Bloch: *Schelomo*
> **Lloyd Webber, Menuhin, Royal Philharmonic Orchestra.** Philips 416354 [DDD] + *Enigma Variations*
> **Ma, Previn, London Symphony Orchestra.** Sony 39541 [53333] [DDD] + Walton: Cello Concerto
> **Schmidt, Frühbeck de Burgos, London Symphony Orchestra.** IMP PCD 930 [DDD] + Vaughan Williams: *Fantasia on a Theme by Thomas Tallis, Fantasia on "Greensleeves"*
> **Starker, Slatkin, Philharmonia Orchestra.** RCA Victor Red Seal 61695 [DDD] + Walton: Cello Concerto; Delius: *Caprice and Elegy*

Enigma Variations, Op. 36

A brilliant tour-de-force, this set of variations both humorous and mysterious is one of the best-orchestrated pieces anyone has written. It is also the apotheosis of Elgar's love for riddles. Each of the 14 variations is a musical portrait of a friend, his wife, or himself. Originally the persons were disguised under pseudonyms or initials, but they have all long since been identified.

There is a theme for the variations to be built on, but Elgar insisted there was another, unheard theme which is woven through the work. Many have striven since the premiere in 1899 to figure this riddle out, and every year or two someone claims to have the "proof" that explains it. The main clue Elgar gave was that it was so obvious he was amazed no one had guessed it. But he took the answer, if there is one, to his grave. As years passed he grew more and more irritable over the constant speculation. "There is nothing to be gained....by solving the enigma," he wrote; "the listener should hear the music as music."

My own belief is that there is no "enigma." I think it was a publicity stunt to call attention to the piece, or a private joke which got out of hand, and Elgar was too embar-

——— *Some CDs may be available only through importers.* ———

rassed or ashamed to admit it. Why else would he never reveal the answer, and become so crotchety about being badgered? Or, he may have had an idea about an imaginary counterpoint that could be inferred, but forgot later what it was! There are just as many possibilities in this direction as there are when assuming Elgar was serious. But, in this eternal puzzle, you may believe whatever you wish.

> **Boult, London Philharmonic Orchestra.** EMI 64748 [ADD] + Holst: *The Planets*
> **A. Davis BBC Symphony Orchestra.** Teldec 73279 [DDD] + *Cockaigne* Overture, *Introduction and Allegro, Serenade for Strings*
> **Gibson, Scottish National Orchestra.** Chandos 6504 [ADD] + *Pomp and Circumstance* Marches
> **Menuhin, Royal Philharmonic Orchestra.** Philips 416354 [DDD] + Cello Concerto
> **Previn, Royal Philharmonic Orchestra.** Philips 416813 [DDD] + *Pomp and Circumstance* Marches

Pomp and Circumstance March in D, Op. 39, No. 1

There are five marches in the Op. 39 set, all of them grandiose in the way only the British can be, but No. 1 has always been the favorite. Its main theme, which the composer rightly pointed out "comes once in a lifetime," has become (with words added to it) virtually a second British national anthem. In America, it frequently serves more prosaically to accompany high school graduates down the aisle during their final ceremonies.

> **Gibson, Scottish National Orchestra.** Chandos 6504 [ADD] + *Enigma Variations*
> **Previn, Royal Philharmonic Orchestra.** Philips 416813 [DDD] + *Enigma Variations*
> **Solti, London Philharmonic Orchestra.** (Nos. 1, 4, 5) London [Decca] 430447 [ADD] + Holst: *The Planets*

Symphony No. 1 in A-flat, Op. 55

"The greatest symphony of modern times," said conductor Hans Richter, who led the premiere in 1908. Audiences agreed. They begged to hear it again, and within a year it had been given a hundred times around the world. This was the greatest success Elgar ever had. It has a beautiful slow theme which recurs throughout the symphony, marked *nobilmente e semplice* ("with nobility and simplicity"). It is so striking and characteristic that the word *nobilmente* has come to signify the essential spirit of Elgar's musical art.

——— *U.S. labels and numbers are given first, U.K. in [brackets] when needed.* ———

Boult, London Philharmonic Orchestra. EMI 64013 + *Serenade for Strings, Chanson de matin, Chanson de nuit*
Haitink, Philharmonia Orchestra. EMI Doublefforte 69761 (2) [ADD] + Symphony No. 2, *Pomp & Circumstance* March No. 5
Handley, London Philharmonic Orchestra. Classics for Pleasure 9018 [ADD]
Judd, Hallé Orchestra. IMP [Carlton Classics] PCD 2019 [DDD]

Gabriel Fauré (1845-1924)

Fauré was the least exhibitionistic, the most classical—to the point of being branded "Hellenistic"—of the Late Romantics. His response to the perceived bankruptcy of Romanticism was to transcend it by looking both backward (to 18th-century ideals of form and restraint) and forward (not to overthrowing tradition, but to finding new ways to handle the tried and true materials). The art he developed was eminently civilized. Not everyone had patience with this gentle approach; one famous pianist slammed the lid down on Fauré's music, muttering that it was "too damned polite."

This apostle of restraint and gentility was the last of six children born to a father who was the last in several generations of butchers. He was "discovered" by an old blind woman of the village, who heard the boy improvising over the keyboard in an old chapel and convinced his parents to send him, at the age of nine, to the then-new Niedermeyer School. Papa Fauré was worried about the expense, but when Louis Niedermeyer heard the boy play he waived all fees.

After Niedermeyer's death, Fauré came under the tutelage of Saint-Saëns. They were only ten years apart in age, and became lifelong friends. This was the beginning of a chain of connections between Fauré and most of the important French composers of his era: nearly 40 years later, Fauré would become the teacher of Ravel.

Meanwhile, however, his career moved slowly but steadily. After fighting in the Franco-Prussian War he returned to the Ecole Niedermeyer as a teacher. Over the years he worked frequently as a professional organist, working his way up to professor of composition at the Paris Conservatory, of which he became the Director in 1905.

No sooner, however, had he reached the pinnacle of respect and recognition than he began to grow deaf. Nevertheless, he produced many of his finest works in the last 20 years of his life, during which time his hearing diminished gradually to zero. During World War I he and his wife moved to a town in the Pyrenees, near his birthplace. There he lived out his last days, composing to the end as he gazed at the mist-covered mountains, hearing the music only in his private and isolated world of imagination.

——— *All CDs listed are considered approximately equal in (high) merit.* ———

Pelléas et Mélisande, Op. 80

A few years before Debussy wrote his opera on Maurice Maeterlinck's play, Fauré contributed incidental music for a London production starring one of the great actresses of that era, Mrs. Patrick Campbell. The suite has four sections, *Prélude, Fileuse* ("The Spinner"), *Sicilienne*, and *Death of Mélisande*. Pelléas, indeed, gets short shrift in this mysteriously evocative music, the composer focusing almost exclusively on the heroine.

Dutoit, Montreal Symphony Orchestra. London [Decca] 421440 [DDD] + *Requiem, Pavane*

Fournet, Netherlands Radio Symphony Orchestra. Denon 73675 [DDD] + Chausson: Symphony in B-flat

Tortelier (violin and conductor), Ulster Orchestra. Chandos 8952 [DDD] + *Pavane;* Chausson: *Poème, Poème de l'amour et de la mer*

Requiem, Op. 48

Fauré's acknowledged masterpiece was written in bits and pieces over several years, but came together as a unified work in memory of his father, who died in 1885. It is one of the few Requiems which fulfill the promise of the implied command: Rest. Unfailingly tranquil, it presents Death as the Comforter, not a thing to be feared. Fauré drops the traditional *Dies irae* section describing the terrors of the Last Judgment and ends uniquely with the *In Paradisum* ("May the angels receive thee in Paradise"), a musical setting which could serve as a dictionary definition for the word "exquisite."

Best, English Chamber Orchestra, Corydon Singers. Hyperion 66292 [DDD] + 4 short choral pieces

Dutoit, Montreal Symphony Orchestra and Chorus. London [Decca] 421440 [DDD] + *Pelléas et Mélisande, Pavane*

Gardiner, Orchestre Révolutionnaire et Romantique, Monteverdi Choir. Philips 438149 [DDD] + *Les Djinns, Madrigal;* Debussy: *3 Chansons de Charles d'Orléans;* Ravel: *3 Chansons;* Saint-Saëns: 3 songs

Giulini, Philharmonia Orchestra and Chorus. Deutsche Grammophon 419243 [DDD] + Ravel:*Pavane for a Dead Princess*

Hickox, London Symphony Orchestra and Chorus. Carlton Classics 6600092 [30366 0009] [DDD] + Bernstein: *Chichester Psalms*

Legrand, Philharmonia Orchestra, Ambrosian Singers. Teldec 90879 [DDD] + Duruflé: *Requiem*

Rutter, City of London Sinfonia, Cambridge Singers. Collegium 109 [DDD] + 6 short choral works

———— *CDs listed are solid, central choices, not necessarily "the greatest."* ————

Summerly, Oxford Camerata and Schola Cantorum. Naxos 8.550765 [DDD]
+ other choral works

Engelbert Humperdinck (1854-1921)

Humperdinck was not even remotely related to the Anglo-American pop singer allegedly of the same name. Arnold Dorsey, looking for a "stage name" that people would remember, seemed to think old Engelbert was so unknown that nobody would make the connection. Apparently, the gamble largely paid off: I once read in an "Ask the Expert" newspaper column a letter from one of the singer's fans inquiring as to whether Engelbert Humperdinck was his real name. "No," replied the Expert, "he just made it up."

The real Engelbert Humperdinck was a promising student of composition who became an assistant to Richard Wagner at Bayreuth, serving as stage manager at the premiere of Parsifal. Later he resumed his studies, becoming at last a professor, first in Spain, then in his native Germany.

Although he composed a number of operas and incidental music scores, his only enduring success was *Hänsel und Gretel*. Ironically, he wrote the music with great reluctance at first, after being badgered by his sister to help with a children's play she had written based on the Grimm fairy tale. The score came to the attention of Richard Strauss who immediately recognized it as a masterpiece and arranged for its production at Weimar in 1893. Since then it has become the closest thing there is to a perennial Christmas opera, especially of course in German-speaking countries.

Hänsel und Gretel

The musical style of this enchanting children's classic is greatly under the influence of Wagner, and is surprisingly dense and heavy considering the subject matter. Nevertheless, the absence of any patronizing of its young listeners seems only to endear it to them the more. Children are, as their elders often forget, far more perceptive than they are normally credited to be.

C. Davis, Murray, Dresden State Orchestra. Philips 438013 (2) [DDD]
Karajan, Schwarzkopf, Philharmonia Orchestra. EMI Studio 69293 (2) (mono) [ADD]
Runnicles, Larmore, Bavarian Radio Symphony Orchestra. Teldec 94549 [DDD]
Tate, von Otter, Bavarian Radio Symphony Orchestra. EMI 54022 (2) [DDD]

───── *Some famous CDs are not listed because currently out of print.* ─────

Vincent d'Indy (1851-1931)

Vincent d'Indy was an aristocrat from the cradle to the grave. Able to trace his ancestry to King Henri IV, and entitled to be addressed as Vicomte d'Indy, he took his caste seriously, both personally and professionally. Fame and fortune were to be his, but were never his motivations. "An artist," he said in his speech inaugurating the Schola Cantorum, "knows that his mission is to serve." Very noble, but one might wonder how someone who went on to insist that the artist "must be touched by sublime charity" could at the same time be the most blatant anti-Semite of the composers, not excluding Wagner.

In fact, d'Indy was one of the most complex and contradictory men in music history. Extremes of behavior ran in his family. His mother died in childbirth and he was reared for 21 years by a musical grandmother who alternated draconian music instruction with spontaneous bursts of doting affection. Young Vincent's childhood dream was not music, however, but the military; he was thrilled to lead a bayonet charge during the Franco-Prussian War in 1870, and to the end of his long life drove friends to despair by repeatedly re-staging the Battle of Waterloo.

He also studied initially for the law, but gave it up and decided to concentrate on music, the love of which had been simmering inside him since he heard some Beethoven piano sonatas at the age of eight. He enrolled in the Paris Conservatory, but rebelled against its starchy atmosphere and undertook private study with César Franck.

He became Franck's bulldog, championing his teacher's theories and music against all detractors throughout his career. He also became the most passionate French advocate of Wagnerism. Fed up by the Conservatory, he helped found a rival insitution, the Schola Cantorum, in 1894. He taught there till his death, though in 1912 he was reconciled with the Conservatory after some reforms were made, and he taught some classes there also.

Piously, devoutly Catholic, he scorned not only Jews but democracy. Though a brilliant scholar he was curiously indiscriminate about artistic talent; he professed to see no difference in quality between Beethoven and Meyerbeer, and thought neither Debussy nor Ravel had any future.

Yet he was scrupulously honest in his dealings, and unfailingly courteous, even to those he despised. Though widely disliked, he was just as universally respected. Despite his regimentation and dogmatism, he insisted that his students be exposed to all ideas and styles, no matter how much he might personally detest them.

In his day his music was generally regarded as cerebral and cacophonous. Although he espoused the Franckian system of cyclical form, he struck out in his own directions and cannot be said to imitate anyone else; his style might be characterized as a hybrid of neo-Classicism and late Romanticism, with some intimations of Impressionism! His influence however was not through his works, but through his surprisingly open-minded molding of pupils as distinguished (and as different from their teacher) as Erik Satie, Arthur Honegger, Georges Auric, and Albert Roussel—and even, briefly, Cole Porter!

————— *Catalog numbers are subject to change without notice.* —————

Symphony on a French Mountain Air, Op. 25

The one composition which has kept d'Indy's name unfailingly before the concertgo-ing public is truly a beautiful work; not really a symphony but a piano concerto, it rings wonderful changes on a tune in the style of an Alpine shepherd song.

> **Dutoit, Montreal Symphony Orchestra.** London [Decca] 430278 [DDD] +
> Franck: Symphony in D Minor
> **Munch, Boston Symphony Orchestra.** RCA Victor Gold Seal 6805 [ADD] +
> Berlioz: Overture to *Béatrice et Bénedict*; Franck: Symphony in D Minor (with
> Monteux, Chicago Symphony Orchestra)

Ruggero Leoncavallo (1857-1919)

Leoncavallo had his fifteen minutes of fame, but it was set in the midst of many instances of poverty, disappointment, and defeat. His one surviving work, *Pagliacci* ("Clowns"), con-tains what is probably the most famous tenor aria ever written, "Vesti la giubba." Ironically, its sentiments mirrored Leoncavallo's life: "On with the show! Put on your costume; the people pay, they want to laugh. So laugh, clown, and they will applaud; laugh at the sorrow that tears your heart." Perhaps it was personal experience that enabled the composer to make this one moment so searing and convincing.

Born in Naples, the son of a judge, he studied at the Bologna Conservatory. He entrusted his first opera and all his money to an alleged impresario who ran off with the funds, leaving the 20-year-old destitute. He took to the streets, singing and playing the piano for pennies. Eventually he found a decent job as a pianist in Egypt, but a revolt against the British made life dangerous for foreigners and he had to disguise himself as an Arab to escape the country, riding a horse to Port Said for 24 solid hours.

His last money having been spent on ship fare, he found himself penniless again, but got by playing the piano in Parisian cabarets and writing popular songs. Desperate to claim the attention he felt his talent deserved, he remembered an incident of his youth when an actor, playing opposite his unfaithful wife in a drama, actually killed her on stage. He decided to write a one-act opera in the manner of Mascagni, whose mini-tragedy *Cavalleria Rusticana* had recently been a smash success.

Persistence won the day: Leoncavallo got the publisher Sonzogno to endorse him, and Pagliacci had its premiere in 1892 under the baton of an up-and-coming conductor named Arturo Toscanini. Almost no one in that first audience had any idea who Leoncavallo was, but they shook the rafters at the end of the opera. The scene was described by all who were there as pandemonium.

Leoncavallo was headline material the next day and became the toast of the opera world. Alas, with one partial exception, he never had another hit. Failure followed upon

———— Since CDs can change label and number, use artists as main reference. ————

failure, and in the end he was more bitter than before, having lost all that he had struggled so hard to win.

Leoncavallo's name is inextricably associated with that of Mascagni, since their two famous operas are almost always performed as a pair. But though they are the two icons of the so-called Verismo (realism) school of opera, they were far from identical. Leoncavallo was the better trained artist, and he was subtler; all of his work is more refined and poetic than Mascagni's, and some who know his other works have claimed him as a better craftsman even than Puccini. In fact, Leoncavallo wrote his own *La Bohème*, an opera based on the same book as Puccini's, but it came out a year later and was lost in the shuffle.

Pagliacci

In *Pagliacci*, one is gripped from the moment that the character Tonio appears before the curtain and sings the insinuating Prologue, warning the audience of the emotions to come, to the final wrenching shock, as Canio, the clown, having stabbed his wife in front of an initially uncomprehending audience, lets the bloody knife fall to the floor while quietly intoning one of the most famous lines in opera: "La commedia è finita." It could be the inscription on Leoncavallo's tomb.

> **Muti, Carreras, Philharmonia Orchestra, Ambrosian Opera Chorus.** EMI 63650 (2) + Mascagni: *Cavalleria Rusticana*
> **Serafin, di Stefano, Callas, La Scala Orchestra and Chorus.** EMI 56287 (2) (mono) [ADD] + Mascagni: *Cavalleria Rusticana*

Gustav Mahler (1860-1911)

When asked as a child what he wanted to be when he grew up, Mahler replied: "A martyr." He became possibly the most driven of all the great composers. In his nine completed symphonies, an unfinished tenth, and the "symphony-disguised-as-a-song-cycle" *Das Lied von der Erde*, he deliberately sought to stretch the definition of a symphony to the breaking point. Cast in unusual structures, Mahler's symphonies are vast in scope (No. 3 is the longest symphony in the repertory), employ sometimes gargantuan instrumental forces, often include vocal solos and choral parts, and flirt with various high-flown programmatic and philosophical concepts. The symphony, to Mahler, was "a world," a vehicle through which he sought to give voice to the "complete man."

His lifelong preoccupation with the themes of suffering and death, and the riddle of how to transcend them, seemed to take root early. His parents had an unhappy marriage, and many of his siblings died in childhood. Once when his father was brutalizing his mother, young Gustav fled the house, only to be enchanted by hearing a hurdy-gurdy playing "O, du lieber Augustin." Ever after, he was fascinated by the fact that childlike innocence and inhuman cruelty can coexist so intimately; it was a subject he explored as the first composer to be treated by Sigmund Freud.

Mahler's musical training was enriched by studies in philosophy and the new discipline of psychology. Over time he became an ever more impassioned and idealistic person, tormented by his embattled relations with musicians and orchestras. His career centered on conducting, not composing, his ascent was rapid, and he was eventually acknowledged as one of the greatest conductors in the world.

During his ten years as director of the Vienna Court Opera he appeared to perform miracles; the works he conducted seemed, his admirers said, "Herrlich wie am ersten Tag" ("Glorious as on the first day"). Nevertheless he was vilified in the press, a victim of intrigues and anti-Semitism, hated by his enemies because of his unbending belief in himself, his arrogance with orchestra players, his perfectionism, and his sarcastic tongue.

In 1906 he suffered the death of a daughter, then shortly after was diagnosed with a terminal heart condition. Unable to take any more of Vienna he came to New York City as conductor of both (!) the Metropolitan Opera and the New York Philharmonic Orchestra. Pressured to go easy on the musicians, lighten his programs, and hobnob with wealthy socialites, he found no peace. Under the strain of disappointment and an unrelenting concert schedule, he collapsed. Returned to Europe, he died in a nursing home waving his finger like a baton and murmuring the name of his God: "Mozart."

Except for the premiere of his Eighth Symphony, Mahler had few successes in his lifetime as a composer. His huge symphonies, with their heaven-storming passages juxtaposed against music of childlike innocence, seemed grotesque to most listeners, a hodgepodge of bombast and naiveté. Hysteria and bathos are charged against him even today; but especially since being championed so convincingly by Leonard Bernstein in the 1960s, Mahler's music has become a major force in the concert halls of the world.

Almost overnight the attitude towards his works among critics and audiences alike changed from ridicule to awe, and today most see (and hear) him as one of the most significant figures in the transition from Romanticism to Modernity, and the first great composer to voice both the anguish and hope of the 20th century.

Das Lied von der Erde

"The Song of the Earth" was completed in 1909, the first major work since the doctor had given him his death warrant. It is a symphony in all but name, with the addition of two solo vocal parts which are settings of Chinese poems about youth, beauty, loneliness, and leavetaking. The awareness of approaching death is contrasted with a poignant love of nature and life.

Klemperer, Ludwig, Wunderlich, Philharmonia Orchestra and Chorus. EMI 47231 [ADD]

——— *[DDD] indicates newest recordings; [ADD] or [AAD] are reissues.* ———

Leppard, Baker, Mitchinson, BBC Northern Sinfonia. BBC Radio Classics 9120 [ADD]

Symphony No. 1 in D "Titan"

Mahler's first symphony began life as a giant symphonic poem, which he revised to fulfill a commission from the Budapest Philharmonic. As with many of his earlier works he first provided a program, then later withdrew it as something that would only mislead listeners. It is still one of his more popular works, youthful and poetic, almost Schubertian in places, and highly personal. Much of its thematic material is borrowed from his earlier song cycle, *Lieder eines fahrenden Gesellen* ("Songs of a Wayfaring Lad"). The composer was 29 when he conducted its premiere in 1889.

Abbado, Berlin Philharmonic Orchestra. Deutsche Grammophon 431769 [DDD]

Bernstein, Concertgebouw Orchestra. Deutsche Grammophon 427303 [DDD]

Horenstein, London Symphony Orchestra. Unicorn 2012 [AAD]

B. Walter, Columbia Symphony Orchestra. CBS [Sony] 37235 [ADD]

Symphony No. 2 in C Minor, "Resurrection"

Several years passed after the first symphony before Mahler completed his second, a work on an altogether larger scale. There are five movements, with vocal parts in the last two. The theme of the work is the impermanence of life and how faith can intervene to help mankind transcend sorrow. The final movement unites soprano, alto, and chorus in Klopstock's *Resurrection Ode* ("Rise again, my dust, after a short rest"), followed by Mahler's own words on faith in a future life. The symphony was first performed in 1895 with Richard Strauss conducting.

Bernstein, New York Philharmonic Orchestra. Deutsche Grammophon 423395 (2) [DDD]

Blomstedt, San Francisco Symphony Orchestra. London [Decca] 443350 (2) [DDD]

Haitink, Berlin Philharmonic Orchestra. Philips 438935 (2) [DDD]

Jansons, Oslo Philharmonic Orchestra. Chandos Collect 6595/6 (2) [DDD]

Klemperer, Philharmonia Orchestra. EMI Studio 69662 [ADD]

Rattle, City of Birmingham Symphony Orchestra. EMI 47962 (2) [DDD]

———— CDs go in and out of print; availability of all listed items is not assured. ————

Symphony No. 4 in G

Mahler's most cheerful and, with the first, shortest symphony is the most popular of them all, which fact it is perhaps as well he does not know. It is laid out parallel with the four verses of the song "The Heavenly Life" from *Das Knaben Wunderhorn*, which Mahler set separately as a song cycle. The four-movement structure and the use of folk-like idioms make this symphony almost Haydnesque; at least in comparison to the others!

Maazel, Battle, Vienna Philharmonic Orchestra. CBS 44908 [DDD]

Previn, Ameling, Pittsburgh Symphony Orchestra. EMI 65179 [ADD] + Schubert: 3 songs (with Ameling)

Solti, Te Kanawa, Chicago Symphony Orchestra. London [Decca] 410188 [DDD]

Szell, Raskin, Cleveland Orchestra. Sony Essential Classics 46535 [ADD] + *Lieder eines fahrenden Gesellen* (with von Stade, A. Davis, London Philharmonic Orchestra)

Wit, Russell, Polish National Radio Symphony Orchestra. Naxos 8.550527 [DDD]

Symphony No. 8 in E-flat, "Symphony of a Thousand"

The nickname comes from the number of performers. Mahler himself led the premiere just eight months before his death, though he had written the symphony four years earlier. The performance (1910) was a triumph, the 1,000 performers joining the 3,000 people in the audience in a 30-minute ovation at the end.

The score calls for a children's choir, a large male choir, two large female choirs, a pipe organ, two pianos, a huge orchestra augmented by bells, and extra brass choir, and for good measure a mandolin! Despite its length the symphony is divided into just two parts, the first a setting of the medieval hymn *Veni, creator Spiritus* ("Come, creating Spirit"), the second the closing scene from Goethe's *Faust.* It is not the longest symphony (that was Mahler's Third), but it is the largest.

Gielen, Frankfurt Opera House and Museum Orchestra and Chorus. Sony Essential Classics 48281 [ADD]

Morris, Symphonica of London. IMP [Carlton Classics] DPCD 1019 [DDD]

Solti, Chicago Symphony Orchestra and Chorus. London [Decca] 414493 [ADD]

Tennstedt, London Philharmonic Orchestra and Chorus. EMI 47625 (2) [DDD]

———— *Some CDs may be available only through importers.* ————

Symphony No. 9 in D

Mahler's last completed symphony is his most despairing. It has the conventional four movements, but they are long, and the last is an adagio, as in Tchaikovsky's *Pathétique*. It is the composer's tormented valedictory to life; frequently quoted throughout the work is a little theme from Beethoven's *Les Adieux* ("Farewell") piano sonata.

Barbirolli, Berlin Philharmonic Orchestra. EMI Studio 63115 [ADD]
Bernstein, Vienna Philharmonic Orchestra. Deutsche Grammophon 419208 (2) [DDD]
Inbal, Frankfurt Radio Symphony Orchestra. Denon 1566/7
Judd, Mahler-Jugend Orchestra. Nuova Era 6906/7 (2) [DDD] + Adagio from Symphony No. 10 (with European Community Youth Orchestra)
Karajan, Berlin Philharmonic Orchestra. Deutsche Grammophon "Karajan Gold" 439024 (2) [DDD]
B. Walter, Vienna Philharmonic Orchestra. Dutton Labs 5005 [ADD] (mono)

Pietro Mascagni (1863-1945)

Mascagni led a life similar in many ways to Ruggero Leoncavallo, with whom his name will be ever entwined. He grew up in poverty and obscurity, had one huge success in opera, continued to compose but met subsequently mostly with failure, and spent his last days in bitterness and regret.

Showing musical talent as a youth, he was sent to the Milan Conservatory by a wealthy nobleman on whom his early compositions had made an impression. But Mascagni hated the school and dropped out to become conductor of a small traveling opera troupe. For several years he lived hand to mouth, teaching piano, and tossing manuscripts of one-act operas in a drawer.

In 1889 the Sonzogno publishing house announced a competition for a one-act opera. Mascagni thought he had no chance, but his wife fished out the score of *Cavalleria Rusticana* and secretly dropped it in the mail. It won the first prize, and the promise of a performance in Rome in 1890.

The premiere was one of the great sensations in opera history. Mascagni had to take 40 curtain calls. The cheering audience followed him out of the theater and set up camp in front of his apartment building. With the door blocked, the composer had to be pulled through a window to get inside. Parades were held in his honor, and he was invested with the royal Order of the Crown. *Cavalleria Rusticana* was staged with unprecedented rapidity in opera houses around the world.

Like Leoncavallo, Mascagni had high hopes of many more years of triumph, but out of 14 more operas he had only sporadic, and relatively mild, successes. His last pitiful try for the spotlight was as virtual court composer for Mussolini. He wrote songs glorifying Fascism and enjoyed Il Duce's fulsome praise and patronage.

But after the Nazis were thrown out, and Mussolini was hanged upside down, Mascagni's property was confiscated and his reputation ruined. Despised, he spent his last months in a cheap hotel, vainly trying to disavow his Fascist sympathies. Looking back on the glory days of his big hit with *Cavalleria*, the composer lamented: "I was crowned before I was king!"

Cavalleria Rusticana

Despite Mascagni's personal humiliation, his beloved opera never lost its hold on the public, and it is still a standard of the repertoire. The first opera of a movement that came to be called "Verismo" ("realism"), *Cavalleria Rusticana* moves swiftly with gut-wrenching vividness through its brief length to tell a tale of Sicilian passion, jealousy, and death. The most famous single passage is not an aria but the orchestral Intermezzo, which wordlessly sums up the poignant emotion of the story.

Cellini, Bjørling, RCA Victor Orchestra, Robert Shaw Chorale. RCA Victor Gold Seal 6510 [ADD]

Levine, Domingo, National Philharmonic Orchestra (Washington, DC). RCA Victor Red Seal 3091 [ADD]

Muti, Carreras, Philharmonia Orchestra, Ambrosian Opera Chorus. EMI 63650 (2) + Leoncavallo: *Pagliacci*

Serafin, di Stefano, Callas, La Scala Orchestra and Chorus. EMI 56287 (2) (mono) [ADD] + Leoncavallo: *Pagliacci*

Giacomo Puccini (1858-1924)

Puccini came from a long line of church musicians from Lucca, Italy. The first one we know of, also named Giacomo, was born in 1712. Puccini's grandfather, Domenico, was a contemporary of Beethoven and composed a piano concerto which has been recorded. But church and pianos were not for the last and greatest of the line: "I was born many years ago," he wrote near the end of his life, "and the Almighty touched me with his little finger and said 'Write for the theater—mind, only for the theater!' And I have obeyed the supreme command."

He tried at first to follow the family tradition, but his irresponsible and impish nature fought against it. When playing organ improvisations in church he would interpolate opera arias, scandalizing the priests. As a teenager he walked 13 miles to see the new opera by Verdi, *Aida*, and that was it. He stopped his foolishness and became a serious student at the Milan Conservatory.

—————*All CDs listed are considered approximately equal in (high) merit.* —————

For almost ten years after graduation he lived in dire poverty, living on beans and raw onions and the pity of friends. In those days he was a close friend of Mascagni, from whom he absorbed the spirit of the Verismo movement, and whose success in 1890 with *Cavalleria Rusticana* inspired him. Then the triumph of *Manon Lescaut* in 1893 launched Puccini's meteoric career.

From then on he had almost uninterrupted success, bringing one hit after another to the world's stages. Somehow he found the key to continually touching listeners' hearts, which his friends Mascagni and Leoncavallo had been unable to do. Audiences proclaimed him the successor to Verdi. Some critics, however, carped at what they considered sentimentality, vulgarity, and bad taste. His music was described as unoriginal and shallow.

Puccini's defenders chalk a lot of that up to elitism: he may have targeted his audience, playing up to their love of passionate emotions and caressing melodies, but he was only doing his job, and doing it superlatively well. Indeed, despite much critical hesitation about Puccini over the years, his reputation as a good musician, skilled orchestrator, inspired melodist, and deft psychologist has been slowly but constantly rising.

He had an infallible instinct for the stage, despite raging inner doubts as to his worth and place in history. "Next to Wagner," he once said, "we are all mandolin players." His insecurity was mitigated by spending money. He took up the pose so often seen in his photographs: a dapper rake, elegantly suited, cigarette dangling from one hand, mustache trimmed, bowler hat atilt. He loved fine food and wine, fast women and cars.

Despite his profligacy and philandering he lost neither his wife nor his public. When he succumbed to a heart attack following cancer surgery, a performance of *La Bohème* was underway in Rome. The news arrived at the opera house and the conductor stopped the orchestra. After a moment he lifted his baton again and the musicians began playing the *Funeral March* by Chopin. The audience silently stood, weeping, and then quietly filed from the hall. Audiences ever since have been shedding tears for Puccini and for his heroines, and for the intensely poignant music he gave them.

La Bohème

A story about young bohemians in love with love, *La Bohème* is one of the handful of most popular operas ever written. Already long since a hit with classical music fans, it reached an even wider audience when a scene was featured in the film *Moonstruck*. This opera is the prototype of the so-called "soap" operas.

Beecham, de los Angeles, RCA Victor Symphony Orchestra and Chorus. EMI 58236 (2) (mono)

Karajan, Freni, Berlin Philharmonic Orchestra. London [Decca] 421049 (2) [ADD]

Pappano, Vaduva, Philharmonia Orchestra. EMI 56120 (2) [DDD]

———— *CDs listed are solid, central choices, not necessarily "the greatest."* ————

Serafin, Tebaldi, St. Cecilia Academy Orchestra and Chorus. London [Decca]
425534 (2) [ADD]
Solti, Caballé, London Philharmonic Orchestra. RCA Victor Red Seal 0371
(2) [DDD]

Madama Butterfly

A fiasco at its premiere, *Madama Butterfly* was one of the few Puccini operas to flop.
The composer made a few revisions, and within three months it was a hit like all his others.
Puccini actually studied Japanese music to lend a tinge of authenticity to the score. The
story concerns a typical Puccini heroine, a woman who kills herself rather than suffer
shame at the hands of a faithless lover. This solution to infidelity seemed to please Puccini
greatly, for he used it repeatedly.

Barbirolli, Scotto, Santa Cecilia Academy Orchestra and Chorus. EMI 69654
(2) [ADD]
Karajan, Freni, Vienna Philharmonic Orchestra and Chorus. London [Decca]
417577 (3) [ADD]
Leinsdorf, Moffo, Rome Opera Chorus and Orchestra. RCA Victor Red Seal
4145 (2) [ADD]
Patané, Kincses, Hungarian State Opera Orchestra and Chorus. Hungaroton
12256/7 (2) [ADD]
Serafin, Tebaldi, St. Cecilia Academy Chorus and Orchestra. London [Decca]
425531 (2) [ADD]
Sinopoli, Freni, Philharmonia Orchestra, Ambrosian Opera Chorus.
Deutsche Grammophon 423567 (3) [DDD]

Tosca

A woman flings herself from a tower in despair after her lover has been treacherously
executed by a brutal police chief whom she has stabbed to death after he tried to violate
her. A "shoddy little shocker" of a story, Joseph Kerman called it. It is the most *verismo*
("realistic") of Puccini's operas, and second in popularity only to *La Bohème*. Although
musically inferior to several of his other works, it makes a strong impression in performance, demonstrating the composer's unerring sense of what works in the theater.

De Sabata, Callas, La Scala Orchestra and Chorus. EMI 56304 (2) (mono)
[ADD]
[Barring a miracle, this is the only version I will ever list for *Tosca* in this particular book, which
means to start you on the right path in classical music. Since there is no question of this being the

——— *Some famous CDs are not listed because currently out of print.* ———

greatest *Tosca* ever recorded—in fact, it is very likely the greatest recording ever made of *any* opera—I consider it foolish to place lesser deities beside it, whatever their merits. Start here; then go whither you wish. If you think that "stereo," or "digital," etc., is more important than Maria Callas at the peak of her genius, I cannot help you.]

Turandot

Considered by many Puccini's masterpiece, *Turandot* shows an advanced sophistication in handling the orchestra. Its rather peculiar story set in a mythical China is framed by music of great power, alternating with unusual poetry and delicacy–that is, as far as it goes, for Puccini died before finishing it. The rather perfunctory conclusion we hear today was tacked on by another hand.

Mehta, Sutherland, London Philharmonic Orchestra, John Alldis Choir. London [Decca] 414274 (2) [ADD]

Molinari-Pradelli, Nilsson, Rome Opera Chorus and Orchestra. EMI 69327 (2) [ADD]

Serafin, Callas, La Scala (Milan) Chorus and Orchestra. EMI 56307 (2) [ADD]

Richard Strauss (1864-1949)

Richard Strauss once said he could describe a fork in music. That one quip, lightly tossed off, manages to sum up the whole esthetic and attitude of a composer who was both programmatic and pragmatic. "I am unable," he said, "to write without a program to guide me."

He knew better than anyone else how to imitate life and nature in music, but also how to turn up a dollar. Jokes were told about his tight-fisted ways. His son: "Papa, how much did you get for the rehearsal tonight?" Strauss, teary: "Now I know you are my boy!" Gustav Mahler's wife Alma once sat next to him at one of those rehearsals, and noted in her diary: "Strauss thought of nothing but money. The entire time he held a pencil and calculated the profits to the last pfennig."

He went through life sure of his talent and unperturbed by criticism. He wrote a giant tone poem, *Ein Heldenleben* ("A Hero's Life") which he frankly admitted was about his own career. A few years later he composed the *Symphonia Domestica*, which is meant to portray himself, his wife, and infant son at home, giving baby a bath, making love, having a spat, and so on. When his self-absorption was challenged he replied that "I don't see why I shouldn't write a symphony about myself; I find myself quite as interesting as Napoleon or Alexander the Great."

Egomaniac he may have been, but his pragmatism let him stand curiously outside himself and reflect unsparingly on his own failings. At the end of his career he assessed

——— Catalog numbers are subject to change without notice. ———

himself more shrewdly than any critic: "I may not be a first-rate composer, but I am a first-rate second-rate composer." He did not argue with his musical nemesis, Claude Debussy, who admitted after hearing *Ein Heldenleben* that Strauss was "very nearly a genius." Strauss asked no more of life than that: just pay him his fee!

Richard Strauss (totally unrelated, by the way, to Johann Strauss and his brood) was the son of a famous French horn player, Franz Strauss, from whom he seems to have derived his utter self-assurance. Rehearsing a work with Wagner, the elder Strauss obstinately refused to change the way he played a passage. Flying into a rage, Wagner stormed off stage, leaving the orchestra in an embarrassed silence. Finally Franz Strauss rose, looked around serenely, and said "I have put him to flight!"

Young Richard studied music, especially conducting, under Hans von Bülow, and picked up influences from Berlioz and Brahms, but most of all Liszt and Wagner. He developed into one of the great conductors of the early 20th century, and had his first compositional success in his early 20s with the tone poem *Don Juan*. A succession of further orchestral works, constructed like Liszt and orchestrated like Wagner, won him headline coverage as the natural heir to their legacies.

The Wagnerites, in particular, were thrilled to see the Master's theories vindicated in the brilliantly colorful works of this disciple. Some, in fact, dared to suggest Strauss was even greater, for he wrote orchestral works as well as operas. Just as with Wagner, a kind of cult grew up around Strauss in his lifetime. His flamboyant music, contrasted with his bourgeois persona, his sudden fame and enormous financial success, and the sometimes shocking subject matter of his music, such as the "decadent" opera *Salome*, made titillating newspaper copy, and he was regularly billed as the world's greatest composer.

He seems to have been utterly apolitical and amoral. He stayed in Germany during World War II and accepted the post of president of the Reich Music Chamber. He didn't seem to see anything much wrong with the Nazis, but he also defended his Jewish friends, much to the dismay of Hitler and Goebbels. He just didn't seem to quite get the point. His mind was elsewhere, reliving the past, contemplating more important issues such as whether words or music should dominate in an opera. When the war was over he seemed bewildered by the defeat and destruction, and wrote another tone poem, *Metamorphosen*, to express his sorrow at all the damaged buildings.

As he grew old, his works became bigger and more densely orchestrated, but he had nothing new to say. In fact, he drew back from the forward-looking harmonies of *Salome* and *Elektra* to write music more acceptable to the masses, such as *Der Rosenkavalier* with its neo-Johann Straussian waltzes.

Yet his style remains strikingly distinct and personal. No one can hear more than a few bars of his music and not know Strauss wrote it. With all their ostentation and pretension, their sometimes obscure symbolism, and a tendency towards excess in everything, Strauss's works continue to fascinate and entertain, if more by ingenuity and calculation than anything from the heart. Strauss was, after all, a truly great second-rate composer.

——— *Since CDs can change label and number, use artists as main reference.* ———

Also sprach Zarathustra (Thus Spake Zarathustra), Op. 30

Intrigued and inspired by the "superman" theories of Nietzsche, this was one of Strauss's less famous tone poems until the opening measures created a sensation in the 1968 film *2001—A Space Odyssey* (which Arthur Schlesinger, Jr. characterized as "morally pretentious, intellectually obscure, and inordinately long," just the things that detractors say about much of Strauss). Many people still listen only to those few bars and then turn the player off. Too bad Stanley Kubrick didn't use the whole piece.

Blomstedt, Dresden State Orchestra. Denon 2259 [DDD] + *Don Juan*

Haitink, Concertgebouw Orchestra. Philips Duo 442281 (2) [ADD] + *Death and Transfiguration, Don Juan, Ein Heldenleben, Till Eulenspiegel, Rosenkavlier* Waltzes (with Jochum conducting)

Karajan, Berlin Philharmonic Orchestra. Deutsche Grammophon "Karajan Gold" 439016 [DDD] + *Don Juan*

Karajan, Berlin Philharmonic Orchestra. Deutsche Grammophon Originals 447441 [ADD] + *Don Juan, Till Eulenspiegel, Dance of the Seven Veils* from *Salome*

Karajan, Berlin Philharmonic Orchestra. London [Decca] Classic Sound 448582 [ADD] + *Don Juan, Till Eulenspiegel, Dance of the Seven Veils* from *Salome*

Kempe, Dresden State Orchestra. EMI 68110 (2) [ADD] + *Death and Transfiguration, Don Juan, Ein Heldenleben, Rosenkavalier* Waltzes, *Dance of the Seven Veils* from *Salome, Till Eulenspiegel*

[As this book went to press, the excellent Kempe double set was available only in the U.K., as two CDs for the price of one. It was not simultaneously released in the U.S. If purchased in the U.S. through an importer the deep discount might not apply.]

Mackerras, Royal Philharmonic Orchestra. RPO [Tring] 071 + *Don Juan, Till Eulenspiegel*

Previn, Vienna Philharmonic Orchestra. Telarc 80167 [DDD] + *Don Juan, Death and Transfiguration*

Reiner, Chicago Symphony Orchestra. RCA Victor Gold Seal 60930 [ADD] + *Rosenkavalier* Waltzes (arr. Reiner), *Le Bourgeois gentilhomme*

Reiner, Chicago Symphony Orchestra. RCA Victor Gold Seal 61494 [ADD] + *Ein Heldenleben*

Solti, Berlin Philharmonic Orchestra. London [Decca] 452604 [DDD] + *Till Eulenspiegel, Dance of the Seven Veils* from *Salome*

Solti, Chicago Symphony Orchestra. London [Decca] Jubilee 430445 [ADD] + *Don Juan, Till Eulenspiegel*

——— Artists are listed alphabetically, not in order by critical ranking. ———

Death and Transfiguration (Tod und Verklärung), Op. 24

Strauss thought up his own scenario for this one: a dying artist lets his past play before his mind's eye, then senses an approaching redemptive joy. On his death bed Strauss whispered to his daughter-in-law, "Alice, it's funny, but dying is just as I imagined it in *Tod und Verklärung!*"

> **Blomstedt, Dresden State Orchestra.** Denon 73801 [DDD] + *Till Eulenspiegel, Metamorphosen*
>
> **Haitink, Concertgebouw Orchestra.** Philips Duo 442281 (2) [ADD] + *Also sprach Zarathustra, Don Juan, Ein Heldenleben, Till Eulenspiegel, Rosenkavlier* Waltzes (with Jochum conducting)
>
> **Karajan, Berlin Philharmonic Orchestra.** Deutsche Grammophon Originals 447422 [ADD] + *Metamorphosen, 4 Last Songs* (with Janowitz)
>
> **Kempe, Dresden State Orchestra.** EMI 68110 (2) [ADD] + *Also sprach Zarathustra, Don Juan, Ein Heldenleben, Rosenkavalier* Waltzes, *Dance of the Seven Veils* from *Salome, Till Eulenspiegel*
>
> [As this book went to press, the excellent Kempe double set was available only in the U.K., as two CDs for the price of one. It was not simultaneously released in the U.S. If purchased in the U.S. through an importer the deep discount might not apply.]
>
> **Previn, Vienna Philharmonic Orchestra.** Telarc 80167 [DDD] + *Also sprach Zarathustra, Don Juan*
>
> **Szell, Cleveland Orchestra.** Sony Essential Classics 53511 [ADD] + *Dance of the Seven Veils* from *Salome, Symphonia Domestica*

Don Juan, Op. 20

Strauss's seminal success (no pun intended) was inspired by a poem on the legendary lover by Nikolaus Lenau, in which Don Juan is the type of a superhero brimming with the life-force (an image dear to Nietzsche and much German philosophy of the time), who is undone only by excess.

> **Blomstedt, Dresden State Orchestra.** Denon 2259 [DDD] + *Also sprach Zarathustra*
>
> **Haitink, Concertgebouw Orchestra.** Philips Duo 442281 (2) [ADD] + *Also sprach Zarathustra, Death and Transfiguration, Ein Heldenleben, Till Eulenspiegel, Rosenkavlier* Waltzes (with Jochum conducting)
>
> **Karajan, Berlin Philharmonic Orchestra.** Deutsche Grammophon Galleria 429717 [ADD] + *Ein Heldenleben*

———— *[DDD] indicates newest recordings; [ADD] or [AAD] are reissues.* ————

Karajan, Berlin Philharmonic Orchestra. Deutsche Grammophon "Karajan Gold" 439016 [DDD] + *Don Juan*

Karajan, Berlin Philharmonic Orchestra. Deutsche Grammophon Originals 447441 [ADD] + *Also sprach Zarathustra, Till Eulenspiegel, Dance of the Seven Veils* from *Salome*

Karajan, Berlin Philharmonic Orchestra. London [Decca] Classic Sound 448582 [ADD] + *Also sprach Zarathustra, Till Eulenspiegel, Dance of the Seven Veils* from *Salome*

Kempe, Dresden State Orchestra. EMI 68110 (2) [ADD] + *Also sprach Zarathustra, Death and Transfiguration, Ein Heldenleben, Rosenkavalier* Waltzes, *Dance of the Seven Veils* from *Salome, Till Eulenspiegel*

[As this book went to press, the excellent Kempe double set was available only in the U.K., as two CDs for the price of one. It was not simultaneously released in the U.S. If purchased in the U.S. through an importer the deep discount might not apply.]

Mackerras, Royal Philharmonic Orchestra. RPO [Tring] 071 [DDD] + *Also sprach Zarathustra, Till Eulenspiegel*

Previn, Vienna Philharmonic Orchestra. Telarc 80167 [DDD] + *Also sprach Zarathustra, Death and Transfiguration*

Solti, Chicago Symphony Orchestra. London [Decca] Jubilee 430445 [ADD] + *Also sprach Zarathustra, Till Eulenspiegel*

Szell, Cleveland Orchestra. Sony Essential Classics 48272 [ADD] + *Till Eulenspiegel; Ein Heldenleben* (with Ormandy, Philadelphia Orchestra)

Don Quixote, Op. 35

One of Strauss's most graphically illustrated tone poems, *Don Quixote* is nevertheless cast in the form of a mammoth set of variations on a cello theme. This tune represents the delightfully mad hero, who for Strauss symbolizes all who go through life chasing an illusion. By purely musical means Strauss suggests the bleating of sheep, the battle with the windmills, and many other elements of the Cervantes story. It is one of the composer's most stunning bag of tricks, yet also one of his best-written and subtlest scores.

du Pré, Boult, New Philharmonia Orchestra. EMI 55528 [ADD] + Lalo: Cello Concerto

Janigro, Reiner, Chicago Symphony Orchestra. RCA Victor Gold Seal 61796 [ADD] + *Burleske* (with pianist Byron Janis)

Munroe, Bernstein, New York Philharmonic Orchestra. Sony 47625 [ADD] + *Dance of the Seven Veils* from *Salome, Festival Prelude*

Tortelier, Kempe, Berlin Philharmonic Orchestra. EMI 68736 [ADD] + *Till Eulenspiegel*

——— *CDs go in and out of print; availability of all listed items is not assured.* ———

Ein Heldenleben (A Hero's Life), Op. 40

Much in the way that Wagner mocked his adversaries in *Die Meistersinger*, Strauss pilloried his in this depiction of himself standing up to his querulous and insipid critics, affirming life, love, and vigor, and at the end achieving spiritual illumination as well as domestic bliss. The concept may be a bit overbaked, but as music it is one of his most vital and well-structured compositions.

Haitink, Concertgebouw Orchestra. Philips Duo 442281 (2) [ADD] + *Also sprach Zarathustra, Death and Transfiguration, Don Juan, Till Eulenspiegel*; *Rosenkavlier* Waltzes (with Jochum conducting)

Karajan, Berlin Philharmonic Orchestra. Deutsche Grammophon Galleria 429717 [ADD] + *Don Juan*

Kempe, Dresden State Orchestra. EMI 68110 (2) [ADD] + *Also sprach Zarathustra, Death and Transfiguration, Don Juan, Rosenkavalier* Waltzes, *Dance of the Seven Veils* from *Salome, Till Eulenspiegel*

[As this book went to press, the excellent Kempe double set was available only in the U.K., as two CDs for the price of one. It was not simultaneously released in the U.S. If purchased in the U.S. through an importer the deep discount might not apply.]

Ormandy, Philadelphia Orchestra. Sony Essential Classics 48272 [ADD] + *Don Juan, Till Eulenspiegel* (with Szell, Cleveland Orchestra)

Reiner, Chicago Symphony Orchesta. RCA Victor Gold Seal 61494 [ADD] + *Also sprach Zarathustra*

Sawallisch, Philadelphia Orchestra. EMI Classics 56149 [DDD] + Oboe Concerto

Der Rosenkavalier: Waltz Suite

"The Cavalier of the Rose," with text by Strauss's frequent collaborator Hugo von Hofmannsthal, is his best-loved opera, a deliberate throwback to the glittering days of the Waltzing Strausses, and an antidote to his harsh and shocking operas, *Salome* and *Elektra*. For the composer, ever eager to show off, it was his way of demonstrating that he could successfully capture every mood and genre. The many waltz tunes strewn through the long score have been gathered into concert suites by various arrangers and by Strauss himself.

Jochum, Concertgebouw Orchestra. Philips Duo 442281 (2) [ADD] + *Also sprach Zarathustra, Death and Transfiguration, Don Juan, Ein Heldenleben, Till Eulenspiegel* (with Haitink conducting)

Kempe, Dresden State Orchestra. EMI 68110 (2) [ADD] + *Also sprach Zarathustra, Death and Transfiguration, Don Juan, Ein Heldenleben, Dance of the Seven Veils* from *Salome, Till Eulenspiegel*

——— **Some CDs may be available only through importers.** ———

[As this book went to press, the excellent Kempe double set was available only in the U.K., as two CDs for the price of one. It was not simultaneously released in the U.S. If purchased in the U.S. through an importer the deep discount might not apply.]

Reiner, Chicago Symphony Orchestra. RCA Victor Gold Seal 60930 [ADD] + *Also sprach Zarathustra, Le Bourgeois gentilhomme*

Salome: Dance of the Seven Veils

In the opera, Salome executes a sensual dance to win King Herod's acquiescence to her demand for the head of John the Baptist. This is one role generally off-limits to the more corpulent sopranos. The dance is a striking bit of pseudo-orientalia, though one may note that underlying the feverish hothouse sensuality is a Viennese waltz!

Bernstein, New York Philharmonic Orchestra. Sony 47625 [ADD] + *Don Quixote, Festival Prelude*

Karajan, Berlin Philharmonic Orchestra. Deutsche Grammophon Originals 447441 [ADD] + *Also sprach Zarathustra, Till Eulenspiegel, Don Juan*

Karajan, Berlin Philharmonic Orchestra. London [Decca] Classic Sound 448582 [ADD] + *Also sprach Zarathustra, Till Eulenspiegel, Don Juan*

Kempe, Dresden State Orchestra. EMI 68110 (2) [ADD] + *Also sprach Zarathustra, Death and Transfiguration, Don Juan, Ein Heldenleben, Rosenkavalier* Waltzes, *Till Eulenspiegel*

[As this book went to press, the excellent Kempe double set was available only in the U.K., as two CDs for the price of one. It was not simultaneously released in the U.S. If purchased in the U.S. through an importer the deep discount might not apply.]

Solti, Berlin Philharmonic Orchestra. London [Decca] 452604 [DDD] + *Also sprach Zarathustra, Till Eulenspiegel*

Szell, Cleveland Orchestra. Sony Essential Classics 53511 [ADD] + *Death and Transfiguration, Symphonia Domestica*

Till Eulenspiegel's Merry Pranks, Op. 28

For many people, even Strauss detractors, this is his most acceptable orchestral work. Late in his life one of his quasi-acolytes asked him if he realized that in this work he had approached the metaphysical limits of humor. "Nothing of the kind," the composer snorted, "I just wanted the people in the hall to have a good laugh for once." Strauss himself was tiring of the pseudo-intellectual gobbledy-gook with which his admirers attempted to deify him.

Till Owl-Glass was a real person, a medieval rake who had a reputation for thumbing his nose at authority. In later legend he was credited with ever more outlandish feats of impudence, which are portrayed in Strauss's tone poem. At the end he is hanged for his rascality, but his ghost returns to give the judge the raspberries.

Blomstedt, Dresden State Orchestra. Denon 73801 [DDD] + *Death and Transfiguration, Metamorphosen*

Haitink, Concertgebouw Orchestra. Philips Duo 442281 (2) [ADD] + *Also sprach Zarathustra, Death and Transfiguration, Don Juan, Ein Heldenleben; Rosenkavlier* Waltzes (with Jochum conducting)

Karajan, Berlin Philharmonic Orchestra. Deutsche Grammophon Originals 447441 [ADD] + *Also sprach Zarathustra, Dance of the Seven Veils* from *Salome, Don Juan*

Karajan, Berlin Philharmonic Orchestra. London [Decca] Classic Sound 448582 [ADD] + *Also sprach Zarathustra, Dance of the Seven Veils* from *Salome, Don Juan*

Kempe, Berlin Philharmonic Orchestra. EMI 68376 [ADD] + *Don Quixote* (with Tortelier)

Kempe, Dresden State Orchestra. EMI 68110 (2) [ADD] + *Also sprach Zarathustra, Death and Transfiguration, Don Juan, Ein Heldenleben, Rosenkavalier* Waltzes, *Dance of the Seven Veils* from *Salome*

[As this book went to press, the excellent Kempe double set was available only in the U.K., as two CDs for the price of one. It was not simultaneously released in the U.S. If purchased in the U.S. through an importer the deep discount might not apply.]

Mackerras, Royal Philharmonic Orchestra. RPO [Tring] 071 [DDD] + *Also sprach Zarathustra, Don Juan*

Solti, Berlin Philharmonic Orchestra. London [Decca] 452604 [DDD] + *Also sprach Zarathustra, Dance of the Seven Veils* from *Salome*

Solti, Chicago Symphony Orchestra. London [Decca] Jubilee 430445 [ADD] + *Also sprach Zarathustra, Don Juan*

Szell, Cleveland Orchestra. Sony Essential Classics 48272 [ADD] + *Don Juan; Ein Heldenleben* (with Ormandy, Philadelphia Orchestra)

———— *All CDs listed are considered approximately equal in (high) merit.* ————

The Moderns
(ca. 1915-Present)

The term "modern" is self-defeating, since everything is modern to those who are contemporaneous with it. Once a definable period is past, it of course becomes the Ancient time or the Medieval time, and so on. If the Modern period in music is defined as the 20th century, then it is about to conclude and be renamed. But what? Not the Atonal period, or 12-Tone period, or Neo-Classical Period, or any name derived from any of the many other -isms and -ologies that have made up the era, for no one of them has dominated the times.

Leonard Bernstein dubbed it the Age of Anxiety, and perhaps that will do as well as any other. Although it is clear to every listener that music of the 20th century differs from all that went before, at least in degree, it is difficult to find one thread that unites its disparate styles into a coherent pattern.

If there is one technical element that stands out it is dissonance. There simply has been greater latitude for composers to use dissonance as an expressive tool ever since the loosening of tonal relations in Wagner's music, but of course that would apply to the Late Romantics as well. To get beyond them we must take into account the totality of several other changes, subtle and overt: a de-emphasis of melody, an increase in the angularity of rhythms, greater freedom of form.

Yet none of these quite enables us to add up to that thing we call the Modern style in classical music. The missing element in the equation is *angst,* that uniquely 20th century pervasive feeling that somehow things are not quite right, that doom is possibly right around the corner. Angst is a 20th-century term born of two World Wars, economic depressions, the discovery of the id, the invention of the Bomb, and all the other dreadful things we all know about only too well. A preoccupation with the sufferings of humanity began to permeate all the arts early in the 20th century; it is evident not only in music, but as well in literature and in painting, particularly the German Expressionists. Arnold Schoenberg actually subtitled his one-act monodrama *Erwartung* ("Expectation") as *Angsttraum*—"a dream of angst."

Certainly our lives have their happy and optimistic moments as well, but these tend not to be the things that inspire great art. And surely there was angst in previous ages; it is just that it was not a matter of public record. The bad things that happened long ago were interpreted in the arts as Tragedy, a somewhat remote and idealized form of suffering, reserved for those who were noble by birth or soul, forbidden to the vulgar. Even the composers who did not fill their works with angst can often be understood as reacting to it, as in the sardonic humor of Satie or Prokofiev, the retreat into mysticism of Holst, or the transcendentalism of Ives.

It is the very democratization of the Modern world that has permitted the development of a wide diversity of styles and forms of expression, in art music as elsewhere, and made a pat definition of the age so hard to enunciate. There have been broad trends, such as Impressionism and Expressionism and lately Minimalism, but no overarching umbrella to shelter them all.

Just as democratization legitimized a variety of "serious" art forms, it obviously did the same for the manifestations of popular culture. Ragtime, jazz, blues, popular song and their various offshoots could claim integrity and dignity right alongside the works of the "long-hair" composers; in fact, by the early 1960s the term "long-hair" had completely reversed itself and become applied to the Beatles and their kin instead of Franz Liszt and his.

One negative result of all this diffusion and fragmentation has been a widening gap between popular and "art" cultures, so that in the minds of many they have come to be enemies rather than neighbors. So-called classical music has often been supported for the wrong reasons, as a symbol of affluence or aristocracy, a sign that its aficionados are a loftier breed of intellect and social position, a type of thinking I have always found repulsive (and which, quite rightly, repulses advocates of popular culture).

There have been art composers who have successfully incorporated popular styles in their works, e.g. Ravel, Milhaud, and Villa-Lobos, and composers like Gershwin and Grofé who came from the opposite direction, evolving their art out of popular song towards traditional "classical" forms, but none of these has bridged the gap between two cultures. The classical side often sees these pop elements as acceptable only if they are legitimized by classical composers; the pop side considers such re-creations to be prettified and eviscerated petrifactions of what ought to be a living art of the people.

Much of the art music of the 20th century was born out of a sense of alienation—not only from popular culture, but also from the art culture of the past. It was this sensation that pushed Arnold Schoenberg over the edge, leading him to develop a music that was as unrelated as possible to either of them. His was the major single break with the past and it influenced many, though not all, of the later classical composers. (The fact that the other leading iconoclast, Igor Stravinsky, converted to the Schoenberg camp late in his career only increased the sense of alienation and betrayal for many younger composers.)

The "atonal" system developed by Schoenberg, and which he preferred to call, more accurately, "pantonal," avoids the traditional key system with its sense of tonal centers, and with the dissonances always "resolving" into consonances. Each tone is now considered democratic, independent of the others, never subservient. This led naturally to Schoenberg's invention of the 12-tone (or "serial") system, emphasizing the equality of all 12 notes of the chromatic scale (including all the sharps and flats), and using a predetermined sequence of all the notes (a "tone row") as the theme of every composition.

Although atonality and the tone-row system are not necessarily identical, they are popularly lumped together under the "atonal" designation. In this sense, we can say that atonalism is a prominent feature of the music of Schoenberg, Berg, and Webern, the leading members of the so-called Second Viennese School, and occurs occasionally in the works of many other later composers, especially Stravinsky in his last period. Much atonal music

——— *Some famous CDs are not listed because currently out of print.* ———

is also defined as Expressionistic, denoting the interpretation of inner feelings or psychological states.

Although Stravinsky began as a neo-Romantic, his significant "middle period" exemplified neo-Classicism, a style which few other composers directly imitated. Some of Hindemith's music fits this description, while other of it belongs to the category of *Gebrauchsmusik*, or "functional music."

Impressionism, a style that suggests rather than delineates, is derived from the works of Debussy in the previous period, and is noted mainly in the 20th century in the works of Ravel and Respighi.

Nationalism, strongly influenced by folk music, was a stylistic theory carried over from the 19th century but updated for the 20th with modernized techniques. Some composers who fall naturally in this category are Bartók, Bloch, Enesco, de Falla, Janáček, Khachaturian, Kodály, Nielsen, Sibelius, Vaughan Williams, and Villa-Lobos.

Neo-Romanticism was of course a carry-over as well, and is often applied to the major work of Barber, Hanson, and Rachmaninov.

One branch of the French school emphasized polytonality, a system which keeps the old key system but has two or more frequently mixed together. Composers who belonged to this movement or derived from it include Milhaud, Honegger, Satie, and to a lesser extent Poulenc. The American composer Virgil Thomson may be considered an offshoot of this style.

Polytonality flourished in the 1920s, as did jazz and the American popular song, types which strongly influenced the music of Bernstein, Gershwin, Grofé, and Rodrigo.

Primitivism might be the category for Carl Orff and a number of lesser composers; it is also an occasionally accurate description for composers such as Bartók, Kodály, and Prokofiev.

In addition to all these, a number of eminent Modern composers do not fit snugly into any standard pigeonholes. Among these could be named Britten, Copland, Holst, Prokofiev, Shostakovich, and Walton, all of whom are reasonably Modern and not terribly conservative but sometimes all or none of the above. All of them somehow managed to find distinctive musical personalities while not subscribing fully to any one school or style.

Having said all this, it must be added that in the democratic musical world of the 20th century, hardly any of the composers named is exclusively identified with one style; almost all of them at least occasionally mix in something from a technique with which they are not normally associated. And just to confuse everything, there is Charles Ives, who was at one and the same time a proto-serialist, polytonalist, nationalist, Impressionist, primitivist, neo-Romantic!

Samuel Barber (1910-1981)

Barber was not so much a Romantic, as he was always billed, but an Emotionalist. His works vary in style. They may all sound "Romantic" to musicologists who listen to 12-tone and aleatoric music all day (in fact, Barber used 12-tone technique in several of his works), but they sound fairly modern to the average concert-goer.

Born in West Chester, Pennsylvania, Barber was a nephew of Louise Homer, a "golden age" contralto at the Metropolitan Opera, and he inherited a bit of voice himself: he not only took singing lessons but made a record of his own setting of Matthew Arnold's poem *Dover Beach*.

His music study began early: at seven he was writing piano pieces, and at eight he was writing his mother: "To begin with, I was not meant to be an athelet [sic] I was meant to be a composer. And will be, I'm sure....Don't ask me to try to forget this...and go and play foot-ball. —Please— Sometimes I've been worrying about this so much that it makes me mad! (not very)."

This early penchant for whimsy stayed with him. He became a gourmand with a special interest in soups, and once expressed a wish to be buried "with a sprinkling of croutons over my coffin."

At age 12 he got a paying job as a church organist. Unfortunately, the choirmaster one day demanded little Sam hold a note longer than the score indicated. He refused, and was fired. Two years later he was admitted into the first class of the new Curtis Institute in Philadelphia. That city's great orchestra premiered his overture *The School for Scandal* when he was 23.

In the 1930s he twice won the Pulitzer Prize for Music, and the American Prix de Rome, which allowed him to study in Italy. One Italian who noticed him was Arturo Toscanini, who conducted the premieres of two of his orchestral works, including the Adagio for Strings, which Barber had arranged from a movement of his String Quartet No. 1. Among Barber's other best-known works are his Violin Concerto, the ballet *Medea*, and the three *Essays for Orchestra*.

Adagio for Strings

This serene but dirge-like piece has a gently winding theme that fixes one's attention because it never goes where you think it will, and yet seems inevitable once it gets there. It first became nationally known when played on the radio at the announcement of President Franklin Roosevelt's death. It served the same function after the assassination of President Kennedy, and got renewed exposure as the theme of the film Platoon (as well as *Lorenzo's Oil* later on).

——— *Since CDs can change label and number, use artists as main reference.* ———

Bernstein, Los Angeles Philharmonic Orchestra. Deutsche Grammophon 427806 [DDD] + Bernstein: *Candide* Overture, *On the Town*, Symphonic Dances from *West Side Story*

Levi, Atlanta Symphony Orchestra. Telarc 80250 [DDD] + *Essays* 1, 2; *Knoxville: Summer* of 1915

Marriner, Academy of St. Martin-in-the-Fields. EMI 64306 [ADD] + Copland: *Fanfare for the Common Man, Quiet City*, et al.; Thompson: *The Plow that Broke the Plains; Autumn*

Slatkin, St. Louis Symphony Orchestra. EMI 49463 [DDD] + Overture to *The School for Scandal, Essays for Orchestra* 1-3, *Meditation and Dance of Vengeance* from *Medea*

Slatkin, St. Louis Symphony Orchestra. Telarc 80059 [DDD] + Vaughan Williams: *Fantasia on a Theme by Thomas Tallis; Satie: Trois Gymnopédies; Fauré: Pavane*, etc.

Zinman, Baltimore Symphony Orchestra. Argo 436288 [DDD] +Symphony No. 1, *Essays for Orchestra, Music for a Scene from Shelley*, Overture to *The School for Scandal*

Béla Bartók (1881-1945)

Bartók was, along with Mussorgsky, the most original of all the "nationalist" composers. He called himself "a son of the Hungarian plains," and virtually everything he wrote is suffused with the idiom and temperament of his country. Although he was an expert on Hungarian folk music, he seldom quoted an actual tune in his compositions; his object was to merge authentic folk elements with traditional compositional forms to create a new mode of expression. And this he accomplished.

He was found to have perfect pitch as a child, and his mother, a piano teacher, started him on the instrument when he was five. At age 11 he was giving recitals. He studied at the Budapest Academy of Music and composed some music much influenced by Franz Liszt and Richard Strauss.

In 1905 he and his friend Zoltán Kodály, who was to become the other most famous Hungarian composer of the 20th century, took an Edison recording machine around the countryside and began studying and collecting folk songs. (His other hobby, by the way, was collecting insects.) From then on Bartók began to develop his distinctive style, terse and rugged, often dissonant and sometimes savage.

People became alarmed at his music: when his *Bear Dance* was played in 1912, critic Philip Hale wrote that "the composer was regarded with a certain indulgence by the audience as, if not stark mad, certainly an eccentric person." There was some truth to that. Serious since childhood, Bartók had a morose streak all his life; he seemed to take pleasure in bad news, and disbelieve the good.

———— *Artists are listed alphabetically, not in order by critical ranking.* ————

His works received few performances in his own country, and in 1939, when his mother died and it looked as if the Nazis would be rolling through at any time, he moved to the United States. He was awarded an ethnomusicology position at Columbia University at a small salary. He and his wife had to live frugally, although not, as legend already has it, in dire poverty.

In the early 1940s he began to ail mysteriously. He had leukemia, although the doctors kept telling him they could make no diagnosis. Despite almost constant pain, weight loss, and fevers, Bartók composed some of his greatest works at this time, including one of his rare audience successes, the Concerto for Orchestra. He died in New York City, despairing that he had not done all he wanted to do. Ironically, his reputation began to soar shortly after his death, and within a few years he was universally recognized as one of the greatest composers of the Modern era.

Concerto for Orchestra

Bartók's most popular composition was commissioned by the Koussevitzky Foundation, following a suggestion made by the conductor Fritz Reiner and the violinist Joseph Szigeti, both also Hungarians. Composed in 1943, it was Bartók's last, and largest, orchestral work. It was a great success, and though seriously ill the composer at last had the satisfaction of receiving an ovation.

Dorati, London Symphony Orchestra. Mercury Living Presence 432017 [ADD] + *Dance Suite, Two Portraits, Mikrokosmos* (exc.)

Haitink, Concertgebouw Orchestra. Philips Duo 438812 (2) [ADD] + Piano Concertos 1-3 (with Kovacevich, C. Davis, London Symphony Orchestra, BBC Symphony Orchestra), Violin Concerto No. 2 (with Szeryng, C. Davis, London Symphony Orchestra)

Järvi, Royal Scottish National Orchestra. Chandos 8947 [DDD] + Enesco: *Romanian Rhapsodies* 1, 2

Levine, Chicago Symphony Orchestra. Deutsche Grammophon 429747 [DDD] + *Music for Strings, Percussion and Celesta*

Rattle, City of Birmingham Symphony Orchestra. EMI 55094 [DDD] + *The Miraculous Mandarin* Suite

Reiner, Chicago Symphony Orchestra. RCA Living Stereo 61504 [ADD] + *Music for Strings, Percussion, and Celesta, Hungarian Sketches*

Solti, Chicago Symphony Orchestra. London [Decca] 417754 [DDD] + Mussorgsky: *Pictures at an Exhibition*

————— *[DDD] indicates newest recordings; [ADD] or [AAD] are reissues.* —————

Concerto No. 3 for Piano

Bartók knew he was dying when he wrote this concerto as a parting gift to his wife Ditta Pásztory, a pianist also. He worked on it literally up to the minute he was taken for the last time to the hospital. The final 17 bars were completed from sketches by Bartók's pupil Tibor Serly. The middle Adagio movement is particularly famous for its moving nocturnal tranquillity.

Anda, Fricsay, Berlin Radio Symphony Orchestra. Deutsche Grammophon 447399 [ADD] + Piano Concertos 1, 2
Donohoe, Rattle, City of Birmingham Symphony Orchestra. EMI 54871 [DDD] + Piano Concertos No. 1, 2
Kovacevich, C. Davis, London Symphony Orchestra. Philips Duo 438812 (2) [ADD] + Piano Concertos 1, 2 (with BBC Symphony Orchestra in No. 2); Violin Concerto No. 2 (with Szeryng, C. Davis, London Symphony Orchestra); Concerto for Orchestra (with Haitink, Concertgebouw Orchestra)
Jandó, Ligeti, Budapest Symphony Orchestra. Naxos 8.550771 [DDD] + Piano Concertos 1, 2

Music for Strings, Percussion and Celesta

Uniquely constructed, imaginatively orchestrated, and memorably communicative, this work is a frequent candidate for the greatest single work of music written in the 20th century. It really does have everything. A wide variety of materials, from folk rhythms to outer-space sounds to a fugue of which Bach would be proud, are somehow tightly integrated into a seamless whole that manages to be both intellectual and emotional. Professors and peasants alike can appreciate it.

Levine, Chicago Symphony Orchestra. Deutsche Grammophon 429747 [DDD] + *Concerto for Orchestra*
Marriner, Academy of St. Martin-in-the-Fields. London [Decca] 448577 [ADD] + *Divertimento*; Shostakovich: Piano Concerto No. 1 (with Ogdon, Wilbraham)
Reiner, Chicago Symphony Orchestra. RCA Living Stereo 61504 [ADD] + *Concerto for Orchestra, Hungarian Sketches*

[The Levine is included for diehard digitarians, the Marriner because of its Shostakovich coupling (*q.v.*). Otherwise, the Reiner would have been another rare example in this book of a recording which is generally considered so superior as to make listing any others as possible first purchases seem foolish. This is the best there is, ever has been, and probably will be unless Reiner comes back. (And if there is anything to his legends, he may: members of the orchestra told "It was so cold that..." stories about the great but not ingratiating conductor for years after his death, the best-known being "Fritz Reiner was so mean that...he fired two of the pallbearers at his own funeral.")]

─────── *CDs go in and out of print; availability of all listed items is not assured.* ───────

Quartets (6)

Written over a span of 30 years, these greatest of modern quartets are an inseparable family group, providing a portrait of the composer in microcosm. Some, like No. 3, are very demanding of the listener; you might start with No. 2, one of Bartók's most beautiful (almost Romantic) works.

Emerson Quartet. Deutsche Grammophon 423657 (2) [DDD]
Tokyo String Quartet. RCA Victor Red Seal 68286 (3) [DDD] + Janáček: String Quartets Nos. 1, 2

Alban Berg (1885-1935)

Berg was the outstanding student of Arnold Schoenberg, the originator of the 12-tone, or "atonal" system of music. He was so good that many would say he outdistanced his master.

He was born into comfortable circumstances, the son of a merchant, and descendant of Bavarian court officials. His mother's side had some musical background, but Alban at first lagged behind his piano-playing sister and singing brother. At age 14 he started taking a real interest and by the next year was writing songs. At the same time his father died and he had the first attack of what would be lifelong bronchial asthma. He failed his final exams at school, and tried to commit suicide after a love affair.

He recovered enough to take a civil service job, but gave it up in 1906 to devote himself to music after coming under the influence of Arnold Schoenberg, whose methods he adopted (this was, however, before the notorious 12-tone system was completely formulated; Berg's first truly atonal work was the *Lyric Suite*, in 1926). He married in 1911. World War I interrupted his progress, but soon he was composing again and came to international attention with his Expressionist opera Wozzeck (1925).

The rise of the Nazis led to more problems after 1933, with performances of his works curtailed and his income as well. He became so poor he could not have his teeth fixed. In the autumn of 1935 a bee stung him on the back. An abscess formed which was lanced, but it returned in a couple of months, probably exacerbated by Berg's run-down condition. Systemic blood poisoning developed, and despite operations and blood transfusions the composer died on Christmas eve in his wife's arms. He was 51.

Concerto for Violin

Inspired by the tragic death of Manon Gropius, 18-year-old daughter of Gustav Mahler's widow by her second husband, this greatest of 20th-century violin concertos was commissioned by violinist Louis Krasner, who later became a distinguished professor at Syracuse University, and whom I was privileged to know during three of those years. (Dr.

——— *Some CDs may be available only through importers.* ———

Krasner's 1938 world-premiere monophonic recording, though in execrable sound, is available for archival purposes on the GM label, catalog number 2006.)

Mutter, Levine, Chicago Symphony Orchestra. Deutsche Grammophon 437093 [DDD] + Rihm: *Time Chant*
Perlman, Ozawa, Boston Symphony Orchestra. Deutsche Grammophon 447445 [ADD] + Stravinsky: Violin Concerto; Ravel: *Tzigane*
Zehetmair, Holliger, Philharmonia Orchestra. Teldec 97449 [DDD] + Janáček: Violin Concerto; Hartmann: *Concerto Funèbre*
Zukerman, Boulez, London Symphony Orchestra. Sony 68331 [ADD] + Chamber Concerto, 3 Pieces for Orchestra, Op. 6 (with some differing artists)

Three Pieces for Orchestra, Op. 6

Prelude, Round Dance, and *March* make up this group of pieces written in 1915 and dedicated to Arnold Schoenberg on his 40th birthday. The *Prelude* begins and ends with mysterious soft noises on the percussion, with the orchestra presenting a theme in between. The *Round Dance* (*Reigen*) is built on waltz rhythms and recalls Mahler's peasant dances. The *March* is a brutal affair with terrifying climaxes.

Boulez, London Symphony Orchestra. Sony 68331 [ADD] + Chamber Concerto, Violin Concerto (with Zukerman)
Dorati, London Symphony Orchestra. Mercury Living Presence 432006 [ADD] + Schoenberg: 5 Pieces for Orchestra, Op. 16, *Lulu* Suite; Webern: 5 Pieces for Orchestra, Op. 10
Levine, Berlin Philharmonic Orchestra. Deutsche Grammophon 419781 [DDD] + Schoenberg: 5 Pieces for Orchestra, Op. 16; Webern: 6 Pieces for Orchestra, Op. 6

Wozzeck

Despite his genius, Berg was a superstitious man. He was obsessed about the number 23 after his first asthma attack occurred on the 23rd of July, 1900. One evening in Vienna he was fascinated by a performance of fragments of a drama by Georg Büchner, an Early Romantic playwright who died in 1837 at the age of 23. Berg decided he had to set this symbolic work to music. Although the opera was attacked by many critics it grew in public favor and had 166 performances in 29 cities within a decade. Today it is one of the few modern operas that can be said to have taken a regular place in the repertoire.

———— *U.S. labels and numbers are given first, U.K. in [brackets] when needed.* ————

Böhm, Fischer-Dieskau, Berlin German Opera Orchestra. Deutsche
  Grammophon 435705 (3) [ADD]
Dohnányi, Wächter, Vienna Philharmonic Orchestra. London [Decca]
  417348 (2) [DDD] + Schoenberg: *Erwartung*

Leonard Bernstein (1918-1990)

Bernstein was a media phenomenon as well as a great musician. I say musician because it is
still being argued whether he was a great composer. Certainly he was an enormously talented one, but his exact position in the pantheon is not yet universally accepted. But he was a
star. From the fateful night when he substituted for ailing Bruno Walter as conductor of
the New York Philharmonic in 1943, he was news. The dashing, flamboyant youth was in
the papers the next day, and ever since.

Bernstein was born in Lawrence, Massachusetts. His father, Sam, a Russian Jewish
immigrant, wanted his son to join him in the beauty supply business, but from age ten,
when his aunt Clara gave the family an old upright piano, Lenny had ears only for music.
He later studied at Harvard (with Walter Piston), the Curtis Institute (with Fritz Reiner),
and at Tanglewood (with Serge Koussevitzky)–in other words, with three of the greatest
musicians within a thousand miles.

From 1944, when he wrote the ballet (and later musical) *Fancy Free*, to 1957, the year
of his triumph with *West Side Story*, Bernstein was most active on Broadway, and in films
(e.g., *On the Waterfront*, 1954).

After 1958, when he was appointed music director of the New York Philharmonic, his
activities veered more towards the "serious" repertoire, both in composing and conducting.
And what conducting! Leaping into the air, gyrating, he was the classical equivalent of Elvis
Presley. Some critics rolled their eyes, but Bernstein said a good conductor should be an
actor, and his often brilliant performances were his best defense.

His showmanship extended to a series of television programs in the 1960s, introduc-
ing classical music to the "masses," and resulting in his well-known book *The Joy of Music*,
which has had so many imitators; and, to a series of Harvard lectures which were recorded
in a huge box of LPs and sold right along with his numerous music recordings.

In the 1960s he also championed the music of Gustav Mahler to such an extent that it
raised that composer's profile from a rather obscure sideshow to the forefront of discussion,
interest, and orchestra programming around the world. Bernstein seemed to identify with
Mahler's anguished questioning of the Meaning of Life, and he wrote his own tortured
symphony with the subtitle "The Age of Anxiety."

Over the years he won Grammys and Emmys and Tonys but never fully won the
endorsement of the academic community. He had the image of a fast liver, a little on the
wild side, "very New York," and he died of emphysema brought on by years of cigarette
smoking. All the same, he could lead the Vienna Philharmonic in a Brahms symphony and

——— All CDs listed are considered approximately equal in (high) merit. ———

bring down the house. He was America's Renaissance man of many musics, and it will be a while till we can evaluate him without the stardust in our eyes.

Candide: Overture

It had everything: a great story by Voltaire, a libretto hammered out by Dorothy Parker, John LaTouche, Lillian Hellman, and Richard Wilbur, music by Leonard Bernstein and a premiere in 1956 directed by Tyrone Guthrie. And still it flopped! Bernstein revised it in 1973, and again in 1982, but though its fortunes have improved, it's still the Overture that everybody knows, and the rest remains far down the track. That Overture, though, is as snappy and sassy as classical music gets.

> **Bernstein, Los Angeles Philharmonic Orchestra.** Deutsche Grammophon 427806 [DDD] + *On the Town*, Symphonic Dances from *West Side Story*; Barber: *Adagio for Strings*; Gershwin: *Rhapsody in Blue*
> **Bernstein, New York Philharmonic Orchestra.** Sony 47529 [ADD] + Symphonic Dances from *West Side Story*; Gershwin: *Rhapsody in Blue*, *An American in Paris*.

Chichester Psalms for Chorus and Orchestra

Both devotional and jazzy, this is easily the greatest choral work by an American composer. It was written in 1965 and continues to have a visceral impact on listeners.

> **Bernstein, New York Philharmonic Orchestra.** CBS [Sony] 44710 [ADD] + Poulenc: *Gloria*; Stravinsky: *Symphony of Psalms*
> **Shaw, Atlanta Symphony Orchestra and Chorus.** Telarc 80181 [DDD] + *Missa Brevis*; Walton: *Belshazzar's Feast*
> **Hickox, London Symphony Orchestra and Chorus.** Carlton Classics 6600092 [30366 00092] [DDD] + Fauré: *Requiem*

Dances from West Side Story

Bernstein's greatest musical dates from 1957 on Broadway, and was later made into a successful film. The suite of dances is popular as a concert piece.

> **Bernstein, Los Angeles Philharmonic Orchestra.** Deutsche Grammophon 427806 [DDD] + *Candide* Overture, *On the Town*; Barber: *Adagio for Strings*; Gershwin: *Rhapsody in Blue*

———— *CDs listed are solid, central choices, not necessarily "the greatest."* ————

Bernstein, New York Philharmonic Orchestra. Sony 47529 [ADD] + *Candide*
Overture; Gershwin: *Rhapsody in Blue, An American in Paris*

Ernest Bloch (1880-1959)

Bloch both benefitted and suffered from being stereotyped as a "Hebraic composer." One
one hand it called attention to an important part of his heritage which he wanted to
explore, share, and make universal, and on another it tended to limit his credibility when
he wanted, especially in later life, to be known as well for music with no apparent Jewish
roots at all.

He was born to a clock merchant in Geneva, Switzerland and began his music study at
age 14. In short order he was composing; by age 16 he had completed an *Oriental
Symphony*. He had little luck getting his works performed, however, and in his early 20s
returned to help his father as a salesman and bookkeeper. In the evenings he composed as
assiduously as ever.

To his amazement, his first composition to be accepted for performance was not one
of his short pieces or chamber works, but a full-length opera on Shakespeare's *Macbeth*,
which premiered at the famous Opéra-Comique in Paris in 1910. In the audience was the
great critic (and I do not say that often!) Romain Rolland, who was so impressed he traveled to Geneva to meet the composer. He was taken aback to find Bloch buried in ledger
books and receipts. Encouraging him to strike out on his own, Rolland said "I will answer
for your becoming one of the masters of our time."

Bloch was fired now to create, and his first impulse was to write those works which
expressed, as he said, "the complex, glowing, agitated soul that I feel vibrating through the
Bible"—Schelomo (Solomon), the *Israel Symphony*, the *Baal Shem* Suite, the *Trois Poèmes
Juifs*.

In 1916 Bloch, accompanied by his wife and children, left for the U.S. to become conductor of a touring dance program. Almost immediately his music came to the attention of
well-placed musicians and in just a few months an all-Bloch concert was being given at
Carnegie Hall! He made the papers, always described as "the composer of Hebraic music."

But Bloch was ready for new challenges. In no way did he wish to repudiate his previous work or his spiritual heritage (although he suffered a crisis of faith during World War
II), but he wanted to prove he was more than a provincial composer. Over the succeeding
years he wrote both chamber and programmatic works with no overt Jewish connotations,
winning a prize for his epic rhapsody *America*, a setting of Walt Whitman verses written to
honor his adopted land.

In addition to composing, Bloch taught at the Mannes School of Music in New York
City, became the first director of the Cleveland Institute of Music (1920-25), then director
of the San Francisco Conservatory until he received an endowment in 1931 which made it
possible for him to concentrate entirely on composing. He returned to Switzerland for a

——— *Some famous CDs are not listed because currently out of print.* ———

while, then moved to France and Italy, until the anti-Semitic wave of the late 1930s swept him back the the U.S.

He settled in Agate Beach, Oregon, overlooking the Pacific, where he lived out his remaining 20 years of life, continually composing, continually developing, always learning and seeking new challenges. But it is still the "Hebraic" works of his young years— amounting only to about a quarter of his output—which listeners today remember most vividly, for their sensuous melodies and haunting harmonies seem to blaze forth from a richly passionate mind and soul.

Schelomo—Rhapsody for Cello and Orchestra

Far and away Bloch's most famous composition, *Schelomo* ("Solomon") is an evocation of the ancient king's court and personality, inspired largely by the *Book of Ecclesiastes*. There are suggestions of Solomon's power and pomp, the cries of slaves and warriors, dances of wives and courtiers; but woven throughout is the sad yearning of the king's reluctant wisdom: "I have seen all the works that are done under the sun, and behold, all is vanity...."

P. Fournier, Wallenstein, Berlin Philharmonic Orchestra. Deutsche Grammophon Resonance 429155 [ADD] + Dvořák: Cello Concerto; Bruch: *Kol Nidrei*

Harnoy, Mackerras, London Philharmonic Orchestra. RCA Victor Gold Seal 60757 [DDD] + Bruch: *Adagio on Celtic Themes*, etc.

Isserlis, Hickox, London Symphony Orchestra. Virgin Ultraviolet 61125 [DDD] + Elgar: Cello Concerto

Ma, Zinman, Baltimore Symphony Orchestra. Sony 57961 [DDD] + Bartók: Viola Concerto; Albert: Cello Concerto

Benjamin Britten (1913-1976)

Britten was the Golden Boy of 20th-century English music—composer, pianist, conductor, founder of festivals, master of many styles, witty and prolific, darling of the critics, popular with the public, good or great at everything he tried, seldom stumbling.

The youngest of four children, he was a musical prodigy, composing a full-length oratorio at the age of nine. At 12 he became a student of the composer Frank Bridge, honoring him a few years later with his first major work, the *Variations on a Theme of Frank Bridge*.

Studies at the Royal College of Music were followed by a stint writing incidental music for documentary films, which primed him for his later theatrical work and introduced him to the poet W. H. Auden, who was a major influence. There followed a sojourn in the U.S. with the tenor Peter Pears, who was to become his lifelong companion and artistic collaborator. Here he wrote several important works including the *Sinfonia da Requiem*.

—— *Catalog numbers are subject to change without notice.* ——

He returned to England in 1942 with a commission in his pocket from the Koussevitzky Foundation to write an opera. *Peter Grimes* had its sensational premiere in 1945, being acclaimed the greatest English opera since Purcell's *Dido and Aeneas*, a judgment which still stands after 50 years. A demand for more operas followed and in the ensuing years Britten produced a number of fine stage works, although none quite repeated the success of the first.

He and Pears founded the Aldeburgh Festival in 1948 and Britten acted as its director until his death. It was a venue for many important performances of his own and other compositions. Britten was also active as a pianist and conductor. In the latter capacity he made many distinguished recordings, some of his own works of course, but also such things as one of the best sets ever made of Bach's *Brandenburg Concertos*.

Britten made a conscious effort to vary his style, ranging from the transparency of the *Simple Symphony* to complex experimental works such as *The Turn of the Screw* with its quasi-Schoenbergian harmonies. He seldom strayed far from what the public could readily absorb, while retaining just enough subtleties and academic touches to please the critics. This desire to please everybody does often give his music an unsettling air of calculation.

An unusual aspect of this composer was his emphasis on music for young people. Besides his famous Guide to the *Orchestra*, he wrote the song cycles *A Charm of Lullabies* and *Who Are These Children?*, the cantata *Saint Nicolas*, the "miracle play" *Noyes Fludde*, and an introduction to opera for children, *The Little Sweep*.

Serenade for Tenor, Horn, and Strings, Op. 31

The term "serenade" in this work implies not a lover's song to his beloved, but the older technical sense of "night music," when a serenade was a suite of instrumental pieces played at a person's house, preceded and followed by a march. The vocal part in Britten's composition comprises settings of six poems by Cotton, Tennyson, Blake, Ben Jonson, Keats, and Anonymous (15th century).

Rolfe-Johnson, M. Thompson, B. Thompson, Scottish National Orchestra.
    Chandos 8657 [DDD] + *Les Illuminations;* Quatre Chansons
Pears, Tuckwell, Britten, London Symphony Orchestra. London [Decca]
    417153 [ADD] + *Les Illuminations, Nocturne*

Young Person's Guide to the Orchestra, Op. 34

In case anyone might think this title too flippant or popular, Britten judiciously gave it an alternate, *Variations and Fugue on a Theme of Henry Purcell*, which would be more acceptable to academics. It was originally written as the score for a documentary film on the instruments of the orchestra. The first concert performance was given in 1946.

———— *Since CDs can change label and number, use artists as main reference.* ————

There is a narrative written by Eric Crozier which is still sometimes used, but the work makes its points so clearly that many feel the addition of words is not only superfluous but positively disruptive. I certainly don't care for it when things are just getting going and the music stops while an actor intones "Now this is the tuba, you little morons," or words to that effect.

The theme is taken from Purcell's incidental music to a play called *Abdelazar*, or *The Moor's Revenge*. It is an incredibly fertile tune, and its final statement on the brass is one of the exciting moments in orchestral music.

Britten, London Symphony Orchestra. London [Decca] 417509 [ADD] + *Simple Symphony, Variations on a Theme of Frank Bridge*

Connery (narrator), Dorati, Royal Philharmonic Orchestra. London [Decca] Phase 4 Stereo 444104 [ADD] + Prokofiev: *Peter and the Wolf, Lt. Kijé* Suite

A. Davis, BBC Symphony Orchestra. Teldec British Line 73126 [DDD] + *4 Sea Interludes* and *Passacaglia* from *Peter Grimes, Variations and Fugue on a Theme by Frank Bridge*

Hickox, Bournemouth Symphony Orchestra. Chandos 9221 [DDD] + *Suite on English Folk Tunes, Johnson over Jordan, 4 Sea Interludes* from *Peter Grimes*

Previn, Royal Philharmonic Orchestra. Telarc 80126 [DDD] + *Courtly Dances* from *Gloriana*; Prokofiev: *Peter and the Wolf*

Aaron Copland (1900-1990)

Copland became known as the Dean of American Composers at a surprisingly early stage in his long career. By the time he was 25 two major American orchestras had performed his works, by 35 he was already an entry in every music history book, and by 45 he was acclaimed as the greatest American composer.

This was an extraordinary ascent for one who was born in a drab neighborhood of Brooklyn without any real exposure to musical culture. Copland's attraction to art music was almost instinctive, and he was only 16 when he determined to become a composer. His first lessons were uninspiring and it was not until he was able to save enough to travel to Paris, where he came under the tutelage of Nadia Boulanger, that his talent found its proper direction.

Back in America he was noticed, and subsequently promoted, by Serge Koussevitzky, conductor of the Boston Symphony Orchestra and a vigorous champion of new music. A Guggenheim Fellowship freed Copland from drudge jobs so that he could concentrate on composing, and for a while he concentrated on complex works in an avant-garde idiom.

In the mid-1930s he reassessed his esthetic. "It seemed to me," he later wrote, "that we composers were in danger of working in a vacuum. Moreover, an entirely new public for music had grown up around the radio and phonograph. It made no sense to ignore them

——— *Artists are listed alphabetically, not in order by critical ranking.* ———

and to continue writing as if they did not exist. I felt that it was worth the effort to see if I couldn't say what I had to say in the simplest possible terms."

The result was those classics of Americana that have endeared Copland to a worldwide audience: the ballets *Appalachian Spring* (which won the Pulitzer Prize), *Rodeo*, and *Billy the Kid*; and the brief but unforgettable *Fanfare for the Common Man*, which has become a virtual calling card for the nation. In these works Copland managed, without sacrificing intellectual integrity, to create a sound-world that evokes unmistakably American poetic images: cowboys, the Wild West, farm life, the small town, and the hardy pioneers such as the Pennsylvania Shakers who possessed a wisdom that Aaron Copland took to heart and passed on:

> *'Tis a gift to be simple,*
> *'Tis a gift to be free.*

Appalachian Spring

Composed as a ballet for Martha Graham, this work had its premiere in the Library of Congress in 1944. It was originally entitled *Ballet for Martha*. The present title was taken from a poem by Hart Crane. The scenario concerns a young Pennsylvania Shaker couple celebrating their new farmhouse in springtime. The old Shaker hymn, "The Gift to Be Simple," was made world-famous through this ballet.

Bernstein, New York Philharmonic Orchestra. (suite) Sony 47543 [ADD] + *Fanfare for the Common Man, Billy the Kid, Rodeo, Symphony No. 3*

Copland, Boston Symphony Orchestra. (suite) RCA Living Stereo 61505 [ADD] + *The Tender Land Suite*; Gould: *Fall River Legend, Latin American Symphonette*

Davies, St. Paul Chamber Orchestra. (suite) Pro Arte 3429 [DDD] + *Short Symphony*; Ives: Symphony No. 3

Dorati, Detroit Symphony Orchestra. (complete) London [Decca] Jubilee 430705 [DDD] + *Rodeo, El Salón México*

Kunzel, Cincinnati Pops. (suite) Telarc 80339 [DDD] + *Billy the Kid, Rodeo, Fanfare for the Common Man, Quiet City*

Mehta, Los Angeles Philharmonic Orchestra. (suite) London [Decca] Double 448261 (2) [ADD/DDD] + *Fanfare for the Common Man, Lincoln Portrait* (with Gregory Peck, narrator); *Ceremonial Fanfare* (with Philip Jones Brass Ensemble); *Dance Symphony, El Salón México* (with Dorati, Detroit Symphony Orchestra); *Music for Movies* (with Howarth, London Sinfonietta); *Quiet City* (with Marriner, Academy of St. Martin-in-the-Fields); Exc. from *Old American Songs* (with Horne, Carl Davis, English Chamber Orchestra)

——— *[DDD] indicates newest recordings; [ADD] or [AAD] are reissues.* ———

Orpheus Chamber Orchestra. (suite in chamber version) Deutsche Grammophon 427335 [DDD] + *3 Latin American Sketches, Quiet City, Short Symphony*
Schenck, Atlantic Sinfonietta. (complete chamber version for 13 instruments) Koch 7019 [DDD] + Barber: *Cave of the Heart*
Susskind, London Symphony Orchestra. (complete) Everest 9003 [AAD] + Gershwin: *An American in Paris;* Gould: *Spirituals*
L. Slatkin, St. Louis Symphony Orchestra. (complete) EMI 64315 + *Billy the Kid, Rodeo, Dance Panels*

Billy the Kid

Although "Western" ballets have become rather common currency, they all descend from *Billy the Kid,* first produced in 1938. The music employs authentic cowboy tunes, but filtered through Copland's distinctive imagination. The concert suite from the complete ballet was arranged by the composer.

Bernstein, New York Philharmonic Orchestra. Sony 47543 [ADD] + *Appalachian Spring Suite, Fanfare for the Common Man, Rodeo, Symphony No. 3*
Kunzel, Cincinnati Pops. Telarc 80339 [DDD] + *Appalachian Spring, Rodeo, Fanfare for the Common Man, Quiet City*
Schwarz, Seattle Symphony Orchestra. *Out West,* Delos 3104 [DDD] + *Rodeo;* Grofé: *Grand Canyon* Suite
L. Slatkin, St. Louis Symphony Orchestra. EMI 64315 + *Appalachian Spring, Rodeo*

Fanfare for the Common Man

At the beginning of World War II the conductor of the Cincinnati Symphony Orchestra, Eugene Goossens, commissioned ten composers to write patriotic fanfares. Only Copland's has thrived since, and the composer himself re-used it at the beginning of the last movement of his Third Symphony.

Bernstein, New York Philharmonic Orchestra. Sony 47543 [ADD] + *Appalachian Spring* Suite, *Billy the Kid, Rodeo, Symphony No. 3*
Kunzel, Cincinnati Pops. Telarc 80339 [DDD] + *Billy the Kid, Appalachian Spring, Rodeo, Quiet City*
Marriner, Academy of St. Martin-in-the-Fields. EMI 64306 [ADD] + *Quiet City, et al.;* Barber: Adagio for Strings; Thompson: *The Plow that Broke the Plains; Autumn*

—————— *CDs go in and out of print; availability of all listed items is not assured.* ——————

Mehta, Los Angeles Philharmonic Orchestra. (suite) London [Decca] Double
448261 (2) [ADD/DDD] + *Appalachian Spring, Lincoln Portrait* (with Gregory
Peck, narrator); *Ceremonial Fanfare* (with Philip Jones Brass Ensemble); *Dance
Symphony, El Salòn México* (with Dorati, Detroit Symphony Orchestra); *Music
for Movies* (with Howarth, London Sinfonietta); *Quiet City* (with Marriner,
Academy of St. Martin-in-the-Fields); Exc. from *Old American Songs* (with
Horne, Carl Davis, English Chamber Orchestra)

Rodeo

Copland's other "Western ballet" is altogether more cheerful than *Billy the Kid*, being a
love story instead of the saga of a bloodthirsty killer. Its premiere took place in 1942 at the
Metropolitan Opera House. The four sections are marked "Buckaroo Holiday," "Corral
Nocturne," "Honky Tonk Interlude and Saturday Night Waltz," and (most famously)
"Hoe-Down."

Bernstein, New York Philharmonic Orchestra. Sony 47543 [ADD] +
   Appalachian Spring Suite, *Fanfare for the Common Man, Billy the Kid, Symphony
   No. 3*
Dorati, Detroit Symphony Orchestra. London [Decca] Jubilee 430705 [DDD]
   + *Appalachian Spring, El Salòn Mexico*
Kunzel, Cincinnati Pops. Telarc 80339 [DDD] + *Billy the Kid, Appalachian
   Spring, Fanfare for the Common Man, Quiet City*
Schwarz, Seattle Symphony Orchestra. *Out West*, Delos 3104 [DDD] + *Billy
   the Kid*; Grofe: *Grand Canyon* Suite
L. Slatkin, St. Louis Symphony Orchestra. EMI 64325 + *Appalachian Spring,
   Billy the Kid*

Georges Enesco (1881-1955)

As he is immediately identifiable as the Greatest Composer of Romania, it would be easy to
let Enesco stay in that easy-to-remember pigeonhole. But he keeps popping back out,
reminding us that he was a composer of many styles, of which Romantic nationalism was
just one.

He was as precocious as any composer ever was, starting to teach himself the violin at
age three. By age seven he had written several sonatas and gave his first public concert at
eight. The director of the Vienna Conservatory not only accepted the boy before the normal age of admission, but let him live in his home where he was the darling of all the
famous musicians in town, including Brahms.

Enesco completed his studies in Paris under Fauré and Massenet, both of whom proclaimed him a genius, and it was there that he began using the French spelling of his Romanian name (originally Enescu, and often listed that way—it's not a misprint). By 1910 he was widely recognized as a great composer, conductor, and violinist (I am listening to his recording of the Bach Sonatas and Partitas for Solo Violin as I write this), and he was the teacher of Yehudi Menuhin.

Enesco's early works are heavily influenced by Brahms and Wagner. Later he adopted a neo-Classical style, then began integrating Romanian folk idioms into his works, and finally experimented with several avant-garde techniques including polytonality and microtonal music.

He was a fervent idealist and an apostle of hard work, encouraging musical culture in Romania and laboring to bring it to the attention of the wider world. His eclectic style made it difficult to place him precisely, and as Enesco ruefully realized, "People get annoyed when they can't really classify you." Nevertheless he left a rich legacy of stimulating and often beautiful music which well repays investigation.

Romanian Rhapsody No. 1, Op. 11

World acclaim greeted Enesco with the joint premiere of his two *Romanian Rhapsodies* in Paris in 1908. The first rhapsody especially, with its slow buildup to whirlwind peasant dances, never fails to thrill. Although written for a quick buck, it's a great piece of its kind, and although hardly indicative of the composer's vast canvas it will, one may hope, intrigue you enough to make you wonder about all the rest of his work.

Bernstein, New York Philharmonic Orchestra. Sony 47572 [ADD] + Liszt: *Les Préludes, Hungarian Rhapsodies* (sel.); Brahms: *Hungarian Dances* (sel.)
Dorati, London Symphony Orchestra. Mercury Living Presence 432015 [ADD] + Liszt: *Hungarian Rhapsodies* (6)
Järvi, Royal Scottish National Orchestra. Chandos 8947 [DDD] + *Romanian Rhapsody* No. 2; Bartók: *Concerto for Orchestra*

Manuel de Falla (1876-1946)

Falla put Spain on the classical music map at last, after centuries of lassitude. Not since Tomás Luis de Victoria in the Renaissance had this important European country participated in serious music culture much beyond the zarzuela, or Spanish operetta (which though delightful isn't very serious).

Falla was born into a highly cultured family in Cadiz, starting piano study with his mother and later advancing to the Madrid Conservatory. There he studied in preparation for a career as a piano virtuoso, but another influence intervened. He came under the spell of his composition teacher, Felipe Pedrell, a fervent nationalist who encouraged study of Spanish folk song and dance and their integration into art music.

In 1905 Falla won first prize in a competition with his folk opera *La vida breve*. Two years later he left for Paris where he became friends with Claude Debussy, and hobnobbed generally with the leading lights of the intense musical activity going on there: Fauré, Ravel, Dukas, and others. Debussy's influence was as significant as Pedrell's to his compositional style, and indeed Falla is sometimes counted among the Impressionists.

After seven years of absorbing all musical France had to offer Falla returned to Spain and spent more years traveling his native land, studying its music and folklore. The first major product of the integration of all these elements was the ballet *El amor brujo*, the orchestral suite from which, including the inescapable *Ritual Fire Dance*, remains Falla's most popular work.

Subsequently his position as Spain's major composer was solidified with the piano concerto *Nights in the Gardens of Spain*, and the ballet *The Three-Cornered Hat*. Although hardly a prolific composer, Falla maintained a high level of integrity and quality in all his work, which is characterized by vivid poetic feeling and intensely picturesque atmosphere.

Falla was a small, natty man, very dark of complexion (Debussy called him "le petit espagnol tout noir"), and of melancholy disposition. His punctilious adherence to a strict personal schedule with each day's chores done at an exact predetermined time, including dinner at midnight, drove even his domestic help away. He had an aversion to wealth and honors, and for 17 years lived in a modest house in Granada.

In addition, Falla was a superstitious hypochondriac who refused to see visitors during the full moon and was terrified of drafts. He was deeply religious, and at first supported Franco during the Spanish Civil War, believing the insurgents were a danger to the Church. But only a year after being appointed president of the Institute of Spain by the victorious Generalissimo, Falla became disillusioned and moved to Argentina, where he grew ever more frail and died in 1946.

El amor brujo

"Love, the Magician" is a gypsy ballet with a part for soprano. It first became a success in 1928 in Paris. The music is languorous and passionate and includes the famous *Ritual Fire Dance*. The scenario concerns the legend of a dead lover's ghost which appears every time a new lover tries to replace him. The spell is broken by a magic kiss after the ghost has been distracted by another girl.

Dutoit, Tourangeau, Montreal Symphony Orchestra. London [Decca] Ovation 430703 [DDD] + *Nights in the Gardens of Spain* (with De Larrocha); Rodrigo: *Concierto de Aranjuez*

———— *All CDs listed are considered approximately equal in (high) merit.* ————

Giulini, de los Angeles, Philharmonia Orchestra. EMI 64746 [ADD] + *Three-Cornered Hat* (sel.), *Nights in the Gardens of Spain* (with Soriano, Frühbeck de Burgos)

Maazel, Bumbry, Berlin Radio Symphony Orchestra. Deutsche Grammophon Originals 447414 [ADD] + Exc. from *The Three-Cornered Hat*; Stravinsky: *Firebird* Suite

Reiner, L. Price, Chicago Symphony Orchestra. RCA Living Stereo 62586 [ADD] + 3 Dances from *The Three-Cornered Hat*, Exc. from *La vida breve*; Albéniz: *Iberia*, etc.; Granados: *Intermezzo* from *Goyescas*

Simon, Walker, London Symphony Orchestra. Chandos 8457 [DDD] + *Nights in the Gardens of Spain* (with Fingerhut), Exc. from *La vida breve*

Nights in the Gardens of Spain

The title provides pretty much all the commentary that is needed. Not quite a piano concerto, but a set of impressionistic orchestral pieces with the piano wandering through the gardens of the imagination. Nights! Gardens! Spain! Get it?

De Larrocha, Dutoit, Montreal Symphony Orchestra. London [Decca] 430703 [DDD] + *El amor brujo*; Rodrigo: *Concierto de Aranjuez*

Fingerhut, Simon, London Symphony Orchestra. Chandos 8457 [DDD] + *El amor brujo*, Exc. from *La vida breve*

Rosenberger, Schwarz, London Symphony Orchestra. Delos 3060 [DDD] + *Three-Cornered Hat* (sel.)

Rubinstein, Ormandy, Philadelphia Orchestra. RCA Victor Gold Seal 61863 [ADD] + Saint-Saëns: Piano Concerto No. 2; Franck: *Symphonic Variations*

Soriano, Frühbeck de Burgos, New Philharmonia Orchestra. EMI 64746 [ADD] + *El amor brujo*, *Three-Cornered Hat* (sel.) (with Giulini conducting)

The Three-Cornered Hat: Dances

Falla's other ballet is best known through excerpted dances. *El Sombrero de tres picos* was commissioned by the legendary impresario Serge Diaghilev and had an overwhelming success at its premiere in London in 1919. The story is adapted from a classic Spanish novel by Pedro del Alarcón.

Giulini, Philharmonia Orchestra. EMI 64746 [ADD] + *El amor brujo*, *Nights in the Gardens of Spain* (with Soriano, Frühbeck de Burgos)

Maazel, Bumbry, Berlin Radio Symphony Orchestra. Deutsche Grammophon Originals 447414 [ADD] + *El amor brujo*; Stravinsky: *Firebird* Suite

————— *CDs listed are solid, central choices, not necessarily "the greatest."* —————

Reiner, Chicago Symphony Orchestra. RCA Living Stereo 62586 [ADD] + *El amor brujo* (with L. Price), Exc. from *La vida breve*; Albéniz: *Iberia*, etc.; Granados: *Intermezzo* from *Goyescas*

Schwarz, London Symphony Orchestra. Delos 3060 [DDD] + *Nights in the Gardens of Spain* (with Rosenberger)

George Gershwin (1898-1937)

Gershwin is almost unique in music history in showing that so-called popular idioms can be made as distinctive and durable as any art or "classical" music. He effectively blurred the lines that once demarcated these two supposedly separate worlds, bringing dignity to jazz and popular song, and making the classical sphere less fearsome to the masses without trivializing it.

He had an unremarkable childhood in New York City, playing street hockey and rooting for the Giants. He even belonged to a gang, and thought boys who liked music were "Maggies." His father was a small-time businessman who variously ran a cigar store, pool hall, Turkish bath, and bookie operation.

One day, when he was ten and playing ball outside P.S. No. 25 on the Lower East Side, he was struck by the sounds of a violin coming from the school auditorium. A local prodigy (and later concert violinist), Max Rosen was playing Dvořák's *Humořesque*. Young George was intrigued and soon made friends with Maxie, pumping him for information on music.

Before he knew it he was taking piano lessons and assiduously studying the Great Masters. Nevertheless, his teachers were alarmed by his continuing attachment to popular songs, ragtime, and jazz, and his irritable defense of them. Gershwin actually loved the classics, but he believed in the music of his milieu too, and was determined to prove it had value.

At age 16 he became a publicist for the Tin Pan Alley publishing firm of Remick. In his spare time he often practiced Bach preludes and fugues. One day a fellow "plugger" asked if he was studying to be a concert pianist. "No," Gershwin replied seriously, "I'm practicing to become a popular-song composer."

Soon he got a job at $35 a week writing songs for a rival publisher, Harms (with lyrics, as always, by his older brother Ira), and one of them, "Swanee," became a million-seller after being sung by Al Jolson in the show *Sinbad*. Gershwin was on his way. By age 23 he was the toast of Broadway, and even London, with songs that are now true classics of American popular culture pouring from him in profusion. A decade later, *Of Thee I Sing* became the first musical to win the Pulitzer Prize.

But the work that established Gershwin's international fame, and made the serious music world take him at least semi-seriously, was *Rhapsody in Blue*, commissioned by bandleader Paul Whiteman in 1924, and orchestrated by Ferde Grofé. Suddenly jazz was respectable, and composers around the world were swept up in the new craze: Ravel,

——— *Some famous CDs are not listed because currently out of print.* ———

Milhaud, Kurt Weill and many others picked up the jazz bug and wrote concert works that incorporated its idioms.

The tables of critical opinion had now turned upside down, and Gershwin's music was praised by Vaughan Williams and Bartók. Arnold Schoenberg became a regular tennis partner. Always looking to improve his technical skills Gershwin asked for lessons, but the leader of the avant-garde refused: "I would only make you a bad Schoenberg, and you're such a good Gershwin already."

Going from one triumph to another on stage and screen, Gershwin became a true workaholic, often staying up all night composing, oblivious to everything around him except his beloved cigars. He never married because he was too busy to do so. At parties he would do nothing but play his own music on the piano. After one such marathon of monopoly, pianist Oscar Levant asked "If you had to do it all over again, George, would you still fall in love with yourself?"

When, at the height of his fame, he began complaining of headaches it was chalked up to overwork, even when he collapsed. But a second collapse led to the discovery of a brain tumor. He underwent surgery immediately, but died in the hospital. Since then, however, the world has not stopped being in love with George Gershwin's music.

An American in Paris

Gershwin speaks: "My purpose here is to portray the impressions of an American visitor in Paris as he strolls about the city, listens to the various street noises, and absorbs the French atmosphere." The visitor was, of course, Gershwin himself, who traveled to France in 1928, hoping to pick up a few pointers on theory and orchestration. Mostly, however, he strolled around the city, listened to the various street noises, and...you get the picture. Speaking of pictures, *An American in Paris* was made into an Academy Award-winning film in 1951 starring Gene Kelly.

Bernstein, New York Philharmonic Orchestra. CBS 42264 [ADD] + *Rhapsody in Blue*; Grofé: *Grand Canyon* Suite

Bernstein, New York Philharmonic Orchestra. Sony 47529 [ADD] + *Rhapsody in Blue*; Bernstein: *Candide* Overture, Symphonic Dances from *West Side Story*

Fiedler, Boston Pops Orchestra. RCA Living Stereo 68792 [ADD] + *Rhapsody in Blue*, Concerto in F, *Variations on "I Got Rhythm"*

Previn, Pittsburgh Symphony Orchestra. Philips 412611 [DDD] + *Rhapsody in Blue*, Piano Concerto in F

Susskind, London Symphony Orchestra. Everest 9003 [AAD] + Copland: *Appalachian Spring*; Gould: *Spirituals*

Porgy and Bess

The original play was by DuBose Heyward. He and his wife Dorothy collaborated with Ira Gershwin to produce the libretto for this magnificent folk opera, which had its premiere in 1935. It is Gershwin's largest work, and probably his masterpiece. The composer had grown up in Harlem and absorbed a great deal from black musicians, including "Fats" Waller and Art Tatum. He lavished almost three years of work on his opera, but at first critical opinion was divided. Acclaim was universal only years after Gershwin's death, *Porgy and Bess* becoming the first American opera ever presented at La Scala, Milan, the world's greatest opera house. It was also a hit in the Soviet Union.

Rattle, London Philharmonic Orchestra. EMI 56220 (3) [DDD]

Rhapsody in Blue

Bandleader Paul Whiteman had enormous faith in Gershwin's ability to write in the larger forms, but the composer was reluctant to accept the invitation to write a symphonic work for a planned concert of experimental jazz at the Aeolian Hall in New York City. He only gave in after Whiteman announced in the papers that it was going to happen. Again, Gershwin's own evaluation of the piece: "I hear it as a sort of musical kaleidoscope of America—of our vast melting-pot, of our incomparable national pep, our blues, our metropolitan madness."

> **Bernstein, Los Angeles Philharmonic Orchestra.** Deutsche Grammophon 427806 [DDD] + Barber: *Adagio for Strings*; Bernstein: *Candide* Overture, *On the Town*, Symphonic Dances from *West Side Story*
> **Bernstein, New York Philharmonic Orchestra.** CBS [Sony] 42264 [ADD] + *An American in Paris*, Piano Concerto in F
> **Bernstein, New York Philharmonic Orchestra.** Sony 47529 [ADD] + *An American in Paris*; Bernstein: *Candide* Overture, Symphonic Dances from *West Side Story*
> **Previn, Pittsburgh Symphony Orchestra.** Philips 412611 [DDD] + *An American in Paris*, Piano Concerto in F
> **Wild, Fiedler, Boston Pops Orchestra.** RCA Living Stereo 68792 [ADD] + *An American in Paris*, Concerto in F, *Variations on "I Got Rhythm"*

——— *Since CDs can change label and number, use artists as main reference.* ———

Ferde Grofé (1892-1972)

As mentioned above under the Gershwin entry, Grofé orchestrated that composer's greatest hit, *Rhapsody in Blue*. He was another American who came up through the ranks of popular music, especially dancebands. One of his "serious" works, the *Grand Canyon* Suite, is also one of the most popular works ever written by an American, and his *Mississippi* Suite is hardly less appealing. But if you will ask any musicologist or academic or critic to name the top ten American composers I guarantee you will never hear him mentioned. Perhaps he should have stuck with his baptismal name, Ferdinand Rudolph von Grofé.

He was born in New York City. His father was a baritone and an actor, his mother a cellist. His maternal grandfather was principal cellist of the Los Angeles Sympphony Orchestra for some 25 years, and before that played next to Victor Herbert in the Metropolitan Opera Orchestra. An uncle was a distinguished violinist.

The family moved to Los Angeles only a year after Ferdinand was born. His mother taught him to read music at age five, and soon he was accompanying her cello playing from the piano. The father died when Ferde was seven and his mother moved to Leipzig, Germany for three years to submerge her grief in further music study.

After they returned to California, the young Grofé undertook a study of as many musical instruments as he could master, from the violin to the marimbaphone, and at 17 he was paid for his first commercial work, a march commissioned for an Elks convention. Now Grofé was able to make a living with music, although at first he played a lot of dance halls and hotels, eventually working his way up to playing viola with the Los Angeles Symphony.

He did some Hollywood mood music work, during which he met the great band-leader Paul Whiteman who took Grofé on as a pianist and arranger in 1920. Their first hit, "Whispering," sold a million and a half copies (I treasure my original 78 rpm copy!). Then came the opportunity to orchestrate Gershwin's masterpiece.

After the successful premiere of the *Grand Canyon* Suite in 1931, Grofé struck out on his own, leading his own orchestra, guesting, doing independent arranging, teaching orchestration at the Juilliard School, and writing a long series of orchestral suites such as the *Hudson River, Death Valley, World's Fair, Aviation*, and *Hollywood* Suites. There was even a *Rudy Vallee* Suite, provoking my friend, music librarian and polymath Rex Levang, to suggest that Grofé's range extended "from Death Valley to Rudy Vallee."

There is always a temptation to snicker at Grofé because of his unsophisticated con-cepts and his frank pandering to audience love of visual connotations tacked on to music. When the idea is executed so lovingly and skillfully, however, it seems ungenerous to deny listeners the melodic and harmonic pleasures of this kind of very literal program music.

For those who would find fault, I direct their attention to the barking dogs in Vivaldi's *The Four Seasons*, the ticking clock in Haydn's Symphony No. 101, or (my favorite) the

—— Artists are listed alphabetically, not in order by critical ranking. ——

athletic amphibians in the great aria "Their land brought forth frogs" from Handel's oratorio *Israel in Egypt*, to name just a few of the composers who would have been proud to write the *Aviation* Suite, if only they had known what an airplane was.

Grand Canyon Suite

Grofé conceived his most famous suite, not surprisingly, while viewing the great natural wonder in 1922, but seven years later when he began to write there were other images mixing themselves in his imagination: memories of a thunderstorm that frightened him as a boy (*Cloudburst*), the rhythm of a piledriver outside his Chicago hotel (*On the Trail*), looking at the sky on the ninth hole of a golf course in New Jersey (*Sunset*). Presumably the other movements, *Sunrise* and *Painted Desert*, were inspired only by the Grand Canyon. At any rate the suite was a complete success at its 1931 premiere; Grofé was anointed the "prime minister of jazz," and his diplomatic coup has since traveled the world.

Bernstein, New York Philharmonic Orchestra. CBS 42264 [ADD] +
   Gershwin: *An American in Paris, Rhapsody in Blue*
Dorati, Detroit Symphony Orchestra. London [Decca] 430712 [ADD] +
   Gershwin (arr. Bennett) *Porgy and Bess: Symphonic Picture*
Kunzel, Cincinnati Pops. Telarc 80086 [DDD] + Gershwin: *Catfish Row*
Schwarz, Seattle Symphony Orchestra. *Out West*, Delos 3104 [DDD] +
   Copland: *Billy the Kid, Rodeo*

Howard Hanson (1896-1981)

Hanson was born in Wahoo, Nebraska, the home town of two other eminent Americans of the same era, Hollywood producer Darryl F. Zanuck and Detroit Tigers first baseman Sam Crawford. His parents were Swedish immigrants; Hanson wrote his Symphony No. 1 "Nordic" in honor of his Scandinavian roots. His mother was his first teacher. Later he received a degree from Northwestern University and at age 20 was appointed professor of theory and composition at the College of the Pacific in San Jose, California. Only two years after that he was named Dean of the Conservatory of Fine Arts.

In 1920 he became the first Fellow selected by the American Academy of Rome to study three years in Italy. On his return he was immediately named director of the Eastman School of Music in Rochester, New York, where he continued until his retirement in 1964. He made the school one of the finest such institutions in the world, and for many years held there an annual festival of American music to encourage and exhibit native composers.

He was a notable conductor, making several recordings of his own and other music. He won numerous awards, including the Pulitzer Prize for his Symphony No. 4 (1944). His style is neo-Romantic, and he has a better claim on that label than Samuel Barber, who

———— [DDD] indicates newest recordings; [ADD] or [AAD] are reissues. ————

so often wears it instead. His comet is temporarily out of view, but time will bring it around again one day.

Symphony No. 2, "Romantic," Op. 30

Hanson's most beloved work was written to celebrate the 50th season of the Boston Symphony Orchestra, who first played it in 1930 under Serge Koussevitzky. It is still regarded as one of the finest native American symphonic works.

> **Hanson, Eastman Rochester Symphony Orchestra.** Mercury Living Presence 432008 [ADD] + Symphony No. 1, *Song of Democracy*
> **Schwarz, Seattle Symphony Orchestra.** Delos 3073 [DDD] + Symphony No. 1, *Elegy in Memory of Koussevitzky*

Paul Hindemith (1895-1963)

Hindemith ran away from home as a youth when his parents would not hear of his making music his career. He earned a living playing in theater and cafe orchestras while attending the Frankfurt Conservatory, becoming one of the most rapidly developing students, and after a brief stint in the German army became concertmaster of the Frankfurt Opera Orchestra.

He founded the Amar String Quartet and attracted notice with some of his chamber works in the early 1920s. Few modern composers have devoted more of their energies to chamber music, both as composer and performer (Hindemith was an outstanding violist). From 1926 on, after the success of his opera *Cardillac*, Hindemith was acknowledged as a leading German composer (second only to Richard Strauss), and he became an esteemed teacher at the Berlin Hochschule.

At this time he began writing those works for which he coined the term *Gebrauchsmusik* ("functional music"), and which have haunted his reputation ever since. He did not, contrary to legend, stop writing works of high artistic inspiration, but supplemented them with pieces written frankly for mass comsumption and educational purposes. These works, limited in number and intended use, have been cited by many detractors over the years as proving that Hindemith was a workaday composer. "I felt," Hindemith wrote in *A Composer's World*, "like the sorcerer's apprentice who had become the victim of his own conjurations: The slogan *Gebrauchsmusik* hit me wherever I went, it had grown to be as abundant, useless, and disturbing as thousands of dandelions in a lawn."

Despite his fame, Hindemith ran afoul of the Nazis. He had married a Jew, he had Jewish friends, he made recordings with Jews, and although he was not Jewish he staunchly refused to abandon any of them. Dr. Goebbels immediately discovered Hindemith's music to be both degenerate and obscene. Wasn't there an aria in one of his operas that was sung

—— CDs go in and out of print; availability of all listed items is not assured. ——

in a bathtub? Even worse, it was written in "the most atrocious dissonance of musical impotence."

Hindemith fled Germany in 1935, spending about a year in Turkey, then coming to the U.S. at the invitation of Elizabeth Sprague Coolidge, a great patron of the arts. He taught at Yale for several years and continued composing, producing some of his finest works. He took up residence in Zurich, Switzerland in 1953, but died back in Frankfurt in 1963, leaving nearly 500 works in the catalog of his life's toil.

His reputation suffered greatly after the war, many composers of the younger generation seeing Hindemith as a musician who had abandoned his earlier progressive ideas and unfairly attacked the avant-garde movement. He was considered a fuddy-duddy who did not deserve the eminence and adulation he received in official quarters; he thus became a symbol of hypocrisy and reaction, and the label of *Gebrauchsmusik* was smeared unfairly over all his output.

Hindemith himself once said that 80 percent of his music was bad, but if it were not for that portion, the 20 percent that was good would never have been written. I rather like the estimation of Donald Francis Tovey (one of the few musicologists who is actually fun to read), who said of Hindemith: "As far as I can judge, his music does not bore many people, though it annoys some. He is never very long, he thumps no tubs, and he makes the best of modern life."

Mathis der Maler (Symphony)

Not really a symphony at all, this work is a suite of three sections excerpted from Hindemith's opera of the same name, which premiered in Switzerland in 1938. It is a dramatic allegory about the artist's dilemma in society, framed in the context of the historical defeat of German liberalism during the Peasants' Revolt of the early 16th century, subjects which did not endear the composer to the Nazi Party. The story is told through the life of the historical painter Matthias Grünewald, and each of the "symphony's" movements depicts a panel of the artist's altar-piece at the monastery church of Isenheim.

Bernstein, Israel Philharmonic Orchestra. Deutsche Grammophon 429404 [DDD] +*Symphonic Metamorphosis of Themes by Weber, Concert Music*, Op. 50

Blomstedt, San Francisco Symphony Orchestra. London [Decca] 421523 [DDD] + *Symphonic Metamorphosis of Themes by Weber, Trauermusik*

Kletzki, Suisse Romande Orchestra. London [Decca] Enterprise 433081 [ADD] + *Symphonic Metamorphosis on Themes by Weber* (with Abbado conducting the London Symphony), Violin Concerto (with Oistrakh, violin, and Hindemith conducting)

Sawallisch, Philadelphia Orchestra. EMI 55230 [DDD] + *Symphonic Metamorphosis on Themes by Weber, Nobilissima Visione*

——— *Some CDs may be available only through importers.* ———

Szell, Cleveland Orchestra. Sony 53258 [ADD] + *Symphonic Metamorphosis*; Walton: *Variations on a Theme by Hindemith*

Symphonic Metamorphosis of Themes by Weber

While teaching at Yale in 1943, Hindemith came across a volume of four-hand piano music by Carl Maria von Weber, and agreeing with your author that Weber is unjustly neglected, decided to make an orchestral work out of some of the themes. He did alter some of them a bit to suit his purposes, but they are very recognizable, and the piquant and brilliant orchestration of the resulting four-movement suite is quite in a class by itself.

Abbado, London Symphony Orchestra. London [Decca] Enterprise 433081 [ADD] + *Mathis der Maler* Symphony (with Kletzki and Suisse Romande Orchestra), Violin Concerto (with Oistrakh, violin, and Hindemith conducting)
Abbado, London Symphony Orchestra. London Classic Sound 448579 [ADD] + Janáček: Sinfonietta; Prokofiev: Symphony No. 3
Bernstein, Israel Philharmonic Orchestra. Deutsche Grammophon 429404 [DDD] + *Mathis der Maler* Symphony, *Concert Music*, Op. 50
Blomstedt, San Francisco Symphony Orchestra. London [Decca] 421523 [DDD] + *Mathis der Maler* Symphony, *Trauermusik*
Sawallisch, Philadelphia Orchestra. EMI 55230 [DDD] + *Mathis der Maler* Symphony, *Nobilissima Visione*
Szell, Cleveland Orchestra. Sony 52358 [ADD] + *Mathis der Maler* Symphony; Walton: *Variations on a Theme by Hindemith*

Gustav Holst (1874-1934)

For much of his life, Holst was a frail, remote, mystical soul who, despite the enormous popularity of his suite *The Planets*, sought to avoid fame rather than curry it.

He came from a long line of musicians with Russian, German, and Swedish roots. His father was a piano teacher when Gustav was born in Cheltenham. At 17 he began studies in London at the Royal College of Music, where he met and started a lifelong friendship with Ralph Vaughan Williams. Musically, he fell under the spell of Wagner, from which he was not to recover for a decade.

Neuritis forced him to give up a planned career as a pianist and he took up the trombone instead. He supported a wife and children for a while by playing in shows and bands, but in 1903 tried to make a go of it as a composer. His fees from published works were insufficient, however, and he turned to teaching, which occupied him the rest of his life except on weekends, when he tried to get in a little composing. Despite the burden teaching signified for him, he was often praised by his students as an enthusiastic and inspiring instructor.

Holst had abandoned Wagnerism by 1906 and took up study of his national roots—Henry Purcell, the madrigal composers of the English Renaissance, and folksong. Another deep interest was Hindu philosophy and literature, which reflected itself in such works as the opera *Savitri* and the *Hymns from the Rig Veda*. He went so far as to learn Sanskrit at the School of Oriental Languages so that he could translate the ancient texts himself.

His one notable public success was the introduction of *The Planets* in 1918, which dismayed him because he was afraid it would create expectations of more in the same vein, whereas Holst was always looking to do something new and different. (He refused the suggestion of one of the work's admirers that he follow up with a suite on the wives of King Henry VIII.) A proper composer, he said, should "pray for failure." He never considered *The Planets* anywhere near his best work, but much of his other music only bewildered audiences.

Holst's health deteriorated after a fall in 1923, and he spent his last years more and more reclusively, sometimes withdrawing deeply into himself. He continued to compose however till the year before his death, and he bequeathed also to the world his brilliant daughter Imogen, an outstanding teacher and musician, and author of a fascinating biography of her father.

The Planets

This seven-movement suite has nothing to do with Greek mythology, but rather the symbolic astrological meanings of the planets. The associations are self-explanatory: "Mars, the Bringer of War," etc. Despite the obscurity of much of his other music, Holst's planetary suite has soared very near the top of the classical charts and only grows in interest with the advance of recording technology, to which it responds brilliantly. The last planet, incidentally, is Neptune (the Mystic), since Pluto had not been discovered when the music was written.

Boult, London Philharmonic Orchestra. EMI Studio 64748 [ADD] + Elgar: *Enigma Variations*
Dutoit, Montreal Symphony Orchestra. London [Decca] 417553 [DDD]
Gardiner, Philharmonic Orchestra. Deutsche Grammophon 445860 [DDD] + Grainger: *The Warriors*
Handley, Royal Philharmonic Orchestra. RPO [Tring] 007 [DDD] + *St. Paul's Suite*
Judd, Royal Philharmonic Orchestra. Denon 75076 [DDD]
Solti, London Philharmonic Orchestra. London [Decca] Jubilee 430447 [ADD] + Elgar: *Pomp and Circumstance* Marches 1, 4, 5

———— *All CDs listed are considered approximately equal in (high) merit.* ————

Arthur Honegger (1892-1955)

Honegger is today one of the most thoroughly neglected of the great composers, which ought, I think, to make him all the more interesting to explore. He is one of those who is difficult to pinpoint, which doesn't help his popular acceptance. You can't say he is conservative or avant-garde, and there is no one of his works that is universally known. He is a composer you need to hear a great deal of before you can decide whether he is for you or not.

He was born in France, but of Swiss parents, and he kept his Swiss citizenship all his life. He was groomed as a musician from childhood and received academic training both at the Zurich and Paris Conservatories. He started attracting notice for his compositions by 1916, and was soon made notorious by his apparent association with the Group of Six (*Les Six*) consisting of composers who supposedly shared an inconoclastic viewpoint despising both the excessive rhetoric of Romanticism and the pallid intellectualism of the atonalists.

Honegger, religious and serious by nature, was an ill fit for this group, if there ever was one, for it was really little more than a concept of the music critic Henri Collet. They had no meetings, they actually shared remarkably few viewpoints, and in any case they "disbanded" not long after they allegedly got together. By the 1930s Honegger specifically renounced any association with *Les Six*; nevertheless, we still read in music textbooks that he was a leading member of this group!

Between the two world wars Honegger created a body of music that defies easy categorization. His style smacks of neo-Classicism, but he liberally employs bitonality. There are hints of Impressionism in his work, a dab of the modern Russians here and there, sharp rhythms, lots of polyphony, references to medieval chant and French folk song. It comes out not sounding terribly individual, but not particularly derivative either.

One minute he was writing *Pacific 231* which describes a railroad train, or *Rugby*, a picture of the sport (the piece actually had its premiere in a football stadium), the next he was composing *Le Roi David*, an atmospheric if occasionally turgid oratorio based on the Bible (it was once his biggest success, but seems to have faded greatly). Whether any of this is anything we should worry about is another matter.

Reading over what I have just written it sounds as if I have a fairly low opinion of Honegger, but that is not true. He is a favorite composer of mine partly because he is so frustratingly eclectic and elusive. What holds his work together is spirituality and seriousness of purpose. And there is something fascinating and touching in following his journey through the history of music, trying to find his own voice. I believe future generations will find his five symphonies to be his most lasting legacy, especially the moving Second, written during the occupation of Paris during World War II.

———— CDs listed are solid, central choices, not necessarily "the greatest." ————

Pacific 231

"I have always loved railway engines passionately," Honegger once unguardedly told an interviewer. "For me they are living beings, and I love them in the same way as other men love women or horses." This remark came back to haunt him many a time. The name and number are taken from a type of locomotive engine, although the thought of connecting it to a train actually came after the fact, for the piece was originally written simply as an exercise in suggesting motion in general. But audiences loved it at once, and professed to be able to hear the gentle heaving of the engine at rest, the strain of picking up speed, and finally the sleek engine thundering through the night (not the day, mind you!).

> **Ansermet, Suisse Romande Orchestra.** London [Decca] Classic Sound 448576 [ADD] + Dukas: *The Sorcerer's Apprentice*; Chabrier: *España*; Debussy: *La Mer*; Ravel: *Boléro, La Valse*
>
> **Jansons, Oslo Philharmonic Orchestra.** EMI 55122 [DDD] + Symphonies Nos. 2, 3
>
> **Plasson, Toulouse Capitole Orchestra.** Deutsche Grammophon 435438 [DDD] + *Pastorale d'été, Rugby, Horace victorieux, Tempest* Prelude, *Mermoz* (excerpts from film score)

Symphony No. 2

Although Honegger worked assiduously for the Resistance during World War II, the Nazis seem to have left him alone to compose without any special hindrance. The Second Symphony has just three movements, the first exhibiting a mood of despair with a note of defiance, the second laden with lamenting. The third movement starts in agitation, and develops into what one might take to be the march of storm-troopers' boots. Then as from afar, rising like a prayer over the din, is heard a trumpet nobly intoning Bach's chorale "How brightly shines the morning star." The contrast is dramatically effective, and the symphony ends with a brief burst of hope and light.

> **Jansons, Oslo Philharmonic Orchestra.** EMI 55122 [DDD] + Symphony No. 3; *Pacific 231*
>
> **Karajan, Berlin Philharmonic.** Deutsche Grammophon Originals 447435 [ADD] + Symphony No. 3; Stravinsky: Concerto in D
>
> **Munch, Boston Symphony Orchestra.** RCA Victor Gold Seal 60685 [ADD] + Symphony No. 5; Milhaud: *La Création du Monde, Suite Provençale*
>
> [As we go to press, RCA is planning to delete the above title. It will be useless to argue, as these decisions are always made by financial officers, not artistic directors. Despite this I am leaving it in my book, as no other recording can match it for this repertoire and you may have a chance to pick it up as remaindered, or possibly later on as a reissue under a different number.]

——— *Some famous CDs are not listed because currently out of print.* ———

Schwarz, Seattle Symphony Orchestra. Delos 3121 [DDD] + R. Strauss: *Metamorphosen*; Webern: *Langsamer satz* (arr. Schwarz)

Charles Ives (1874-1954)

Ives was not only one of the great eccentrics in the history of music, he was on the face of it one of the most unlikely eccentrics. If I were to greet the first visitors from Mars and tell them that one of the greatest, possibly the most original, of American composers of symphonic and vocal and chamber music was the originator of "estate planning" and headed one of the nation's largest and most successful insurance agencies, I would probably be hustled aboard ship and have my tonsils removed (of course that might happen anyway).

He was born in Danbury, Connecticut, the ninth generation from one of the original settlers of New Haven, and descendant and relative of several successful businesspeople. The major exception was Ives's father, who followed a musical career; General Ulysses S. Grant is reported to have remarked to President Lincoln that the George Ives band was the best in the entire Union Army. This remarkable man experimented in his spare time with every kind of sound-combination, including polytonality and quarter-tone music, and this in the last quarter of the 19th—not the 20th—century.

The elder Ives died at age 49. Charles often spoke in later years of his devastation, and it is reasonable to suppose that he had a strong desire to expand on his father's efforts. Bored with the orthodoxy of his music classes at Yale, the young Ives tried out his iconoclastic ideas on the organ of the New Haven church where he played Sunday service.

After college he married and went into the insurance business, finding it to accord with his humanitarian impulses. For 20 years, from 1898 until he suffered a severe heart attack in 1918, he composed in the evenings and on weekends. His activities were restricted thereafter, although he did not retire until 1930, and he lived to the age of 79.

Beginning in about 1922 some of Ives's music began to circulate among interested musicians and gradually some of the works received performances and critical acclaim. In 1945 he was elected to the National Institute of Arts and Letters, and two years later his Symphony No. 3 was awarded the Pulitzer Prize—42 years after it was composed! (He gave the money away, commenting that "prizes are for mediocrity.")

By the 1960s his reputation had raised him almost to cult status. His works were extensively recorded and programmed and books were written about his extraordinary life, colorfully flavored with his pithy and often pungent Yankee observations. When a man in the audience booed at a concert of modern music, Ives stood up and shouted "Stop being such a God-damned sissy!"

Much of his own music was truly decades ahead of its time in its exploration of atonalism, aleatoric ("chance") techniques, polytonal writing, and other means of expression, and by the time Ives was appreciated all of these had become common currency through the work of other composers. Although he belatedly received the admiration he was due, many critics caution that much of his work was by nature naive and by necessity incomplete, unsophisticated, or arbitrary. It has been discovered also that some of the "modernisms" in Ives's music were "tipped in" by the composer years after the original date of composition!

Symphony No. 2

This may be easy-listening Ives, but it painlessly introduces his wild and hyper-American imagination in palatable form under the cover of a Brahmsian orchestration. It is a stew of everything from *Turkey in the Straw* to *Columbia, the Gem of the Ocean*, seasoned with wrong notes, shocking chords, bad phrasing, and general nose-thumbing, but inexplicably endearing and even, by the end, deeply moving.

Bernstein, New York Philharmonic Orchestra. Sony 47568 [ADD] + Symphony No. 3, *Central Park in the Dark*
Bernstein, New York Philharmonic Orchestra. Deutsche Grammophon 429220 [DDD] + *Central Park in the Dark, The Unanswered Question,* 4 other pieces

Three Places in New England

Written between 1902 and 1914 but not performed until 1930, this "cycle" of three tone poems is one of Ives's few works to appeal even to Europeans, who seem to find most of his music incomprehensible. The three "places" are: Boston Common; Putnam's Camp, Redding, Connecticut; and The Housatonic [River] at Stockbridge. The most famous, or infamous, moment occurs in the second piece when Ives creates the illusion of two brass bands passing each other while playing at different tempi!

Orpheus Chamber Orchestra. Deutsche Grammophon 439869 [DDD] + *The Unanswered Question;* Symphony No. 3, *et al.*
Sinclair, Orchestra of New England. Koch 37025 [DDD] + 8 other short representative works
Tilson Thomas, Boston Symphony Orchestra. Deutsche Grammophon 423243 [ADD] + Symphony No. 4, *Central Park in the Dark* (with Ozawa conducting)

Leoš Janáček (1854-1928)

Janáček was past 60 when he began to achieve acclaim. His opera *Jenůfa* had finally had a successful production, and his creative vigor was renewed by a love affair with a much younger woman. The diverse strands of his career now came together in one fair cloth, and at an age when many are ready to retire he created a string of masterpieces including the Sinfonietta, two string quartets, four operas, and the *Glagolitic Mass*.

The climb to success had been not only long but arduous. Janáček was the ninth of 14 children born to a Moravian village schoolmaster. He eked out a living for years as a teacher and conductor, attracting little notice as a composer. He had one son and one daughter, each of whom died young. His first six decades comprised a history of personal tragedy and professional obscurity.

His boyhood training had taken place under a priest who wrote music, and he later studied organ at the College of Music in Prague; in spite of this Janáček was at best an agnostic, and his Mass is a pantheistic celebration of nature. One critic thought that Janáček, "now that he is old and a firm believer," must have mended his ways, but the enraged composer (now 72) sent the critic a postcard: "No old man, no believer." A couple of years later, near death, he augmented the statement with "till I see for myself." He refused in fact to grow old, and one of his freshest, finest works is a wind sextet titled *Youth*, which he wrote at the age of 70.

Janáček's unique style and sound-world were formed to a great extent out of the Moravian countryside and its folk music. "I want," he once wrote, "to be in direct contact with the clouds; I want to feast my eyes on the blue of the sky; I want to gather the sun's rays into my hands, I want to plunge myself in shadow, I want to pour out my longings to the full: all directly."

He was provincial in the best sense, his personal language flowering by virtue of being isolated from the musical currents of his time. The composers who did interest and affect him were those who strove hardest to bring everyday reality into their esthetic: Leoncavallo, Mascagni, and above all Mussorgsky. These were in turn filtered through his own psyche, which was characterized by a nervous irascibility tempered by a tender compassion for the earth and its creatures.

Only in recent years has Janáček, much like his spiritual forebear Mussorgsky, been recognized for the originality and genius of his music: modern, yet eminently accessible; "primitive," yet subtle and sophisticated, romantic yet angular and astringent. His dramatic flair blazes powerfully in his amazing operas, ranging from *The Cunning Little Vixen*, in which half the characters are animals, to *The Makropoulos Affair*, the tale of a 300-year-old woman, to *From the House of the Dead*, an uncompromising transcription of Dostoyevsky's portrait of life in a Siberian prison.

Sinfonietta

First performed in 1926, the work was inspired by fanfares that Janáček heard at a military band concert in a park. It is a five movement suite with a brilliantly original and effec-

—— *Artists are listed alphabetically, not in order by critical ranking.* ——

tive construction, and one of the most striking openings in all of music. These fanfares will get your attention (and hold it).

Abbado, London Symphony Orchestra. London Classic Sound 448579 [ADD]
+ Hindemith: *Symphonic Metamorphosis*; Prokofiev: Symphony No. 3

Lenárd, Slovak Radio Symphony Orchestra (Bratislava). Naxos 8.550411
[DDD] + *Taras Bulba, Lachian Dances*

Mackerras, Vienna Philharmonic Orchestra. London [Decca] Jubilee 430727
[DDD] + *Taras Bulba*; Shostakovich: *Age of Gold* Suite (with Haitink conducting Shostakovich)

Rattle, Philharmonia Orchestra. EMI 47504 [DDD] + *Glagolitic Mass*

Aram Khachaturian (1903-1978)

Khachaturian is the best-known composer of Armenian origin or ancestry, and yes, there are others: Richard Yardumian and Alan Hovhaness being reasonably well-known examples. And we could discuss the life and works of Gomidas Vartabed, but that definitely belongs to another book.

Khachaturian was a nationalist, folk-oriented composer who followed the Soviet party line (one of his less-loved works in the West is his *Ode to Stalin*) but managed not to have all of his creativity smothered by its restrictive demands. That alone should be cause for admiration.

He was born in Tiflis, son of a bookbinder, and had almost no formal music training until age 19, when he was able to enroll in a school in Moscow; he had been listening, however, even as a child, to the indigenous music surrounding him. He studied cello and composition at the Gnessin School and was subsequently admitted to the Moscow Conservatory. He was in his 30s before gaining international recognition for his single piano and violin concerti. Khachaturian's forms are loose and rhapsodic, his melodies long and sinuous, his orchestrations barbarically colorful—thus arousing the wrath of musicologists but making a direct and welcome appeal to the average listener.

Gayne: Suite

One of the best-known modern ballets, *Gayne* (or *Gayaneh*, as it often appears in an alternative transliteration), was first performed by the Kirov Ballet in 1942. The scenario presents morally edifying themes as enacted by peasants on an Armenian collective farm. The dictates of Socialist Realism are now grist for parody, but the music continues to delight. The *Saber Dance* is only the most famous of numerous highly enjoyable dances.

—— *[DDD] indicates newest recordings; [ADD] or [AAD] are reissues.* ——

Järvi, Scottish National Orchestra. Chandos 8542 [DDD] + *Masquerade* Suite, Piano Concerto (with Orbelian)
Khachaturian, London Symphony Orchestra. Classics for Pleasure 4634 [ADD] + *Spartacus* Suite; Glazunov: *Autumn* from *The Seasons*
Tjeknavorian, Armenian Philharmonic Orchestra. (5 dances) ASV 773 [DDD] + *Spartacus* Suite, *Masquerade* Suite; Ippolitov-Ivanov: *Caucasian Sketches*

Zoltán Kodály (1882-1967)

Kodály has been overshadowed in music history by his friend Béla Bartók, but like him he was an avid scholar of Hungarian folk music and incorporated his discoveries into original works in a colorful and memorable way. He was not as intellectual or original as Bartók, but he had plenty to offer on his own more modest terms.

Kodály spent his childhood and youth in rural Hungary, his ears catching the indigenous music of the countryside. His serious study began at age 18 when he entered the Budapest Conservatory. It was here that he made friends with Bartók, and subsequently joined him in rummaging all over Hungary collecting and publishing the native folk music. Kodály later wrote that "The vision of an educated Hungary, reborn from the people, rose before us." The influence of this music changed Kodály from a neo-Brahmsian composer to one of striking neo-primitivism, though of a far more genteel brand than Bartók's.

His output was relatively sparse, but it spanned nearly the whole of his venerable life. His first performed work was an overture he wrote in elementary school and he wrote a symphony at the age of 80. His many years of researching, teaching, and composing made him a major cultural hero in Hungary, where he was for long more honored than his expatriate colleague Bartók, not least because of his warmer and more avuncular personality. Kodály also developed a method of music education which is now used in many countries.

During World War II Kodály, who was married to a Jew, worked for the anti-Nazi underground in his occupied country. His activities helping Jews to escape were discovered by the Gestapo, but because of his eminence and popular esteem he was left relatively unhindered. The Nazis feared a general uprising if Kodály were arrested.

Háry János: Suite

Háry János is a kind of Hungarian Baron Munchausen—an eccentric old gentlemen who vividly recalls marvelous exploits he never actually performed. His story is told in a colorful opera which is almost never heard outside of Hungary except in the orchestral suite extracted from it. The six movements showcase nearly every good quality Kodály had to offer: tenderness, humor, bracing rhythms, memorable tunes, exotic orchestration. It is an endearing memorial to a noble and intelligent artist.

Antal, Hungarian State Orchestra. Naxos 8.550142 [DDD] + "Hungarian Concert"

Dorati, Minneapolis Symphony Orchestra. Mercury Living Presence 432005 [ADD] + *Dances of Galánta, Dances of Marosszék* (with Philharmonia Hungarica); Bartók: *Hungarian Sketches, Romanian Dances*

Dutoit, Montreal Symphony Orchestra. London [Decca] 444322 [DDD] + *Dances of Galánta, Dances of Marosszék, Peacock* Variations

Szell, Cleveland Orchestra. Sony Essential Classics 48162 [ADD] + Prokofiev: *Lt. Kijé* Suite; Mussorgsky: *Pictures at an Exhibition*

Darius Milhaud (1892-1974)

Milhaud became, at the death of Ravel, the most famous French composer. He was also the most prolific (writing some 600 works) and, in the words of his fellow composer and fervent admirer Virgil Thomson, "one of the most completely calm of modern masters."

Born in Aix-en-Provence, a beautiful and ancient town on the Mediterranean, Milhaud showed musical precocity at an early age and studied at the Paris Conservatory with Widor and Dukas, and at the Schola Cantorum with d'Indy. He became friends with the poet Paul Claudel, who was also a diplomat, and joined him for over a year as an attaché to the French legation in Brazil. There he became entranced by the tango and other indigenous music, whose spirit and form he often integrated into his later compositions. Another strong influence was American jazz, incorporation of which into concert works became a kind of specialty which enhanced his reputation in the 1920s.

After returning to France he was anointed as one of "The Six," that notorious but artificial group of composers who stood for insouciant insubordination in the world of music. He was distinguished from the others not only by his incredible industry, but by his melodic and technical fluency, personal charm, and effective use of polytonality (another specialty, as it turned out). He was, said Arthur Honegger, "the most gifted of us all." He was also noted for his wide culture and deep religiosity.

Milhaud, who proudly described himself as "a Frenchman from Provence, and by religion a Jew," fled the Nazi invasion of France with his wife in 1940, joining the faculty of Mills College in California. Although returning to France after the war, he regularly returned to the U.S., teaching at Mills and, in the summers, at Aspen, Colorado. He maintained a rigorous and active career over a long life, despite being confined to a wheelchair for more than 30 years due to severe arthritis. He is buried, as he wished, in his beloved Aix, under the Mediterranean sun.

——— *Some CDs may be available only through importers.* ———

La Création du Monde

A work for 18 instruments, including saxophone, "The Creation of the World" is a chamber-ballet telling an African story of first things. The original stage design and costumes were by Fernand Léger. The music was directly modeled after New Orleans-style jazz that Milhaud heard and closely studied while visiting Harlem.

Bernstein, National Orchestra of France. EMI 47845 + *Le boeuf sur le toit, Saudades do Brasil*

Munch, Boston Symphony Orchestra. RCA Victor Gold Seal 60685 [ADD] + *Suite Provenéale*; Honegger: Symphonies 2, 5

[As we go to press, RCA is planning to delete the above title. It will be useless to argue, as these decisions are always made by financial officers, not artistic directors. Despite this I am leaving it in my book, as no other recording can match it for this repertoire and you may have a chance to pick it up as remaindered, or possibly later on as a reissue under a different number.]

Nagano, Lyon Opera Orchestra. Erato 45820 [DDD] + *Le boeuf sur le toit*, Harp Concerto

Zedda, Lausanne Chamber Orchestra. Virgin Ultraviolet 61206 [DDD] + Debussy: *Danse, Sarabande*; Prokofiev: *Sinfonietta*

Carl Nielsen (1865-1931)

Nielsen is one of the best examples in music of a "progressive conservative." He was not opposed to modernisms, but he saw no reason to reject the past; he cherished his freedom to use all the materials and styles that music has offered and bend them to his will. And that he was able from the humblest beginnings to rise in today's estimation to one of the great symphonists is testament to a will that was powerful indeed.

He was born, of peasant stock, on the Danish island of Funen, in the same year as another great Scandinavian composer, Jean Sibelius. As a youth he picked up the rudiments of music and at 18 enrolled in the Copenhagen Conservatory. His best instrument was the violin, which he played in the Royal Opera Orchestra until 1905, three years before he became its conductor. He also taught at the Royal Danish Conservatory, becoming its director one year before his death.

As a composer, his early influences were the German Romantics, especially Brahms. He subsumed the treasury of Danish folk music as well, but can hardly be called a nationalistic composer in the usual sense. As much as anything, he built his esthetic on his experiences with nature. He avoided schools and movements and -isms; his guide was not a manual of composition, but his inner self. He mastered the tools of his trade and employed them however necessary to communicate his message.

What he had to say was essentially optimistic. His own life was as well-adjusted as any composer's ever was: he had a model marriage (no pun intended—his wife was a sculptor), many friends, and a marvelous wit which is often reflected in his music. Although there is plenty of conflict in his work, it is nearly always underpinned by a glowing faith in nature and life.

Nielsen's international recognition came well after his death, as it gradually dawned on music lovers that here was not a mere provincial, but a composer for the ages, perhaps most memorably in his six symphonies. These are works of tremendous structural integrity and often raw emotional power.

Symphony No. 4, Op. 29, "Inextinguishable"

Second only to No. 5 in fame, the Fourth Symphony is in four movements played without break, symbolizing the perpetual overlapping growth of all life implied in the subtitle, and celebrated in the music. It was first performed in 1916.

Blomstedt, San Francisco Symphony Orchestra. London [Decca] 421524 [DDD] + Symphony No. 5

Karajan, Berlin Philharmonic Orchestra. Deutsche Grammophon 445518 [DDD] + Sibelius: *Tapiola*

Rattle, Philharmonia Orchestra. EMI 64737 [ADD] + *Pan and Syrinx*; Sibelius: Symphony No. 5

Symphony No. 5, Op. 50

Only two movements comprise this unique, and many would say greatest, Nielsen symphony. The first encapsulates a virtual "war" between the side drum and the rest of the orchestra, a portrayal of conflict wholly original and once heard, quite unforgettable; the second movement is a foil to the first, moving on to vigorous affirmation.

Blomstedt, San Francisco Symphony Orchestra. London [Decca] 421524 [DDD] + Symphony No. 4

Carl Orff (1892-1982)

Orff is known to the general public for only one composition, *Carmina Burana*, but it is one of the most popular works written by anyone in the 20th century. Despite this, and the fact that he developed one of the most distinctive and instantly recognizable styles in the history of music, he has been one of the most critically reviled composers.

——— *All CDs listed are considered approximately equal in (high) merit.* ———

He was born in Munich and spent virtually his entire life there, scion of a family with generations of military and scholarly connections. His music studies, largely self-didactic, led him for the first half of his life to concentrate on teaching, research, and conducting. He was one of the founders of a music school in Munich in 1925, and is noted for his series *Schulwerk* which sought to teach music to children by leading them through the evolution of Western music, starting with simple scales and rhythms. He continued teaching this method after founding the Orff Institute in Salzburg in 1961, and the system is still widely used today.

He did compose music in earlier years, mostly in imitation of other composers, particularly Schoenberg and Richard Strauss. In his early 40s he repudiated these derivative works, withdrawing or destroying most of them, and abandoning the line he had previously followed from Wagner to the 12-tone school. He looked now to the Renaissance and Baroque, especially Monteverdi and Bach, for inspiration, although he also professed admiration for Stravinsky.

In addition to *Carmina Burana* (with which, he said, "my collected works begin"), Orff wrote a number of operatic and stage works which uniquely feature large percussion ensembles and much spoken dialogue. His later style emphasizes driving, repetitive rhythms and a blend of old folk idioms with modern or even jazzy elements.

The undeniably catchy rhythms and clear melodies of Orff's music have not endeared him to classical music academics, who generally feel he panders too much to popular taste. Another complaint is that his scholarly theories are little more than simple-minded commonplaces dressed up in fancy language (his style was once characterized as "neo-Neanderthal"). Orff was further tainted in many minds by his celebrity during the Nazi period in Germany, although he denied being political and was generally considered rehabilitated after World War II.

Perhaps the fairest estimate of the composer was written in a 1956 *New Yorker* article by Winthrop Sargeant: "I am not sure how great a composer Mr. Orff is. There are times when he seems to me a sort of rich man's banjo player. But one thing about his music strikes me very forcibly; it is never tiresome or dull."

Carmina Burana

First produced in 1937, Orff's big hit was designated a "scenic cantata," and he intended it not just to be sung but pantomimed as well with scenery on stage. The text is adapted from poems unearthed in an old monastery in the 19th century, revealing the monks to have been rather more worldly than their vows should allow. The title means simply "Songs of Burana," that being the old Latin name of the Bavarian town where the monastery was situated. The work itself is in three sections: "In Springtime," "In the Tavern," and "The Court of Love."

——— *CDs listed are solid, central choices, not necessarily "the greatest."* ———

Blomstedt, San Francisco Symphony Orchestra and Chorus. London [Decca] 430509 [DDD]

Frühbeck de Burgos, New Philharmonia Orchestra and Chorus. EMI 64328
+ Ravel: *Boléro*

Jochum, German Opera Orchestra and Chorus. Deutsche Grammophon Galleria 423886 *or* Deutsche Grammophon Originals 447437 [ADD]

Ormandy, Philadelphia Orchestra, Rutgers University Choir. Sony Essential Classics 47668 [ADD]

Ozawa, Berlin Philharmonic Orchestra, Berlin Cathedral Choir, etc. Philips 422363 [DDD]

Previn, London Symphony Orchestra and Chorus. EMI 56444 [ADD]

Francis Poulenc (1899-1963)

Poulenc was called by a friend, in a bit of French overstatement, "part monk, part gutter-snipe." Certainly he was a mass of contradictions—one moment deeply religious and serious, the next frivolously impudent—both in his life and music; his compositions ranged from the *Four Motets for a Time of Penitence* to a song cycle called *Banalités*. The fastidious and the ludicrous were equal components of his manner and method.

Born into a well-to-do family, Poulenc showed outstanding musical ability as a youth and studied piano with Ricardo Viñes, the most famous interpreter of Debussy's keyboard works. His formal training after that was spotty, but he began to attract notice with his piquant compositions and his association with the group of *enfants terribles* known as "Les Six," which included also Milhaud and Honegger.

His dog face and droll wit endeared him to French high society, among whom he spent many evening hours at parties where he absorbed that heightened sense of the ridiculous which peeks out from so many of his works. On the other hand, the death of a dear friend in a car accident in 1936 led Poulenc to a revival of his childhood Catholic piety, which informs other of his compositions, most notably his moving opera *Dialogues des Carmelites*.

He wrote little purely orchestral or symphonic music, preferring the marriage of words and music, which he called "an act of love." He wrote a large number of songs, almost all for his friend the baritone Pierre Bernac, and they are among the finest written in the 20th century. He also excelled in short piano works, choral music, and ballet.

His often casual and breezy style was looked at askance by many critics. "When he has nothing to say," wrote David Drew of Poulenc, "he says it." But this composer was seldom seeking to utter profundities. He looked upon himself as an entertainer, and said that in his opinion music "should humbly seek to please." Those who can appreciate an art devoid of bombast and enlivened by irreverence, always accessible to the lay listener, may find a kindred soul in Poulenc.

——————— *Some famous CDs are not listed because currently out of print.* ———————

Concerto in G Minor for Organ, Strings, and Timpani

Popular, oddly enough, almost everywhere but France, Poulenc's Organ Concerto was written in 1938. It was commissioned, as were other works, by a notable patron of the arts, the Princesse Edmond de Polignac (who was, more prosaically perhaps, an heiress of the Singer Sewing Machine Co. fortune). It is neo-Baroque in concept.

Duruflé, Prêtre, ORTF Orchestra. EMI 47723 [ADD] + *Gloria, 4 Motets for a Time of Penitence*
Hurford, Dutoit, Philharmonia Orchestra. London [Decca] 436546 [DDD] + Piano Concerto, 2-Piano Concerto

Gloria in G

The Koussetitzky Foundation commissioned this work, a 20th-century tribute perhaps to Vivaldi. It is distinguished by melodic beauty, rhythmic variety, and a unique atmosphere comprising both gaiety and mystery. Few moments in music are more spontaneously joyful than the *Laudamus Te* section of the Poulenc *Gloria*.

Bernstein, New York Philharmonic Orchestra. CBS [Sony] 44710 [ADD] + Stravinsky: *Symphony of Psalms*; Bernstein: *Chichester Psalms*
Prêtre, ORTF Orchestra and Chorus. EMI 47723 [ADD] + Organ Concerto (with Duruflé), *4 Motets for a Time of Penitence*
Rutter, City of London Sinfonia, Cambridge Singers. Collegium 108 [DDD] + *4 Motets for a Time of Penitence, et al.*

Serge Prokofiev (1891-1953)

By one measure, Prokofiev could be considered the greatest composer of the 20th century, for he wrote at least one acknowledged masterpiece in most of the standard forms:

Symphony (Nos. 1 and 5)
Piano Concerto (No. 3)
Piano Sonata (No. 6)
Violin Sonata (No. 2)
Ballet (*Romeo and Juliet*)
Opera (*War and Peace*)
Orchestral suite (*Scythian* Suite)

to suggest a few. And just for an encore he created some of the greatest film scores (e.g. *Ivan the Terrible, Alexander Nevsky*), turning those into great cantatas as well, and topping it

——— Catalog numbers are subject to change without notice. ———

all off by writing a masterpiece of children's music, *Peter and the Wolf*. Although few musicologists would go so far as to rate Prokofiev above Stravinsky or Bartók, I would suggest that despite his fame and popularity he is still not taken as seriously as he deserves.

Paradox and irony were virtually life principles for Prokofiev. He was one of the first major artists to leave the Soviet Union after the 1917 revolution, and one of the few to return of his free will. After he returned he was widely regarded in the West as a Russian propagandist, while in his homeland he came under severe censure for creating "cacophony" and for appealing to "distorted tastes." He was one of the few great composers since Mahler to invest his music with humor, but he could match anyone in the evocation of poignant sorrow. He could be one of the most uncompromisingly dissonant of composers, or one of the most lyrical and romantic.

Prokofiev was born in comfortable circumstances in Ukraine and was a happy, gifted child. He wrote his first work, called "Hindu Galop," at age five, and by nine had completed two (!) operas in piano score. He was admitted to the St. Petersburg Conservatory at age 13, studying there with Liadov, Rimsky-Korsakov, and Tcherepnin, the last-named giving his young pupil a taste for many styles, from Haydn to the moderns.

He began to experiment with modern harmonies and orchestration, finding in them a distinctive language in which to express his vein of fantasy and irony, often veering towards the acerbic (one of his piano suites is frankly titled *Sarcasms*). Some of the more avant-garde works, such as the Symphony No. 2, are hard on the ears even today: John Michel, of the American Composers Forum, once characterized it to me as "like going around in a washing machine with a bunch of rocks." At the premiere of the *Scythian* Suite (1916), conservative composer Alexander Glazunov ran from the hall, his hands over his ears, and one of the violinists in the orchestra told a friend "My wife is sick and I have to buy medicine; otherwise I would never agree to play this crazy music."

Prokofiev left Russia in 1918 to undertake a U.S. tour. His brilliant piano playing was applauded, but his compositions were condemned as "Bolshevism in music." He spent the 1920s in Paris, where his style was found far more acceptable, even chic. After 15 years abroad he returned to the Soviet Union where he remained until his death, mixing and matching his output, i.e., composing works of originality and integrity alongside frankly jingoistic garbage designed to placate the Soviet censors.

At its best, Prokofiev's sound is distinctive, his melodies and rhythms especially being memorable. He possessed both wit and warmth, despite his early reputation for acidic irony and grotesquerie. And in an era when so many composers were preoccupied with theories and messages and attitudes, he composed prolifically as one who simply felt and understood music instinctively and possessed a natural communicative power.

—— *Since CDs can change label and number, use artists as main reference.* ——

Alexander Nevsky, Op. 78

Sergei Eisenstein's classic 1938 epic historical film was scored by Prokofiev, who later created this cantata from various elements in the original, augmented by a text drawn up by Prokofiev and a collaborator. It is written for mezzo-soprano, chorus and orchestra, and is a work of truly cinematic power. The final chorus, "Alexander's Entry into Pskov," is thrilling enough to make you into a Russian patriot, at least for a few minutes.

Abbado, London Symphony Orchestra and Chorus. Deutsche Grammophon Originals 447419 [DDD] + *Lt. Kijé* Suite, *Scythian* Suite
Järvi, Scottish National Orchestra and Chorus. Chandos 8584 [DDD] + *Scythian* Suite
Previn, Los Angeles Philharmonic Orchestra, Master Chorale of Orange County. Telarc 80143 [DDD] + *Lt. Kijé* Suite
Reiner, Chicago Symphony Orchestra. RCA Victor Gold Seal 60176 [ADD] + *Lt. Kijé* Suite; Glinka: *Russlan and Ludmila* Overture
L. Slatkin, St. Louis Symphony Orchestra and Chorus. Vox Box 5021 (2) [ADD] + *Lt. Kijé* Suite, *Ivan the Terrible*

Concerto No. 3 in C for Piano, Op. 26

Bravura and sophistication characterize Prokofiev's most popular concerto, which had its premiere in Chicago about the same time as his ill-fated opera *The Love for Three Oranges*, in 1921. It is recognizably Russian in its lyricism, fervor and drama, although without the more extravagant gestures of the Romantics.

Argerich, Abbado, Berlin Philharmonic Orchestra. Deutsche Grammophon 415062 [ADD] + Tchaikovsky: Piano Concerto No. 1 (with Dutoit conducting)
Argerich, Abbado, Berlin Philharmonic Orchestra. Deutsche Grammophon Originals 447438 [ADD] + Ravel: Piano Concerto in G, *Gaspard de la nuit*
Cliburn, Hendl, Chicago Symphony Orchestra. RCA Living Stereo 62691 [ADD] + Schumann: Piano Concerto in A Minor (with Reiner conducting)
Cliburn, Kondrashin, Symphony of the Air. RCA Victor Red Seal 6209 [ADD] + Rachmaninov: Piano Concerto No. 3
Graffman, Szell, Cleveland Orchestra. CBS 37806 [ADD] + Piano Concerto No. 1, Piano Sonata No. 3
Janis, Kondrashin, Moscow Philharmonic Orchestra. Mercury Living Presence 434333 [ADD] + Rachmaninov: Piano Concerto No. 3; recital
Paik, Wit, Polish National Radio Symphony Orchestra. Naxos 8.550566 [DDD] + Piano Concertos 1, 4

—————*Artists are listed alphabetically, not in order by critical ranking.*—————

Rodriguez, Tabakov, Sofia Philharmonic Orchestra. Elan 2220 [DDD] + Rachmaninov: Piano Concerto No. 3

Lieutenant Kijé Suite, Op. 60

A misplaced punctuation mark accidentally "creates" a (fictitious) Lieutenant Kijé, whose existence must then be documented to avoid embarrassing the Tsar. Such is the droll conceit of a 1933 film for which Prokofiev was perfectly suited to write the music. The suite takes the imaginary hero from birth to death, all tongue-in-cheek.

Abbado, London Symphony Orchestra. Deutsche Grammophon Originals 447419 [DDD] + *Alexander Nevsky, Scythian* Suite

Dorati, Netherlands Radio Philharmonic Orchestra. London [Decca] Phase 4 Stereo 444104 [ADD] + *Peter and the Wolf;* Britten: *Young Person's Guide to the Orchestra*

Marriner, London Symphony Orchestra. Philips Duo 442278 (2) [ADD] + *Love for Three Oranges* Suite; *Peter and the Wolf* (with McCowen, Haitink, Concertgebouw Orchestra); Exc. from *Romeo and Juliet* (with de Waart, Rotterdam Philharmonic Orchestra); *Scythian* Suite, Symphony No. 1 (with Previn, Los Angeles Philharmonic Orchestra)

Ormandy, Philadelphia Orchestra. CBS [Sony] Odyssey 39783 [ADD] + *Love for Three Oranges* Suite, Symphony No. 1

Previn, Los Angeles Philharmonic Orchestra. Telarc 80143 [DDD] + *Alexander Nevsky*

L. Slatkin, St. Louis Symphony Orchestra. Vox Box 5021 (2) [ADD] + *Alexander Nevsky, Ivan the Terrible*

Reiner, Chicago Symphony Orchestra. RCA Victor Gold Seal 60176 [ADD] + Prokofiev: *Alexander Nevsky;* Glinka: *Russlan and Ludmila* Overture

Szell, Cleveland Orchestra. Sony Essential Classics 48162 [ADD] + Kodály: *Háry János* Suite; Mussorgsky: *Pictures at an Exhibition*

Yuasa, London Philharmonic Orchestra. Classics for Pleasure 2214 [DDD] + Rimsky-Korsakov: *Scheherazade*

The Love for Three Oranges: Suite, Op. 33b

The full-length satirical fairytale opera from which the suite derives was written in America, premiering in Chicago in 1921 to booing and hissing. It is still seldom heard today, quite unjustly, for it is filled with wonderful music as the popular six-movement suite indicates. Ironically for a work emanating from the Soviet Union, the famous March

—— [DDD] indicates newest recordings; [ADD] or [AAD] are reissues. ——

served for many years in the U.S. as the theme of the popular radio and television show
The FBI in Peace and War.

> **Marriner, London Symphony Orchestra.** Philips Duo 442278 (2) [ADD] + *Lt.
> Kijé* Suite; *Peter and the Wolf* (with McCowen, Haitink, Concertgebouw
> Orchestra); Exc. from *Romeo and Juliet* (with de Waart, Rotterdam
> Philharmonic Orchestra); *Scythian* Suite, Symphony No. 1 (with Previn, Los
> Angeles Philharmonic Orchestra)
>
> **Ormandy, Philadelphia Orchestra.** CBS [Sony] Odyssey 39783 [ADD] + *Lt.
> Kijé* Suite, Symphony No. 1
>
> **Skrowaczewski, Minnesota Orchestra.** Vox Box 3016 (3) [ADD] + *Romeo and
> Juliet* (sel.), *Scythian* Suite; Stravinsky: *Firebird* Suite, *Petrushka, Le sacre du
> printemps*

Peter and the Wolf, Op. 67

The famous tale of heroic Peter and his animal friends (and enemy) was written by
Prokofiev himself. A narrator speaks between and over the musical parts, in which each
character is labeled with a signature theme and further identified by a specific instrument
or group of instruments: Peter is a string quartet, the cat is a clarinet, the wolf is three
French horns, and so on.

> **Abbado, Sting, Chamber Orchestra of Europe.** Deutsche Grammophon 429396
> [DDD] + Symphony No. 1, *Overture on Hebrew Themes,* March, Op. 99
>
> **Bernstein, New York Philharmonic Orchestra.** CBS [Sony] 37765 + Saint-
> Saëns: *Carnival of the Animals*
>
> **Connery, Dorati, ConneryRoyal Philharmonic Orchestra.** London [Decca]
> Phase 4 Stereo 444104 [ADD] + *Lt. Kijé* Suite; Britten: *Young Person's Guide to
> the Orchestra*
>
> **Haitink, Concertgebouw Orchestra.** Philips Duo 442278 (2) [ADD] + *Lt. Kijé*
> Suite, *Love for Three Oranges* Suite (with Marriner, London Symphony
> Orchestra); Exc. from *Romeo and Juliet* (with de Waart, Rotterdam
> Philharmonic Orchestra); *Scythian* Suite, Symphony No. 1 (with Previn, Los
> Angeles Philharmonic Orchestra)
>
> **Licata, Gielgud, Royal Philharmonic Orchestra.** RPO [Tring] 046 [DDD] +
> Saint-Saëns: *Carnival of the Animals;* Bizet: *Jeux d'enfants*
>
> **Previn, Royal Philharmonic Orchestra.** Telarc 80126 [DDD] + Britten: *Young
> Person's Guide to the Orchestra, Courtly Dances* from *Gloriana*
>
> **Stamp, Gielgud, Academy of London.** Virgin Classics 59533 [DDD] + Saint-
> Saëns: *Carnival of the Animals;* Mozart: *Eine kleine Nachtmusik*

—— *CDs go in and out of print; availability of all listed items is not assured.* ——

Romeo and Juliet, Op. 64

Prokofiev actually arranged and conducted these suites before the complete ballet was ever staged. It had been written for the Kirov Ballet but was unaccountably shelved for several years. Finally in 1940 it achieved a production followed by international fame, and today it is generally acknowledged as the greatest full-length ballet composed since Tchaikovsky. All recordings listed are of suites or extended excerpts from the work.

> **de Waart, Rotterdam Philharmonic Orchestra.** (exc.) Philips Duo 442278 (2) [ADD] + *Lt. Kijé* Suite, *Love for Three Oranges* Suite (with Marriner, London Symphony Orchestra); *Peter and the Wolf* (with McCowen, Haitink, Concertgebouw Orchestra); *Scythian* Suite, Symphony No. 1 (with Previn, Los Angeles Philharmonic Orchestra)
>
> **Dorati, London Symphony Orchestra.** (suites) Mercury Living Presence 432004 [ADD] + Mussorgsky: *A Night on Bald Mountain*
>
> **Levi, Cleveland Orchestra.** (suites + exc.) Telarc 80089 [DDD]
>
> **Pesek, Royal Liverpool Philharmonic Orchestra.** (sel.) Virgin 59278 [DDD]
>
> **Salonen, Berlin Philharmonic Orchestra.** (sel.) Sony 42662 [DDD]
>
> **Skrowaczewski, Minnesota Orchestra.** (sel.) Vox Box 3016 (3) [ADD] + *Love for Three Oranges* Suite; Stravinsky: *Firebird* Suite, *Petrushka, Le sacre du printemps*
>
> **Solti, Chicago Symphony Orchestra.** (exc.) London [Decca] 430731 + Symphony No. 1
>
> **Tilson Thomas, San Francisco Symphony Orchestra.** (exc.) RCA Victor Red Seal 68288 [DDD]

Symphony No. 1 in D, Op. 25, "Classical"

Prokofiev's intention here was to create a work that might have been written by Haydn had he been born in Russia in the 20th century. Its bracing instrumentation and lively synthesis of old and new have made it a concert favorite.

> **Abbado, Sting, Chamber Orchestra of Europe.** Deutsche Grammophon 429396 [DDD] + *Peter and the Wolf* (with Sting), *Overture on Hebrew Themes, March,* Op. 99
>
> **Karajan, Berlin Philharmonic Orchestra.** Deutsche Grammophon 437253 [ADD] + Symphony No. 5
>
> **Ormandy, Philadelphia Orchestra.** CBS [Sony] Odyssey 39783 [ADD] + *Lt. Kijé* Suite, *Love for Three Oranges* Suite
>
> **Orpheus Chamber Orchestra.** Deutsche Grammophon 423624 [DDD] + Bizet: Symphony in C; Britten: *Simple Symphony*

——— *Some CDs may be available only through importers.* ———

Previn, Los Angeles Philharmonic Orchestra. Philips Duo 442278 (2) [ADD]
+ *Scythian* Suite; *Lt. Kijé* Suite, *Love for Three Oranges* Suite (with Marriner, London Symphony Orchestra); *Peter and the Wolf* (with McCowen, Haitink, Concertgebouw Orchestra); Exc. from *Romeo and Juliet* (with de Waart, Rotterdam Philharmonic Orchestra)

Previn, Los Angeles Philharmonic Orchestra. Philips Solo 442399 [DDD] +
Symphony No. 5

Solti, Chicago Symphony Orchestra. London [Decca] Jubilee 430446 +
Mussorgsky: *Pictures at an Exhibition*; Tchaikovsky: Overture *1812*

Solti, Chicago Symphony Orchestra. (exc.) London [Decca] 430731 + *Romeo and Juliet* (exc.)

Tilson Thomas, London Symphony Orchestra. Sony 48239 [DDD] +
Symphony No. 5

Symphony No. 5, Op. 100

Written during World War II, the Fifth Symphony is a broad and heroic work inspired by the self-sacrifice of the Russian people. Basically noble in tone throughout, its progress is colored with occasional melancholy, but it concludes in jubilation.

Karajan, Berlin Philharmonic Orchestra. Deutsche Grammophon 437253 [ADD] + Symphony No. 1

Previn, Los Angeles Philharmonic Orchestra. Philips Solo 442399 [DDD] +
Symphony No. 1

Tilson Thomas, London Symphony Orchestra. Sony 48239 [DDD] +
Symphony No. 1

Sergei Rachmaninov (1873-1943)

Rachmaninov is the best possible illustration of how unsatisfactory it is to lump all the composers of the 20th century into the "modern" category. Although his creative career encompassed all the discoveries and revolutions of Debussy, Stravinsky, Schoenberg and the rest, he completely ignored them. Every bar of his music could have been written by a contemporary of Tchaikovsky and hardly anyone would notice the difference. For this reason he has never been a favorite of critics, who are paid to notice people who do completely new and outrageous things, although he has become one of the most beloved composers of the general public.

The fifth of six children, Rachmaninov at first grew up pampered by a doting mother and an aristocratic father who was an excellent pianist. Hard times came however, when

Sergei was only nine; his parents separated and only a year later he was enrolled in the St. Petersburg Conservatory. In two more years he was off to the more prestigious Moscow Conservatory where he made rapid progress in piano and composition while often chafing under the drudgery of routine lessons and rigid discipline.

At first he struggled with trying to make a living at music. A success here and there would be more than offset by a fiasco, such as that which greeted his first symphony. He often sank into depressions which interrupted his work (Stravinsky once described him as "six feet of gloom"). He had to undergo three months of hypnosis before he could resume work on his great Piano Concerto No. 2. He did, however, manage to sustain a lifelong happy marriage.

In 1918 Rachmaninov and his family sailed for America, leaving behind a Bolshevik society with which they had no sympathy. From now until his death Rachmaninov would be especially active as a concert pianist—one of a handful of the greatest of all time. He recorded all of his performances of his own concerti, and continued composing, although his muse seemed to wane in later years.

In 1931 he bought a house in Switzerland, on Lake Lucerne, where he was able to enjoy his passion for speedboats and fast cars. He sent money to causes he supported in Russia and eventually was "forgiven" by the Soviet authorities for writing "decadent bourgeois" music.

Despite his often unfavorable reputation among musicologists, caused by his utter lack of interest in inventing anything new, Rachmaninov was a more than competent musical architect, an inspired melodist, and a great orchestrator. He set high standards for himself and although his music may be conservative, relative to that of his contemporaries, it is not trivial or weak in any way.

50 years have passed since the experts were predicting a swift oblivion for Rachmaninov. "Artificial and gushing," was the description of his music in one edition (now revised) of the venerable *Grove's Dictionary of Music and Musicians.* "The enormously popular success some few of Rachmaninov's works had in his lifetime is not likely to last," the author droned on. But half a century later Rachmaninov is more popular than ever, and has taken his place in the pantheon of great composers as firmly as most of the Old Masters.

Concerto No. 2 in C Minor for Piano, Op. 18

"Full Moon and Empty Arms" was the 1940s hit pop song cribbed from the last movement of this most romantic of all piano concertos. Nevertheless it has survived all efforts to water it down, and despite its melodic prodigality and lush scoring it has enough integrity to keep the vultures well away from its long-predicted demise. If you do not want to leap to your feet cheering at the last dramatic bars of this music, you are probably not cut out for Rachmaninov's world.

——— *All CDs listed are considered approximately equal in (high) merit.* ———

Ashkenazy, Previn, London Symphony Orchestra. London [Decca] Jubilee 417702 [ADD] + *Rhapsody on a Theme by Paganini*

Ashkenazy, Previn, London Symphony Orchestra. London [Decca] Double 436386 (2) [ADD] + Piano Concerto No. 3, *Rhapsody on a Theme by Paganini*, 5 Preludes, 3 *Etudes-tableaux*

Cliburn, Reiner, Chicago Symphony Orchestra. RCA Victor Red Seal 55912 [ADD] + Tchaikovsky: Piano Concerto No. 1 (with Kondrashin conducting)

Cliburn, Reiner, Chicago Symphony Orchestra. RCA Living Stereo 61961 [AAD] + Beethoven: Piano Concerto No. 5

Gutiérrez, Maazel, Pittsburgh Symphony Orchestra. Telarc 80259 [DDD] + Piano Concerto No. 3

Jandó, Lehel, Budapest Symphony Orchestra. Naxos 8.550117 [DDD] + *Rhapsody on a Theme by Paganini*

Janis, Dorati, Minneapolis Symphony Orchestra. Mercury 432759 [ADD] + Piano Concerto No. 3, Prelude in C-sharp Minor, etc.

Katchen, Solti, London Symphony Orchestra. London [Decca] Weekend Classics 417880 or London [Decca] Classic Sound 448604 [ADD] + *Rhapsody on a Theme by Paganini*; Dohnányi: Variations on a Nursery Song (with Boult conducting London Philharmonic)

[Weekend Classics version omits the Dohnányi, but is cheaper.]

Rubinstein, Reiner, Chicago Symphony Orchestra. RCA Victor Red Seal 4934 [ADD] + *Rhapsody on a Theme by Paganini*

Wild, Horenstein, Royal Philharmonic Orchestra. Chandos 6507 [ADD] + Piano Concerto No. 3

Concerto No. 3 in D Minor for Piano, Op. 30

The composer was soloist at the premiere in 1909, in New York City. Walter Damrosch conducted on that occasion, but a month later the orchestra was led by none less than Gustav Mahler. As fervent as anything by Rachmaninov, the third piano concerto is actually quite similar to the second, only denser and more difficult to play. Incidentally, the composer stopped playing it after he heard Vladimir Horowitz, seeing that he had been beaten at his own game.

Argerich, Chailly, Berlin Radio Symphony Orchestra. Philips 446673 [ADD] + Tchaikovsky: Piano Concerto No. 1 (with Kondrashin conducting)

Ashkenazy, Previn, London Symphony Orchestra. London [Decca] Double 436386 (2) [ADD] + Piano Concerto No. 2, *Rhapsody on a Theme by Paganini*, 5 Preludes, 3 *Etudes-tableaux*

——— *CDs listed are solid, central choices, not necessarily "the greatest."* ———

Cliburn, Kondrashin, Symphony of the Air. RCA Victor Red Seal 6209
[ADD] + Prokofiev: Piano Concerto No. 3

Gutiérrez, Maazel, Pittsburgh Symphony Orchestra. Telarc 80259 [DDD] +
Piano Concerto No. 2

Horowitz, Reiner, RCA Symphony Orchestra. RCA Victor Gold Seal 7754
[ADD] + Piano Sonata No. 2, three short pieces

Janis, Dorati, London Symphony Orchestra. Mercury Living Presence 432759
[ADD] + Piano Concerto No. 2, Prelude in C-sharp Minor, etc.

Rodriguez, Tabakov, Sofia Philharmonic Orchestra. Elan 2220 [DDD] +
Prokofiev: Piano Concerto No. 3

Wild, Horenstein, Royal Philharmonic Orchestra. Chandos 6507 [ADD] +
Piano Concerto No. 2

Rhapsody on a Theme of Paganini, Op. 43

Rachmaninov took the 24th Caprice for solo violin of Niccolò Paganini as the theme
for this set of 24 variations, in which the theme is frequently contrasted with the *Dies Irae*
melody from Gregorian Chant. This ostensible tribute to the violinist/composer who was
often alleged to be the Devil, with reference to the end of the world as described in the
medieval Requiem liturgy, is actually one of Rachmaninov's more light-hearted compositions! Perhaps only a man so naturally lachrymose could make dismal things seem so cheerful. The 18th variation, by the way, is the "famous" one, and there truly is no passage of
Romantic music more Romantic.

Ashkenazy, Previn, London Symphony Orchestra. London [Decca] Jubilee
417702 [ADD] + Piano Concerto No. 2

Ashkenazy, Previn, London Symphony Orchestra. London [Decca] Double
436386 (2) [ADD] + Piano Concerto Nos. 1, 2; 5 Preludes, 3 *Etudes-tableaux*

Jandò, Lehel, Budapest Symphony Orchestra. Naxos 8.550117 [DDD] +
Piano Concerto No. 2

Katchen, Solti, London Symphony Orchestra. London [Decca] Weekend
Classics 417880 *or* London [Decca] Classic Sound 448604 [ADD] + Piano
Concerto No. 2; Dohnányi: Variations on a Nursery Song (with Boult con-
ducting London Philharmonic)
[Weekend Classics version omits the Dohnányi, but is cheaper]

Rubinstein, Reiner, Chicago Symphony Orchestra. RCA Victor Red Seal 4934
[ADD] + Piano Concerto No. 2

———— *Some famous CDs are not listed because currently out of print.* ————

Symphony No. 2 in E Minor, Op. 27

The composer conducted the first performance in 1908. The symphony was an instant success and remains one of the most beloved in the standard repertoire. Often suffused with melancholy, it is resplendent with hard-won affirmation at the end.

Jansons, St. Petersburg Philharmonic Orchestra. EMI 55140 [DDD] + Vocalise, Scherzo in D Minor

Litton, Royal Philharmonic Orchestra. Virgin Classics 59548 [DDD] + *Vocalise*

Paray, Detroit Symphony Orchestra. Mercury Living Presence 434368 [ADD] + Franck: Symphony in D Minor

Rozhdestvensky, London Symphony Orchestra. IMP [Carlton Classics] PD 904 [DDD]

Temirkanov, St. Petersburg Philharmonic Orchestra. RCA Victor Red Seal 61281 [DDD] + *Vocalise*

Maurice Ravel (1875-1937)

Ravel was the most elegant composer of the century, maybe of all time. His dapper wardrobe and wavy hair were a perfect foil to his finely-wrought music, which Stravinsky called the product of "a Swiss clockmaker." Indeed Ravel openly sought technical perfection, fully aware that no one ever achieves it. His music is as meticulously chiseled as were his own Basque cheekbones, but the oft-heard implication that his music is therefore dry and unfeeling is disproved by a few minutes' listening.

The son of a railway engineer, Ravel began piano lessons at age seven. He spent 15 years at the Paris Conservatory, studying with Gabriel Fauré among others. By 1905 he had composed several fine works, including the *Pavane for a Dead Princess* and his Quartet in F, yet four years in a row he had been passed over for the prestigious Prix de Rome which he hoped to win. Finally there was such an uproar from prominent musicians across France that the Conservatory's director, Théodore Dubois, was forced to resign (he was replaced by Fauré).

Two years later, scandal again put Ravel in the spotlight when a song cycle he had written stirred accusations that he was plagiarizing Debussy, a charge long since dropped by the jury of history. In any case, Ravel was now famous and lived up to his reputation by turning out a succession of masterpieces. By World War I he was widely acknowledged as France's greatest composer—even though he was wholly Basque and Swiss by descent.

Ravel was hardly over five feet in height. He was emotionally reserved; he never married, but loved children and animals, seeming to be more comfortable with them than with adult humans. Sometimes while dining with friends he would sit silently for a long time and then suddenly squawk loudly like a parrot. His small villa was filled with tiny curios and mechanical toys which he loved to show off to a select circle of friends. He loved good food and strong cigarettes.

In 1932 he suffered a slight injury in a taxi accident. Within a few months he began experiencing strange symptoms: his muscles seemed to atrophy, he could barely hold a pen, and eventually he was paralyzed. Suspecting a brain tumor, surgeons operated on him. No tumor was found, but in a few days Ravel was dead.

Alborada del gracioso

Somewhat clumsily translated as "The Jester's Morning Song," this virtuosic evocation of strumming guitars and bursting sunrise is Ravel's orchestration of one of five pieces for solo piano originally published as *Miroirs*, a word impossible for English speakers to pronounce.

> **Cluytens, Paris Conservatory Orchestra.** EMI 69165 (2) [ADD] + *Boléro, Pavane for a Dead Princess, Rapsodie espagnole, La valse, Ma Mère l'Oye, Le tombeau de Couperin, Valses nobles et sentimentales, et al.*
>
> **Dutoit, Montreal Symphony Orchestra.** London [Decca] 410010 [DDD] + *Boléro, Rapsodie espagnole, La valse*
>
> **Dutoit, Montreal Symphony Orchestra.** London [Decca] 421458 (4) [ADD/DDD] + *Boléro, Daphnis et Chloé* (complete), *Pavane for a Dead Princess, Rapsodie espagnole, La valse, Ma Mère l'Oye, Le tombeau de Couperin, Valses nobles et sentimentales*; Piano Concerto in G, Piano Concerto for the Left Hand (with Rogé), *et al.*
>
> **Haitink, Amsterdam Concertgebouw Orchestra.** Philips Duo 438745 (2) [ADD] + *Boléro, Rapsodie espagnole, La valse, Daphnis et Chloé* Suite No. 2, *Pavane for a Dead Princess, Valses nobles et sentimentales, Le tombeau de Couperin, Ma Mère l'Oye, Menuet antique*
>
> **Karajan, Orchestre de Paris.** EMI 64357 [ADD] + *La valse, Boléro,* Debussy: *La mer* (with Berlin Philharmonic Orchestra)
>
> **López-Cobos, Cincinnati Symphony Orchestra.** Telarc 80171 [DDD] + *Boléro, Rapsodie espagnole, La valse, Valses nobles et sentimentales*
>
> **Maazel, New Philharmonia Orchestra.** EMI Seraphim 68539 (2) [ADD] + *Boléro, Pavane for a Dead Princess, Valses nobles et sentimentales;* Mussorgsky: *Pictures at an Exhibition;* Debussy: *La mer, Nocturnes* (with Previn, Royal Philharmonic Orchestra)
>
> **Martinon, Orchestre de Paris.** EMI Doublefforte 68610 (2) [ADD] + *Boléro, Pavane for a Dead Princess, Rapsodie espagnole, La valse, Le tombeau de Couperin, Ma Mère l'Oye, Valses nobles et sentimentales,* et al.

———— *Since CDs can change label and number, use artists as main reference.* ————

Paray, Detroit Symphony Orchestra. Mercury Living Presence 432003 [ADD] + *Pavane for a Dead Princess, Rapsodie espagnole, La valse, Le tombeau de Couperin*; Ibert: *Escales*

Reiner, Chicago Symphony Orchestra. RCA Victor Gold Seal 60179 [ADD] + *Pavane for a Dead Princess, Rapsodie espagnole, Valses nobles et sentimentales*; Debussy: *Ibéria* from *Images pour orchestre*

Tortelier, Ulster Orchestra. Chandos 8850 [DDD] + *Rapsodie espagnole*; Debussy: *Images pour orchestre*

Boléro

"Yes, it is my masterpiece," an exasperated Ravel once snapped to Honegger, "unfortunately, it contains no music." *Boléro* was written to be danced by Ida Rubinstein, who starred in the balletic premiere of 1928. It was premiered two years earlier as a concert piece by Arturo Toscanini and brought the audience cheering to its feet. Since then it has remained at or very near the top of the Classical Hit Parade, and has become associated in the popular mind as the ultimate in chic sensuality.

Ansermet, Suisse Romande Orchestra. London [Decca] Classic Sound 448576 [ADD] + *La Valse*; Dukas: *The Sorcerer's Apprentice*; Chabrier: *España*; Debussy: *La mer*; Honegger: *Pacific 231*

Bychkov, Orchestre de Paris. Philips 438209 [DDD] + *Rapsodie espagnole, Daphnis et Chloé* Suite No. 2, *La valse, Pavane for a Dead Princess*

Cluytens, Paris Conservatory Orchestra. EMI 69165 (2) [ADD] + *Alborada del gracioso, Pavane for a Dead Princess, Rapsodie espagnole, La valse, Ma Mère l'Oye, Le tombeau de Couperin, Valses nobles et sentimentales, et al.*

Dutoit, Montreal Symphony Orchestra. London [Decca] 410010 [DDD] + *Alborada del gracioso, Rapsodie espagnole, La Valse*

Dutoit, Montreal Symphony Orchestra. London [Decca] 430714 [DDD] + *Daphnis et Chloé* Suite No. 2, *Pavane for a Dead Princess*, La valse

Dutoit, Montreal Symphony Orchestra. London [Decca] 421458 (4) [ADD/DDD] + *Alborada del gracioso, Daphnis et Chloé* (complete), *Pavane for a Dead Princess, Rapsodie espagnole, La valse, Ma Mère l'Oye, Le tombeau de Couperin, Valses nobles et sentimentales*; Piano Concerto in G, Piano Concerto for the Left Hand (with Rogé), *et al.*

Frühbeck de Burgos, New Philharmonia Orchestra and Chorus. EMI 64328 + Orff: *Carmina Burana*

Haitink, Amsterdam Concertgebouw Orchestra. Philips Duo 438745 (2) [ADD] + *Alborada del gracioso, Rapsodie espagnole, La valse, Daphnis et Chloé*

——— *Artists are listed alphabetically, not in order by critical ranking.* ———

Suite No. 2, *Pavane for a Dead Princess, Valses nobles et sentimentales, Le tombeau de Couperin, Ma Mère l'Oye, Menuet antique*

Jean, Slovak Radio Symphony Orchestra (Bratislava). Naxos 8.550173 [DDD] + *Daphnis et Chloé* Suite No. 2, *Ma Mère l'Oye Suite, Valses nobles et sentimentales*

Karajan, Berlin Philharmonic Orchestra. Deutsche Grammophon Galleria 427250 [ADD] + *Daphnis et Chloé* Suite No. 2; Debussy: *La mer, Prelude to the Afternoon of a Faun*

Karajan, Berlin Philharmonic Orchestra. *Famous Ballets,* London [Decca] Double 437404 (2) [ADD] + Chopin: *Les Sylphides,* Delibes: *Coppélia* Suite, Gounod: *Faust* ballet music, Offenbach: Exc. from *Gaité Parisienne,* Tchaikovsky: *Sleeping Beauty* Suite

Karajan, Berlin Philharmonic Orchestra. Deutsche Grammophon "Karajan Gold" 439013 [DDD] + *Rapsodie espagnole*; Mussorgsky: *Pictures at an Exhibition*

Karajan, Berlin Philharmonic Orchestra. Deutsche Grammophon Originals 447426 [ADD] + Mussorgsky: *Pictures at an Exhibition*; Debussy: *La mer*

Karajan, Berlin Philharmonic Orchestra. EMI 64357 [ADD] + Debussy: *La mer*; Ravel: *Alborada del gracioso, La valse* (with Orchestre de Paris)

López-Cobos, Cincinnati Symphony Orchestra. Telarc 80171 [DDD] + *Alborado del gracioso, Rapsodie espagnole, La valse, Valses nobles et sentimentales*

Maazel, New Philharmonia Orchestra. EMI Seraphim 68539 (2) [ADD] + *Alborada del gracioso, Pavane for a Dead Princess, Valses nobles et sentimentales;* Mussorgsky: *Pictures at an Exhibition*; Debussy: *La mer, Nocturnes* (with Previn, Royal Philharmonic Orchestra)

Martinon, Orchestre de Paris. EMI Doublefforte 68610 (2) [ADD] + *Alborada del gracioso, Pavane for a Dead Princess, Rapsodie espagnole, La valse, Le tombeau de Couperin, Ma Mère l'Oye, Valses nobles et sentimentales, et al.*

Monteux, London Symphony Orchestra. Philips 442542 [ADD] + *Pavane for a Dead Princess, Rapsodie espagnole, La valse, Ma Mère l'Oye* (complete)

Rattle, City of Birmingham Symphony Orchestra. EMI Red Line 69830 [DDD] + *Daphnis et Chloé* (complete)

Concerto in G for Piano

French clarity is joined here with jazzy riffs to create a piano concerto with two crisp outer movements enclosing a nocturne that ripples like a moonlit lake. Ravel conducted the first performance in 1932, with Marguerite Long at the piano.

Argerich, Abbado, Berlin Philharmonic Orchestra. Deutsche Grammophon Originals 447438 [ADD] + *Gaspard de la nuit*; Prokofiev: Piano Concerto No. 3

————— *[DDD] indicates newest recordings; [ADD] or [AAD] are reissues.* —————

De Larrocha, L. Slatkin, St. Louis Symphony Orchestra. RCA Victor Red Seal 60985 [DDD] + Concerto for the Left Hand, *Valses nobles et sentimentales*, Sonatine

Fowke, Baudo, London Philharmonic Orchestra. Classics for Pleasure 4667 [ADD] + *La valse*, Piano concerto for the left hand, *Valses nobles et sentimentales* (piano solo version)

Michelangeli, Gracis, Philharmonia Orchestra. EMI 49326 [ADD] + Rachmaninov: Piano Concerto No. 4

Mok, Simon, Philharmonia Orchestra. Cala 1005 [DDD] + *Daphnis et Chloé* Suite No. 2, *Pavane for a Dead Princess, Rapsodie espagnole, et al.*

Rogé, Dutoit, Montreal Symphony Orchestra. London [Decca] 421458 (4) [ADD/DDD] + Piano Concerto for the Left Hand; *Alborada del gracioso, Boléro, Daphnis et Chloé* (complete), *Pavane for a Dead Princess, Rapsodie espagnole, La valse, Ma Mère l'Oye, Le tombeau de Couperin, Valses nobles et sentimentales, et al.*

Daphnis et Chloé

Premiered in 1912, Ravel's *real* masterpiece (see *Boléro*) was commissioned by the impresario Serge Diaghilev as a vehicle for his ballet superstar, Vaslav Nijinsky. The book is based on the Greek myth of two rustic lovers who are separated, then reunited by the god Pan. The work's proportions are as elegant as any Greek temple, its orchestration the most shimmering of Ravel's career, the flow and surge of evocative harmony and melody irresistible, and the finale, in which sheets of sound crash over the consciousness like Aegean tidal waves, is overwhelming. Ravel created two suites from the complete score, of which No. 2 is most often heard as an independent concert piece.

Bychkov, Orchestre de Paris. (Suite No. 2) Philips 438209 [DDD] + *Rapsodie espagnole, La valse, Boléro, Pavane for a Dead Princess*

Dutoit, Montreal Symphony Orchestra. (complete) London [Decca] 400055 [DDD]

Dutoit, Montreal Symphony Orchestra. (Suite No. 2) London [Decca] 430714 [DDD] + *Boléro, Pavane for a Dead Princess, La valse*

Dutoit, Montreal Symphony Orchestra. (complete) London [Decca] 421458 (4) [ADD/DDD] + *Alborada del gracioso, Boléro, Pavane for a Dead Princess, Rapsodie espagnole, La valse, Ma Mère l'Oye, Le tombeau de Couperin, Valses nobles et sentimentales;* Piano Concerto in G, Piano Concerto for the Left Hand (with Rogé), *et al.*

Haitink, Amsterdam Concertgebouw Orchestra. (Suite No. 2) Philips Duo 438745 (2) [ADD] + *Alborada del gracioso, Rapsodie espagnole, La valse, Boléro,*

Pavane for a Dead Princess, Valses nobles et sentimentales, Le tombeau de Couperin, Ma Mère l'Oye, Menuet antique

Jean, Slovak Radio Symphony Orchestra (Bratislava). Naxos 8.550173 (Suite No. 2) [DDD] + *Boléro, Ma Mère l'Oye Suite, Valses nobles et sentimentales*

Karajan, Berlin Philharmonic Orchestra. (Suite No. 2) Deutsche Grammophon Galleria 427250 [ADD] + *Boléro;* Debussy: *La mer, Prelude to the Afternoon of a Faun*

Monteux, London Symphony Orchestra. (complete) London [Decca] Classic Sound 448603 [ADD] + *Rapsodie espagnole, Pavane for a Dead Princess*

Munch, Boston Symphony Orchestra. (complete) RCA Living Stereo 61846 [ADD]

Rattle, City of Birmingham Symphony Orchestra. EMI Red Line 69830 [DDD] + *Boléro*

Simon, Philharmonia Orchestra. Cala 1005 [DDD] + Piano Concerto in G (with Mok), *Pavane for a Dead Princess, Rapsodie espagnole,* et al.

Tortelier, Ulster Orchestra. (complete) Chandos 8893 [DDD] + Debussy: *Prelude to the Afternoon of a Faun*

Pavane pour une infante défunte (Pavane for a Dead Princess)

As with many Ravel orchestral hits, this one started life as a piano solo, written when he was only 21. It was orchestrated in 1910 and was an immediate success. When asked the significance of the title, Ravel replied that he just liked the way it sounded. In response to a student who played the piano version too slowly, he is reported to have said "Please remember that I have written a pavane for a deceased princess, not a deceased pavane for a princess."

Bernstein, New York Philharmonic Orchestra. CBS [Sony] 37769 [ADD] + Dukas: *Sorcerer's Apprentice;* Saint-Saëns: *Danse macabre, Bacchanale* from *Samson et Dalila;* Chabrier: *España;* Offenbach: *Overture to Orpheus in the Underworld*

Bychkov, Orchestre de Paris. Philips 438209 [DDD] + *Rapsodie espagnole, Daphnis et Chloé Suite No. 2, La valse, Boléro*

Cluytens, Paris Conservatory Orchestra. EMI 69165 (2) [ADD] + *Alborada del gracioso, Boléro, Rapsodie espagnole, La valse, Ma Mère l'Oye, Le tombeau de Couperin, Valses nobles et sentimentales,* et al.

Dutoit, Montreal Symphony Orchestra. London [Decca] 430714 [DDD] + *Boléro, Daphnis et Chloé Suite No. 2, La valse*

Dutoit, Montreal Symphony Orchestra. London [Decca] 421458 (4) [ADD/DDD] + *Alborada del gracioso, Boléro, Daphnis et Chloé* (complete),

Rapsodie espagnole, La valse, Ma Mère l'Oye, Le tombeau de Couperin, Valses nobles et sentimentales; Piano Concerto in G, Piano Concerto for the Left Hand (with Rogé), *et al.*

Giulini, Philharmonia Orchestra. Deutsche Grammophon 419243 [DDD] + Fauré: *Requiem*

Haitink, Amsterdam Concertgebouw Orchestra. Philips Duo 438745 (2) [ADD] + *Alborada del gracioso, Rapsodie espagnole, La valse, Boléro, Daphnis et Chloé* Suite No. 2, *Valses nobles et sentimentales, Le tombeau de Couperin, Ma Mère l'Oye, Menuet antique*

Maazel, New Philharmonia Orchestra. EMI Seraphim 68539 (2) [ADD] + *Boléro, Pavane for a Dead Princess, Valses nobles et sentimentales;* Mussorgsky: *Pictures at an Exhibition;* Debussy: *La mer, Nocturnes* (with Previn, Royal Philharmonic Orchestra)

Martinon, Orchestre de Paris. EMI Doublefforte 68610 (2) [ADD] + *Alborada del gracioso, Boléro, Rapsodie espagnole, La valse, Le tombeau de Couperin, Ma Mère l'Oye, Valses nobles et sentimentales, et al.*

Monteux, London Symphony Orchestra. London [Decca] Classic Sound 448603 [ADD] + *Daphnis et Chloé, Rapsodie espagnole*

Monteux, London Symphony Orchestra. Philips 442542 [ADD] + *Boléro, Rapsodie espagnole, La valse, Ma Mère l'Oye* (complete)

Orpheus Chamber Orchestra. Deutsche Grammophon 449186 [DDD] + *Le tombeau de Couperin;* Satie: *Gymnopédies* 1, 3; Fauré: *Masques et bergamasques*

Paray, Detroit Symphony Orchestra. Mercury Living Presence 432003 [ADD] + *Alborada del gracioso, Rapsodie espagnole, Le tombeau de Couperin, La valse;* Ibert: *Escales*

Reiner, Chicago Symphony Orchestra. RCA Victor Gold Seal 60179 [ADD] + *Alborada del gracioso, Rapsodie espagnole, Valses nobles et sentimentales;* Debussy: *Ibéria* from *Images pour orchestre*

Simon, Philharmonia Orchestra. Cala 1005 [DDD] + Piano Concerto in G (with Mok), *Daphnis et Chloé* Suite No. 2, *Rapsodie espagnole, et al.*

Quartet in F

Despite charges that Ravel copied Debussy, this Quartet is one of his few works to betray any direct influence. In any case, he dedicated it not to Debussy, but to Fauré. It is a work of ingenious refinement; the critic Roland-Manuel proclaimed it "a miracle of grace and tenderness." All choices listed are coupled with the Debussy Quartet, a natural partner.

Alban Berg Quartet. EMI 47347 [DDD] + Debussy: Quartet in G Minor
Carmina Quartet. Denon 75164 [DDD] + Debussy: Quartet in G Minor

——— *U.S. labels and numbers are given first, U.K. in [brackets] when needed.* ———

Hagen Quartet. Deutsche Grammophon 437836 [DDD] + Debussy: Quartet in G Minor; Webern: String Quartet

Juilliard Quartet. Sony 52554 [DDD] + Debussy: Quartet in G Minor; Dutilleux: Quartet

Orpheus Quartet. Channel Classics 3892 [DDD] + Debussy: Quartet in G Minor; Dutilleux: *Ainsi la nuit*

Quartetto Italiano. Philips Silver Line 420894 [ADD] + Debussy: Quartet in G Minor

Rapsodie espagnole

Published in 1907, this work established Ravel as a master of orchestration as well as an authentic Spanish style, endorsed by no less an expert than Manuel de Falla (*q.v.*). The four sections are labeled *Prelude to the Night, Malagueña, Habañera*, and *Festival.*

Bychkov, Orchestre de Paris. Philips 438209 [DDD] + *Daphnis et Chloé* Suite No. 2, *La Valse, Boléro, Pavane for a Dead Princess*

Cluytens, Paris Conservatory Orchestra. EMI 69165 (2) [ADD] + *Alborada del gracioso, Boléro, Pavane for a Dead Princess, La valse, Ma Mère l'Oye, Le tombeau de Couperin, Valses nobles et sentimentales, et al.*

Dutoit, Montreal Symphony Orchestra. London [Decca] 410010 [DDD] + *Alborado del gracioso, Boléro, La valse*

Dutoit, Montreal Symphony Orchestra. London [Decca] 421458 (4) [ADD/DDD] + *Alborada del gracioso, Boléro, Daphnis et Chloé* (complete), *Pavane for a Dead Princess, La valse, Ma Mère l'Oye, Le tombeau de Couperin, Valses nobles et sentimentales*; Piano Concerto in G, Piano Concerto for the Left Hand (with Rogé), *et al.*

Haitink, Amsterdam Concertgebouw Orchestra. Philips Duo 438745 (2) [ADD] + *Pavane for a Dead Princess, La valse, Boléro, Daphnis et Chloé* Suite No. 2, *Valses nobles et sentimentales, Le tombeau de Couperin, Ma Mère l'Oye, Menuet antique*

Karajan, Berlin Philharmonic Orchestra. Deutsche Grammophon "Karajan Gold" 439013 [DDD] + *Boléro*; Mussorgsky: *Pictures at an Exhibition*

López-Cobos, Cincinnati Symphony Orchestra. Telarc 80171 [DDD] + *Alborada del gracioso, Boléro, La valse, Valses nobles et sentimentales*

Martinon, Orchestre de Paris. EMI Doublefforte 68610 (2) [ADD] + *Alborada del gracioso, Boléro, Pavane for a Dead Princess, La valse, Le tombeau de Couperin, Ma Mère l'Oye, Valses nobles et sentimentales, et al.*

Monteux, London Symphony Orchestra. London [Decca] Classic Sound 448603 [ADD] + *Daphnis et Chloé, Pavane for a Dead Princess*

———*All CDs listed are considered approximately equal in (high) merit.*———

Monteux, London Symphony Orchestra. Philips 442542 [ADD] + *Boléro, Pavane for a Dead Princess, La valse, Ma Mère l'Oye* (complete)

Paray, Detroit Symphony Orchestra. Mercury Living Presence 432003 [ADD] + *Alborada del gracioso, Pavane for a Dead Princess, Le tombeau de Couperin, La valse,* Ibert: *Escales*

Reiner, Chicago Symphony Orchestra. RCA Victor Gold Seal 60179 [ADD] + *Alborada del gracioso, Pavane for a Dead Princess, Valses nobles et sentimentales;* Debussy: *Ibéria* from *Images pour orchestre*

Simon, Philharmonia Orchestra. Cala 1005 [DDD] + Piano Concerto in G (with Mok), *Daphnis et Chloé* Suite No. 2, *Pavane for a Dead Princess, et al.*

Tortelier, Ulster Orchestra. Chandos 8850 [DDD] + *Alborada del gracioso;* Debussy: *Images pour orchestre*

Trio for Piano, Violin & Cello (1914)

A magical score of half-tints, glimpses of dreams, and exotic rhythms, this is one of Ravel's greatest works, yet until it was featured in the film *Un coeur en hiver* ("A Heart in Winter") it was little remarked by a wider public. It represents the summing up of his emotions and esthetic before they were irrevocably altered by illness and the First World War.

Ashkenazy, Perlman, Harrell. London [Decca] 444318 [DDD] + Debussy: Sonatas 1, 3

Beaux Arts Trio. Philips 411141 [ADD] + Chausson: Piano Trio

Borodin Trio. Chandos 8458 [DDD] + Debussy: Sonatas 2, 3

Joachim Trio. Naxos 8.550934 [DDD] + Debussy: Piano Trio; Schmitt: *Très lent*

Rouvier, Kantorow, Muller. Erato 45920 [DDD] *Un coeur en hiver. Ravel Trios and Sonatas,* Erato 45920 [DDD] + Sonata for violin and cello, Sonata for violin and piano, *Berceuse sur le nom de Gabriel Fauré*

La Valse

One of Ravel's most popular orchestral works, the exact intent of which is uncertain. It is usually interpreted as a kind of remembrance of the Viennese waltz as in a lovely but gradually more disturbed dream, then brutally shattered at the end as, presumably, World War I breaks out with the crack of a gun.

Ansermet, Suisse Romande Orchestra. London [Decca] Classic Sound 448576 [ADD] + *Boléro;* Dukas: *The Sorcerer's Apprentice;* Chabrier: *España;* Debussy: *La mer;* Honegger: *Pacific 231*

——— *Some famous CDs are not listed because currently out of print.* ———

Baudo, London Philharmonic Orchestra. Classics for Pleasure 4667 [ADD] + Piano Concerto in G, *Valses nobles et sentimentales* (piano solo version), Piano Concerto for the Left Hand (with Fowke)

Bychkov, Orchestre de Paris. Philips 438209 [DDD] + *Rapsodie espagnole, Daphnis et Chloé* Suite No. 2, *Boléro, Pavane for a Dead Princess*

Cluytens, Paris Conservatory Orchestra. EMI 69165 (2) [ADD] + *Alborada del gracioso, Boléro, Pavane for a Dead Princess, Rapsodie espagnole, Ma Mère l'Oye, Le tombeau de Couperin, Valses nobles et sentimentales, et al.*

Dutoit, Montreal Symphony Orchestra. London 430714 [DDD] + *Boléro, Pavane for a Dead Princess, Daphnis et Chloé* Suite No. 2

Dutoit, Montreal Symphony Orchestra. London 410010 [DDD] + *Alborada del gracioso, Boléro, Rapsodie espagnole*

Dutoit, Montreal Symphony Orchestra. London [Decca] 421458 (4) [ADD/DDD] + *Alborada del gracioso, Boléro, Daphnis et Chloé* (complete), *Pavane for a Dead Princess, Rapsodie espagnole, Ma Mère l'Oye, Le tombeau de Couperin, Valses nobles et sentimentales*; Piano Concerto in G, Piano Concerto for the Left Hand (with Rogé), *et al.*

Haitink, Amsterdam Concertgebouw Orchestra. Philips Duo 438745 (2) [ADD] + *Pavane for a Dead Princess, Rapsodie espagnole, Boléro, Daphnis et Chloé* Suite No. 2, *Valses nobles et sentimentales, Le tombeau de Couperin, Ma Mère l'Oye, Menuet antique*

Karajan, Orchestre de Paris. EMI 64357 [ADD] + *La valse; Boléro*, Debussy: *La mer* (with Berlin Philharmonic Orchestra)

López-Cobos, Cincinnati Symphony Orchestra. Telarc 80171 [DDD] + *Alborada del gracioso, Boléro, Rapsodie espagnole, Valses nobles et sentimentales*

Maazel, New Philharmonia Orchestra. EMI Seraphim 68539 (2) [ADD] + *Alborada del gracioso, Boléro, Pavane for a Dead Princess, Valses nobles et sentimentales;* Mussorgsky: *Pictures at an Exhibition*; Debussy: *La mer, Nocturnes* (with Previn, Royal Philharmonic Orchestra)

Martinon, Orchestre de Paris. EMI Doublefforte 68610 (2) [ADD] + *Alborada del gracioso, Boléro, Pavane for a Dead Princess, Rapsodie espagnole, Le tombeau de Couperin, Ma Mère l'Oye, Valses nobles et sentimentales, et al.*

Monteux, London Symphony Orchestra. Philips 442542 [ADD] + *Boléro, Pavane for a Dead Princess, Rapsodie espagnole, Ma Mère l'Oye* (complete)

Paray, Detroit Symphony Orchestra. Mercury 432003 [ADD] + *Alborada del gracioso, Pavane for a Dead Princess, Le tombeau de Couperin;* Ibert: *Escales*

Ottorino Respighi (1879-1936)

Respighi was the leading exponent of Impressionism in Italy, although his talent was not comparable to Debussy's. He was the author of a great deal of music that borders on the tawdry, but at his best he was a brilliant orchestrator and arranger.

Respighi was born into a musical family, studied at first with his father, and later on with both Max Bruch and Nikolai Rimsky-Korsakov. Eventually he became a professor of composition at the famous Academy of Saint Cecilia in Rome, and was appointed its director in 1923.

He was among the few Italian composers who emphasized symphonic music over opera, although he wrote several of those as well. He was a talented scene painter, as his three famous tone poems attest, but also a wonderful transcriber of other people's music, as in the *Ancient Airs* and his colorful ballet *La boutique fantasque* after Rossini.

Respighi would be more comfortably numbered among the Late Romantics than among the Moderns, had he not been born so late. He had little interest in 20th-century techniques of composition. "Why," he once asked and interviewer, "should I use new techniques when one still has so much to say through the language of conventional music?" To be sure, one does find in Respighi the occasional snippet of avant-gardism, but it never forms an essential part of his style. For the most part, that is a result of blending the influences of Richard Strauss, the Impressionists, and the Russian nationalists. Eclectic perhaps, but often vastly entertaining.

Ancient Airs and Dances

In Respighi's day most of the Italian Renaissance composers were entirely unknown to the general public, and preserving their work through modern orchestral transcriptions could be seen as a perfectly reasonable act of homage. Many such arrangements have disappeared in recent years as the original music has been restored and performed on authentic instruments, yet Respighi's three suites of *Ancient Airs and Dances* have survived quite vigorously. This is because they are transcriptions of a very high order, and can stand as independent, interesting works right alongside the originals.

Dorati, Philharmonia Hungarica. Mercury Living Presence 434304 [ADD]
Gee, Australian Chamber Orchestra. Omega 1007 [DDD] + *The Birds*: Suite
López-Cobos, Lausanne Chamber Orchestra. Telarc 80309 [DDD] + *Botticelli Tryptych*
Orpheus Chamber Orchestra. (suites 1 and 3 only) Deutsche Grammophon 437533 [DDD] + *The Birds, Botticelli Tryptych*
Wolff, Saint Paul Chamber Orchestra. Teldec 91729 [DDD] + *The Birds*: Suite, *Botticelli Tryptych*

——— *Since CDs can change label and number, use artists as main reference.* ———

Fountains of Rome; Pines of Rome; Roman Festivals

Respighi's three famous tone poems were written at different times, but form a natural tryptych and are often recorded as a group. These works clearly echo Respighi's lessons with Rimsky-Korsakov. *The Fountains of Rome* is the earliest piece, first performed in 1917, and remains the most popular. It was inspired by four of Rome's many beautiful fountains, whose names are attached to each of the movements of the music. *The Pines of Rome*, conceived as a sequel to the earlier work, was first heard in 1924 and has similar pictorial associations. Arturo Toscanini led the first performance of *Roman Festivals*, an evocation of Ancient Rome, in 1929. It has been somewhat less popular than the other two, the writing being rather more harsh (but then, how *can* you write when describing Christians being ripped to pieces by the lions?).

Bátiz, Royal Philharmonic Orchestra. Naxos 8.550539 [DDD]
Gatti, St. Cecilia Academy National Orchestra. Conifer Classics 51292 [DDD]
Maazel, Pittsburgh Symphony Orchestra. Sony 66843 [DDD]
Marriner, Academy of St. Martin-in-the-Fields. Philips 432133 [DDD]
Muti, Philadelphia Orchestra. EMI 47316 [DDD]
Reiner, Chicago Symphony Orchestra. (*Pines* and *Fountains* only) RCA Living
   Stereo 68079 [ADD] + Debussy: *La Mer*
Tortelier, Philharmonia Orchestra. Chandos 8989 [DDD]

Joaquin Rodrigo (1901-   )

Rodrigo is alive and well at age 96 as I write these words, and let us salute him. He is basically one of those one-horse composers, known worldwide for his *Aranjuez* Concerto, but falling off rapidly after that. He can be considered one of the best of the minor composers of the 20th century.

He was born in Sagunto, Spain, and though blind from the age of three studied music, eventually with Dukas at the Schola Cantorum in Paris. He was encouraged to compose by Manuel de Falla, and developed a suave and melodious style based on colorful Hispanic idioms.

He has written a number of concerti for various instruments, but his name is most intimately associated with the guitar. During the Spanish Civil War he lived in France and Germany, but returned to Madrid in 1939. Spain has awarded him many honors, and he has successfully toured the world with his music.

———— *Artists are listed alphabetically, not in order by critical ranking.* ————

Concierto de Aranjuez

Perhaps the most famous of all guitar concerti, this work inspired by the Aranjuez region of Spain is highly impressionistic and evocative, especially in its celebrated Adagio movement. It liberally employs jazz idioms.

Bonell, Dutoit, Montreal Symphony Orchestra. London [Decca] 430703 [DDD] + Falla: *El amor brujo, Nights in the Gardens of Spain*
Kraft, Ward, Northern Chamber Orchestra. Naxos 8.550729 [DDD] + Villa-Lobos: Guitar Concerto; Castelnuovo-Tedesco: Guitar Concerto
P. Romero, Marriner, Academy of St. Martin-in-the-Fields. Philips 432828 [ADD] + *Fantasia pará un gentilhombre*, Concierto Madrigal for 2 Guitars (with Angel Romero)
Söllscher, Orpheus Chamber Orchestra. Deutsche Grammophon 429232 [DDD] + *Fantasia pará un gentilhombre*; Villa-Lobos: Guitar Concerto
J. Williams, Frémaux, Philharmonia Orchestra. CBS 45648 + *Fantasia pará un gentilhombre*; Albéniz: guitar pieces

Erik Satie (1866-1925)

Satie was one of the most unconventional of all the composers, even for a Frenchman. His influence on a younger generation of his confreres was ultimately more significant than his own compositions; composer and author Eric Salzman deftly described Satie as "a remarkable innovator with a great deal of genius if little talent."

As a youth he studied at the Paris Conservatory but, impatient with academia, dropped out after a year. He began writing piano pieces with peculiar titles such as *Flabby Preludes for a Dog, Sketches and Exasperations of a Big Boob Made of Wood,* and *Dessicated Embryos.* Unnoticed by most critics amongst the whimsy were harmonies which anticipated those of Debussy.

Satie earned a living playing popular tunes at the Black Cat Cafe in the Montmartre district, dismissed by the musical establishment as a charlatan. He came under the influence of the Symbolist poets, as well as the Rosicrucians. He started his own religion, called The Metropolitan Church of Jesus the Leader, and held services in a dingy room furnished with rotting chairs.

Only a few musicians, notably those who came to be known as the Group of Six, and who came to regard Satie as their spiritual godfather, understood that his purpose was to deflate the pretensions of the German Romantic school with its giant structures and somber philosophical gestures. Satie wanted to return music to a simpler, more economical esthetic, shorn of all empty rhetoric and leavened by wit.

——— [DDD] indicates newest recordings; [ADD] or [AAD] are reissues. ———

Past age 40 Satie realized that his message was impaired by his lack of technical prowess. He therefore enrolled in the Schola Cantorum and studied for three years with Vincent d'Indy and Albert Roussel. Subsequently he composed works larger in scope than heretofore.

In his last years he sought both solitude and poverty. He took rooms in a Paris suburb, where he became affectionately known as "le bon maestro d'Arcueil." He lived in total squalor, preferring to identify with the disenfranchised of the world. And he continued to write his unique music, naughty and sardonic and impudent and just a little mad. It is no accident that Satie became a hero to the counterculture of the 1960s, for whom the first *Gymnopédie* was almost a theme song.

Trois Gymnopédies

Written originally for piano solo in 1888, the first and third of these pieces were later orchestrated by Debussy. The title refers to dances that were performed by naked boys as part of rituals at ancient Greek festivals. The melodies have a distinctly "timeless" quality, and the harmonies are most original.

(Piano) **McCabe.** Emergo 3970 or Saga 3393 + other short pieces
(Orchestral) **Orpheus Chamber Orchestra.** (Nos. 1, 3) Deutsche Grammophon 449186 [DDD] + Ravel: *Pavane for a Dead Princess, Le Tombeau de Couperin;* Fauré: *Masques et bergamasques*
(Piano) **Ortiz.** IMP [Carlton Classics] PCD 846 [DDD] + Debussy: *Clair de lune,* 6 other pieces, and pieces by 5 other French composers
(Piano) **Pöntinen.** BIS 317 [DDD] + other short pieces
(Piano) **Rogé.** London [Decca] 410220 [DDD] + other short pieces
(Orchestral) **L. Slatkin, St. Louis Symphony Orchestra.** Telarc 80059 [DDD] + Barber: *Adagio for Strings;* Vaughan Williams: *Fantasia on a Theme by Thomas Tallis;* Fauré: *Pavane,* etc.

Arnold Schoenberg (1874-1951)

Schoenberg did more than any other composer to single-handedly change the sound of 20th-century music. He was the most significant theorist of his age and the founder of the so-called Second Viennese School made up of the atonal or 12-tone composers.

Schoenberg's father ran a shoe shop in Vienna and sang in a choral society. Although there was little money for lessons, Arnold learned to play violin, viola, and cello as a child, learning mostly through a friend. The father died when Arnold was 16 and he took a bank job to support his mother and younger sister. At 21 he decided to make his living somehow

———— CDs go in and out of print; availability of all listed items is not assured. ————

in music. He got a job conducting a chorus and in so doing met the composer Alexander von Zemlinsky, who introduced him to Wagner's music, gave him the only formal training he ever had, was a lifelong influence, and in 1901 became his brother-in-law.

Schoenberg and his wife moved to Berlin where the composer received moral and monetary assistance from Richard Strauss. The couple, now with a daughter, went back to Vienna in 1903 where Schoenberg began his teaching career. Alban Berg and Anton Webern were among his first students; they were to become, with Schoenberg, the Unholy Trinity of Atonalism. Gustav Mahler also befriended Schoenberg, and his departure for America in 1907 was a blow to the budding young composer.

More disappointments, however, were in the offing. In 1908 his wife ran off with a mutual friend, and although she was persuaded to return, the friend committed suicide. Schoenberg now began to write his "atonal" works—a misnomer, as they are not without tones or pitches, but simply do not follow the conventional tonal system—and immediately suffered critical abuse, which in turn impacted negatively on his teaching income. He was also the victim of anti-Semitic propaganda (despite the fact that he had converted to Protestant Christianity in 1898) and was almost murdered by a neighbor.

These difficulties led the Schoenbergs to return to Berlin, where fortunes improved, again aided by Richard Strauss who got Schoenberg a teaching position. World War I interrupted his career again as he was called to military service. At the end of the war he settled in Vienna once more and soon began to develop his "12-tone method," an abitrary system of tonal relationships whose main advantage was to provide an escape hatch from the perceived bondage of the traditional major-minor key system.

Schoenberg's first wife died in 1923 and he remarried. The pair, who were to have three children together, moved back to Berlin where Schoenberg wrote several important works and taught at the Prussian Academy. This very successful interlude was shattered by the advent of the Nazis in 1933. Schoenberg fled to Paris, where he returned proudly to his original Jewish faith prior to moving on to the U.S., where, within a year, he was appointed a professor at UCLA. He became an American citizen in 1941.

Although Schoenberg was in a very real sense the "father of modern music," he was well-grounded in the past. When asked who his teachers had been he liked to answer "Haydn and Mozart." But he also knew his Brahms and Wagner, and even Johann Strauss (he re-orchestrated some of the famous waltzes). He insisted that his music was a natural outgrowth of the Late Romantic tradition, and justifiably argued that his new technique should be called not "atonal" but "pantonal." This new music was highly complex, dissonant, melodically jagged, and rhythmically asymmetrical, and has never won the affections of the public, who generally find it ugly and disagreeable. It has remained almost exclusively the domain of musical cognoscenti.

——— *Some CDs may be available only through importers.* ———

Chamber Symphony No. 1 in E, Op. 9

Scored for 15 solo instruments, five strings and ten winds, this work is still only mid-way between the older diatonic tradition and Schoenberg's simmering atonalism. Although difficult to play with good balance, it is a fast and exciting piece which has become one of the composer's most-recorded works.

Orpheus Chamber Orchestra. Deutsche Grammophon 429233 [DDD] +
Chamber Symphony No. 2, *Verklärte Nacht*
Rattle, City of Birmingham Symphony Orchestra. EMI 55212 [DDD] +
Variations for Orchestra, *Erwartung*

Five Pieces for Orchestra, Op. 16

When this work was first heard in London in 1912, Schoenberg provided a program note that said "This music seeks to express all that swells in us subconsciously like a dream." One critic wrote the next day that it was, perhaps, music of the future "and we hope, of a distant one." Trying to drum up enthusiasm, Schoenberg gave in to the public demand for pictures with their music and gave the movements subtitles such as "Yesteryears" and "Summer Morning by a Lake." That made it all better.

Barenboim, Chicago Symphony Orchestra. Teldec 98256 [DDD] + *Verklärte Nacht*, misc. solo piano pieces
Dorati, London Symphony Orchestra. Mercury Living Presence 432006 [ADD] + Berg: 3 Pieces for Orchestra, *Lulu* Suite; Webern: 5 Pieces for Orchestra, Op. 10
Levine, Berlin Philharmonic Orchestra. Deutsche Grammophon 419781 [DDD] + Berg: 3 Pieces for Orchestra; Webern: 6 Pieces, Op. 6

Variations for Orchestra, Op. 31

Dating from 1928, this is a full-fledged 12-tone composition, and actually is beautiful once you adjust your ears to the style. The nine variations are easy to follow as they are each in a different mood and tempo. It was premiered under the baton of the great Wilhelm Furtwängler and caused quite a row (no pun intended) in the audience.

Boulez, BBC Symphony Orchestra. Sony 48464 [ADD] + *Verklärte Nacht*, *Die glückliche Hand*
Karajan, Berlin Philharmonic Orchestra. Deutsche Grammophon 415326 [ADD] + *Verklärte Nacht*

——— *U.S. labels and numbers are given first, U.K. in [brackets] when needed.* ———

Rattle, City of Birmingham Symphony Orchestra. EMI 55212 [DDD] + Chamber Symphony No. 1, *Erwartung*

Verklärte Nacht, Op. 4 (Transfigured Night)

Schoenberg was 25 when he wrote this post-Wagnerian Expressionist tone poem for string sextet. Later he arranged it for string orchestra. It is inspired by a poem of Richard Dehmel, recounting the confession of a woman to her lover, as they stroll in the moonlight, that she is having a child by her unloved husband.

Although hardly typical of Schoenberg's mature style (there is not a single "tone-row" in it), it remains his most popular work, basically Late Romantic in style, but beautiful and affecting, whatever we call it. All versions listed are for string orchestra.

Barenboim, Chicago Symphony Orchestra. Teldec 98256 [DDD] + 5 Pieces for Orchestra, Op. 16, misc. solo piano pieces

Boulez, BBC Symphony Orchestra. Sony 48464 [ADD] + Variations for Orchestra, *Die Glückliche Hand*

Holliger, Chamber Orchestra of Europe. Teldec 77314 [DDD] + Chamber Symphony No. 2, *Incidental Music for an Imaginary Film Score*

Karajan, Berlin Philharmonic Orchestra. Deutsche Grammophon 415326 [ADD] + Variations for Orchestra, Op. 31

Krivine, Sinfonia Varsovia. Denon 79442 [DDD] + Wagner: *Siegfried Idyll;* R. Strauss: *Metamorphosen*

Orpheus Chamber Orchestra. Deutsche Grammophon 429233 [DDD] + Chamber Symphonies Nos. 1, 2

Dmitri Shostakovich (1906-1975)

Shostakovich was among the greatest 20th-century composers, but also among the most variable. His works range rather incredibly from sublime masterpieces to unredeemable junk. Partly this was a result of the need to tapdance around the shifting demands of the Communist arbiters of taste, but it was due also to a natural tendency in Shostakovich to veer from the noble to the trivial and back again. It was just as well, for his vulgar impulse often resulted in some minor masterpiece of light music, such as his whimsical transcription of "Tea for Two;" on the other hand, it could produce a symphony as vapidly bombastic as No. 12.

Shostakovich was born in St. Petersburg to a well-off family. His father was a mining engineer, his mother a talented pianist who trained Dmitri and his two sisters in the basics of music. By age 12 it was obvious that the boy was extraordinarily gifted and he audi-

———— All CDs listed are considered approximately equal in (high) merit. ————

tioned successfully before Alexander Glazunov, then director of the St. Petersburg Conservatory.

Upon graduation he completed his First Symphony which made him instantly famous; the "boy genius" was hailed around the world. In fact, the symphony was no mere harbinger of coming greatness, it was already great. But the young composer was dissatisfied with it and gave up composing for a while to follow a career as pianist. The urge to compose returned in less than two years, however, and he proceeded to turn out symphonies, operas, chamber music, and solo piano works at a healthy pace.

In 1936 he first ran seriously up against Soviet authorities when his grimly satirical opera *Lady Macbeth of Mtzensk District* was excoriated as a "muddle instead of music....the music quacks, grunts, growls and suffocates itself" (so said a *Pravda* article that appeared shortly after Joseph Stalin had seen the opera). The composer, the article warned, "could end very badly." Shostakovich quickly backtracked, withdrawing his Fourth Symphony which was close to being premiered. Thenceforward he was ever on the alert against going too far for the liking of the Socialist Realism crowd.

He redeemed himself, at least temporarily, with the Symphony No. 5 in 1937. In this tour-de-force Shostakovich created a great work that satisfied officialdom in its exterior qualities but at the same time reached poetic depths within. He did so well with this juggling act that instead of "ending very badly" he won the Stalin Prize in 1940 for his Piano Quintet. (History repeated itself when Shostakovich was condemned in 1948 for "ideological weakness," then won the Stalin Prize again for an oratorio praising the dictator's reforestation program.)

The artistic atmosphere lightened somewhat after Stalin's death in 1953, but Shostakovich continued for another 20 years to balance his more intellectual productions with jolly patriotic drivel, just to be safe. The dichotomy is even more noticeable when one compares his sardonically witty works, written à la Prokofiev, with those that express a profoundly tragic despair; it is sometimes difficult to believe the same person wrote them, but the paradox may be chalked up to his Jekyll and Hyde existence.

Four years after the death of Shostakovich a book of his purported memoirs as "told to" one Solomon Volkov was published in New York. In it the author claims that his capitulations to the Soviet system were a subterfuge and that his music was a disguised protest against a murderous regime. There is good reason however to believe that the book is a hoax, and so, even in death, the mystery of which Shostakovich was the real one persists.

Concerto No. 1 for Piano, Trumpet, and Orchestra, Op. 35

One of the composer's lighter works, this unusual concerto for two oddly paired soloists brims with cheerfulness, even exhilaration, from beginning to end. It was premiered in 1933 in St. Petersburg, and in America a year later under Leopold Stokowski.

——— *CDs listed are solid, central choices, not necessarily "the greatest."* ———

Alexeev, Jones, Maksymiuk, English Chamber Orchestra. Classics for Pleasure 4547 [DDD] + Piano Concerto No. 2, *The Unforgettable Year* 1919, *The Assault on Beautiful Gorky*

Ogdon, Wilbraham, Marriner, Academy of St. Martin-in-the-Fields. London [Decca] 448577 [ADD] + Bartók: *Music for Strings, Percussion, and Celesta; Divertimento*

Previn (in Shostakovich No. 1), **Vacchiano, Bernstein** (in Shostakovich No. 2), **Bernstein, New York Philharmonic Orchestra.** Sony 47618 [ADD] + Piano Concerto No. 2; Poulenc: 2-Piano Concerto

Quartet No. 8 in C Minor for Strings, Op. 110

Shostakovich wrote 15 string quartets, of which this is by far the best known for its intense expression of anguish. It was inspired by the destruction of Dresden in World War II, leading the composer to dedicate it to "the memory of the victims of fascism and war." When it was first played for him he is said to have buried his face in his hands and sobbed.

Beethoven Quartet. Koch/Consonance 81-3006 [ADD] + Quartets Nos. 7, 15
Borodin Quartet. Virgin Classics 59041 [DDD] + Quartets Nos. 3, 7
Eder Quartet. Naxos 8.550973 [DDD] + Quartets Nos. 1, 9
Kronos Quartet. Nonesuch 79242 [DDD] + Crumb: *Black Angels;* Ives: *They Are There;* Marta: *Doom;* Tallis: *Spem in Alium* (arr. quartet)
Manhattan String Quartet. ESS.A.Y 1009 [DDD] + Quartets 6, 7
Voces Intimae String Quartet. BIS 26 [AAD] + Piano Trio No. 2, 7 Romances

Quintet in G Minor for Piano and Strings, Op. 57

A neo-Classical work in five movements of considerable expressive variety, this work speaks from the heart and is written with great skill and sensitivity. It is considered by some the composer's finest chamber work, and possibly the best written in Russia in the 20th century.

Borodin Trio, Zweig, Horner. Chandos 8342 [DDD] + Piano Trio No. 2
Nash Ensemble. Virgin Classics 59312 [DDD] + Piano Trio No. 2; 4 Waltzes for Flute, Clarinet & Piano

Symphony No. 5, Op. 47

The symphony that saved the composer's neck in 1937 has become not only his greatest hit, but one of the most popular symphonies ever written, surely the most beloved of

——— *Some famous CDs are not listed because currently out of print.* ———

the 20th century. It is similar in atmosphere to Beethoven's Fifth, with its majestic opening, followed later by an intensely introspective slow movement exploding into a brilliant finale that comes up like a sunburst. Most listeners take the finale as triumphantly life-affirming, but the dubious *Memoirs* claim it actually symbolizes "fate crushing the brave."

Ashkenazy, Royal Philharmonic Orchestra. London [Decca] 421120 [DDD] + 5 Fragments for Orchestra, Op. 42

Bernstein, New York Philharmonic Orchestra. CBS [Sony] 37218 [ADD]

Järvi, Scottish National Orchestra. Chandos 8650 [DDD] + Ballet Suite No. 5 from *The Bolt*

Levi, Atlanta Symphony Orchestra. Telarc 80215 [DDD] + Symphony No. 9

Mravinsky, Leningrad Philharmonic Orchestra. Praga 250085 [ADD] + Symphony No. 9

Rahbari, Belgian Radio and Television Orchestra. Naxos 8.550427 [DDD] + Symphony No. 9

Temirkanov, St. Petersburg Philharmonic Orchestra. RCA Victor Red Seal 68548 [DDD] + Symphony No. 9

Symphony No. 10 in E Minor, Op. 93

Not so popular as No. 5, the 10th Symphony is nevertheless considered by many connoisseurs to be a more significant and powerful work. It is imbued with an almost constant nervous energy culminating in a grand peroration. It was written in 1953. One of its attractions is that it seems to be "saying something"—one is compelled to believe that there is an underlying program. But just what that might be, the composer never let on.

Jansons, Philadelphia Orchestra. EMI 55232 [DDD] + Mussorgsky: *Songs and Dances of Death*

Karajan, Berlin Philharmonic Orchestra. Deutsche Grammophon "Karajan Gold" 439036 [DDD]

Mravinsky, Leningrad Philharmonic Orchestra. BMG Melodiya 25198 [ADD] + Symphony No. 6

Skrowaczewski, Hallé Orchestra. IMP [Carlton Classics] PCD 2043 [DDD]

Trio No. 2 in E Minor for Piano, Violin and Cello, Op. 67

Shostakovich is often at his best in his chamber works. This trio, written in 1944, was prompted by the death of a close friend and is largely somber in tone. Its four movements sustain melancholy for nearly half an hour without ever losing the listener's attention, so vivid is the work's expressive power.

——— *Catalog numbers are subject to change without notice.* ———

Borodin Trio. Chandos 8342 [DDD] + Piano Quintet
Nash Ensemble. Virgin Classics 59312 [DDD] + Piano Quintet; 4 Waltzes for
Flute, Clarinet & Piano
Palsson, Tellefsen, Helmerson. BIS 26 [AAD] + Quartet No. 8, 7 Romances
Stern, Ma, Ax. CBS 44664 [DDD] + Cello Sonata, Op. 40

Jean Sibelius (1865-1957)

Sibelius made a reputation as a symphonist and tone poet, but above all as the Finnish
national composer-laureate. He was able to capture the distinctive national idiom and
transmit (and transmute) it to a worldwide audience hanging on his every note.

His father, a medical doctor, died of cholera when Johan was only two. (I say Johan
because that was his birth name. He adopted "Jean" from a sea-captain uncle who had
Frenchified his name while abroad.) He started piano at nine, but much preferred the violin, which he began at 15. As a youth he sometimes sat from dawn to dusk beside a lake,
experimenting on his fiddle and burning with the dream of becoming a great virtuoso. His
first composition, written at age ten, was entitled *Water Drops.*

As a teen-ager he read the epics of Homer in ancient Greek and the odes of Horace in
Latin (this was before the invention of television). He was interested in astronomy and pro-
ficient in mathematics. His mother wanted him to study law at the University of Helsinki,
but after a year there he was certain that music was his destiny and enrolled in the
Conservatory, where he was an outstanding student. A scholarship took him on to Berlin
and later Vienna, where he studied composition.

Returning to Finland, Sibelius steeped himself in the old myths and the national epic,
the *Kalevala* (with whose meter Americans are familiar from Longfellow's *The Song of
Hiawatha,* which borrowed it outright). At age 26 he won nationwide recognition with his
giant tone poem *Kullervo,* based on ancient legends. Soon he was producing outstanding
works of nationalistic inspiration and teaching violin and theory at the Conservatory.

In 1897 the Finnish government provided him with a stipend which enabled him to
devote all his time to composing, and in 1899 the publication of *Finlandia* made him the
international cultural spokesperson for his country.

Many in those days assumed that the music of Sibelius was built on authentic folk
melodies, but the truth is that every melody was completely original. As with most of the
great nationalist composers, Sibelius was so imbued with his native culture that he could
evoke it without copying literally from source material. In his great tone poems he obviously called on literary inspiration, but his symphonies are "pure" music; in the symphony, he
once said, "music begins where words leave off."

The "folk" strain of his muse began to fade after the turn of the century and his works
took on a more inward and personal nature. At the same time he was overindulging in cigars and liquor and struggling with constant debt. An illness in 1908 darkened his outlook

———— Since CDs can change label and number, use artists as main reference. ————

and forced him to give up his addictions for a while, but his concentration on work increased. His financial problems gradually faded as he toured the major music centers, conducting his works and receiving numerous honors along the way.

World War I seriously interrupted his career, and the Finnish civil war in 1918 forced Sibelius temporarily from his home. His output declined precipitously and by the mid-1920s he was essentially a recluse, back on tobacco and booze.

He lived on for another 30 years in silence, holed up in his lakeside home, hinting regularly that he was writing an Eighth Symphony, but more likely struggling with the bottle. Asked what he was doing all those years he answered: "Creating my masterpiece." But when he died in his 91st year, there was nothing. He was buried in the garden, next to his beloved wife of more than 60 years.

Concerto in D Minor for Violin, Op. 47

In his earlier years Sibelius was himself a violinist, but it was only long after he had stopped playing that he wrote his sole concerto for the instrument, and as it turns out it is one of the finest composed in the 20th century. The first movement is rhapsodic, the middle lyrically emotional, and the last a vigorous dance—Tovey called it "a polonaise for polar bears."

Accardo, C. Davis, Boston Symphony Orchestra. Philips Duo 446160 (2) [ADD] + *Finlandia, The Swan of Tuonela, Tapiola,* Symphonies Nos. 3, 6, 7

Chung, Previn, London Symphony Orchestra. London [Decca] Classic Sound 425080 [ADD] + Tchaikovsky: Violin Concerto

Heifetz, Hendl, Chicago Symphony Orchestra. RCA Victor Red Seal 61744 [ADD] + Prokofiev: Violin Concerto No. 2; Glazunov: Violin Concerto

Kang, Leaper, Czechoslovak Radio Symphony Orchestra, Bratislava. Naxos 8.550329 [DDD] + short pieces by Svendsen, Sinding, Halvorsen

Kennedy, Rattle, City of Birmingham Symphony Orchestra. EMI 54559 [DDD] + Symphony No. 5

Lin, Salonen, Philharmonia Orchestra. CBS 44548 [DDD] Nielsen: Violin Concerto

Little, Handley, Royal Liverpool Philharmonic Orchestra. Classics for Pleasure Eminence 2203 [DDD] + Brahms: Violin Concerto

Midori, Mehta, Israel Philharmonic Orchestra. Sony 58967 [DDD] + Bruch: *Scottish Fantasy*

Mutter, Previn, Dresden State Orchestra. Deutsche Grammophon 447895 [DDD] + Serenades Nos. 1, 2; Humoresque No. 1

Perlman, Previn, Pittsburgh Symphony Orchestra. EMI 47167 [ADD] + Sinding: Suite

———*Artists are listed alphabetically, not in order by critical ranking.*———

Rachlin, Maazel, Pittsburgh Symphony Orchestra. Sony 53272 [DDD] + Serenade No. 2, *En Saga*

Repin, Krivine, London Symphony Orchestra. Erato 98537 [DDD] + Tchaikovsky: Violin Concerto

Stern, Ormandy, Philadelphia Orchestra. Sony 66829 [ADD] + Tchaikovsky: Violin Concerto

Vengerov, Barenboim, Chicago Symphony Orchestra. Teldec 13161 [DDD] + Nielsen: Violin Concerto

Finlandia, Op. 26

Easily the most impassioned, inspiring piece of national music ever written, *Finlandia* was written as the finale to a historical tableau. Its famous chorale is one of the best-known melodies in the world, and fitted out with words it has become the Finnish national song.

Ashkenazy, Boston Symphony Orchestra. London [Decca] 436566 [DDD] + Symphony No. 2, *Valse triste, Romance* in C

Barbirolli, Hallé Orchestra. EMI 69205 [ADD] + *Valse Triste, Karelia* Suite, *Pohjola's Daughter, Lemminkäinen's Return*

C. Davis, Boston Symphony Orchestra. Philips Solo 442389 [ADD] + Symphony No. 2, *Swan of Tuonela, Valse triste*

C. Davis, Boston Symphony Orchestra. Philips Duo 446160 (2) [ADD] + Violin Concerto (with Accardo) *The Swan of Tuonela, Tapiola,* Symphonies Nos. 3, 6, 7

Karajan, Berlin Philharmonic Orchestra. *Valse Triste,* Deutsche Grammophon "Karajan Gold" 439010 [DDD] + *Valse triste, The Swan of Tuonela;* Grieg: *Peer Gynt* (exc.), *Holberg* Suite

Mackerras, Royal Philharmonic Orchestra. RPO [Tring] 013 [DDD] + Symphony No. 2, *Karelia* Suite

Swan of Tuonela

Like *Finlandia* originally part of a larger work, *The Swan of Tuonela* is best known now as an independent tone poem. It describes a mythical swan said to sing as it floats down the dark river of Tuonela, the Hell of Finnish folklore.

C. Davis, Boston Symphony Orchestra. Philips Solo 442389 [ADD] + Symphony No. 2, *Finlandia, Valse triste*

C. Davis, Boston Symphony Orchestra. Philips Duo 446160 (2) [ADD] + Violin Concerto (with Accardo) *Finlandia, Tapiola,* Symphonies Nos. 3, 6, 7

———— *[DDD] indicates newest recordings; [ADD] or [AAD] are reissues.* ————

Jansons, Oslo Philharmonic Orchestra. EMI 54804 [DDD] + Valse triste, Symphony No. 2, *Andante festivo*

Karajan, Berlin Philharmonic Orchestra. *Valse Triste,* Deutsche Grammophon "Karajan Gold" 439010 [DDD] + *Valse triste, Finlandia;* Grieg: *Peer Gynt* (exc.), *Holberg* Suite

Symphony No. 2 in D, Op. 43

Despite the composer's protestations about "pure" symphonic music, the suspicion is inescapable that this beloved symphony was inspired by northern winds howling through pine forests and mighty waves breaking over granite crags, so vividly does it "speak." Sibelius freely admitted that the rugged climate and scenery of Finland was one of his innermost creative stimuli.

Ashkenazy, Boston Symphony Orchestra. London [Decca] 436566 [DDD] + *Finlandia, Valse triste,* Romance in C

Barbirolli, Royal Philharmonic Orchestra. Chesky 3

C. Davis, Boston Symphony Orchestra. Philips Solo 442389 [ADD] + *Finlandia, Swan of Tuonela, Valse triste*

C. Davis, Boston Symphony Orchestra. Philips Duo 446157 (2) [ADD] + Symphonies Nos. 1, 4, 5

C. Davis, London Symphony Orchestra. RCA Victor Red Seal 68218 [DDD] + Symphony No. 6

Gibson, Scottish National Orchestra. Chandos 6556 [DDD] + Symphony No. 5

Jansons, Oslo Philharmonic Orchestra. EMI 54804 [DDD] + *The Swan of Tuolema, Valse triste, Andante festivo*

Järvi, Gothenburg Symphony Orchestra. BIS 252 [DDD] + *Romance* in C

Karajan, Berlin Philharmonic Orchestra. EMI Studio 69243 [DDD]

Mackerras, Royal Philharmonic Orchestra. RPO [Tring] 013 [DDD] + *Finlandia, Karelia* Suite

Ormandy, Philadelphia Orchestra. Sony Essential Classics 53509 [ADD] + Symphony No. 7

Symphony No. 5 in E-flat, Op. 82

Broad in scope and noble in tone, the Fifth Symphony radiates a serene power. Its famous ending, with huge brass chords evoking a giant striding over mountains, is one of the composer's most arresting inspirations.

——— *CDs go in and out of print; availability of all listed items is not assured.* ———

C. Davis, Boston Symphony Orchestra. Philips Duo 446157 (2) [ADD] + Symphonies Nos. 1, 2, 4

C. Davis, London Symphony Orchestra. RCA Victor Red Seal 61963 [DDD] + Symphony No. 3

Gibson, Scottish National Orchestra. Chandos 6556 [DDD] + Symphony No. 2

Rattle, City of Birmingham Symphony Orchestra. EMI 54559 [DDD] + Violin Concerto (with Nigel Kennedy)

Rattle, Philharmonia Orchestra. EMI 64737 [ADD] + Nielsen: Symphony No. 4, *Pan and Syrinx*

Valse triste

Sibelius's brother-in-law Arvid Järnefelt wrote a play called *Death* for which the composer contributed incidental music. The haunting "sad waltz" is danced by a dying woman in her last dream.

Ashkenazy, Boston Symphony Orchestra. London [Decca] 436566 [DDD] + Symphony No. 2, *Finlandia*, Romance in C

Barbirolli, Hallé Orchestra. EMI 69205 [ADD] + *Finlandia*, *Karelia* Suite, *Pohjola's Daughter*, *Lemminkäinen's Return*

C. Davis, Boston Symphony Orchestra. Philips Solo 442389 [ADD] + Symphony No. 2, *Finlandia*, *The Swan of Tuonela*

Jansons, Oslo Philharmonic Orchestra. EMI 54804 [DDD] + *The Swan of Tuonela*, Symphony No. 2, *Andante festivo*

Karajan, Berlin Philharmonic Orchestra. *Valse Triste*, Deutsche Grammophon "Karajan Gold" 439010 [DDD] + *The Swan of Tuonela*, *Finlandia*; Grieg: *Peer Gynt* (exc.), *Holberg* Suite

Igor Stravinsky (1882-1971)

Stravinsky was, if not the greatest (and many would call him so), certainly the most famous composer of the 20th century. He was to music as his friend Picasso was to painting—the dominating figure of his art, the icon of Modernism, a symbol and a signpost of the times. But there is a peculiar phenomenon about his career: the works for which he is best known were written mostly between the ages of 28 and 30. He continued to compose for nearly 60 more years, revered and deferred to by Academia, but hardly any of these more "advanced" works have won affection from the public.

——— *Some CDs may be available only through importers.* ———

Although Stravinsky, son of an opera singer, loved music from childhood, there was little in his first years to indicate the famous composer to come. He studied piano as a child but at his father's insistence undertook a course in law at St. Petersburg University. Not until age 20 did he firmly decide on a career as a composer. He studied with Rimsky-Korsakov for six years, producing such works as a very conventional symphony, and four children by his wife, who was his first cousin.

The big break came in 1910, when the impresario Serge Diaghilev turned to Stravinsky after another composer had defaulted on a commission to write a ballet on the Russian legend of the fire-bird. Stravinsky wrote the score hurriedly; it was a sensation, made the composer world-famous, and tormented him the rest of his life by remaining his most popular work.

There followed another successful ballet, *Petrushka*, and then in 1913 a famous scandal with the highly dissonant and primitivistic *Le Sacre du printemps* (always called in English *The Rite of Spring*, but more properly *The Consecration of Spring*). There was a near-riot in the hall as apostles of the avant-garde shouted at, and came to blows with, defenders of the old traditions.

Stravinsky and his wife were in Switzerland when the Russian Revolution broke out, and they decided not to go home. Diaghilev lured Stravinsky back to his Ballets Russe for another commission, *Pulcinella*, but the composer was changing his style, turning away from his Russian nationalist roots to the more pan-European idiom of neo-Classicism. This remained his style between the two World Wars and there was a great deal of carping that he had abandoned his original manner.

Burdened with debt, Stravinsky began touring in the 1920s as a pianist and conductor to make money. His travels took him all over Europe and to North and South America. He became a French citizen in 1934 and soon after published an autobiography. Within the next five year his mother died, and his wife and one daughter succumbed to tuberculosis. On top of these tragedies, war was on the horizon, so Stravinsky accepted an invitation to lecture for a year at Harvard University and moved permanently to the U.S., where he remarried and changed citizenship once again. The couple soon settled in Hollywood.

During World War II Stravinsky wrote little of importance, and up until 1953 his chief product was the opera *The Rake's Progress*, on which he worked for three years. Then he became friends with Robert Craft, a young musician who was to become (and is in part to this day) his shadow and alter ego and prime minister to the world, acting as a secretary, advisor, conductor and interpreter of his works, biographer, and general apologist.

It was Craft who introduced Stravinsky to the methods of the 12-tone composers which he had previously ignored. Stravinsky was particularly taken with the spare purity of Anton Webern and soon he had forsaken neo-Classicism to become a serial, or "atonal" composer. This was even less popular with the general public than his neo-Classicism had been, but Stravinsky forged calmly ahead. He was denounced by many of his previous

———— U.S. labels and numbers are given first, U.K. in [brackets] when needed. ————

admirers for capitulating to the "enemy," while leading composers of the newer avant-garde, such as Pierre Boulez, now ridiculed Stravinsky as a poseur and opportunist.

Stravinsky was a precisionist in everything he did, and the often cool detachment and streamlined logic of his music tends to appeal most to those who are of his temperament. His inspirations did not flow, as Beethoven recommended, "from the heart to the heart," but from the brain to the brain. However one feels about him, he was one of the most influential composers of the past century, and despite his three changes of style, his works are stamped with a distinctive individuality. Only Schoenberg matches him in historical significance, and between them they managed to think up the majority of techniques which have made the Moderns clearly different from the Romantics.

Today, a quarter of a century after his death, Stravinsky occupies very nearly the same position he did for much of his life: venerated by most of the intelligentsia but, except for the early neo-Romantic ballets, avoided by the average listener.

Firebird Suite

The suite of highlights is much more often heard in concert than the complete ballet, for all the really "good music" is in the short version. The point has been made, however, that the glorious final flight of the fire-bird can seem unprepared if what precedes it is too short. Nevertheless, it is traditional to start with the Suite and my recommendations are so restricted.

> **Chung, Paris Opera-Bastille Orchestra.** Deutsche Grammophon 437818 [DDD] + Rimsky-Korsakov: *Scheherazade*
>
> **Haitink, London Philharmonic Orchestra; Markevitch, London Symphony Orchestra.** Philips Duo 438350 (2) [ADD] + *Petrushka, Le sacre du printemps, Apollon musagète*
>
> **Shaw, Atlanta Symphony Orchestra.** Telarc 80039 [DDD] + Borodin: Overture and *Polovtsian Dances* from *Prince Igor*
>
> **Skrowaczewski, Minnesota Orchestra.** Vox Box 3016 [ADD] + *Petrushka, Le sacre du printemps*; Prokofiev: *Romeo and Juliet* (sel.), *Love for Three Oranges* Suite
>
> **Stravinsky, Columbia Symphony Orchestra.** CBS (Sony) 39015 [ADD] + *Le sacre du printemps, Petrushka* Suite

Petrushka (complete)

Petrushka is a wooden puppet. All the puppets in a show are regularly brought to life by a magician, until Petrushka is slain by one of the other characters. At the end of the bal-

——— *All CDs listed are considered approximately equal in (high) merit.* ———

let his ghost returns to terrorize the magician. The music, laden with folk tunes authentic and simulated, is full of atmosphere. Unlike *The Firebird*, *Petrushka* is almost always heard complete, although in the composer's 1947 revision instead of the 1911 original. Take note on albums which you are buying since they are substantially different; you may prefer one over the other, or wish to have both if it becomes a favorite work. (Those listed are the 1947 score unless indicated otherwise.)

Boulez, New York Philharmonic Orchestra. (1911 score) CBS 42395 [AAD] + *Le sacre du printemps*

Chailly, Royal Concertgebouw Orchestra. London [Decca] 443774 [DDD] + *Pulcinella* Suite

Haitink, London Philharmonic Orchestra; Markevitch, London Symphony Orchestra. Philips Duo 438350 (2) [ADD] + *Firebird* Suite, *Le sacre du printemps*, *Apollon musagète*

Skrowaczewski, Minnesota Orchestra. Vox Box 3016 (3) [ADD] + *Firebird* Suite, *Le sacre du printemps*; Prokofiev: *Romeo and Juliet* (sel.), *Love for Three Oranges* Suite

Stravinsky, Columbia Symphony Orchestra. CBS (Sony) 42433 [ADD] + *Le sacre du printemps*

Le sacre du printemps (The Rite of Spring)

In this case there is no question of revisions or versions: the complete, unexpurgated ballet that shocked the first audience and the world back in 1913 remains untouchable. Stravinsky claimed to have dreamed the scenario, "a solemn pagan rite: wise elders, seated in a circle, watching a young girl dance herself to death." Imitation of Russian folksong is again an important element, but this time the presentation overwhelms the senses. A huge orchestra pummels the listener with screaming dissonances and bone-breaking rhythms. It was terribly Modern in 1913 but by 1941 had been domesticated by Walt Disney as music for cartoon dinosaurs. Our ears are well-used to these sounds by now, but *The Rite of Spring* remains both a historical signpost in the development of music, and a vivid, exciting composition.

Boulez, Cleveland Orchestra. CBS 42395 [AAD] + *Petrushka* (1911 score)

Craft, London Symphony Orchestra. Koch 7359 [DDD] + *Apollon musagète*

Haitink, London Philharmonic Orchestra; Markevitch, London Symphony Orchestra. Philips Duo 438350 (2) [ADD] + *Firebird* Suite, *Petrushka*, *Apollon musagète*

Karajan, Berlin Philharmonic Orchestra. Deutsche Grammophon 429162 [ADD] + Mussorgsky: *Pictures at an Exhibition*

——— *CDs listed are solid, central choices, not necessarily "the greatest."* ———

Muti, Philadelphia Orchestra. EMI 64516 + Mussorgsky: *Pictures at an Exhibition*

Rattle, City of Birmingham Symphony Orchestra. EMI 49636 [DDD] + *Apollo*

Skrowaczewski, Minnesota Orchestra. Vox Box 3016 [ADD] + *Firebird* Suite, *Petrushka*; Prokofiev: *Romeo and Juliet* (sel.), *Love for Three Oranges* Suite

Stravinsky, Columbia Symphony Orchestra. CBS [Sony] 39015 [ADD] + *Firebird* Suite, *Petrushka* Suite

Stravinsky, Columbia Symphony Orchestra. CBS [Sony] 42433 [ADD] + *Petrushka* (complete)

Symphony of Psalms

It isn't easy to get beyond Stravinsky's "Russian period" when trying to introduce people to his music, but I wanted to include at least one of the best works from his neo-Classical (middle) period. The most famous of these is surely the *Symphony of Psalms*, a setting of Biblical passages in Latin with an atmosphere of ancient times—hard to get more "Classical" than that.

Bernstein, New York Philharmonic Orchestra. CBS [Sony] 44710 [ADD] + Bernstein: *Chichester Psalms*; Poulenc: *Gloria*

Stravinsky, CBC Symphony Orchestra, Toronto Festival Singers. CBS [Sony] 42434 [ADD] + Symphony in 3 Movements, Symphony in C

Tilson Thomas, London Symphony Orchestra and Chorus. Sony 53275 [DDD] + Symphony in C, Symphony in 3 Movements

Virgil Thomson (1896-1989)

Thomson was one of America's most stimulating, thoughtful, original, and long-lived composers and critics. He created the first really distinctive American opera, he composed distinguished film scores, he wrote witty and perceptive critiques of the American musical scene for many years, and was still active at age 93.

Thomson's ancestors came West from Virginia as pioneers in the 19th century. Southern Baptists, they fought on the Confederate side in the Civil War. Virgil was born in Kansas City, Missouri into a morally strict family of modest cultural attainments. Somehow he gravitated to music and was composing piano pieces with names like *The Chicago Fire* at age four.

As he developed into a young man, his music abilities were augmented by a precocious talent for crafting prose. After serving briefly in World War I he enrolled at Harvard

—— *Some famous CDs are not listed because currently out of print.* ——

University, and came under the spell of Erik Satie's music. Soon he was an enthusiastic Francophile and studied with Nadia Boulanger in Paris for a year. He was thrilled to meet Satie and to discover the music of the Group of Six who followed his path, overthrowing Romantic orthodoxy by mixing jazz and dance-hall tunes with serious compositional techniques. It was a perfect fit for Thomson, who found a unique style by blending the French classical tradition with his heritage of nostalgic middle-Americana.

In the mid-1920s he returned to Paris and became friends with the poet Gertrude Stein and her circle of progressive artists whom she named "the lost generation." Their collaborative opera, *Four Saints in Three Acts*, enjoyed a major success in 1934, despite its avant-garde text and deceptively simple music. Thomson's fame was secured. The production, coordinated by John Houseman, choreographed by Frederick Ashton, and designed by the painter Florine Stettheimer, with an all-black cast, became a legend in American theatrical history.

From 1940 to 1954 Thomson was chief music critic of the New York *Herald Tribune*, contributing brilliant insights on American concert life and composers and championing contemporary music. His wit was incisive and he was not averse to turning it on himself: he defined a music critic as one who "seldom kisses, but always tells."

During this period he continued to compose, producing the ballet *Filling Station*, film scores for the documentaries *The Plow that Broke the Plains* and *The River* and a mythical opera about the early crusader for women's rights, Susan B. Anthony, called *The Mother of Us All*. Another admired work is his score to the film *Louisiana Story*, which won the Pulitzer Prize in 1949. His fascinating autobiography was published in 1966.

A surprising number of music histories give little space to this venerable and lovable genius, treating him as a marginal figure with no distinctive profile. Nothing, in my opinion, could be farther from the truth. His melodiously deceptive surfaces, like Mozart's, merely overlie an ocean of refined sensibility. His music is elegantly crafted, yet warm and human. It is richly evocative of an America half real, half imagined, but vividly recreated out of nostalgia and sincere affection.

The Plow that Broke the Plains

The 1936 documentary film gave Thomson his first chance to write for the cinema, and it was revelatory. Instead of the plush, sleazy imitations of Late Romantic composers which were common up until then, Thomson provided clean, lean music of simple dignity and unvarnished sincerity. Bits of jazz and blues here jostle with cowboy songs, banjo chords, and even a few thumps on the old washtub to help tell the story of the Way West.

Kapp, Philharmonia Virtuosi. ESS.A.Y 1005 [DDD] + *The River*
Marriner, Academy of St. Martin-in-the-Fields. EMI 64306 [ADD] + *Autumn*;
    Barber: *Adagio for Strings*; Copland: *Fanfare for the Common Man*, *Quiet City*,
    et al.

——————— *Catalog numbers are subject to change without notice.* ———————

Stokowski, Symphony of the Air. Vanguard Classics 8013 [ADD] + *The River*, Stravinsky: *The Soldier's Tale*

Ralph Vaughan Williams (1872-1958)

Vaughan Williams could be a bit deceiving. His gentle nature was disguised behind a frame as big and burly as a bear, and his genius as a symphonist—one of the greatest in the 20th century—was sometimes obscured by a perception that he was but a provincial composer of folk-inspired idyllic landscapes.

He did belong in part to the English "pastoral school," which was not necessarily a bad thing, although most of its composers are considered of secondary importance. But if he was one, he was the greatest one. And he went far beyond the merely nationalistic by seeking out the universal message latent in his native idiom.

Vaughan Williams (for that was his surname, British style) grew up in a cultured household and was introduced to art music at an early age. He studied at the Royal College of Music with Sir Hubert Parry, and later abroad with both Max Bruch and Maurice Ravel. By age 19 he had published his first composition.

By 1901 he had become intensely interested in the English folksong tradition and resolved to incorporate it into his creative work. With his friend Gustav Holst he traveled around the countryside collecting indigenous music and writing it down. He also lectured and contributed scholarly articles on the subject. In 1906 he edited the *English Hymnal*. He served in World War I, then returned to the Royal College of Music as an instructor. In 1921 he added conducting the London Bach Choir to his already busy schedule, which had become crowded with composing ever more successful works—symphonic, vocal, choral, and operatic.

His career simply expanded with a slow, tranquil grace straight through to his 86th year, when he died shortly after completing his Ninth Symphony. Long before the end he had become the "grand old man of English music," the most important British composer between Elgar and Britten.

Vaughan Williams developed his own distinctive style, blending the folk traditions with a more advanced type of rhythm and harmony. He was a modern composer, but conservative, uninterested either in Schoenberg's atonalism or Stravinsky's neo-isms. Up until 1935 his style favored the folk-pastoral idiom; after the Fourth Symphony, however, a more rugged and abstract vein was often apparent in his music.

Fantasia on a Theme by Thomas Tallis

First written in 1910, later twice revised, and not published until 1921, this work for double string orchestra and solo quartet was well worth the wait. The original tune, taken from one of Tallis's psalter settings of 1567, is treated in a beautifully evocative manner,

——— Since CDs can change label and number, use artists as main reference. ———

overwhelming in emotional power. Along with the shorter and simpler *Fantasia on "Greensleeves,"* it is probably the most internationally beloved work by any English composer. I might not go as far as one British writer who called it "the greatest work of music ever written," but I wouldn't ridicule the choice either; it's in the running at least.

Abravanel, Utah Symphony Orchestra. Vanguard Classics 4071 [08.4053.71] [ADD] + *Fantasia on "Greensleeves," 5 Variants on "Dives and Lazarus," Flos Campi*

Barbirolli, Sinfonia of London, Allegri String Quartet. EMI 47537 [ADD] + *Fantasia on "Greensleeves"*; Elgar: *Introduction and Allegro, et al.*

Boughton, English String Orchestra. Nimbus 7013 [DDD] + *Fantasia on "Greensleeves," The Wasps* Overture, *The Lark Ascending,* Oboe Concerto, *5 Variants of "Dives and Lazarus"*

Boult, London Philharmonic Orchestra. EMI 64017 [ADD] + Symphony No. 2

Frühbeck de Burgos, London Symphony Orchestra. IMP [Carlton Classics] PCD 930 [DDD] + *Fantasia on "Greensleeves"*; Elgar: Cello Concerto (with Schmidt)

Haitink, London Philharmonic Orchestra. EMI 49394 [DDD] + Symphony No. 2

Menuhin, English Chamber Orchestra. Arabesque 6568 [DDD] + *Fantasia on "Greensleeves", The Lark Ascending, Variants of "Dives and Lazarus"*

Previn, Royal Philharmonic Orchestra. Telarc 80158 [DDD] + Symphony No. 5

L. Slatkin, St. Louis Symphony Orchestra. Telarc 80059 [DDD] + Barber: *Adagio for Strings*; Satie: *Trois Gymnopédies*; Faure: *Pavane,* etc.

Warren-Green, London Chamber Orchestra. Virgin Ultraviolet 61126 [DDD] + *Fantasia on "Greensleeves", The Lark Ascending*; Elgar: *Introduction and Allegro, Serenade for Strings*

Symphony No. 2, "London"

Although not the greatest Vaughan Williams symphony, the "London" makes a most attractive introduction to the other eight. It is frankly programmatic, each of its four movements being almost an independent tone poem. The first suggests the city coming to vibrant life after a foggy dawn. Vaughan Williams described the second as "Bloomsbury Square on a November afternoon." The third movement evokes Westminster Embankment at night, with the sounds of the Strand heard from a distance. The finale is in two sections, the first a solemn march which works up to a powerful climax, the second (after an expec-

——— *Artists are listed alphabetically, not in order by critical ranking.* ———

tant interlude in which we hear Big Ben chiming) a cruise down the rippling Thames ending, apparently, at dawn, with the music which opened the symphony.

Bakels, Bournemouth Symphony Orchestra. Naxos 8.550734 [DDD] + *The Wasps* Overture

Barbirolli, Hallé Orchestra. EMI 64197 [ADD] + Symphony No. 8

Boult, London Philharmonic Orchestra. EMI 64017 [ADD] + *Fantasia on a Theme by Thomas Tallis*

A. Davis, BBC Symphony Orchestra. Teldec British Line 90858 [DDD] + Symphony No. 8

Haitink, London Philharmonic Orchestra. EMI 49394 [DDD] + *Fantasia on a Theme by Thomas Tallis*

Handley, Royal Liverpool Philharmonic Orchestra. Classics for Pleasure Eminence 2209 [DDD] + Symphony No. 8

Previn, London Symphony Orchestra. RCA Victor Gold Seal 60581 [ADD] + *Concerto Accademico, The Wasps* Overture

Previn, Royal Philharmonic Orchestra. Telarc 80158 [DDD] + *The Lark Ascending*

Symphony No. 5 in D

The composer dedicated this serene yet expansive symphony to his fellow-composer Jean Sibelius whom he greatly admired. It belongs to the "pastoral" part of his work but is in no way wispy or weak. The last movement, a passacaglia, ends in quiet ecstasy.

Barbirolli, London Symphony Orchestra. EMI 65110 [ADD] + Bax: *Tintagel*

Boult, London Philharmonic Orchestra. EMI 64018 [ADD] + Symphony No. 3 (with New Philharmonia Orchestra)

Handley, Royal Liverpool Philharmonic Orchestra. Classics for Pleasure Eminence 9512 [DDD] + *Flos campi*

Previn, London Symphony Orchestra. RCA Victor Gold Seal 60586 [ADD] + Bass Tuba Concerto, *3 Portraits* from *The England of Elizabeth*

Previn, Royal Philharmonic Orchestra. Telarc 80158 [DDD] + *Fantasia on a Theme by Thomas Tallis*

Heitor Villa-Lobos (1887-1959)

Villa-Lobos was at least as colorful a man as was his music. One of the few composers to favor having his picture taken in a pin-striped suit with a fat cigar jutting from his jaw,

--- *[DDD] indicates newest recordings; [ADD] or [AAD] are reissues.* ---

looking like a 30s movie gangster, Villa-Lobos was the most famous Brazilian classical composer, and probably the most prolific composer of the 20th century. Counts of his compositions range from 1,600 to more than 2,500; no one is absolutely sure of the figure since he was prone to give a manuscript away as a souvenir and toss off a new one to replace it.

His father was Latino, his mother Indian. The father, a schoolteacher, was an amateur musician who tutored his son in cello and clarinet, but died when Heitor was only 11. The boy continued as best he could, teaching himself to play an old piano, figuring out the guitar, naively playing the violin by holding it upright like a cello. (Years later he was asked what instruments he could play. "I *can't* play the oboe," he answered remorsefully.)

Villa-Lobos spent much of his youth on the streets, taking in the sounds and rhythms of Afro-Brazilian musicians. He started writing his own music at 12, and made money playing guitar in theaters and coffee houses. At 18 he set out across the country to discover "the Brazilian soul" in music, from jungle chants to urban popular song. Among his many adventures he claimed to have narrowly escaped being boiled alive by cannibals.

In 1919, pianist Artur Rubinstein was touring South America. Rubinestein was quite the movie buff and took in the cinema one evening in Rio. He was intrigued by the music accompanying the silent film. Discovering it to be the work of a young native musician, Rubinstein sought him out. A few days later Villa-Lobos showed up at the pianist's hotel room with a group of friends and put on a concert of his works.

Rubinstein was so impressed he arranged to send Villa-Lobos to Paris for professional study; but when he got there, in typical style, he put on a concert of his music instead of attending to his studies. "I didn't come here to learn from you," he proclaimed, "I have come to show you what I have done!"

Villa-Lobos returned to Brazil internationally famous and was made director of the Department of Artistic and Musical Education. Among his more notorious pedagogical projects was a choir of over 30,000 schoolchildren singing patriotic music in a soccer stadium, Villa-Lobos conducting them with a Brazilian flag. The composer was becoming equally well-known as an educator and national icon, and for his almost superhuman energy (he founded his own music conservatory and in his leisure time became the billiards champion of Rio de Janeiro).

In subsequent years he traveled frequently to France (and occasionally the U.S.) to conduct his works, and of course continued composing assiduously, seeking ever more unusual combinations of instruments and sonorities (one work is scored for soprano, three metronomes, and orchestra). He invented two characteristic musical forms, the *Bachiana Brasileira*, a suite in which Brazilian folk elements are treated as if composed by Bach, and the *chôro*, a kind of serenade evoking music of the Brazilian street bands.

Mostly self-taught, but imbued with a wide-ranging musical culture from bird-calls to Bach, Villa-Lobos was one of those rare composers who created a style so personal and unique that few have dared to copy it.

Bachiana Brasileira No. 5 for Soprano and Eight Celli

The two movements of this piece were written several years apart, from 1938 to 1945. The opening Aria, a conception perhaps of how Bach would have written the *Air on the G String* if he were Brazilian, immediately became Villa-Lobos's signature composition. Its Portuguese text describes the moon rising through lustrous clouds at midnight.

Gomez, Pleeth Cello Octet. Hyperion 66257 [DDD] + *Bachiana Brasileira* No. 1; Suite for Voice and Violin (with Manning); Bach: 2 Preludes and Fugues from *The Well-Tempered Clavier* (arr. Villa-Lobos)

Hendricks, Bátiz, Royal Philharmonic Orchestra. EMI 47433 [DDD] + *Bachianas Brasileiras* Nos. 1, 7

Concerto for Guitar and Orchestra

Villa-Lobos wrote a large body of great music for classical guitar. The Concerto was created as recently as 1951. It nostalgically recalls the composer's days playing in the street bands of Rio.

Kraft, Ward, Northern Chamber Orchestra. Naxos 8.550729 [DDD] + Rodrigo: *Concierto de Aranjuez*; Castelnuovo-Tedesco: Guitar Concerto

P. Romero, Marriner, Academy of St. Martin-in-the-Fields. Philips 416357 [DDD] + Castelnuovo-Tedesco: Guitar Concerto; Rodrigo: *Sones*

Söllscher, Orpheus Chamber Orchestra. Deutsche Grammophon 429232 [DDD] + Rodrigo: *Concierto de aranjuez, Fantasia pará un gentilhombre*

William Walton (1902-1983)

Walton may be said to have continued the tradition of Elgar in British music up to the present. In developing an original voice, neither radical nor unduly conservative, he managed to remain both distinctively personal and English. Although he wrote relatively few works (just one in each genre, except for his two symphonies), an unusually high proportion of them are frequently performed and widely admired.

Walton's parents were singing teachers from Lancashire from whom the boy naturally picked up a great deal about music: he once said he could sing Handel's *Messiah* before he could talk. At age ten he won a scholarship to Christ Church Cathedral Choir School. As an undergraduate at Oxford he became friends with the colorful Sitwell family of literati, Sacheverell, Osbert—and Edith, whose *Façade* poems led to Walton's *succès de scandale* in 1923 with his jaunty musical setting.

—————— *Some CDs may be available only through importers.* ——————

Walton's academic career was short by failure in algebra; he later said this contributed to his avoidance of the "slide-rule school" of composition. Nevertheless, his unusual musical talent attracted the attention and encouragement of composer Ferruccio Busoni, conductor Ernest Ansermet, and musicologist Edward Dent.

His first important composition, a Piano Quartet, was published when he was 17, and his String Quartet was performed at an important festival of modern music when he was still only 21. A succession of fine works followed, including concertos for viola and violin, two symphonies, the cantata *Belshazzar's Feast*, the opera *Troilus and Cressida*, and distinctive scores for several films including Shakespeare's *Hamlet, Richard III, and Henry V.*

Walton was knighted in 1951, and the next year contributed two stirring, neo-Elgarian marches for the coronation of Elizabeth II. In his later years he and his wife lived on the Mediterranean island of Ischia where he continued even more leisurely his slow, meticulous creation of fine music.

Belshazzar's Feast

Walton's early choral training stood him in good stead for this cantata, one of the most vivid and memorable of its kind. The Biblical verses, compiled by Osbert Sitwell, recount the fall of Babylon and the "handwriting on the wall." It was first performed in 1931 and while occasionally sniffed at by critics for its conservative idiom, has only grown more popular with the years.

Hickox, London Symphony Orchestra and Chorus. Classics for Pleasure Eminence 2225 [DDD] + *In Honour of the City of London*

Litton, Bournemouth Symphony Orchestra and Chorus. London [Decca] 448134 [DDD] + *Coronation March, Crown Imperial, Henry V* Suite

Previn, London Symphony Orchestra and Chorus. EMI 64723 + *Portsmouth Point* Overture, *Scapino* Overture, *Improvisations on an Impromptu of Benjamin Britten*

Previn, Royal Philharmonic Orchestra and Chorus. Carlton Classics 6701862 [30367 01862] or RPO 7013 [8001] [DDD] + *Henry V* Suite

Shaw, Atlanta Symphony Orchestra and Chorus. Telarc 80181 [DDD] + Bernstein: *Chichester Psalms, Missa Brevis*

Symphony No. 1 in B-flat Minor

Brooding or conflicting for most of its length, this work finally wins through to affirmation in the great symphonic tradition, but its sound-world is uniquely Waltonian: nobly "English," but tonally ambiguous, unified by an undercurrent in the bass. The effect is compellingly dramatic.

———— U.S. labels and numbers are given first, U.K. in [brackets] when needed. ————

Handley, Royal Liverpool Philharmonic Orchestra. ASV Quicksilva 6093 [DDD] + *Spitfire Prelude and Fugue*

Mackerras, London Symphony Orchestra. Classics for Pleasure Eminence 2206 [DDD] + Symphony No. 2

Previn, London Symphony Orchestra. RCA Victor Gold Seal 7830 [ADD] + Vaughan Williams: Overture to *The Wasps*

[Another RCA classic scheduled for extinction by the accounting department (*see* under Honegger: Symphony No. 2 and Milhaud: *La création du monde*), this is one of the most famous recordings of a 20th-century work ever made, and in fact is often listed as one of the "100 greatest recordings" of all time. This of course is of no consequence to accountants, who would as readily tear down the Taj Mahal or the Lincoln Memorial if to do so would generate revenue. Unlike them, I prefer to leave the listing in my book; perhaps you can find the disc in an estate sale.]

Previn, Royal Philharmonic Orchestra. Telarc 82016 [DDD] + *Crown Imperial, Orb and Sceptre*

Thomson, London Philharmonic Orchestra. Chandos 8862 [DDD] + *Varii Capricci*

Anton Webern (1883-1945)

Webern enables me to draw this survey of the history of classical music and its recordings to a close almost in silence; not because Webern was unimportant, but because his music was so quiet, his output so miniscule, his life so uneventful, his demise so pitiful.

He was born in Vienna and received a doctorate from the University in 1906, thus becoming the first composer to start out with a degree in musicology. At first he was a devoted Wagnerian, even composing a piece for soprano and orchestra called *Siegfried's Sword* (unfinished).

But in 1904 he met Arnold Schoenberg. He signed on as his first pupil, and so he remained the rest of his life, turning into the most single-minded follower of the atonal, and later, 12-tone, school. Those who find this music harsh or difficult might contemplate the fact that Webern had a pathological fear of noise, and the slightest deviation from perfection of pitch or volume was torture to him.

He was active most of his life as a conductor, ironically often giving outstanding performances of light music such as Johann Strauss waltzes. He was a fanatical perfectionist in every detail of his life; a different conductor had to be engaged to lead the premiere of Berg's Violin Concerto after Webern had used up two of the three allotted rehearsals preparing just the first eight bars of the music! He was neurotically tidy and neat, wrapping his manuscripts in ribbons, and once pointing out about 100 printing errors in a Schoenberg score, all marked in color-coded pencil.

He was a small man with poor eyesight, unprepossessing in appearance at first, but with a charisma born of dedication when he spoke of his ideals, or sat at the piano to demonstrate. He wrote few works, and they are famous for their extreme economy, seldom

———— *All CDs listed are considered approximately equal in (high) merit.* ————

lasting more than a few minutes. They have been called the musical equivalent of Japanese *haiku* poetry.

Webern's music—austere, uncompromising, unadorned, anti-Romantic—was ridiculed by all but the most intellectual and avant-garde musical sophisticates. After Austria was annexed by the Nazis his music was forbidden, his books burned, and he was allowed only enough students to survive. He only escaped slave labor by agreeing to do proofreading for his former publisher.

One evening in 1945, visiting his son-in-law, who had been secretly dabbling in the black market, Webern stepped outside the house to smoke a cigarette. American soldiers were just arriving to arrest his son-in-law, and one of them, trigger-happy, fired three shots at the shadowy figure before him. The composer staggered back into the house and died shortly afterwards.

So ended a life of suffering and rejection, but also of high idealism, with (to rewrite T. S. Eliot) a bang *and* a whimper.

Five Pieces for Orchestra, Op. 10

This entire work, with five precisely designed sections, takes less than five minutes to play! In this short space Webern puts a large number of instrumental soloists (not really a true "orchestra") through a variety of tempi and moods. Anything that could possibly be considered superfluous to the central thesis is stripped away. Webern gave each tiny piece a tiny name: *Prototype, Transformation, Return, Memory,* and *Soul.*

> **Abbado, Vienna Philharmonic Orchestra.** Deutsche Grammophon 431774 [DDD] + 6 Pieces, Op. 6, et al.: Schoenberg: *A Survivor from Warsaw*
> **Dorati, London Symphony Orchestra.** Mercury Living Presence 432006 [ADD] + Berg: 3 Pieces for Orchestra, *Lulu* Suite; Schoenberg: 5 Pieces for Orchestra, Op. 16

Six Pieces for Orchestra, Op. 6

The pieces here are longer than in the previous work, but still quite brief by normal standards. This is Webern's only work scored for large orchestra. The variety of mysterious and striking effects is astonishing.

> **Abbado, Vienna Philharmonic Orchestra.** Deutsche Grammophon 431774 [DDD] + 5 Pieces, Op. 10, et al.: Schoenberg: *A Survivor from Warsaw*
> **Levine, Berlin Philharmonic Orchestra.** Deutsche Grammophon 419781 [DDD] + Schoenberg: 5 Pieces for Orchestra, Op. 16; Berg: 3 Pieces for Orchestra

——— CDs listed are solid, central choices, not necessarily "the greatest." ———

A Minimal Epilogue

Among the many tides and currents washing over the world of music in the last generation, one has become especially notable. Minimalism, as it is called, relies on establishing patterns which are then repeated continually but with slow evolving alterations. An offshoot of Primitivism (see Carl Orff), this music is a reaction against the overly-cerebral music of many 20th-century avant-garde composers and often borrows idioms from ethnic and popular music.

It is, my opinion, too early to give this school full measure in a book such as this which is designed to concentrate on the tried and true; nevertheless, so much has been recorded of, and written about, this music, and it has developed such a large audience, that a brief consideration of some of its leaders is in order.

John Adams (1947-   )

Adams is the composer of this school considered Most Likely to Succeed by many critics; that is, they see his music as definitely lasting beyond the mere fad stage. Partly this is because he stretches the definition of Minimalism to include more elements of the musical palette and thus enrich his expressive range.

The Chairman Dances

Catchy dance music for Chairman Mao may sound a bit *outré*, but so it goes in the Adams opera *Nixon in China,* one of the most talked-about compositions of recent years. The opera is available on a complete recording, but for an introduction stick to this excerpt.

De Waart, San Francisco Symphony Orchestra. Nonesuch 79144 [DDD] + 2 Fanfares, *et al.*

Rattle, City of Birmingham Symphony Orchestra. EMI 55051 [DDD] + *Harmonielehre, Tromba Lontana, Short Ride in a Fast Machine*

Shaker Loops

The title has a double implication, referring both to the religious practices of the American Shakers and to the musical mechanisms of trills and shakes.

Adams, Orchestra of St. Luke's. Nonesuch 79360 [DDD] + Violin Concerto (with Kremer, Nagano, London Symphony Orchestra)

——— *Some famous CDs are not listed because currently out of print.* ———

Warren-Green, London Concert Orchestra. Virgin Classics 59610 [DDD] +
Glass: *Company, Facades;* Reich: *8 Lines;* Heath: *The Frontier*

Philip Glass (1937-   )

Glass is the best known, most recorded, and most orthodox of the Minimalists, sticking to
the repetitive pattern concept to create a hypnotic effect.

Music of Philip Glass

Highlights from various works give an excellent overview.

Various artists. Glassmasters, Sony 62960 (3) [DDD]

Piano Music

Another compilation delineating the Glass style, this disc is played, authoritatively one
must think, by the composer himself.

Glass. CBS 45576 [DDD]

Henryk Górecki (1933-   )

Gorecki is the oldest of this group and shows the closest links to the Primitivists. His
works make few demands on listeners, stressing direct themes and rich harmonies.

Symphony No. 3

Subtitled "The Symphony of Sorrowful Songs," the lyrics comprise the lament of a
mother for her dead son. The work was premiered in 1977.

Upshaw, Zinman, London Sinfonietta. Nonesuch 79282 [DDD]

Anthologies

Here follow selected collections of classical music not otherwise treated under individual composers. These comprise a mix of works by various composers, and/or showcase the talents of one particular artist, or group of artists, in a certain genre or on a specific instrument. Listings are alphabetical by artist within type; as elsewhere in this book, the order of listings does not imply a hierarchy of merit. Likewise, the listings are not meant to be exhaustive, but to suggest some likely first purchases in each category. Be aware also that if your favorite artist seems left out, it may only be because he or she is fully treated under the composer sections and may not even have an "anthology" album to consider.

General

Various artists. *Building a Classical Music Library, Vol. I-IV*, Platinum Disc 6202 (*The Baroque Era*), 6212 (*The Classical Period*), 6222 (*The Early and Mainstream Romantics*), 6232 (*The Late Romantics and The Moderns*) [DDD] (Four CDs keyed to this book, each with 64-69 minutes of music, total of 52 selections.)

Various artists. *Discover Classical Music*, Naxos 8.550008-9 (2) [DDD] (35 selections from Gregorian Chant to Carl Orff from the vast, budget-priced Naxos catalogue, with 60-page booklet guide.)

Various artists. *The Idiot's Guide to Classical Music*, RCA Victor 62641 [ADD] (99 tracks in 73 minutes, presenting "An Index of Classical Music's Greatest Themes," dirt cheap.)

Early Music

Various artists. *Adventures in Early Music*, DHM 68859 (70-minute survey of the history of period performance practice, with 44-page booklet guide)

Various artists. *Gaudeamus Early Music Sampler*, ASV Gaudeamus 1002 [DDD] (Low-priced introduction to a distinguished catalog from England.)

Various artists. *The Early Music Collection*, Naxos 8.504009 (4) [DDD] (Four-CD budget collection with excellent performances, wide variety.)

Various artists. *Introduction to Early Music*, Naxos 8.551203 [DDD] (One-disc distillation of the above.)

[For Medieval and Renaissance anthologies, see listings in the chapter for those periods earlier in this book.]

Baroque

Edlinger, Capella Istropolitana. *Baroque Favorites,* Naxos 8.550102 [DDD] (Music of Bach, Handel, Scarlatti, Vivaldi, others.)

Edlinger, Capella Istropolitana. *Best of Baroque Music,* Naxos 8.550014 [DDD] (Music of Albinoni, Bach, Corelli, Handel, Telemann, others.)

Hogwood, Academy of Ancient Music. *Pachelbel's Canon and Other Baroque Favorites,* L'Oiseau-Lyre 410553 [ADD] (Includes works by Vivaldi, Gluck, Handel, others.)

I Musici. *Baroque Favorites,* Philips Solo 442396 [ADD] (Standard works of Pachelbel, Albinoni, Corelli, Bach, Handel, *et al.*)

Krechek, Capella Istropolitana. *Italian Concerti Grossi,* Naxos 8.550877 [DDD] (The best of an important genre.)

Lamon, Tafelmusik. *Popular Masterworks of the Baroque,* Reference Recordings 13 [DDD] (Handel, Pachelbel, Bach, Purcell, Vivaldi, Telemann played on period instruments, vividly recorded.)

Leppard, English Chamber Orchestra. *Pachelbel's Canon in D and Other Baroque Favorites,* CBS [Sony] 44650 [DDD] (Includes works by Bach, Charpentier, Gluck, Handel, Purcell, Vivaldi, Marcello.)

Menuhin, Bath Festival Orchestra, et al. *The Most Famous Baroque Classics,* EMI Encore 68304 [ADD/DDD] (Unreconstructed non-period performances for those who can't stand "original instruments" but don't want "no-names" either.)

Roberts, His Majesty's Sagbutts and Cornetts. *Grand Tour: Music from 16th- and 17th-Century Italy, Spain & Germany,* Hyperion 66847 [DDD] (Title tells it all; with period instruments, crystalline sound.)

Various artists. *Sunday Paper,* Angel [EMI] 72064 [ADD/DDD] (16 tracks of Pachelbel's *Canon,* Bach's J*esu, Joy of Man's Desiring,* Vivaldi's *The Four Seasons,* and more Baroque standards.)

Various artists. *Great Baroque Favorites,* CBS [Sony] 38482 [ADD/DDD] (Music of Bach, Handel, Pachelbel, Vivaldi, Albinoni, Purcell, others.)

Various artists. *Favorite Baroque,* Classics for Pleasure 4620 [DDD] (The major standards mixed with a few more adventurous items.)

Various artists. *The Ultimate Baroque Collection,* Erato 92876 [DDD] (Works by Albinoni, Bach, Handel, Pachelbel, Purcell, Telemann, Vivaldi.)

Zukerman, St. Paul Chamber Orchestra. *Baroque Music,* Philips 412215 [DDD] (Handel, Pachelbel, Purcell, Rameau, Telemann, Vivaldi with modern instruments but on an intimate scale.)

——— *Artists are listed alphabetically, not in order by critical ranking.* ———

Orchestral

Academy of St. Martin-in-the-Fields Chamber Ensemble. *Academy Classics*, Chandos 9216 [DDD] (Mozart to Walton, pleasing examples from this beloved group's vast repertoire.)

Fiedler, Boston Pops Orchestra. *Fiedler's Greatest Hits*, RCA Victor 60835 [ADD] (*Stars and Stripes Forever* and all the other signature lollipops of America's classic "pops" conductor.)

Kunzel, Cincinnati Pops Orchestra. *The Very Best of Erich Kunzel & The Cincinnati Pops*, Telarc 80175 [DDD] (Compilation from the many successful albums of the Boston Pops' one serious rival, in brilliant digital sound.

Marriner, Academy of St. Martin-in-the-Fields. *Academy of St. Martin-in-the-Fields*, EMI 47391 [ADD] (Classic collection of characteristic performances, Baroque to Romantic, by the most-recorded conductor in history.)

Orpheus Chamber Orchestra. *Classical Hits*, Deutsche Grammophon 437782 [DDD] (Favorite short works, mostly from Classical and Early Romantic eras.)

Toscanini, NBC Symphony Orchestra, *et al.* *The Toscanini Sampler*, RCA Victor Gold Seal 60340 [ADD] (69 minutes from the 82-CD collection of recordings by the most famous conductor of them all. Hear why.)

Various artists. *The Royal Treasury of Classical Music*, Platinum Disc 08542 (10) [DDD] (Ten-CD set of new recordings by three great British orchestras, the Royal Philharmonic, London Symphony Orchestra, and The Philharmonia, with Adrian Leaper, Frank Shipway, and Philip Gibson variously conducting; an anthology of dozens of classical orchestral favorites at super-budget pricing—about what you'd pay for two full-priced compact discs.)

Ballet

Karajan, Berlin Philharmonic Orchestra. *Famous Ballets*, London [Decca] Double 437404 (2) [ADD] Includes Ravel: *Boléro*; Chopin: *Les Sylphides*, Delibes: *Coppélia* Suite, Gounod: *Faust* ballet music, Offenbach: Exc. from *Gaîté Parisienne*, Tchaikovsky: *Sleeping Beauty* Suite

Various artists. *The Ultimate Ballet Collection*, Erato 996969 [ADD/DDD] (Creative mix of great classical music for the dance.)

Various artists. *Essential Ballet*, London [Decca] 436658 [ADD/DDD] (19 selections from the world of ballet.)

——— *[DDD] indicates newest recordings; [ADD] or [AAD] are reissues.* ———

Opera

Bjørling, Merrill, Milanov, Albanese, Tebaldi. *"The Pearl Fishers" Duet Plus Duets and Scenes by Puccini and Verdi,* RCA Victor Vocal Series 7799 [ADD] (Before "The Three Tenors," this was the biggest-selling operatic album of all time. Find out why before being irretrievably submerged in bad taste.)

Callas. *Operatic Recital,* EMI 47282 (mono) [ADD] (Easily the best single disc of the greatest legend among women singers.)

Caruso. *Enrico Caruso 1873-1921,* Nimbus Prima Voce 7803 [ADD] (20 tracks, 75 minutes of the great voice of recorded music history. Dead for over 70 years, Caruso is still a best seller. Re-live the legend with this smartly packaged introduction to superhuman singing, in sound that has been digitally enhanced for amazing fidelity and clarity. Caution: Play the first three cuts last, as they are mostly of archival interest and don't give the best impression of what's waiting in the following grooves. Only one of my favorite Caruso recordings is not on this disc; close enough for perfection.)

Various artists. *Aria: A Passion for Opera,* EMI 65163 [ADD/DDD] (17 of the greatest scenes and arias, with Callas, Domino, many others.)

Various artists. *Aria II: A Passion for Opera,* EMI 65597 [ADD/DDD] (More of the above.)

Various artists. *The Ultimate Opera Collection,* Erato 91715 [ADD/DDD] (19 tracks from Carreras, Bartoli, Te Kanawa, Upshaw, Horne, Hampson, Caballé, and more.)

Various artists. *Invitation to the Opera,* IMP [Carlton Classics] TCD 1070 (3) [DDD] (Three discs jammed with overtures, arias, scenes, choruses from many operas, good overview.)

Various artists. *Mad about Opera,* London [Decca] 437636 [ADD/DDD] (Selections with Pavarotti, Domingo, Norman, Freni, and more.)

Various artists. *Essential Opera,* London [Decca] 433822 [ADD/DDD] (Pavarotti, Freni *et al.* sing greatest arias from standard operas.)

Various artists. *Essential Opera 2,* London [Decca] 440947 [ADD/DDD] (Continuation of above with Carreras, Sutherland, *et al.*)

Various artists. Prima Voce Sampler, Nimbus Prima Voce 1430 [ADD] (14 selections from this label's great library of great singers of yesteryear—when singers were greater.)

Various artists. *100 Singers, 100 Years at the Met,* RCA Victor Red Seal 61580 (6) [ADD] (As advertised, 100 great singers to choose from, recorded from 1903 to 1980. Almost all are indeed "great," and there is no more concise anthology of such singing upon which one can later expand a collection.)

———— *CDs go in and out of print; availability of all listed items is not assured.* ————

Choral

Chanticleer. *Out of This World,* Teldec 96515 [DDD] (16 choral selections from Thomas Tallis to Bill Evans.)

Christophers, The Sixteen. *The Sixteen at 16: A 16th Birthday Celebration,* Collins Classics 16002 (Renaissance to today with the award-winning ensemble.)

King's College Choir, Cambridge. *Choral Favorites,* Classics for Pleasure 4632 [ADD] (Peerless singing in the great British tradition.)

King's Singers. *20th Anniversary Celebration Sampler,* EMI 69375 [ADD/DDD] (Perfect introduction to these amazing voices who seem at home in everything from classics to pop.)

Gardiner, Monteverdi Singers. *Jubilate Deo!,* Philips 446116 [ADD/DDD] (Baroque and Renaissance sampler from this stalwart choir's 20th anniversary season.)

Rutter, Cambridge Singers. *A Banquet of Voices: Music for Multiple Choirs,* Collegium 123 [DDD] (72 minutes of superb singing, including the Tallis 40-part motet *Spem in alium.*)

Shaw, Robert Shaw Festival Singers, Atlanta Symphony Orchestra & Choruses. *Absolute Heaven: Essential Choral Masterpieces,* Telarc 80458 [DDD] (15 selections without a single duplication of *Passage to Paradise,* see **Various artists** below.)

Various Artists. *Passage to Paradise,* EMI 69241 (2) [ADD/DDD] (33 highlights from great sacred music, the *Hallelujah Chorus* and many more.)

Piano

Cliburn. *My Favorite Encores,* RCA Victor Gold Seal 60276 [ADD] (Show-enders by America's most beloved pianist.)

Gould. *Images,* Sony 62588 (2) [ADD] (All "wrong," all wonderful, by the only pianist before David Helfgott who could do whatever he felt like and get away with it, with a pleasant bonus of playing the correct notes.)

Horowitz. *A Portrait of Vladimir Horowitz,* CBS [Sony] 44797 [ADD] (Highlights from the vast recorded legacy of the King of the Keyboard.)

Michelangeli. *Arturo Benedetti Michelangeli,* EMI 64490 [ADD] (Selected recordings from the repertoire of an eccentric, colorful, and uneven artist who, when he was *on* (as here), was *on.*)

Perahia. *A Portrait of Murray Perahia,* CBS [Sony] 42448 [ADD/DDD] (Highlights from the career of one of the most polished, perceptive, and lyrically poetic pianists of recent years.)

——— *Some CDs may be available only through importers.* ———

Pletnev. *Piano Sampler*, Virgin Classics 59086 [DDD] (Overview of one of the most exciting young pianists on the horizon today.)

Pöntinen. *Music for a Rainy Day*, BIS 300 [DDD] (12 miniatures, thoughtfully selected, atmospherically played by Sweden's young poet of the ivories. Word for today: *rubato.*)

Richter. *The Art of Sviatoslav Richter*, Deutsche Grammophon Double 447355 (2) [ADD] (Excellent overview of one of the giants of the keyboard in the 20th century.)

Rubinstein. *Highlights from the Rubinstein Collection*, RCA Victor Gold Seal 60211 [ADD] (Teasers from the legacy of Horowitz's chief rival, and acknowledged superior in Chopin.)

Various artists. *Für Elise: Solo Piano Favourites*, London [Decca] 417751 [DDD] (Small classics in superb performances by Ashkenazy, Schiff, Lupu, Bolet, De Larrocha, *et al.*)

Organ

Alain. *Famous Music for Organ*, Erato 45976 [ADD/DDD] (Bach's Toccata and Fugue in D Minor and several others by one of the 20th century's greatest organists.)

Cleobury. *The Splendour of King's: Essential Organ Favorites*, Collins Classics 1401 [DDD] (Great organ music on the magnificent organ of King's College, Cambridge, England.)

Hurford. *Organ Spectacular*, London [Decca] 430710 [DDD] (Britain's best-known organist thrills in wall-rattlers.)

Lucas. *Organ Showpieces from St. Paul's Cathedral*, Naxos 8.550955 [DDD] (Outstanding recital of organ greats without a single note of Bach; a feat in itself. Thrifty, too.)

Murray. *An Organ Blaster Sampler*, Telarc 80277 [DDD] (Ten organ hits from Bach to Messiaen.)

Murray, Empire Brass. *Music for Organ, Brass & Percussion*, Telarc 80218 [DDD] (The ultimate in pomp and splendor, plus played loudly through a window it will drive drug dealers out of your neighborhood.)

Harpsichord

Black. *The Essential Harpsichord*, Collins Classics 5024 [DDD] (74 minutes of selections, lively playing.)

Dart, Kipnis, Newman. *Harpsichord Greatest Hits*, CBS [Sony] 68458 [ADD] (Inexpensive collection of 29 favorites, good at the price despite variable sound.)

───── *U.S. labels and numbers are given first, U.K. in [brackets] when needed.* ─────

Kipnis. *A Treasury of Harpsichord Favorites*, Music & Arts 243 [DDD] (32 harpsichord classics played by a master on multiple instruments with period tunings.)

Pinnock. *The Harmonious Blacksmith*, Archiv 413591 [DDD] (Handel's exciting tune headlines this fine collection, though it is far less broad and inclusive than that of Kipnis.)

Brass and Wind Ensemble

Canadian Brass. *Greatest Hits*, RCA Red Seal 4733 [ADD/DDD] (Works by Bach, Mouret, Handel, Pachelbel, Sousa, *et al.*, rounded up from this winning group's many successful albums.)

Empire Brass Quintet. *Royal Brass: Music from the Renaissance & Baroque*, Telarc 80257 [DDD] (Representative brilliance from Telarc's resident brass artists, equal to the best.)

Fennell, Cleveland Symphonic Winds. Telarc 80038 [DDD] (The album that put digital recording [and Telarc recordings] on the map, it's still astonishing musically and sonically. A landmark recording featuring *Handel's Royal Fireworks Music*, Bach's *Fantasia in G*, and two *Suites for Band* by Gustav Holst.)

Trumpet

André, various orchestras. *Maurice André Trumpet Masterpieces*, Deutsche Grammophon Double 413853 (2) [ADD] (Most of the great trumpet concertos played by France's *trompette bien-aimé*.)

Hardenberger, Marriner, Academy of St. Martin-in-the-Fields. *Trumpet Concertos*, Philips 420203 [DDD] (Haydn, Hummel, Hertel, and Stamitz with Sweden's top lips. One of the best classical trumpet CDs ever made.)

Marsalis, Newman, English Chamber Orchestra. *In Gabriel's Garden*, Sony 66244 [DDD] (Varied collection from America's superstar of the trumpet.)

Schwarz. *A Baroque Trumpet Recital*, Nonesuch 71274 [ADD] (When Gerard Schwarz retired from his instrument, America lost its greatest trumpeter but Seattle gained its greatest conductor. A glimpse here of golden days on brass.)

Steele-Perkins, Lamon, Tafelmusik. *Music for Trumpet and Orchestra*, Sony Vivarte 53365 [DDD] (Recital by today's leading player of "period" trumpets.)

Trombone

Lindberg. *10 Year Jubilee*, BIS 638 [DDD] (Celebration of the outstanding classical trombonist, who has done for its repertory what Galway has done for the flute's.)

———*All CDs listed are considered approximately equal in (high) merit.*———

Flute

Galway. *A Portrait*, RCA Victor Red Seal 68142 (2) [DDD] (Double CD set showcasing versatile range of Rampal's only serious rival.)

Rampal. *La Flûte Enchanté*, EMI 69642 (4) [ADD] (Broad survey by the world's greatest flutist [and most-recorded classical artist] of standards from Bach to Honegger.)

Recorder

Petri. *18th-Century Italian Recorder Sonatas*, Philips 412632 (Representative selections from the most famous living performer on the recorder.)

Clarinet

Meyer. *Clarinet Connection: The Great Concertos*, EMI 55155 [DDD] (Mozart, Weber, and Stamitz.)

Bassoon

Smith. *Bassoon Bon-Bons*, ASV 2052 [DDD] (Daniel Smith, the best-known bassoonist of today, shows what his sometimes patronized instrument can do in everything from Bach to Verdi, even Rachmaninov and Chopin.)

Violin

Heifetz. *Selections from The Heifetz Collection*, RCA Victor Gold Seal 62645 [ADD] (18 tracks from Bach to Gershwin laid down by the most famous violinist of the 20th century.)

Perlman. *The Art of Perlman*, EMI 64617 (4) [ADD/DDD] (Highlights from the brilliant career of the most successful violinist of the last generation.)

Vengerov. *Virtuoso Works for Violin and Piano*, Teldec 77351 [DDD] (A baker's dozen of whiz-bang fireworks for the violin, played to perfection by perhaps the brightest star on the violin horizon.)

Cello

Ma. *Portrait of Yo-Yo Ma*, CBS [Sony] 44796 [ADD/DDD] (Selections from this favorite artist's many albums.)

———— *All CDs listed are considered approximately equal in (high) merit.* ————

Rostropovich. *The Rostropovich Edition,* EMI 65701 (3) [ADD] (Most of the greatest cello concertos played by the greatest cellist of recent times, accompanied by some of the greatest conductors—Karajan, Bernstein, Szell, Bernstein, etc.)

Guitar

Bream. *Guitar Greatest Hits,* RCA Victor 62663 [ADD] (My choice for the greatest of them all; he just doesn't *look* like a guitarist!)

Bream. *The Ultimate Guitar Collection,* RCA Victor 33705 (2) [ADD] (More of the above, including the beloved Rodrigo *Concierto de Aranjuez* in a peerless performance.)

Fisk. *The Best of Eliot Fisk,* MusicMasters 67151 [ADD/DDD] (Fascinating selection by one of the best of the younger artists.)

Parkening. The Great Recordings, EMI 54905 (2) [ADD] (42 selections by America's premiere classical guitarist; two and a half hours of music on two discs.)

Romero (Pepe). *Famous Spanish Guitar Music,* Philips 411033 [DDD] (Great program by most famous member of a famous family.)

Romero (Pepe). *Guitar Solos,* Philips 434727 [DDD] (Standard works of Albéniz, Granados, Sor, Tarrega, *et al.*)

Williams. *John Williams' Greatest Hits,* CBS [Sony] 31407 (Classic selections by one of the handful of greatest guitarists in the world.)

Percussion

Glennie, Wordsworth, National Philharmonic Orchestra (London). *Rhythm Song,* RCA Victor 60242 [DDD] (Fascinating performances by the young deaf woman, Evelyn Glennie, of original works and popularized classics for marimba, timpani and other percussion instruments.)

———— *CDs listed are solid, central choices, not necessarily "the greatest."* ————

Classical Music in the Movies

One of the questions I receive most often is "What was that music they used in..." (so-and-so film). "It sounded so familiar, but I couldn't quite place it." When it's a standard work of classical music, I feel I should try to locate it. Here is a list of famous music that shows up in numerous famous movies. The list is by no means complete or exhaustive; it only attempts to answer some of the more commonly-asked inquiries.

The order is alphabetical by film, with the year indicated (so that there is no confusion among multiple movies with the same title). I have listed at least some of the classical music that appears within each film, but not necessarily every work quoted therein.

It is important to be aware that very seldom is an entire classical work employed in a movie score; in the great majority of cases you are hearing only an excerpt, and sometimes little more than a few bars of theme, re-orchestrated by persons other than the original composer. Moral: If your only knowledge of classical music is from movies, it's incomplete and distorted at best.

Age of Innocence, The (1993)
Balfe: "I dreamt that I dwelt in marble halls" from *The Bohemian Girl*
Gounod: "Jewel Song" from *Faust*
J. Strauss I: *Radetzky* March
J. Strauss II: *The Emperor* Waltz; *Tales from the Vienna Woods*

Alien (1979)
Hanson: Symphony No. 2
Mozart: *Andante* from *Eine kleine Nachtmusik*

Amadeus (1984)
Mozart: various works, including *Requiem*, Symphonies 25 and 29, Piano Concertos 20 and 21, *Eine kleine Nachtmusik*, and Serenade for 13 Winds

Angie (1994)
Massenet: *Méditation* from *Thaïs*

Apocalypse Now (1979)
Wagner: *Ride of the Valkyries* from *Die Walküre*

Babe (1995)
Saint-Saëns: Symphony No. 3 "Organ"

Babette's Feast (1987)
Mozart: "Là ci darem la mano" from *Don Giovanni*

Badlands (1973)
Orff: *Carmina Burana*
R. Strauss: *Four Last Songs*

Barry Lyndon (1975)
Mozart: March from *Idomeneo*

Breaking Away (1979)
Mendelssohn: *Saltarello* from Symphony No. 4 "Italian"

Brief Encounter (1945)
Rachmaninov: Piano Concerto No. 2

Carmen Jones (1954)
Bizet: *Carmen*

Carlito's Way (1993)
Delibes: *Flower Duet* from *Lakmé*

Chariots of Fire (1981)
Allegri: *Miserere*
Elgar/Parry: "Jerusalem"

Children of a Lesser God (1986)
  Bach: Concerto for Two Violins,
    S.1043
Clockwork Orange, A (1971)
  Beethoven: Symphony No. 9
  Elgar: *Pomp and Circumstance* March
    No. 1
  Rimsky-Korsakov: *Scheherazade*
  Rossini: Overtures to *La gazza ladra,*
    The Barber of Seville, William Tell
Coeur en hiver, Un (1993)
  Ravel: *Modére* from Piano Trio
Court Martial (1955) [UK, **Carrington,**
  V. C.]
  Schubert: Quintet in C
Crimes and Misdemeanors (1989)
  Bach: *English* Suite No. 2
  Schubert: String Quartet No. 15 in
    G Major
Dangerous Liaisons (1988)
  Handel: *Largo* ("Ombra mai fu")
    from *Xerxes*; Organ Concerto No.
    13 "The Cuckoo and the
    Nightingale"
Dark Eyes (1987)
  Rossini: "Una voce poco fa" from
    The Barber of Seville
Dead Poets Society (1989)
  Beethoven: Piano Concerto No. 5
    "Emperor"
Death in Venice (1971)
  Beethoven: *Für Elise*
  Mahler: *Adagietto* from Symphony
    No. 5; "O Mensch" from
    Symphony No. 3
  Mussorgsky: *Lullaby*
  Puccini: "Vogliateme bene" from
    Madama Butterfly
Die Hard (1988)
  Beethoven: Symphony No. 9

Die Hard 2 (1990)
  Sibelius: *Finlandia*
Diva (1981)
  Catalani: "Ebben? Ne andrò lontano"
    from *La Wally*
Dr. Jekyll and Mr. Hyde (1932)
  Bach: Toccata and Fugue in D
    Minor, S.565
Dracula (1931)
  Tchaikovsky: *Swan Lake*
  Wagner: Prelude to Act I, *Die*
    Meistersinger
Draughtsman's Contract, The (1982)
  Purcell: Prelude to Act III, *King*
    Arthur
Driving Miss Daisy (1989)
  Dvořák: *Song to the Moon* from
    Rusalka
Elephant Man, The (1980)
  Barber: *Adagio for Strings*
Elvira Madigan (1967)
  Mozart: *Andante* from Piano
    Concerto No. 21
Equinox (1993)
  Rachmaninov: *Symphonic Dances*
Europeans, The (1979)
  Foster: *French Quadrilles; Old Folks*
    Quadrille; Soirée Polka
  Schubert: 6 Waltzes, Op. 9
  C. Schumann: Piano Trio
Excalibur (1981)
  Orff: "O Fortuna" from Carmina
    Burana
  Wagner: *Siegfried's Funeral March*
    from *Götterdämmerung; Ride of the*
    Valkyries from *Die Walküre;*
    Liebestod from *Tristan und Isolde*
Fame (1980)
  Mozart: Piano Sonata No. 11,
    K.331

Fantasia (1940)
  J. S. Bach: Toccata and Fugue in D
    Minor, S.565
  Beethoven: Symphony No. 6
    "Pastorale"
  Dukas: *The Sorcerer's Apprentice*
  Mussorgsky: *A Night on Bald
    Mountain*
  Ponchielli: *Dance of the Hours* from
    La Gioconda
  Schubert: *Ave Maria*
  Stravinsky: *Le sacre du printemps (The
    Rite of Spring)*
  Tchaikovsky: *The Nutcracker* Suite
Farewell to Arms, A (1932)
  Wagner: *Liebestod* from *Tristan und
    Isolde*
Fatal Attraction (1987)
  Puccini: "Con onore muore" and
    "Un bel dì" from *Madama
    Butterfly*
Father of the Bride (1991)
  J. S. Bach: Minuet and *Badinerie*
    from Orchestral Suite No. 2
  Pachelbel: Canon in D
Fearless (1993)
  Beethoven: *Für Elise*; Piano Concerto
    No. 5 "Emperor"
  Górecki: Symphony No. 3
  Penderecki: *Polymorphia*
Fire Maidens of Outer Space (1955)
  Borodin: *Polovtsian Dances* from
    Prince Igor
Four Weddings and a Funeral (1994)
  Handel: "Arrival of the Queen of
    Sheba" from *Solomon*
Frankie and Johnny (1991)
  Debussy: *Clair de lune*
French Lieutenant's Woman, The (1981)
  Mozart: Piano Sonata No. 17, K.576

Gallipoli (1981)
  Albinoni: *Adagio*
  Bizet: "Au fond du temple saint"
    from *The Pearl Fishers*
Glory (1989)
  Orff: "O Fortuna" from *Carmina
    Burana*
Godfather, The, Part III (1990)
  Mascagni: *Easter Hymn* and
    Intermezzo from *Cavalleria
    Rusticana*
Good Morning, Babylon (1987)
  Rossini: *La gazza ladra* Overture
  Verdi: "La Vergine degl' angeli" from
    La forza del destino
Great Lie, The (1941)
  Tchaikovsky: Piano Concerto No. 1
Great Waltz, The (1938)
  J. Strauss II: various works
Green Card (1990)
  Mozart: Flute Concerto No. 1;
    Concerto for Flute and Harp;
    Clarinet Concerto
**Greystoke: The Legend of Tarzan,
  Lord of the Apes** (1984)
  Elgar: *Pomp and Circumstance* March
    No. 4; Symphony No. 1
Groundhog Day (1993)
  Mozart: Piano Sonata No. 11 in A
    Major, K.331
  Rachmaninov: *Rhapsody on a Theme
    by Paganini*
Guarding Tess (1994)
  Mozart: "Ich gehe, doch rate ich dir"
    from *Abduction from the Seraglio;
    Catalog Aria* from *Don Giovanni*
Hannah and Her Sisters (1986)
  J. S. Bach: Harpsichord Concerto
    No. 5, S.1056
  Puccini: "Sola, perduta, abbandonata"
    from *Manon Lescaut*

Heat and Dust (1983)
  J. Strauss II: Tales from the Vienna
    Woods
  Schumann: "Des Abends" from
    Fantasiestücke, Op. 12
Honeymoon in Vegas (1992)
  Verdi: "La donna è mobile" from
    Rigoletto
Howards End (1992)
  Grainger: *Bridal Lullaby; Mock
    Morris*
Hudsucker Proxy, The (1994)
  Bizet: *Carmen*
  Khachaturian: *Sabre Dance* from
    Gayaneh
Hunger, The (1983)
  Bach: *Gavotte en rondeaux* from
    Partita for Violin Solo No. 3,
    S.1006; Suite No. 1 for Cello Solo
  Delibes: *Flower Duet* from *Lakmè*
  Ravel: *Gaspard de la nuit*
  Schubert: Piano Trio No. 2 in E-flat
    Major, Op. 100
Immortal Beloved (1994)
  Beethoven: various works, including
    Symphonies 3, 5, 6, 7, 9; Piano
    Concerto 5; Piano Sonatas 8
    "Pathétique," 14 "Moonlight";
    Violin Concerto; Violin Sonata 9
    "Kreutzer"; Piano Trio 4 "Ghost";
    Für Elise; Missa Solemnis; String
    Quartet 13, Op. 130; *Christ on the
    Mount of Olives*
  Rossini: Overture to *La gazza ladra*
Indecent Proposal (1993)
  Vivaldi: Violin Concerto No. 8 from
    L'estro armonico
Island of Dr. Moreau, The (1996)
  Bach: Brandenburg Concerto No. 2
  Bach: Concerto for Two Violins,
    S.1043

Jean de Florette (1986)
  Verdi: *La forza del destino* Overture
Jefferson in Paris (1995)
  Charpentier: *In Hoc Festo*
  Corelli: Violin Sonata, Op. 5, No. 12
    "La Folia"
  Duphly: *Courante* in C Minor
Kalifornia (1993)
  Beethoven: Symphony No. 8
Kind Hearts and Coronets (1949)
  Mozart: "Il mio tesoro" from *Don
    Giovanni*
Kramer vs. Kramer (1979)
  Purcell: Trumpet Sonata in D
  Vivaldi: Concerto for Two
    Mandolins
Ladykillers, The (1955)
  Boccherini: Minuet from Quintet,
    G.275
Last Emperor, The (1987)
  J. Strauss II: *The Emperor* Waltz
Lisztomania (1975)
  Liszt: various works
Longest Day, The (1962)
  Beethoven: Symphony No. 5
Lorenzo's Oil (1992)
  Barber: *Adagio for Strings; Agnus Dei*
  Bellini: "Casta Diva" from *Norma*
  Donizetti: "Una furtiva lagrima"
    from *L'elisir d'amore*
  Elgar: Cello Concerto
  Mahler: *Adagietto* from Symphony
    No. 5
  Marcello: Oboe Concerto
  Mozart: *Ave, verum corpus*
Love and Death (1975)
  Prokofiev: *Lt. Kijé* Suite
Love Story (1970)
  Mozart: Piano Sonata No. 12, K.332
Ludwig (1972)
  Wagner: various works

Luna, La (1979)
Verdi: "Ella è pura!" from *Un ballo in maschera*
M. Butterfly (1993)
Puccini: "Un bel dì" from *Madama Butterfly*
Madame Souzatzka (1988)
Beethoven: Piano Sonata No. 23 "Appassionata"
Mahler (1970)
Mahler: various works
Man Without a Face, The (1993)
Puccini: "Ch'ella me creda" from *La Fanciulla del West*
Manhattan (1979)
Gershwin: *Rhapsody in Blue*
Puccini: *Madama Butterfly*
Manon des sources (1986)
Verdi: *La forza del destino* Overture
Midsummer Night's Sex Comedy, A (1982)
Mendelssohn: Incidental Music to *A Midsummer Night's Dream*; Symphony No. 3
Misery (1990)
Beethoven: Piano Sonata No. 14 "Moonlight"
Moderns, The (1988)
Mozart: "Voi che sapete" from *The Marriage of Figaro*
Moonstruck (1987)
Puccini: scenes and arias from *La Bohème*
Mrs. Doubtfire (1993)
Rossini: "Largo al factotum" from *The Barber of Seville*
Mummy, The (1932)
Tchaikovsky: *Swan Lake*
Music Lovers, The (1970)
Tchaikovsky: various works

My Left Foot (1989)
Mozart: "Un'aura amorosa" from *Così fan tutte*
Night Porter, The (1974)
Mozart: *The Magic Flute*
Ordinary People (1980)
Pachelbel: Canon in D
Out of Africa (1985)
Mozart: *Adagio* from *Clarinet Concerto*
Schubert: *The Shepherd on the Rock*
Philadelphia (1993)
Catalani: "Ebben? Ne andrò lontano" from *La Wally*
Cilea: "Io son l'umile ancella" from *Adriana Lecouvreur*
Giordano: "La mamma morta" from *Andrea Chenier*
Picnic at Hanging Rock (1975)
Beethoven: Piano Concerto No. 5 "Emperor"
Platoon (1986)
Barber: *Adagio for Strings*
Pretty Woman (1990)
Verdi: "Sempre libera" from *La Traviata*
Prizzi's Honor (1985)
Donizetti: "Una furtiva lagrima" from *L'Elisir d'amore*
Puccini: "O mio babbino caro" from *Gianni Schicchi*
Rossini: Overture to *The Barber of Seville*
Puppetmaster (1989)
Brahms: Waltz, Op. 39, No. 15
Quiz Show (1994)
Weill: *Morität* ("Mack the Knife") from *The Threepenny Opera*
Raging Bull (1980)
Mascagni: *Intermezzo* from *Cavalleria Rusticana*

Raven, The (1935)
  J. S. Bach: Toccata and Fugue in D
    Minor, S.565
  Dvořák: Symphony No. 9 "From the
    New World"
Right Stuff, The (1983)
  Debussy: *Clair de lune*
Rollerball (1975)
  Albinoni: *Adagio*
  J. S. Bach: Toccata and Fugue in D
    Minor, S.565
  Shostakovich: Symphony No. 5
  Tchaikovsky: *Romeo and Juliet*; Waltz
    from *Sleeping Beauty*
Room with a View, A (1986)
  Puccini: "O mio babbino caro" from
    Suor Angelica; "Il sogno di
    Doretta" from *La Rondine*
Rosemary's Baby (1968)
  Beethoven: *Für Elise*
Salem's Lot (1979)
  Vivaldi: *Winter* from *The Four
    Seasons*
Seven Year Itch, The (1955)
  Rachmaninov: Piano Concerto No. 2
Seventh Veil, The (1946)
  Rachmaninov: Piano Concerto No. 2
Schindler's List (1993)
  J. S. Bach: *English* Suite No. 2
Shawshank Redemption, The (1994)
  Mozart: "Che soave zeffiretto" from
    The Marriage of Figaro
Shine (1996)
  Chopin: Prelude No. 15 in D-flat
    Major "Raindrop"
  Rachmaninov: Prelude in C-sharp
    Minor, Op. 3, No. 2
  Rachmaninov: Piano Concerto No. 3
Shining, The (1980)
  Bartók: *Music for Strings, Percussion
    and Celesta*

Ligeti: *Fontana*
Penderecki: *De natura sonoris;
  Polymorphia; Kanon; Utreja*
Shirley Valentine (1989)
  Stravinsky: *The Firebird*
Short Cuts (1993)
  Herbert: Cello Concerto No. 2
  Stravinsky: *The Firebird*
Silence of the Lambs, The (1991)
  J. S. Bach: *Goldberg Variations*
Somewhere in Time (1980)
  Rachmaninov: 18th Variation from
    Rhapsody on a Theme by Paganini
Song of Norway (1970)
  Grieg: various works
Song of Scheherazade (1947)
  Rimsky-Korsakov: various works
Sophie's Choice (1982)
  Mendelssohn: *Songs Without Words,*
    No. 1
  Schumann: *Kinderscenen*
Star Trek VIII: First Contact (1996)
  Berlioz: *Royal Hunt and Storm* from
    Les troyens
Sunday, Bloody Sunday (1971)
  Mozart: "Soave sa il vento" from *Cos*"
    fan tutte
Sunset Boulevard (1950)
  J. S. Bach: Toccata and Fugue in D
    Minor, S.565
10 (1979)
  Ravel: *Boléro*
Till the End of Time (1946)
  Chopin: Polonaise No. 6, Op. 53
    "Heroic"
Tous les matins du monde (1991)
  Couperin: *Leçons de ténèbres*
  Lully: *Turkish March*
  Marais: viol music
  St.-Colombe: viol music

Trading Places (1983)
Mozart: *Marriage of Figaro* Overture
True Romance (1993)
Delibes: *Flower Duet* from *Lakmé*
Truly Madly Deeply (1991)
J. S. Bach: Solo Cello Suites
2001: A Space Odyssey (1968)
Khachaturian: *Gayaneh*
Ligeti: *Lux aeterna; Atmosphères*
J. Strauss II: *The Blue Danube* Waltz
R. Strauss: *Also sprach Zarathustra*
Unbearable Lightness of Being, The (1988)
Janáček: *Pohadka; On the Overgrown Path; String Quartet No. 1; Idyll* for String Orchestra
Untouchables, The (1987)
Leoncavallo: "Vesti la giubba" from *Pagliacci*
Wall Street (1987)
Verdi: "Questa o quella" from *Rigoletto*

Wayne's World (1992)
Tchaikovsky: *Romeo and Juliet*
Wedding Banquet, The (1993)
Mozart: *Alla turca* from Piano Sonata No. 11, K.331
When Harry Met Sally... (1989)
Mozart: Quintet in E-flat Major for Piano and Winds, K.452
Who Framed Roger Rabbit (1988)
Liszt: *Hungarian Rhapsody* No. 2
Witches of Eastwick, The (1987)
Puccini: "Nessun dorma" from *Turandot*
Wizard of Oz, The (1939)
Mussorgsky: *A Night on Bald Mountain*
Year of Living Dangerously, The (1983)
R. Strauss: "Beim Schlafengehen" from *Four Last Songs*

About the Author

Bill Parker has been a classical music broadcaster, author, and record executive for over 30 years. He was an announcer and producer for several radio stations, principally Minnesota Public Radio where he worked for 17 years, producing both regional and national classical music programs. He has written four previous books, numerous liner notes for record albums, and many newspaper and magazine articles.

He has also worked in the record business as the manager of six record stores, midwestern sales manager for a large classical record distributor, and senior buyer of classical recordings for a major national retailer. His Internet web site, the Classical Music Preview, can be accessed at http://cmp.orbis.net . He also contributes to the Maestro classical music pages of NetRadio Network at http://www.netradio.net .

Bill Parker's favorite quotation is from Sergei Rachmaninov: "Music is enough for a whole lifetime—but a lifetime is not enough for music."

Index

[of major periods of music, and of composers and their works which are treated in detail, with titles and nicknames of "named" compositions. "Generic" titles such as symphony, concerto, sonata, etc., are not listed independently.]

A

Academic Festival Overture (Brahms), 109-110
Adagio for Strings and Organ (Albinoni), 16
Adagio for Strings (Barber), 206-207
Adams, John, 293-294
  Chairman Dances, The, 293
  Shaker Loops, 293-294
Aida (Verdi), 163
Albinoni, Tomaso, 16
  Adagio, 16
Alborada del gracioso (Ravel), 256-257
Alexander Nevsky (Prokofiev), 247
Also sprach Zarathustra (Strauss, R.), 197
American in Paris, An (Gershwin), 225
"American" Quartet (Dvořák), 128
Amor brujo, El (Falla), 222-223
Ancient Airs and Dances (Respighi), 265
anthologies, general, 295
Appalachian Spring (Copland), 218-219
Apprenti sorcier, L' (Dukas), 178-179
Aranjuez Concerto (Rodrigo), 267
"Archduke" Trio (Beethoven), 52
Arlésienne Suites, *L'* (Bizet), 105

B

Bach, Carl Philipp Emanuel, 39-40
  Hamburg Symphonies, 40
Bach, Johann Sebastian, 17-25
  Brandenburg Concertos, 18
  cantatas, 19
  Chromatic Fantasy and Fugue, 20

concertos
  for Harpsichord, 19
  for Violin, 20
  for 2 Violins , 20
  Goldberg Variations, 20-21
  harpsichord music, 20-21
  Italian Concerto, 21
  lute music, 22
  Magnificat in D, 22-23
  Mass in B Minor, 23
  organ music, 23-24
  partitas for harpsichord, 21
  St. Matthew Passion, 24
  sonatas and partitas for solo violin, 22
  Suites for Orchestra, 24-25
  Well-Tempered Clavier, 21
Bachiana Brasileira No. 5 (Villa-Lobos), 289
ballet anthologies, 297
Barber, Samuel, 206-207
  Adagio for Strings, 206-207
Barber of Seville, The (Rossini), 83, 84
Baroque anthologies, 296
Baroque Era, The (ca. 1600-1750), 15-37
  characteristics of, 15-16
  composers, 16-37
Bartered Bride, The Overture and Dances (Smetana), 152
Bartók, Béla, 207-210
  Concerto for Orchestra, 208
  Concerto No. 3 for Piano, 209
  Music for Strings, Percussion and Celesta, 209
  quartets, 210

bassoon anthologies, 302
Beethoven, Ludwig van, 40-52
  concertos
    for piano, 41-43
    for violin, 43
    for violin, cello, piano, 43-44
  overtures, 44
  quartets for strings, 44-45
  sonatas for piano, 45
  Sonata for Violin No. 5, "Spring," 45
  Sonata for Violin No. 9, "Kreutzer," 45
  symphonies (complete), 46-47
  Symphony No. 1, 47
  Symphony No. 2, 47
  Symphony No. 3, "Eroica," 47-48
  Symphony No. 4, 48
  Symphony No. 5, 48-49
  Symphony No. 6, "Pastorale," 49
  Symphony No. 7, 50
  Symphony No. 8, 50-51
  Symphony No. 9, "Choral," 51-52
  Trio No. 6, "Archduke," 52
Bellini, Vincenzo, 72-73
  Norma, 72-73
Belshazzar's Feast (Walton), 290
Berg, Alban, 210-212
  Concerto for Violin, 210-211
  Three Pieces for Orchestra, 211
  Wozzeck, 211-212
Berlioz, Hector, 73-76
  Damnation of Faust, The, 76
  Harold in Italy , 74-75
  Roméo et Juliette, 75
  Symphonie fantastique, 75-76
Bernstein, Leonard, 212-214
  Candide: Overture, 213
  Chichester Psalms, 213
  Dances from *West Side Story*, 213-214
Billy the Kid (Copland), 219
Bizet, Georges, 104-106
  Arlésienne Suites, L', 105
  Carmen, 104-105
  Carmen Suites, 105
  Symphony No. 1 in C, 106
Bloch, Ernest, 214-215

Schelomo—Rhapsody, 215
Blue Danube Waltz, The (Strauss, J., II),
  141
Boccherini, Luigi, 52-53
  Concerto for Cello, 53
Bohème, La (Puccini), 193-194
Boléro (Ravel), 257-258
Boris Gudonov (Mussorgsky), 140
Borodin, Alexander, 106-108
  Prince Igor: Overture, *Polovtsian Dances*,
    107
  Quartet No. 2 in D, 107-108
  Symphony No. 2, 108
Brahms, Johannes, 108-119
  Academic Festival Overture, 109-110
  concertos
    for piano, 110-111
    for violin, 111-112
    for violin and vello, 112
  German Requiem (Ein Deutsches
    Requiem), 113
  Hungarian Dances, 113
  Quintet for Clarinet and Strings, 114
  symphonies (complete), 114-115
  Symphony No. 1, 115
  Symphony No. 2, 115
  Symphony No. 3, 116
  Symphony No. 4, 116-117
  Tragic Overture, 117-118
  Trio for Horn, Violin, and Piano, 118
  Variations on a Theme by Haydn, 118-
    119
Brandenburg Concertos (Bach, J.S.), 18
brass and wind ensemble anthologies, 301
Britten, Benjamin, 215-217
  Serenade for Tenor, Horn, and Strings,
    216
  Young Person's Guide to the Orchestra,
    216-217
Bruch, Max, 119-120
  Concerto No. 1 for Violin, 119-120
Bruckner, Anton, 120-122
  Symphony No. 4, "Romantic," 121
  Symphony No. 7, 121-122
  Symphony No. 8, 122

Symphony No. 9, 122
Byrd, William, 5-6
  choral music, 6
  consort music, 6

C

Candide: Overture (Bernstein), 213
Canon in D (Pachelbel), 30-31
Canzoni for Brass (Gabrieli), 7
Capriccio espagnol (Rimsky-Korsakov),
  144-145
Capriccio italien (Tchaikovsky), 155
Carmen (Bizet), 104-105
Carmen Suites (Bizet), 105
Carmina Burana (Orff), 243-244
Carnaval (Schumann), 96
Carnival of the Animals (Saint-Saëns),
  147-148
Carnival Overture (Dvořák), 127
Cavalleria Rusticana (Mascagni), 192
cello anthologies, 302-303
Chabrier, Emmanuel, 123-124
  España, 123-124
Chairman Dances, The (Adams), 293
Chamber Symphony No. 1 (Schoenberg),
  270
Chausson, Ernest, 124-125
  Poème for Violin and Orchestra, 124-125
  Symphony in B-flat, 125
Chichester Psalms (Bernstein), 213
Chopin, Frédéric, 76-78
  concertos
  for piano, 77-78
  piano anthologies, 78
  Sonata No. 2 for Piano, 78
choral anthologies, 299
"Choral" Symphony (Beethoven), 51-52
Chromatic Fantasy and Fugue (Bach, J.S.),
  20
Clair de lune (Debussy), 156, 157, 160,
  161
clarinet anthologies, 302
Classical Period, The (1750-ca.1820), 36-
  69
  characteristics of the, 39

composers, 39-69
"Classical" Symphony (Prokofiev), 250-
  251
Concierto de Aranjuez (Rodrigo), 267
Copland, Aaron, 217-220
  Appalachian Spring, 218-219
  Billy the Kid, 219
  Fanfare for the Common Man, 219-220
  Rodeo, 220
Coppélia Suite (Delibes), 126
Corelli, Arcangelo, 25
  Concerti Grossi, 25
Coronation of Poppea, The (Monteverdi),
  9-10
Couperin, François, 26
  harpsichord music, 26
Creation, The (Haydn), 56
Création du Monde, Le (Milhaud), 241

D

Damnation of Faust, The (Berlioz), 74
Dance of the Seven Veils from *Salome*
  (Strauss, R.), 201
Dances from *West Side Story* (Bernstein),
  213-214
Danse Macabre (Saint-Saëns), 149-150
Daphnis et Chloé (Ravel), 259-260
Das Lied von der Erde (Mahler), 171, 173
de Falla, Manuel (*see* Falla, Manuel de)
"Death and the Maiden" Quartet
  (Schubert), 88-89
Death and Transfiguration (Strauss, R.),
  198
Debussy, Claude, 171-176
  Images pour orchestre, 172-173
  La Mer, 173-174
  Nocturnes, 174-175
  piano music, 175
  Prélude à l'après-midi d'un faune,
  (Prelude to the Afternoon of a
  Faun)175-176
  Quartet in G Minor, 176
Delibes, Leo, 125-126
  Coppélia Suite, 126
  Sylvia Suite, 126

Delius, Frederick, 176-177
  tone poems, 177
Deutsches Requiem, Ein (Brahms), 113
Dichterliebe (Schumann), 97
Dido and Aeneas (Purcell), 31-32
d'Indy, Vincent (*see* Indy, Vincent d')
Don Giovanni (Mozart), 63-64
Donizetti, Gaetano, 78-79
  Lucia di Lammermoor, 79
Don Juan (Strauss, R.), 198-199
Don Pasquale (Donizetti), 77
Don Quixote (Strauss, R.), 199
Dowland, John, 6-7
  Lachrimae, or Seven Teares 5, 6
  lute music, 7
  lute songs, 7
Dukas, Paul, 178-179
  Sorcerer's Apprentice, The (L'Apprenti
    sorcier), 178-179
Dvořák, Antonin, 126-131
  Carnival Overture, 127
  Concerto for Cello, 127-128
  Quartet No. 12, "American," 128
  Slavonic Dances, 128-129
  Symphony No. 7, 129-131
  Symphony No. 8, 129-131
  Symphony No. 9, "From the New
    World," 130-131

E
Early Music anthologies, 295
Early Romantics, The (ca. 1820-1850),
  71-101
  characteristics of the, 71-72
  composers, 72-101
1812 Overture (Tchaikovsky), 158
Elgar, Edward, 179-182
  Concerto for Cello, 180
  Enigma Variations, 180-181
  Pomp and Circumstance March No. 1,
    181
  Symphony No. 1, 181-182
"Emperor" Concerto (Beethoven), 42-43
Enesco, Georges, 220-221
  Romanian Rhapsody No. 1, 221

Enigma Variations (Elgar), 181-182
"Eroica" Symphony (Beethoven), 47-48
España (Chabrier), 123-124
Exsultate, Jubilate (Mozart), 64

F
Falla, Manuel de, 221-224
  Amor brujo, El, 222-223
  Nights in the Garden of Spain, 223
  Three-Cornered Hat Dances, The, 223-
    224
Falstaff (Verdi), 150
Fanfare for the Common Man (Copland),
  219-220
Fantasia on a Theme by Thomas Tallis
  (Vaughan Williams), 285-286
Fauré, Gabriel, 182-184
  Pelléas et Mélisande, 183
  Requiem, 183-184
Finlandia (Sibelius), 277
Firebird Suite (Stravinsky), 281
Five Pieces for Orchestra (Schoenberg), 270
Five Pieces for Orchestra (Webern), 292
Fliegende Holländer, Der (Wagner), 168
flute anthologies, 302
Flying Dutchman, The (Wagner), 168
Fountains of Rome (Respighi), 266
Four Seasons, The (Vivaldi), 36-37
Franck, César, 131-133
  Sonata in A for Violin and Piano, 132
  Symphony in D Minor, 132-133
"From the New World" Symphony
  (Dvořák), 130-131

G
Gabrieli, Giovanni, 7
  Canzoni for Brass, 7
Gaité Parisienne (Offenbach), 143
Gayne Suite (Khachaturian), 238-239
German Requiem (Brahms), 113
Gershwin, George, 224-226
  American in Paris, An, 225
  Porgy and Bess, 226
  Rhapsody in Blue, 226
Glass, Philip, 294

music of, 294
piano music, 294
Glinka, Mikhail, 80
Ruslan and Ludmila: Overture, 80
Gloria in D (Vivaldi), 37
Gloria in G (Poulenc), 245
Gluck, Christoph Willibald von, 53-54
Orfeo ed Euridice, 54
Goldberg Variations (Bach, J.S.), 20-21
Górecki, Henryk, 294
Symphony No. 3, 294
Grand Canyon Suite (Grofé), 228
"Great" Mass in C (Mozart), 65
"Great" Symphony No. 9 (Schubert), 93
Gregorian Chant, 1-2
Grieg, Edvard, 133-135
Concerto in A Minor for Piano, 134
Peer Gynt Suites Nos. 1, 2, 134-135
Grofé, Ferde, 227-228
Grand Canyon Suite, 228
guitar anthologies, 303

H
Hamburg Symphonies (Bach, C.P.E.), 40
Handel, George Frideric, 26-30
Concertos for Organ, 27-28
Concerti Grossi, 27
Messiah, 28-29
Royal Fireworks Music, 29-30
Water Music, 29-30
Hänsel und Gretel (Humperdinck), 184
Hanson, Howard, 228-229
Symphony No. 2, "Romantic," 229
Harold in Italy (Berlioz), 74-75
harpsichord anthologies, 300-301
Háry János: Suite (Kodály), 239-240
Havanaise (Saint-Saëns), 150
Haydn, Franz Joseph, 54-58
Concerto for Trumpet, 55
Creation, The, 56
Mass No. 11, "Nelson," 56
Quartet in C, "Emperor" (Haydn), 56-57
symphonies, 57-58
"Haydn" Quartets (Mozart), 66

Heldenleben, Ein (Strauss R.), 200
Hero's Life, A (Strauss, R.), 200
Hindemith, Paul, 186, 229-221
Mathis der Maler (Symphony), 230-231
Symphonic Metamorphosis of Themes by Weber, 231
Holst, Gustav, 231-232
Planets, The, 232
Honegger, Arthur, 233-235
Pacific 231, 234
Symphony No. 2, 234-235
Humperdinck, Engelbert, 184
Hänsel und Gretel, 184
Hungarian Dances (Brahms), 113
Hungarian Rhapsodies (Liszt), 138

I
Images pour orchestre (Debussy), 172-173
Incoronazione di Poppea, L' (Monteverdi), 9-10
Indy, Vincent d', 185-186
Symphony on a French Mountain Air, 186
"Inextinguishable" Symphony (Nielsen), 242
Introduction and Rondo Capriccioso (Saint-Saëns), 150
Invitation to the Dance (Weber), 100
Italian Concerto (Bach, J.S.), 21
"Italian" Symphony (Mendelssohn), 84
Ives, Charles, 235-236
Symphony No. 2, 236
Three Places in New England, 236

J
Janáček, Leos, 236-238
Sinfonietta, 237-238
Josquin Desprez, 8
masses and motets, 8

K
Khachaturian, Aram, 238-239
Gayne: Suite, 238-239
Kinderscenen (Schumann), 98
kleine Nachtmusik, Eine (Mozart), 64
Kodály, Zoltán, 239-240

Háry János Suite, 239-240
"Kreutzer" Sonata (Beethoven), 45

L

Lachrimae , or Seven Teares (Dowland), 5, 6
Lakmé (Delibes), 117
Lalo, Edouard, 135-136
  Symphonie espagnole, 136
Lassus, Orlandus, 8-9
  vocal and choral music, 9
Late Romantics, The (ca. 1890-1915),
  171-202
  characteristics of, 171
  composers, 171-202
Leoncavallo, Ruggero, 186-187
  Pagliacci, 187
Lied von der Erde, Das (Mahler), 188-189
Lieutenant Kijé Suite (Prokofiev), 248
Liszt, Franz, 136-139
  concertos for piano, 137
  Hungarian Rhapsodies, 138
  Les Préludes (Symphonic Poem No. 3),
    138
  Sonata in B Minor for Piano, 138-139
"London" Symphony (Vaughan
  Williams), 286-287
Love for Three Oranges Suite, The
  (Prokofiev), 248-249
Lucia di Lammermoor (Donizetti), 79

M

Madama Butterfly (Puccini), 194
Magic Flute, The (Mozart), 64-65
Magnificat in D (Bach, J.S.), 22-23
Mahler, Gustav, 187-191
  Das Lied von der Erde, 188-189
  Symphony No. 1, "Titan," 189
  Symphony No. 2, "Resurrection," 189
  Symphony No. 4, 190
  Symphony No. 8, "Symphony of a
    Thousand," 190
  Symphony No. 9, 191
Mainstream Romantics, The (ca. 1850-
  1890), 103-170
  charcteristics of the, 103-104

composers, 104-170
Marche slave (Tchaikovsky), 156-157
Marriage of Figaro, The (Mozart), 65
Mascagni, Pietro, 191-192
  Cavalleria Rusticana, 192
Mass in B Minor (Bach, J. S.), 23
Mathis der Maler (Symphony)
  (Hindemith), 230-231
Medieval collections, 2-4
Mendelssohn, Felix, 81-84
  Concerto in for Violin, 81-82
  Midsummer Night's Dream, A: Incidental
    Music, 82-83
  Octet, 83
  overtures, 83
  Symphony No. 4, "Italian," 84
Mer, La (Debussy), 173-174
Messiah (Handel), 28-29
Middle Ages and Renaissance, The (ca.
  600-1600), 1-13
  characteristics of, 1
  composers, 1-13
Midsummer Night's Dream, A: Incidental
  Music (Mendelssohn), 82-83
Milhaud, Darius, 240-241
  Création du Monde, Le, 241
Missa Papae Marcelli (Palestrina), 11
Moderns, The (ca. 1915-Present), 203-
  294
  characteristics of, 203-205
  composers, 206-294
Moldau, The (Smetana), 152
Moments Musicaux (Schubert), 88
Monteverdi, Claudio, 9-10
  L'Incoronazione di Poppea (Coronation of
    Poppea, The), 9-10
  madrigals, 10
  Vespro della Beata Vergine (Vespers of
    1610), 10
Moussorgsky, Modeste (*see* Mussorgsky,
  Modest)
movies, classical music in, 305-311
Mozart, Wolfgang Amadeus, 58-69
  concertos
    for clarinet, 60

for flute, 60
for horn, 61
for piano, 61-62
for violin, 63
Don Giovanni, 63-64
Exsultate, Jubilate (Mozart), 64
Magic Flute, The (Die Zauberflöte), 64-65
Marriage of Figaro, The (Le Nozze di Figaro), 65
overtures, 66
Quartets Nos. 14-19 "Haydn," 66
Quintet for Clarinet and Strings, 66
Requiem, 67
Serenade in G ("Eine kleine Nachtmusik"), 67-68
Sinfonia Concertante in E-flat for Violin and Viola, K.364, 68
Sonata No. 11 for Piano, 68
symphonies, 68-69
Music for Strings, Percussion and Celesta (Bartók), 209
Mussorgsky, Modest, 139-142
Boris Gudonov, 140
Night on Bald Mountain, A, 141
Pictures at an Exhibition, 141-142

N
"Nelson" Mass (Haydn), 56
"New World" Symphony (Dvořák), 130-131
Nielsen, Carl, 241-242
Symphony No. 4, "Inextinguishable," 242
Symphony No. 5, 242
Night on Bald Mountain, A (Mussorgsky), 141
Nights in the Gardens of Spain (Falla), 223
Nocturnes (Debussy), 174-175
"Nordic" Symphony (Hanson), 209
Norma (Bellini), 72-73
Nozze di Figaro, Le (Mozart), 65
Nutcracker Suite (Tchaikovsky), 157

O
Offenbach, Jacques, 142-143
Gaité Parisienne, 143

orchestral anthologies, 297
Orfeo ed Euridice (Gluck), 54
Orff, Carl, 242-244
Carmina Burana, 243-244
opera anthologies, 298
organ anthologies, 300
"Organ" Symphony (Saint-Saëns), 150-151
Otello (Verdi), 163-164
Overture *1812* (Tchaikovsky), 158

P
Pachelbel, Johann, 30-31
Canon in D, 30-31
Pacific 231 (Honegger), 234
Paganini, Niccolò, 84-85
Concerto No. 1 for Violin, 85
Pagliacci (Leoncavallo), 187
Palestrina, Giovanni Pierluigi da, 10-11
Missa Papae Marcelli, 11
"Pastorale" Symphony (Beethoven), 49
"Pathètique" Symphony (Tchaikovsky), 161
Pavane for a Dead Princess (Ravel), 260-261
Pavane pour une infante défunte (Ravel), 260-261
Peer Gynt Suites Nos. 1, 2 (Grieg), 134-135
Pelléas et Mélisande (Fauré), 183
percussion anthologies, 303
Péri, La (Dukas), 115
Périchole, La (Offenbach), 132
Peter and the Wolf (Prokofiev), 249
Petrushka (Stravinsky), 281
piano anthologies, 299-300
Pictures at an Exhibition (Mussorgsky), 141-142
Pines of Rome (Respighi), 266
Planets, The (Holst), 232
Plow that Broke the Plains, The (Thomson), 284-285
Poème for Violin and Orchestra (Chausson), 125
Poet's Love (Schumann), 97
Polovtsian Dances (Borodin), 107
Pomp and Circumstance March No. 1 (Elgar), 181

Porgy and Bess (Gershwin), 226

Poulenc, Francis, 244-245

  Concerto for Organ, Strings and
    Timpani, 25

  Gloria in G, 245

Praetorius, Michael, 11

  Terpsichore, 11

Prélude á l'après-midi d'un faune
  (Debussy),175-176

Prelude to the Afternoon of a Faun
  (Debussy), 175-176

Préludes, Les (Liszt), 138

Prince Igor: Overture, Polovtsian Dances
  (Borodin), 107

Prokofiev, Serge, 245-251

  Alexander Nevsky, 247

  Concerto No. 3 for Piano, 247-248

  Lieutenant Kijé Suite, 248

  Love for Three Oranges Suite, The, 248-
  249

  Peter and the Wolf, 249

  Romeo and Juliet, 250

  Symphony No. 1, "Classical," 250-251

  Symphony No. 5, 251

Puccini, Giacomo, 192-195

  Bohème, La, 193-194

  Madama Butterfly, 194

  Tosca, 194-195

  Turandot, 195

Purcell, Henry, 31-32

  Dido and Aeneas, 31-32

  music of, 32

R

Rachmaninov, Sergei, 251-255

  concertos for piano, 252-254

  Rhapsody on a Theme of Paganini, 254

  Symphony No. 2, 255

Rameau, Jean-Philippe, 32-33

  harpsichord music, 32

  orchestral music, 32-33

Rapsodie espagnole (Ravel), 262-263

Ravel, Maurice, 255-264

  Alborada del gracioso, 256-257

  Boléro, 257-258

Concerto in G for Piano, 258-259

Daphnis et Chloé, 259-260

Pavane pour une infante défunte (Pavane
  for a Dead Princess), 260-261

Quartet in F, 261-262

Rapsodie espagnole, 262-263

Trio for Piano, Violin and Cello, 263

Valse, La, 263-264

recorder anthologies, 302

Renaissance collections, 4-5

Requiem (Fauré), 183-184

Requiem Mass (Victoria), 13

Requiem (Mozart), 67

Requiem (Verdi), 164-165

Respighi, Ottorino, 265-266

  Ancient Airs and Dances, 265

  Fountains of Rome, 266

  Pines of Rome, 266

  Roman Festivals, 266

"Resurrection" Symphony (Mahler), 189

Rhapsody in Blue (Gershwin), 226

Rhapsody on a Theme of Paganini
  (Rachmaninov), 254

"Rhenish" Symphony (Schumann), 99

Rigoletto (Verdi), 165

Rimsky-Korsakov, Nikolai, 143-146

  Capriccio espagnol, 144-145

  Russian Easter Overture, 145

  Scheherazade, 145-146

Ring des Nibelungen, Der (Wagner), 169

Rite of Spring, The (Stravinsky), 251, 254

Rodeo (Copland), 220

Rodrigo, Joaquin, 266-267

  Concierto de Aranjuez, 267

Roman Festivals (Respighi), 266

Romanian Rhapsody No. 1 (Enesco), 221

"Romantic" Symphony (Bruckner), 121

"Romantic" Symphony (Hanson), 229

Romeo and Juliet (Prokofiev), 250

Romeo and Juliet Fantasy Overture
  (Tchaikovsky),158-159

Roméo et Juliette (Berlioz), 75

Rosamunde: Incidental Music (Schubert), 90

Rosenkavalier, Der : Waltz Suite (Strauss,
  R.), 200-201

Rossini, Gioacchino, 85-87
Barber of Seville, The, 86-87
overtures, 87
Royal Fireworks Music (Handel), 29-30
Russian Easter Overture (Rimsky-Korsakov), 145
Ruslan and Ludmila: Overture (Glinka), 80

S

Sacre du printemps, Le (Stravinsky), 282-283
Saint-Saëns, Camille, 147-151
Carnival of the Animals, 147-148
concertos
for cello, 148
for piano, 148
for violin, 149
Danse Macabre, 149-150
Havanaise, 150
Introduction and Rondo Capriccioso, 150
Symphony No. 3, "Organ," 150-151
Salome: Dance of the Seven Veils (Strauss, R.), 201
Satie, Erik, 267-268
Trois Gymnopédies, 268
Scarlatti, Domenico, 33-34
sonatas for harpsichord, 33-34
Scenes of Childhood (Schumann), 97-98
Scheherazade (Rimsky-Korsakov), 145-146
Schelomo-Rhapsody (Bloch), 215
Schoenberg, Arnold, 268-271
Chamber Symphony No. 1, 270
Five Pieces for Orchestra, 270
Variations for Orchestra, 270-271
Verklärte Nacht (Transfigured Night), 271
Schubert, Franz, 87-94
Moments Musicaux, 88
Quartet No. 14, "Death and the Maiden," 88-89
Quintet in A, "Trout," 89
Rosamunde: Incidental Music, 90
Sonata No. 21 for Piano, 90-91
songs, 91
Symphony No. 5, 91-92

Symphony No.8, "Unfinished," 92-93
Symphony No. 9, "The Great," 93
Trio No. 1, 93-94
"Wanderer" Fantasy, 94
Winterreise, 94
Schumann, Robert, 95-100
Carnaval, 96
Concerto in A minor for Piano, 96-97
Dichterliebe, 97
Kinderscenen, 97-98
Symphony No. 1, "Spring," 98-99
Symphony No. 2, 99
Symphony No. 3, "Rhenish," 99
Symphony No. 4, 99-100
Serenade for Tenor, Horn, and Strings (Britten), 216
Shaker Loops (Adams), 293-294
Shostakovich, Dmitri, 271-275
Concerto No. 1 for Piano, Trumpet, and Orchestra, 272-273
Quartet No. 8, 273
Quintet in G Minor for Piano and Strings, 273
Symphony No. 5, 273-274
Symphony No. 10, 274
Trio No. 2 for Piano, Violin and Cello, 274-275
Sibelius, Jean, 275-279
Concerto for Violin, 276-277
Finlandia, 277
Swan of Tuonela, 277-278
Symphony No. 2, 278
Symphony No. 5, 278-279
Valse triste, 279
Sinfonietta (Janáček), 237-238
Six Pieces for Orchestra (Webern), 292
Slavonic Dances (Dvořák), 128-129
Sleeping Beauty Suite (Tchaikovsky), 159
Smetana, Bedřich, 151-152
Bartered Bride, The: Overture and Dances, 152
Moldau, The, 152
Song of the Earth, The (Mahler), 188-189
Sorcerer's Apprentice, The (Dukas), 178-179
"Spring" Sonata (Beethoven), 45

"Spring" Symphony (Schumann), 98-99
St. Matthew Passion (Bach, J.S.), 24
Strauss, Johann II, 153
  waltzes, polkas, overtures, 153
Strauss, Richard, 195-202
  Also sprach Zarathustra, 197
  Death and Transfiguration, 198
  Don Juan, 198-199
  Don Quixote, 199
  Heldenleben, Ein, 200
  Rosenkavalier, Der: Waltz Suite, 200-201
  Salome: Dance of the Seven Veils, 201
  Till Eulenspiegel's Merry Pranks, 201-202
Stravinsky, Igor, 279-283
  Firebird Suite, 281
  Petrushka, 281-282
  Sacre du printemps, Le (The Rite of
    Spring), 282-283
  Symphony of Psalms, 283
Swan Lake Suite (Tchaikovsky), 159-160
Swan of Tuonela (Sibelius), 277-278
Sylvia Suite (Delibes), 126
*Symphonic Metamorphosis of Themes by
  Weber* (Hindemith), 231
Symphonie espagnole (Lalo), 136
Symphonie fantastique (Berlioz), 75-76
"Symphony of a Thousand" (Mahler), 190
Symphony on a French Mountain Air
  (d'Indy), 186

T
Tallis, Thomas, 12-13
  church music, 13
Tchaikovsky, Peter Ilyich, 154-161
  Capriccio italien, 155
  Concerto for Violin, 156
  Concerto No. 1 for Piano, 155
  Marche slave, 156-157
  Nutcracker Suite, 157
  Overture *1812*, 158
  Romeo and Juliet Fantasy Overture, 158-
    159
  Sleeping Beauty Suite, 159
  Swan Lake Suite, 159-160
  symphonies, 160-161

Telemann, Georg Philipp, 34-35
  Suite in A Minor for Recorder and
  Strings, 35
Terpischore (Praetorius), 11
Thomson, Virgil, 283-285
  Plow that Broke the Plains, The, 284-285
Three-Cornered Hat: Dances, The (Falla),
  223-224
Three Pieces for Orchestra (Berg), 211
Three Places in New England (Ives), 236
Thus Spake Zarathustra (Strauss, R.), 197
Till Eulenspiegel's Merry Pranks (Strauss,
  R.), 201-202
"Titan" Symphony (Mahler), 189
Tod und Verklärung (Strauss, R.), 198
Tosca (Puccini), 194-195
Tragic Overture (Brahms), 117-118
Transfigured Night (Schoenberg), 271
Traviata, La (Verdi), 165
Tristan und Isolde (Wagner), 1169-170
Trois Gymnopédies (Satie), 268
trombone anthologies, 301
"Trout" Quintet (Schubert), 89
trumpet anthologies, 301
Turandot (Puccini), 195

U
"Unfinished" Symphony (Schubert), 92-93

V
Valkyrie, The (Wagner), 170
Valse, La (Ravel), 263-264
Valse triste (Sibelius), 279
*Variations and Fugue on a Theme of Henry
  Purcell* (Britten), 216-217
Variations for Orchestra (Schoenberg), 270-
  271
Variations on a Theme by Haydn (Brahms),
  118-119
Variations on a Theme by Henry Purcell
  (Britten), 30
Vaughan Williams, Ralph, 285-287
  Fantasia on a Theme by Thomas Tallis,
    285-286
  Symphony No. 2, "London," 286-287

Symphony No. 5, 287
Verdi, Giuseppe, 162-165
  Aida, 163
  Otello, 163-164
  Requiem, 164-165
  Rigoletto, 165
  Traviata, La, 165
Verklärte Nacht (Schoenberg), 271
Vespers of 1610 (Monteverdi), 10
Victoria, Tomás Luis de, 13
  Requiem Mass, 13
Villa-Lobos, Heitor, 287-289
  Bachiana Brasileira No. 5, 289
  Concerto for Guitar, 289
violin anthologies, 302
Vivaldi, Antonio, 35-37
  Four Seasons, The, 17, 36-37
  Gloria in D, 37

W

Wagner, Richard, 166-170
  Flying Dutchman, The (Der fliegende
    Holländer), 168
  orchestral selections, 167-168
  Ring des Nibelungen, Der, 169
  Tristan und Isolde, 169-170

Walküre, Die (The Valkyrie), 170
Walküre, Die (Wagner), 170
Walton, William, 289-291
  Belshazzar's Feast, 290
  Symphony No. 1, 290-291
"Wanderer" Fantasy (Schubert), 94
Water Music (Handel), 29-30
Weber, Carl Maria von, 100-101
  Invitation to the Dance, 100
  overtures, 101
Webern, Anton, 291-292
  Five Pieces for Orchestra, 292
  Six Pieces for Orchestra, 292
Well-Tempered Clavier (Bach, J.S.), 21
West Side Story: Dances (Bernstein), 213-
  214
Winterreise (Schubert), 94
Wozzeck (Berg), 211-212

Y

Young Person's Guide to the Orchestra
  (Britten), 216-217

Z

Zauberflöte, Die (Mozart), 64-65